THREE ORIENTA

NEW RIVERSIDE EDITIONS

Series Editor for the British Volumes
Alan Richardson

Fictions of Empire: Heart of Darkness, Joseph Conrad; *The Man Who Would Be King,* Rudyard Kipling; and *The Beach of Falesá,* Robert Louis Stevenson
edited by John Kucich

Lyrical Ballads and Related Writings, William Wordsworth and Samuel Taylor Coleridge
edited by William Richey and Daniel Robinson

Making Humans: Frankenstein, Mary Shelley, and *The Island of Doctor Moreau,* H. G. Wells
edited by Judith Wilt

Sense and Sensibility, Jane Austen
edited by Beth Lau

Three Oriental Tales: History of Nourjahad, Frances Sheridan; *Vathek,* William Beckford; and *The Giaour,* Lord Byron
edited by Alan Richardson

Three Vampire Tales: Dracula, Bram Stoker; *Carmilla,* Sheridan LeFanu; and *The Vampyre,* John Polidori
edited by Anne Williams

Two Irish National Tales: Castle Rackrent, Maria Edgeworth, and *The Wild Irish Girl,* Sydney Owenson (Lady Morgan)
edited by James M. Smith

Wuthering Heights, Emily Brontë
edited by Diane Long Hoeveler

For a complete listing of our American and British New Riverside Editions, visit our web site at **http://college.hmco.com.**

NEW RIVERSIDE EDITIONS
Series Editor for the British Volumes
Alan Richardson, Boston College

Three Oriental Tales

Complete Texts with Introduction
Historical Contexts • Critical Essays

FRANCES SHERIDAN, History of Nourjahad

WILLIAM BECKFORD, Vathek

LORD BYRON, The Giaour

Edited by Alan Richardson

BOSTON COLLEGE

Houghton Mifflin Company
BOSTON • NEW YORK

Sponsoring Editor: Michael Gillespie
Editorial Associate: Bruce Cantley
Senior Project Editor: Tracy Patruno
Senior Cover Design Coordinator: Deborah Azerrad Savona
Manufacturing Manager: Florence Cadran
Marketing Manager: Cindy Graff Cohen

Cover image: © Corbis

Credits appear on page 328, which is a continuation of the copyright page.

Printed in the U.S.A.

Library of Congress Control Number: 2001090625
ISBN: 0-618-10731-2
2 3 4 5 6 7 8 9-QF-08 07 06 05 04

As part of Houghton Mifflin's ongoing commitment to the environment, this text has been printed on recycled paper.

CONTENTS

ABOUT THIS SERIES
Alan Richardson

The Riverside imprint, stamped on a book's spine or printed on its title page, carries a special aura for anyone who loves and values books. As well it might: by the middle of the nineteenth century, Houghton Mifflin had already established the "Riverside" edition as an important presence in American publishing. The Riverside series of British poets brought trustworthy editions of Milton and Wordsworth, Spenser and Pope, and (then) lesser-known writers like Herbert, Vaughan, and Keats to a growing nation of readers. There was both a Riverside Shakespeare and a Riverside Chaucer by the century's end, titles that would be revived and recreated as the authoritative editions of the late twentieth century. Riverside editions of writers like Emerson, Hawthorne, Longfellow, and Thoreau helped establish the first canon of American literature. Early in the twentieth century, the Cambridge editions published by Houghton Mifflin at the Riverside Press made the complete works of dozens of British and American poets widely available in single-volume editions that can still be found in libraries and homes throughout the United States and beyond.

The Riverside Editions of the 1950s and 1960s brought attractive, affordable, and carefully edited versions of a range of British and American titles into the thriving new market for serious paperback literature. Prepared by leading scholars and critics of the time, the Riversides rapidly became known for their lively introductions, reliable texts, and lucid annotation. Though aimed primarily at the college market, the series was also created (as one editor put it) with the "general reader's private library" in mind. These were paperbacks to hold on to and read again, and the bookshelves of many a "private" library were brightened with the colorful spines of Riverside editions kept long after graduation.

Houghton Mifflin's New Riverside Editions now bring the combination of high editorial values and wide popular appeal long associated with the Riverside imprint into line with the changing needs and desires of twenty-first century students and general readers. Inaugurated in 2000 with the first set of American titles under the general editorship of Paul Lauter, the New Riversides reflect both the changing canons of literature in English and the greater emphasis on historical and cultural context that have helped a new generation of critics to extend and reenliven literary studies. The Series is not only concerned with keeping the classic works of British and American literature alive but grows as well out of the excitement that a broader range of literary texts and cultural reference points has brought to the classroom. Works by formerly marginalized authors, including women writers and writers of color, will find a place in the Series along with titles from the traditional canons that a succession of Riverside imprints helped establish beginning a century and a half ago. New Riverside titles will reflect the recent surge of interest in the connections among literary activity, historical change, and social and political issues, including slavery, abolition, and the construction of "race"; gender relations and the history of sexuality; the rise of the British Empire and of nationalisms on both sides of the Atlantic; and changing conceptions of nature and of the human.

The New Riverside Editions respond to recent changes in literary studies not only in the range of titles but also in the design of individual volumes. Issues and debates crucial to a book's author and original audience find voice in selections from contemporary writings of many kinds as well as in early reactions and reviews. Some volumes will place contemporary writers into dialogue, as with the pairing of Irish national tales by Maria Edgeworth and Sydney Owenson or of vampire stories by Bram Stoker and Sheridan LeFanu. Other volumes provide alternative ways of constructing literary tradition, placing Mary Shelley's *Frankenstein* with H. G. Wells's *Island of Dr. Moreau*, or Lord Byron's *The Giaour*, an "Eastern Tale" in verse, with Frances Sheridan's *Nourjahad* and William Beckford's *Vathek*, its most important predecessors in Orientalist prose fiction. Chronologies, selections from major criticism, notes on textual history, and bibliographies will allow readers to go beyond the text and explore a given writer or issue in greater depth. Seasoned critics will find fresh new contexts and juxtapositions, and general readers will find intriguing new material to read alongside of familiar titles in an attractive format.

Houghton Mifflin's New Riverside Editions maintain the values of reliability and readability that have marked the Riverside name for well over a century. Each volume also provides something new—often unexpected—and each in a distinctive way. Freed from the predictable monotony and rigidity of a set template, editors can build their volumes around the special opportunities presented by a given title or set of related works. We hope that the resulting blend of innovative scholarship, creative format, and high production values will help the Riverside imprint continue to thrive well into the new century.

INTRODUCTION
Alan Richardson

The three major texts here gathered together for the first time, Frances Sheridan's *History of Nourjahad,* William Beckford's *Vathek,* and Lord Byron's *The Giaour,* exemplify three equally significant facets of literary Orientalism in the British tradition. *Nourjahad,* published posthumously in 1767, illustrates the popular appeal of Oriental tales for an audience that sought variety and even exotic escapism within the confines of "moral" fiction. Simultaneously, it reveals how a woman writer could make use of Orientalist motifs and settings to subtly underscore the limitations of the female social sphere and to reimagine the harem as a locus of female empowerment. *Vathek* (1786) remains unparalleled as the most powerful, inventive, and disturbing fantasy in the British Orientalist tradition. Championed and reinterpreted by poets of the English Romantic and French Symbolist movements, most notably George Gordon, Lord Byron and Stéphane Mallarmé, *Vathek* remains a pivotal text for understanding both the Gothic tradition and the transition from neoclassical to Romantic literary modes. The publication of *The Giaour,* in 1813, sealed Byron's reputation as the leading British poet of his generation while establishing the verse "Eastern Tale" as the popular successor to the Orientalist prose tradition culminating in *Vathek.* Together, these three tales illustrate the recurring thematic and ideological concerns as well as the considerable range of the Oriental tale, a range further evidenced by the selections from the *Spectator,* the *Rambler,* Oliver Goldsmith's *Citizen of the World,* and Maria Edgeworth's *Popular Tales* in Part Two of this volume.

The Orientalist vogue in literary writing, which flourished in Britain during the eighteenth and early nineteenth centuries, constituted a crucial element of the larger cultural, scholarly, and administrative enterprise known in retrospect as "Orientalism." Literary Orientalism cannot be understood apart from this larger enterprise, and yet Orientalism is a notoriously vexed topic that has led more than one commentator into the environs of paradox. Edward Said's monumental study, *Orientalism* (1979), the most influential (though by no means the first) exposition of the subject, argued in effect that the "Orient" had always been a constitutive element of the "Western" tradition and that the Orient nevertheless had never existed. As early as Aeschylus's *The Persians* and Euripides's *The Bacchae,* even as early as Homer's *Iliad,* "Western" writers grounded their claims to civilization and their European identity partly on invidious comparison to a barbarous, inarticulate, luxurious, and dangerous "East." But this "Orient," Said claims, was an artificial construct only loosely (when at all) corresponding to the diverse Asian cultures and social groups lumped together as "Oriental." In his view, even the division between Europe and Asia—which constitute a single land mass, the Eurasian continent—is an artificial and ideologically motivated one, a matter of "imaginative geography" (57). Greece, Europe, and ultimately the "West" define themselves against a simultaneously passive and threatening "Orient," which, according to Said, is made to exemplify the negative values—irrationality, cruelty, effeminacy, superstition—that the West wishes to expel or disavow.

Said's model of Orientalism as an invidious, ultimately imperialist discourse enabling Europe to "manage—and even to produce—the Orient politically, sociologically, ideologically, scientifically, and imaginatively" (3) has remained the starting point for numerous analyses of literary Orientalism. Said's *Orientalism* has been equally notable, however, for the significant critiques and qualifications it has provoked, some of them acknowledged by Said himself in later works. Such critics as Lisa Lowe and Sara Suleri have argued, for example, that Said's conception of Orientalism readily became both too monolithic and too rigidly dichotomized to account for the "multiplicity" of Orients envisioned by various writers (Lowe 24) and the "anxiety of empire" that often signifies a sense of European vulnerability in the colonial encounter (Suleri 5). If the West is partly defined by its imaginary construction of the East, then "Europeanness" and "Westernness" are themselves imaginary qualities that risk exposure and revision when placed in contact with "Oriental" societies, cultures, and artifacts. Ziauddin Sardar contends that Orientalism proper arises only with the emergence of Islam as a serious threat to Christian and European supremacy, sparking a "crisis of Western self-knowledge" that finds partial resolution in the wishful construction of an "unfathomable, exotic and erotic" Orient, at once childlike and despotic (2, 17). For Sardar, the sense of cultural threat, however, remains palpable, and Orientalism can include a self-critical "rethinking and remodeling" of European attitudes, a strategic use of the "Orient to reprove Europe" that reaches its peak in the eighteenth century, the era of *Nourjahad* and *Vathek* (37).

Literary works have featured prominently in the debates over Orientalism. Precisely because the Orient is an imaginary projection—a "fabulated, constructed object" in Sardar's words (13)—literary representations of the Orient have served to validate and perpetuate Orientalist stereotypes in a "continuous feedback loop in which the reality of the Orient, any Orient, was quite irrelevant" (Sardar 43). Frances Mannsåker has argued that the stock emotions, scenarios, and character types codified in Orientalist fiction—the cruel and arbitrary despot, the lascivious and untrustworthy harem woman, the supine and superstitious populace, the slothful and corrupt official—shaped the way that European travelers and diplomats perceived and then reported back on the living Eastern societies they encountered (Mannsåker 185). Literary writers can mimic the larger imperial enterprise in featuring Oriental settings and motifs as an "imperial heraldry" incorporating "symbols of the conquered" (Leask, *British* 8), or they can promote imperial and colonial designs by producing and circulating images of Asian "inferiority" (Sardar 48).

Yet literary works, because of their thickness of texture and their imaginative license, can also provide complex, nuanced, and "counterhegemonic" (or, put more simply, "oppositional") depictions of the East (Porter 155, MacKenzie 211). As Europe's primary source for alternative visions of culture, the Orient has long served as both prime "cultural contestant" (Said 1) and "alter-ego" to the Occident (Schwab 4). Even through the distorting lens of Orientalism, the East could provide a critical vantage point from which to criticize Western ideals and institutions, serving to destabilize entrenched European notions. John M. MacKenzie insists that literary and other artistic forms can manifest a degree of "porousness" in relation to Asian thought and culture, resulting in a healthy "contamination" that has enabled European artists to challenge the conventions and restraints of received traditions (208–09). In contrast, John Barrell argues that the very obliteration of Asian cultures within Orientalist writing creates "blank screens" for the wishful projection of European fantasies (8). These "screens" range from the nightmares of imperial anxiety that Barrell finds in the works of Thomas De Quincey to the quasi-pornographic fantasies of European male artists imaginatively let loose in the harem and the representation of homoerotic and other forbidden forms of sexuality under the guise of bizarre Eastern customs or unrestrained Oriental licentiousness. Such representation can unleash oppositional cultural energies, triggering what Dennis Porter terms the "potential ideological irresponsibility of language wherever an eroticized phantasy is granted the freedom to indulge itself in a literary space" (160).

The erotically charged character of much Orientalist fiction emerges as early as Antoine Galland's *Les Mille et une nuits.* (1704–17), the French translation of an Arabic collection of popular tales (*The Thousand and One Nights*) that ignited the eighteenth-century European craze for literary Orientalism. Galland's version was being translated into English as early as 1706, and by 1713 the *Arabian Nights* (as it was known in England) had gone into its fourth edition. Indeed, the cruelty and eroticism, male tyranny and female perfidy that would become staple Orientalist themes can be seen even in the English translation's garrulous full title: *Arabian Nights Entertainments: Consisting of One Thousand and One Stories, Told by The Sultaness of the Indies, to Divert the Sultan from the Execution of a Bloody Vow He Had Made to Marry a Lady Every Day, and Have Her Cut Off Next Morning, to Avenge Himself for the Disloyalty of His First Sultaness, &c.* The collection's running concern with female sexual license becomes overt in the fourteenth night's tale (230–32), in which an erring wife outsmarts the preternaturally clever parrot that her husband has set to spy on her. Yet the tale also highlights the wife's resourceful intelligence and implies that the husband's jealousy is excessive and self-defeating. In this respect, the tale mirrors the larger story that frames the collection, showing how Scheherazade's ingenuity, prodigious memory, and unrivaled gift for narrative finally overcome the obsessive jealousy and extreme misogyny that have rendered the sultan a murderous tyrant. Although the *Arabian Nights* endorsed and helped spread European stereotypes of the Oriental as irrational, cruel, and oversexed, it also offered less predictable images of female initiative and intelligence. In addition it proffered a rich aura of the marvelous and magical at a time when neoclassical prescriptions had rendered European fiction tame by comparison. Many Romantic writers, Samuel Taylor Coleridge, William Wordsworth, and Thomas De Quincey among them, would gratefully attest to the crucial role played by the "Arabian tales" in their early imaginative lives (Ali 40–41).

The instant popularity of *The Thousand and One Nights* guaranteed that a host of imitations would soon follow. François Pétis de la Croix brought out translations of Turkish tales in 1707 and Persian tales in 1710–12, both finding their way into English within a few years. Soon there were "Chinese Tales," "Mogul Tales," "Tartarian Tales," and even "Peruvian Tales," many of them "pseudo-translations" that emerged from the fanciful minds of European imitators (Conant 31–32). Even actual translations like Galland's, however, gave a distinctly European veneer to the tales they presented to an infatuated public. Although Oriental writing was widely supposed to be marked by a lush, metaphorical, "poetic" manner, Galland's French version boasted a Gallic "simplicity, urbanity, and variety of style" that the anonymous English translator faithfully captured, helping to lend a Parisian touch to much of Orientalist writing in English to follow (Ali 12–13). The French also demonstrated, in such original works as Montesquieu's *Persian*

Letters (1721) and Voltaire's *Zadig* (1748), that the conventions and settings of the Eastern tales could be placed in the service of political satire, social critique, and philosophical speculation. The close relation of the French to the English traditions in Orientalist fiction makes it less surprising that Beckford, an English writer, should have chosen to compose *Vathek* in French.

The new "polite" periodicals typified by the *Tatler* (1709–11) and the *Spectator* (1711–14), providing guidance on books and manners as well as entertainment to a growing bourgeois readership, were quick to capitalize on the Orientalist fad. In 1711 the *Spectator* had featured Joseph Addison's celebrated "Vision of Mirzah," a moral allegory set in the "high Hills of *Bagdat,*" and any number of Orientalist contributions followed. One of the most interesting examples from the *Spectator*, pages 232–36 in this volume, was condensed from Ambrose Philips's translation of de la Croix's tales, *The Thousand and One Days,* in 1714. It exemplifies the use of Orientalist fiction to comment on philosophical speculation, in this case Locke's audacious theory of personal identity, which the tale seems to parody but also to lend a certain venerability by suggesting its applicability to a traditional Persian fable. Similarly, Oliver Goldsmith's *Citizen of the World,* initially published in biweekly installments in John Newbery's *Public Ledger* (1760–61), emulates Montesquieu in using an imagined Oriental perspective to relativize and criticize European customs, institutions, and mores. Ironically, one of Goldsmith's many targets is Orientalism itself, as Letter 33 (pages 242–46 in this volume) amusingly demonstrates. Orientalist fiction could be self-critical as well as satirically corrosive in its take on European society and culture, even if the Orient it portrayed was itself largely a European invention.

In addition to its usefulness for satire, philosophical speculation, and cultural critique, the Orientalist tale lent itself to the pronounced moralizing impulse of the times. Joseph Addison's "Mirzah," for example, deploys its Eastern trappings in service of an implicitly Christian meditation on the brevity, uncertainty, and poverty of human life in contrast to the perpetual joys of the afterlife. Samuel Johnson, the preeminent moralist of a didactic age, honed the moral Oriental mode in tales published in the *Rambler*, his own "polite" journal, and perfected it in *Rasselas,* his Orientalist novella of 1759. (Though the action of *Rasselas* begins in Abyssinia—modern Ethiopia—North Africa was readily assimilated within Europe's constructed "Orient" thanks to its history of Muslim influence, as were Muslim-dominated regions of "Europe" such as Albania and Circassia.) The story of Almamoulin from the *Rambler* (1751), included in Part Two, illustrates Johnson's use of the Eastern tale to point his favorite moral message, the vanity of human wishes. It also gives a taste of the pseudo-Oriental style mocked by Goldsmith, though Johnson's use of "Oriental" imagery, forms of address, and figures of speech remains characteristically restrained.

The enduring appeal of the moralized Eastern tale is exemplified by Maria Edgeworth's "Murad the Unlucky," published in her 1804 volume of "popular" stories aimed at the growing audience of readers from the laboring and lower middle classes. Whereas Johnson cautions his "polite" readership against overvaluing wealth and locating happiness in worldly pursuits, Edgeworth promotes the secular virtue of "prudence" for her lower-class audience, with the feckless Murad and his disciplined brother, Saladin, serving as contrasting models in schematic yet entertaining fashion. The narrative taken as a whole rejects the imagined influence of fortune in favor of the predictable consequences of prudent or imprudent behaviors, with obvious application to the lower-class reader targeted for Edgeworth's message of "self-improvement."

In the stories of Almamoulin and of Murad, the moral values are ranked and delivered in ways familiar enough from other didactic works by Johnson and Edgeworth. The Oriental settings and motifs, however, cannot be dismissed as matters of mere backdrop and costuming. The Arabian Nights atmosphere of the marvelous and unexpected, for example, facilitates Johnson's evocation of immense riches and sudden reversals of fortune, while Orientalist stereotyping allows him to exaggerate the "luxury and indulgence" of both Almamoulin and his father (238).[1] Edgeworth, in contrast, works against the marvelous associations touched on in her opening reference to Haroun al Raschid (a central figure in *The Thousand and One Nights*), proffering instead the "far less wonderful" career of prudence and steady application exemplified by Saladin (264). Her reader is implicitly taught to see superstition, fatalism, indolence, and even opium abuse—faults ascribed by bourgeois writers of the time to the British lower classes—as alien and "Oriental" in contrast to the "Christian" and European values Edgeworth embodies in the English soldiers and the "ingenious" French engineer who play incidental but thematically charged roles in the tale (257, 267). Edgeworth's Orient serves as a repository for the negative values she wishes her readers to reject and purge from themselves.

The History of Nourjahad presents an especially rich example of the Orientalist mode lending itself to multiple and conflicting uses. Frances Sheridan (1724–66) was the wife of the actor and theater manager Thomas Sheridan, the mother of the dramatist Richard Brinsley Sheridan, and her-

---

[1]Parenthetical references not otherwise identified are to this New Riverside Edition.

self a successful playwright, although her best-known work is the *Memoirs of Miss Sidney Bidulph* (1761), a sprightly and eventful epistolary novel in the manner of Samuel Richardson's *Clarissa.* Her immersion in the world of the eighteenth-century theater leaves its mark on *Nourjahad,* with its atmosphere of plots, pretense, sudden changes of scene, exotic backdrops, glittering props, and multiple role-playing. For the reader and for Nourjahad himself, however, the theatrical settings and events seem initially a series of marvelous transformations brought on by a "genius" (*jinn* or genie) worthy of the *Arabian Nights.* On one level Sheridan seems to endorse some of the crudest Orientalist stereotypes. Nourjahad is voluptuous, licentious, luxurious, and cruel; Schemzeddin, his patron and the sultan of Persia, appears despotic and puritanically austere. Given the illusion of "inexhaustible riches" and eternal life (29), Nourjahad pushes self-indulgence to pathological extremes, committing sacrilege and murder without compunction. His "boundless' desires are brought within a reasonable compass only after a career of fantastic excess, one that renders him simultaneously tyrannical and feminized, an absolute master enslaved to his progressively debased appetites.

In bestowing on Nourjahad a "natural tendency toward luxury, sensuality, and self-indulgence," Sheridan has been criticized for promoting European values by projecting their contraries onto an imagined East (Mannsåker 184–85). Yet *Nourjahad* can also be read as a displaced criticism of eighteenth-century European social arrangements. Nourjahad's supposedly boundless opportunities for enjoyment, for example, are in fact limited to what can be enjoyed within the confines of a domestic (if palatial) space. He cannot travel, he cannot buy real estate, he cannot enter into a political or professional career; no wonder this harem master grows "effeminate" (33). In fact, Felicity Nussbaum sees Nourjahad's seemingly unique situation as in part an exoticized reflection of the emergent domestic ideology of the period, confining bourgeois women to the "private" sphere and increasingly defining their primary role, after bearing and raising children, in terms of consumerism (see Nussbaum, pages 291–96 in this volume). The Oriental harem provides a stock European fantasy of unchecked male sexual enjoyment, yet it simultaneously evokes the threat of *female* sexuality, including a subversive aura of lesbian desire ("unlawful pleasures") as well (58). Manipulating stock associations between the Oriental and the effeminate, the harem as locus of tyrannical male power and of "unlawful" female desire, the eighteenth-century woman writer could endorse Orientalist stereotypes even in broaching a critique of masculinist European practices. Despite its ambivalent relation to European social arrangements, however, *Nourjahad* retains the basic structure of the moral tale, ending with its hero's ethical awakening and reformation. Sheridan claimed to have imagined the entire plot in a "kind of vision or dream," one that came to her during a wakeful night spent contemplating the importance of the "regulation of the passions" (Lefanu 295).

William Beckford's *Vathek*, published twenty years after *Nourjahad* and two years before the French Revolution, is dreamlike in a more disturbing and violent fashion, giving full play to its hero's passions in an atmosphere of unrestrained desire that frequently verges on the grotesque and horrific. Although the tale is allegedly set in the Middle East, tracing the Caliph Vathek's journey from Samarah (north of Baghdad in Iraq) to Istakhar (north of Shiraz in the heart of Persia, now Iran), *Vathek* yields up a phantasmagoria of "Oriental" associations and motifs. The place names, customs, artifacts, literary references, and religious practices cited by Beckford range promiscuously from the Far East to India and from North Africa to Eastern Europe. Along the way, Beckford manages to evoke and exaggerate a whole set of invidious Orientalist stereotypes, beginning with Vathek himself: tyrant, sensualist, sadist, and devil worshipper. As Guy Chapman notes, the tale's equally crude racism serves as a reminder that Beckford's considerable family fortune—Byron called him "England's wealthiest son"—came in large part from "sugar plantations and slaves in Jamaica" (3). But in its very excess, the proliferation of Orientalist figures and devices may suggest an ironic and potentially critical detachment on Beckford's part. "It revels in all the favorite tropisms and unmasks them at the same time," as one critic puts it (Aravamudan 221). Despite his wealth and social position, Beckford writes out of a profound disenchantment with the social, political, and sexual orthodoxies of eighteenth-century Europe.

Groomed for a political career (his father was lord mayor of London), William Beckford (1760–1843) chose instead a life of connoisseurship, artistic expression, and reverie. "I refuse to occupy my mind with impertinent society," he declares in a letter of 1778; "I will seclude myself if possible from the world, in the midst of the Empire. I am determined to enjoy my dreams, my phantasies and all my singularities, however discordant to the worldlings around" (qtd. Kiely 45). He studied drawing with Alexander Cousins and piano with Wolfgang Amadeus Mozart, became an excellent dancer and musician, and read widely, especially in Orientalist scholarship, travels, and literature. He knew enough Persian and Arabic to render parts of *The Thousand and One Nights* from Arabic into French (Alexander 11). *Vathek* and its copious original notes (worked up by its translator, Samuel Henley, who seems to have gone well beyond Beckford's hints), provides both a compendium and a parody of Orientalist knowledge and made a handy source text for Byron and other later writers. Yet *Vathek* also constitutes a work of self-projection, an early "romantic" exploration of its author's fantasies, obsessions, and desires, replete with autobiographical hints (Kiely 44). As the "projection of an amoral, secret life into the public domain," *Vathek* helps inaugurate the modern concern with the "outlawed self" (Sharafuddin xxxii). In breaking one social rule and literary convention after another, however, *Vathek* has been seen by Mohammed Sharafuddin as deeply unorthodox and cosmopolitan, destabilizing English notions of social identity and opening a space for the "reality and value" of an alien "form of life" (Sharafuddin xxxiv). Paradoxically enough, its Orientalist excesses and unrestrained self-expression have given *Vathek* a certain title not just to cultural criticism but to the possibility of cross-cultural recognition.

Whether or not one grants Beckford this opening to the "*radically* foreign" (Sharafuddin xxxiv), the choice between reading *Vathek* as veiled self-expression and reading it in terms of its ambivalent relation to Orientalism is a false one. In its treatment of sexuality, for example, *Vathek* anticipates the iconoclasm of such Romantic poets as Byron and Percy Bysshe Shelley, not only equipping its hero with the requisite harem but indulging in one forbidden sexual practice after another. Autobiographical matters are clearly involved: to begin with, Beckford carried on a quasi-incestuous adulterous relation with his cousin's wife, Louisa Beckford, often seen as the model for Nouronihar, Vathek's erotic object. Moreover, Beckford lost control of the text of *Vathek* (published by Henley against his wishes, as a supposed "translation" from an anonymous Arabic original, and without the author's final approval) because he was forced into temporary exile to "avoid being prosecuted for pederasty" (Potkay, 296 in this volume). Beckford had carried on a romantic and probably sexual friendship with a young aristocrat, William Courtenay, for several years, until finally surprised in Courtenay's bedroom after raising the suspicions of the family. (The rumor campaign that followed included a reference in a London newspaper, the *Morning Herald,* to "a *Grammatical mistake of Mr. B*——— and the *Hon. Mr. C*———, in regard to the genders" [qtd. Chapman 185].) But alternative forms of sexuality are a staple of Orientalist fiction; even Sheridan's *Nourjahad,* for all its didacticism, hints at lesbian relations in the harem and cross-dresses the hero's love interest as a young man of "more than mortal beauty" (26). Beckford's characteristic exaggeration of "Eastern" sexual license, however autobiographically motivated, makes one part of his text's parodic relation to the Oriental tale and Orientalist scholarship. Yet the pederastic fantasies concerning the thirteen-year-old Gulchenrouz and his fifty boy companions themselves follow a standard Orientalist trajectory, revealing what Sardar calls the "pedophile impulse" that "constructs the Orient as a passive, childlike entity that can be loved and abused, shaped and contained, managed and consumed" (6). In the context of Orientalist fiction, Beckford's private sexual fantasies cannot be disentangled from the cultural fantasy of a supine, infantile, inviting East.

Thanks in part to Henley's mishandling, and perhaps owing to Beckford's sexual frankness as well, the contemporary impact of *Vathek* was minimal compared with its importance for later writers. Stéphane Mallarmé, who issued an edition of Beckford's revised French version in 1876, called it one of the most significant works ever composed in French and "un des jeux les plus fiers de la naissante imagination moderne" ("one of the proudest freaks of the nascent modern imagination"; 561–62). It was Byron, however, who first championed *Vathek,* and his appreciative note at the end of *The Giaour* established its lasting place in British literature a quarter century after its botched debut (Mahmoud 98–100).

Even in launching Beckford's prose Orientalist fantasy into belated prominence, *The Giaour* also impelled a shift from prose to verse as the preferred medium for the Eastern tale in its Romantic incarnation. Robert Southey, the future poet laureate and Byron's literary enemy, had pointed the way with *Thalaba the Destroyer* (1801) and *The Curse of Kehama* (1810), and Walter Savage Landor had transformed Clara Reeve's prose romance "History of Charoba, Queen of Aegypt" into experimental narrative verse still earlier in *Gebir* (1798). It was the wildly popular *Giaour,* however, that established the market not only for Byron's own series of "Turkish Tales," but also for Thomas Moore's *Lalla Rookh* (1817) and other lucrative Orientalist poems. *The Giaour* went through fourteen editions in two years as Byron's "snake of a poem"—"lengthening its rattles every month"—grew from 684 to 1334 lines in the process (Byron, *Letters* 3: 100). Byron followed up with *The Bride of Abydos* (1813), *The Corsair* (1814), *Lara* (1814), and *The Siege of Corinth* (1816), inspiring a renewed vogue for literary Orientalism that made a significant aspect of the cultural movement retrospectively called "Romanticism."

It is noteworthy and rather ironic that Byron would praise *Vathek* for the "correctness of costume," a term referring not just to clothing and related cultural artifacts but more broadly to customs, settings, and literary and religious references (Leask, "Wandering" 176). For unlike Beckford, whose Orient was created almost wholly out of books, George Gordon, Lord Byron (1788–1824) could boast "direct experience" of the Muslim East (Sharafuddin 214). Byron established his early reputation in large part through poetic traveling, visiting the Continent shortly after the end of the Napoleonic Wars and continuing eastward to Albania, Turkey, and Greece (at that time an unruly province of the Ottoman empire). Inevitably, Byron's experience was shaped in advance by Orientalist presuppositions, and his "Eastern tales" are hardly free of the stereotypical motifs found in such earlier writers as Sheridan and Beckford. Sardar calls them "poems of the gratuitous violence, irrational vengeance, and cold-hearted barbarity of Turks" (46) and notes that the pairing of the "barbaric Muslim male" and the "sensual, passive female" in works like *The Giaour* produces a "concrete image of sexuality and despotism and thus inferiority" (48). Sustained readings of *The Giaour,* however, have elicited evidence of Byron's "sympathy," even "amounting to identification," with Turkish manners and Islamic beliefs (Sharafuddin 224–25). (For shock value or otherwise, Byron was fond of claiming he had come near to "turning Mussalman" while in the East [Isaac Disraeli, qtd. Sharafuddin 225].) At the least, Byron seems to have been drawn to the Orient as a "space towards which to escape—and from which to critique and contest"—European modernity with its interrelated capitalist and imperialist agendas (Makdisi 148). Yet even this critical gesture depends to an extent on what Marilyn Butler terms Byron's "romantic" construction of the Orient, valuing the Islamic cultures of Albania and Turkey "precisely for their otherness," their exotic departure from European norms (85).

The otherness that Byron associated with "Oriental" sexuality made no small part of his attraction to the East. Like Beckford before him, Byron was infamous as a sexual outlaw and had been forced into exile, again like Beckford, to avoid an obscure charge that may have included sodomy, then a capital crime (Crompton 196–235). Readings of *The Giaour* tend to focus on the triangular heterosexual relation among the Giaour, Leila, and Hassan, sometimes seen as a national allegory with Leila as Greece caught between two forms of imperialism, Ottoman (Hassan is a Turkish overlord in Greece) and European (the Giaour is a renegade Venetian). That Leila is in fact not Greek but Circassian should at least complicate such readings, though Circassia is itself a region teasingly situated in the uncertain border between East and West.[2] As the object of both men's obsessive desire, Leila brings Hassan and the Giaour into an intimate, if inimical, relation, and Byron is careful to minimize the distance between the Turk and the Venetian rather than to simply oppose them in terms of the expected dichotomy of civilization and barbarism. Regarding Leila's murder at Hassan's behest, the Giaour confesses: "Yet did he but what I had done / Had she been false to more than one" (lines 1062–63).

Significantly, the Giaour remains no less obsessed with Hassan than with Leila, suggesting that heterosexual rivalry, especially in an Orientalist context, can screen or harbor a strong homoerotic attraction. As Suleri has

[2] Byron's Circassia corresponds roughly to the Karachayevo-Cherkesskaya Respublika situated north of Georgia in the modern Russian Federation.

written of British representations of India, narratives of colonialism assume a "predominantly homoerotic cast," giving rise not just to depictions of Oriental "effeminacy" but to a "hysterical attention" providing an "index for the dynamic of complicity that renders the colonizer a secret sharer of the imputed cultural characteristics of the other race" (16). *The Giaour,* though not precisely a colonialist narrative, certainly shares in this dynamic of complicity. Byron's description of the combat between the Giaour and Hassan—insisting that the "last embrace of foes" exceeds in "fervour" the intensity of heterosexual passion (647–50)—reveals the "hysterical attention" that Suleri locates in the male colonial encounter, further complicating Byron's representation of charged and illicit sexuality. Representations of gender relations and sexual desire in *The Giaour* manage both to heighten the conventional opposition of East and West and to throw that opposition into crisis.

The shifting and contradictory character of Byron's represented Orient finds expression as well in the multiple voices and fragmentation of its narrative format. The immediate popularity of *The Giaour* is all the more impressive given its sheer formal challenges. Beginning with Galland's *Les Mille et une nuits,* with its elaborate narrative framing and the disarming gap between its marvelous subject matter and crisp, worldly tone, European writers had made the Oriental tale a vehicle for literary experimentation. Sheridan collapses narrative temporality in daring new ways in *Nourjahad,* as Margaret Doody has detailed in her pioneering essay on "annihilated time" in Sheridan's fiction (excerpted on pages 285–91). Beckford's *Vathek* has impressed critics with its "disturbing" tone of narrative detachment, its creative mingling of Orientalist and Gothic conventions, and its sudden shifts in narrative progression (Kiely 43–64). In *The Giaour,* Byron goes further, shattering the narrative into a mosaic of partial accounts told by diverse speakers, some difficult to identify. According to Sharafuddin, Byron's multiple narrators allow him to represent varied and sometimes opposing viewpoints, expressing "in the very structure of the poem the multiple perspective that constitutes its theme" (243). Leask takes a bleaker view, describing the tale's fragmentation as the "formal equivalent of the cultural degradation" that he locates at the poem's thematic core (*British* 30). Or perhaps the poem's formal dissolution reflects the imminent breakup of the "disintegrating" Ottoman Empire, as Joseph Lew has suggested (178). Presented by Byron himself as the "disjointed fragments" of an older—perhaps oral—popular tale, *The Giaour* confounds temporal as well as geographical boundaries, with allegedly traditional elements welded together in an aggressively modern manner.

The fragmented structure and internal contradictions in these works reflect the ideological fragmentation within literary Orientalism itself.

Although the Oriental tale can indeed function to reinforce, even anticipate, the chauvinism and falsifications of what Said calls "Orientalist discourse" (99), it rarely does so in a single-minded, uncomplicated fashion. European writers from Montesquieu to Byron employed "Oriental" settings, motifs, and attitudes to criticize their own cultures, to challenge or renew literary conventions, and to imagine alternative social, political, and sexual regimes. It would be naive to approach Oriental fiction without acknowledging the larger Orientalist project and the European colonial and imperial designs that impelled it. But the relation of a given tale to Orientalism cannot be determined in advance and is likely to show at least some degree of ambivalence and self-criticism. Nor should Orientalist fiction be reduced altogether to ideology—assuming that one could fully understand its ideological workings apart from its formal commitments and its aesthetic pleasures and provocations. The Orientalist tale is no less challenging or sophisticated for having arisen as a form of popular fiction. The examples in this New Riverside Edition should repay careful attention and repeated reading as they variously amuse and incite, unsettle and beguile.

A NOTE ON THE TEXTS

Alan Richardson

Each of the three major works reprinted in this New Riverside Edition presents a different profile in terms of its textual and compositional history. The most straightforward is Sheridan's *History of Nourjahad,* the first edition of which was published posthumously in 1767 and has remained the text of choice. (There has been no modern edition of Sheridan's works.) This edition follows the first edition closely, with only a few minor (and unnoted) changes in punctuation for greater clarity.

Much more problematic is *Vathek,* composed by Beckford in French in 1782 and translated into English by Samuel Henley, with some assistance from Beckford, in 1785. Henley also supplied the notes, in many but by no means all cases following Beckford's suggestions. In 1786 Henley published his translation against the wishes of Beckford, who wanted the French version to appear first, as *An Arabian Tale, from an Unpublished Manuscript: With Notes Critical and Explanatory.* Beckford, who no longer had access to his original manuscript, obtained a copy of Henley's translation and quickly brought out a retranslation into French (mostly the work of David Levade) published in Lausanne in 1786 but dated 1787. (This version may have drawn on a draft of the lost French manuscript as well.) Unhappy with Levade's work, Beckford, with the help of new assistants, published a revised French version in Paris under the title *Vathek, conte arab* (1787). The text reprinted in this volume, like other modern editions, is based on the English "third edition" of 1816, which incorporates Beckford's corrections of Henley's translation as well as a number of the changes Beckford had made to the third French edition of 1815. In the 1816 edition, Beckford also trimmed Henley's numerous and detailed notes, some more pedantic than informative, to a more manageable though still impressive roster. These revised notes are printed in Part One following the text of *Vathek*, as in all of the early editions, in which they functioned as much to extend and complicate as to illuminate the main text. Annotations to the annotations have been kept to a minimum in order to avoid the appearance of a pedantry rivaling Henley's.

The textual history of *The Giaour* is less complicated despite its many editions. Byron composed the initial version of the poem between September and March of 1813 and published a first edition of 684 lines in June of that year. By December, the poem had gone into its seventh edition and reached its final length of 1334 lines.[1] The text reprinted here follows the twelfth edition (London, 1814), which retains the changes in lines 403 and 407 made for the seventh edition and introduces a new reading of lines 236–37. As with *Vathek,* and for the same reasons, Byron's original notes are printed in a separate section following the poem, as they were presented during Byron's lifetime.

The shorter pieces in Part Two from the *Arabian Nights,* the *Spectator,* Samuel Johnson's *Rambler,* Oliver Goldsmith's *Citizen of the World,* Maria Edgeworth's *Popular Tales,* and Francis Jeffrey's review of *The Giaour,* are based on various early editions and reprints, checked against the earliest editions and most recent scholarly editions available. Original spelling has generally been retained (as it invariably is for the three major texts) although some punctuation has been changed for clarity, and modern typography is consistently used in place of archaic forms such as *æ* ligatures and the eighteenth-century "long *s.*"

---

[1] For a comparison of various editions and a history of textual changes, see the helpful discussion in volume 3 of Jerome J. McGann's edition of Byron's *Complete Poetical Works* (406–14).

LITERARY ORIENTALISM IN BRITAIN, FROM THE *ARABIAN NIGHTS* TO BYRON: A SELECT CHRONOLOGY

1704–17 Antoine Galland's *Les Mille et une nuits* (*The Thousand and One Nights*) freely translated from the Arabic, inaugurates the most intensive era of European literary Orientalism.

1706 *The Arabian Nights Entertainments,* first installment of the anonymous "Grub Street" translation of Galland's *Les Mille* into English, published, with a fourth expanded edition appearing by 1713.

1707 François Pétis de la Croix, *Histoire de la sultane de Perse et des visirs, Contes Turcs* published.

1708 *Turkish Tales,* Consisting of Several Extraordinary Adventures, with *The History of the Sultaness of Persia and the Viziers,* anonymous English translation of *Contes Turcs* published.

1710–12 Pétis de la Croix publishes *Les Mille et une jour, Contes Persans.*

1711 Joseph Addison contributes a number of Orientalist essays and tales to the *Spectator,* including the popular "Vision of Mirzah," No. 159 (1 September).

1714 *The Thousand and One Days: Persian Tales,* translation by Ambrose Philips of *Contes Persans:* "The Story of Fadlallah and Zemroude," condensed from Philips's translation, appears in the *Spectator* 578 (9 Aug.).

1721 Montesquieu's *Lettres persanes* published; translated into English as *Persian Letters* in 1730.

1734 George Sale brings out his translation from the Arabic of the Koran, prefixed by a "Preliminary Discourse" that becomes an important source for Beckford, Byron, and other British Orientalist writers.

1735 George Lyttelton publishes *Letters from a Persian in England to His Friend at Ispahan,* an imitation of Montesquieu.

1736 *Mogul Tales,* anonymous translation from the French edition of T. S. Guellette. Eliza Haywood, *Adventures of Eovaai, Princess of Ijaveo,* published (reissued in 1741 as *The Unfortunate Princess*).

1742 William Collins establishes an important precedent for Orientalist poetry in English with *Persian Eclogues.*

1748 Voltaire, *Zadig* published; translated into English as *Zadig, or The Book of Fate: An Oriental History* the next year.

1750 Samuel Johnson publishes "Hamet and Raschid," the first of a series of "Eastern Tales," in the *Rambler* 38 (28 July), with the story of Nouradin and Almamoulin appearing the following year in 120 (11 May 1751).

1757 Horace Walpole publishes *A Letter from Xo-Ho, a Chinese Philosopher at London to His Friend Lien Chi at Peking.*

1759–60 Johnson publishes *The Prince of Abyssinia: A Tale* (the original title of *Rasselas*), as well as several Oriental tales in his Idler series for the *Universal Chronicle.*

1760–62 Oliver Goldsmith publishes the "Chinese Letters" in biweekly issues of the *Public Ledger,* collected as *The Citizen of the World* in 1762.

1761 John Hawkesworth publishes *Almoran and Hamet: An Oriental Tale.*

1763 Mary Wortley Montagu's "Turkish Embassy Letters," recording her journey to Constantinople in 1717–18, published in a posthumous edition of her *Letters.*

1764 James Ridley, *Tales of the Genii,* published.

1767 Frances Sheridan, *The History of Nourjahad,* published.

1769 Tobias Smollet, *The Orientalist: A Volume of Tales after the Eastern Taste,* published.

1770 Thomas Chatterton publishes his "African Eclogues," modeled on Collins's *Persian Eclogues,* in various periodicals, later collected in his posthumous *Miscellanies* (1778).

1772 Sir William Jones, a prolific Orientalist scholar and pioneering linguist, publishes *Poems Consisting Chiefly of Translations from the Asiatick Languages.*

1774 John Richardson's translation of the *Odes* of Hafiz, a celebrated fourteenth-century Persian poet, published.

1777 Richardson's *Dissertation on the Languages, Literature, and Manners of the Eastern Nations* published; an expanded edition appears the following year.

1782 Jones publishes *The Moallakat, or Seven Arabian Poems.*

1784 Production of Elizabeth Inchbald's *The Mogul Tale, or The Descent of the Balloon,* a farce set in an Eastern seraglio (published in 1788).

1785 Clara Reeve includes an Oriental tale, "The History of Charoba, Queen of Aegypt," as a supplement to *The Progress of Romance,* her history and defense of the novel form. Charles Wilkins produces the first English translation of the Bhagavad Gita (a section of the sacred Hindu epic, the Mahabharata) as *The Bhagavat-Geeta, or Dialogues of Kreeshna and Arjoon.*

1786 Samuel Henley publishes his English translation of *Vathek* against the wishes of William Beckford, who then publishes a retranslation into French in 1787.

1787 Robert Bage, *The Fair Syrian* (novel), published. Inchbald's prison reform drama, *Such Things Are,* set in Sumatra, produced to great popular acclaim (and published the next year).

1789 Jones publishes *Sacontala, or the Fatal Ring: An Indian Drama,* translation of Kalidasa's *Shakuntala* from the Sanskrit.

1790 Ellis Cornelia Knight publishes *Dinarbas, a Tale: Being a Continuation of Rasselas, Prince of Abyssinia.* About this time, Richard Johnson (under the pseudonym "The Rev'd Dr Cooper") publishes the first children's version of *The Thousand and One Nights* as *The Oriental Moralist, or The Beauties of the Arabian Nights Entertainments.*

1792 Hannah Cowley, *A Day in Turkey, or The Russian Slaves,* stage comedy set in a Turkish harem, produced.

1796 Elizabeth Hamilton publishes *Translation of the Letters of a Hindu Rajah,* a novel with a preliminary discourse on the "history, religion, and manners of the Hindoos"; five editions published by 1811.

1797 Samuel Taylor Coleridge writes "Kubla Khan: A Vision in a Dream," which long remains in manuscript but becomes known (through Coleridge's memorable recitations) to William Wordsworth, Mary Robinson, Charles Lamb, and a few other poets and writers, notably Byron, who induces Coleridge to publish it in 1816.

1798 Walter Savage Landor publishes *Gebir,* an experimental epic poem loosely based on Clara Reeve's "History of Charoba, Queen of Aegypt."

1799 *The Works of Sir William Jones,* edited by Anna Maria Jones, published in six volumes; two supplementary volumes follow in 1801 and a new thirteen-volume edition in 1807. *The Story of Al Raoui: A Tale from the Arabic,* sometimes attributed to Beckford, published anonymously.

1800 Mary Pilkington publishes *The Asiatic Princess: A Tale.*

1801 Robert Southey publishes *Thalaba the Destroyer,* an epic-length poem set in the Muslim East.

1804 Maria Edgeworth publishes "Murad the Unlucky" as one of her *Popular Tales.*

1808 M. G. ("Monk") Lewis includes several Oriental tales in his *Romantic Tales. The Poetical Works of Sir William Jones* published in two volumes.

1810 Southey publishes *The Curse of Kehama,* an Orientalist epic poem set in India.

1811 Sidney Owenson (Lady Morgan) publishes *The Missionary,* a novel set in India.

1812 Byron publishes his veiled autobiographical poem *Childe Harold's Pilgrimage,* cantos 1 and 2, and soon finds himself famous; these cantos include "Harold's" visit to Albania, then under the rule of Ali Pacha. Henry Weber gathers translations and imitations of Eastern tales (including Sheridan's *Nourjahad*) in his three-volume *Tales of the East.*

1813 Byron publishes *The Giaour* (June) and *The Bride of Abydos* (December).

1814 Byron publishes *The Corsair* (February) and *Lara* (August).

1815 Byron publishes *Hebrew Melodies.*

1816 Byron publishes *The Siege of Corinth.* Percy Bysshe Shelley publishes his visionary Orientalist poem, *Alastor.* Coleridge publishes "Kubla Khan."

1817 Thomas Moore, *Lalla Rookh,* and James Mill, *History of British India,* published.

1818 Shelley publishes *The Revolt of Islam* (the revised version of *Laon and Cythna,* published the year before and suppressed.)

1819–24 Byron publishes his major work, the comic epic *Don Juan,* in installments over these years; cantos 2 through 6 are set in Greece and in Turkey, where Juan is temporarily immured in a harem.

1820 Thomas Medwin publishes *Oswald and Edwin: An Oriental Sketch.*

1821 Byron, *Sardanapalus* (Orientalist verse drama), and Medwin, *Sketches in Hindoostan,* published.

1821 Thomas De Quincey publishes his "Confessions of an English Opium Eater," including nightmarish Orientalist fantasies, over several numbers of the *London Magazine* and then in book form the following year.

1822 Shelley's dramatic poem *Hellas* stages an allegorical confrontation between Islam and Christianity.

1824 Byron dies at Missolonghi, where he had gone to help finance and personally assist the cause of Greek independence from Ottoman rule.

Part One

THE TALES

The History of Nourjahad

Frances Sheridan

Schemzeddin was in his two and twentieth year when he mounted the throne of Persia. His great wisdom and extraordinary endowments rendered him the delight of his people, and filled them with expectations of a glorious and happy reign. Amongst the number of persons who stood candidates for the young sultan's favour, in the new administration, which was now going to take place, none seemed so likely to succeed, as Nourjahad the son of Namarand. This young man was about the age of Schemzeddin, and had been bred up with him from his infancy. To a very engaging person was added a sweetness of temper, a liveliness of fancy, and a certain agreeable manner of address, that engaged every one's affections who approached him. The sultan loved him, and every one looked on Nourjahad as the rising star of the Persian court, whom his master's partial fondness would elevate to the highest pinnacle of honour. Schemzeddin indeed was desirous of promoting his favourite, yet notwithstanding his attachment to him, he was not blind to his faults; but they appeared to him only such as are almost inseparable from youth and inexperience; and he made no doubt but that Nourjahad, when time had a little more subdued his youthful passions, and matured his judgment, would be able to fill the place of his first minister, with abilities equal to any of his predecessors. He would not, however, even in his own private thoughts, resolve on so important a step, without first consulting with some old lords of his court, who had been the constant friends and counsellors of the late sultan his father. Accordingly having called them into his closet one day, he proposed the matter to them, and desired their opinion. But before they delivered it, he could easily discover by the countenances of these grave and prudent men, that they disapproved his choice. What have you to object to Nourjahad? said the sultan, finding that they all continued silent, looking at each other. His youth, replied the eldest of the counsellors. That objection, answered Schemzeddin, will grow lighter every day. His avarice, cried the second. Thou art not just, said the sultan, in charging him with that; he has no support but from my bounty, nor did

London: Dodsley, 1767. (All notes to *Nourjahad* are provided by the volume editor of this New Riverside Edition.)

he ever yet take advantage of that interest which he knows he has in me, to desire an encrease of it. What I have charged him with, is in his nature notwithstanding, replied the old lord. What hast thou to urge, cried the sultan, to his third adviser? His love of pleasure, answered he. That, cried Schemzeddin, is as groundless an accusation as the other; I have known him from his childhood, and think few men of his years are so temperate. Yet would he indulge to excess, if it were in his power, replied the old man. The sultan now addressed the fourth: What fault hast thou to object to him, cried he? His irreligion, answered the sage. Thou art even more severe, replied the sultan, than the rest of thy brethren, and I believe Nourjahad as good a Mussulman as thyself. He dismissed them coldly from his closet; and the four counsellors saw how impolitic a thing it was to oppose the will of their sovereign.

Though Schemzeddin seemed displeased with the remonstrances of the old men, they nevertheless had some weight with him. It is the interest of Nourjahad, said he, to conceal his faults from me; the age and experience of these men doubtless has furnished them with more sagacity than my youth can boast of; and he may be in reality what they have represented him. This thought disquieted the sultan, for he loved Nourjahad as his brother. Yet who knows, cried he, but it may be envy in these old men? they may be provoked at having a youth raised to that honour to which each of them perhaps in his own heart aspires. We can sometimes form a better judgment of a man's real disposition, from an unguarded sally of his own lips, than from a close observation of years, where the person, conscious of being observed, is watchful and cautious of every look and expression that falls from him. I will sound Nourjahad when he least suspects that I have any such design, and from his own mouth will I judge him.

It was not long before the sultan had an opportunity of executing his purpose. Having past the evening with his favourite at a banquet, where they had both indulged pretty freely, he invited Nourjahad to a walk by moon-light in the gardens of the seraglio.[1] Schemzeddin leaned on his shoulder as they rambled from one delicious scene to another; scenes rendered still more enchanting by the silence of the night, the mild lustre of the moon now at full, and the exhalations which arose from a thousand odoriferous shrubs. The spirits of Nourjahad were exhilerated by the mirth and festivity in which he had passed the day. The sultan's favour intoxicated

---

Mussulman: Muslim.

[1] Seraglio, an Italianate version of *serai,* signifies a large, enclosed dwelling, here the sultan's palace. For European writers, it could also signify the women's quarters or harem or, by extension, the women themselves.

him; his thoughts were dissipated by a variety of agreeable sensations, and his whole soul as it were rapt in a kind of pleasing delirium. Such was the frame of Nourjahad's mind, when the sultan, with an assumed levity, throwing himself down on a bank of violets, and familiarly drawing his favourite to sit by him, said, *Tell me, Nourjahad, and tell me truly, what would satisfy thy wishes, if thou were certain of possessing whatsoever thou shouldst desire?* Nourjahad remaining silent for some time, the sultan, smiling, repeated his question. My wishes, answered the favourite, are so boundless, that it is impossible for me to tell you directly; but in two words, I should desire to be possessed of inexhaustible riches, and to enable me to enjoy them to the utmost, to have my life prolonged to eternity. Wouldst thou then, said Schemzeddin, forego thy hopes of paradise? I would, answered the favourite, make a paradise of this earthly globe, whilst it lasted, and take my chance for the other afterwards.

The sultan, at hearing these words, started up from his seat, and knitting his brow, Be gone, said he, sternly, thou art no longer worthy of my love or my confidence: I thought to have promoted thee to the highest honours, but such a wretch does not deserve to live. Ambition, though a vice, is yet the vice of great minds; but avarice, and an insatiable thirst for pleasure, degrades a man below the brutes.

Saying this, he turned his back on Nourjahad, and was about to leave him; when the favourite catching him by the robe, and falling on his knees, Let not my lord's indignation, said he, be kindled against his slave, for a few light words, which fell from him only in sport: I swear to thee, my prince, by our holy prophet,[2] that what I said is far from being the sentiments of my heart; my desire for wealth extends not farther than to be enabled to procure the sober enjoyments of life; and for length of years, let not mine be prolonged a day, beyond that, in which I can be serviceable to my prince and my country.

It is not, replied the sultan, with a mildness chastened with gravity, it is not for mortal eyes to penetrate into the close recesses of the human heart; thou hast attested thy innocence by an oath; it is all that can be required from man to man; but remember thou hast called our great prophet to witness; him thou canst not deceive, though me thou mayest.

Schemzeddin left him without waiting for his reply; and Nourjahad, exceedingly mortified that his unguarded declaration had so much lessened him in his master's esteem, retired to his own house, which immediately joined the sultan's palace.

---

[2]Muhammad (570–632), the founder of Islam and author of its sacred scripture, the Koran (Quran). In this and other European texts of the period, called Mahomet.

He passed the rest of the night in traversing his chamber, being unable to take any rest. He dreaded the thoughts of losing the sultan's favour, on which alone he depended for his future advancement; and tormenting himself all night with apprehensions of his disgrace, he found himself so indisposed in the morning, that he was unable to leave his chamber. He spent the day in gloomy reflections without suffering any one to come near him, or taking any repast: and when night came, wearied with painful thoughts, and want of sleep, he threw himself on his bed. But his slumbers were disturbed by perplexing dreams. What had been the subject of his anxiety when awake, served now to imbitter and distract his rest: his fancy represented the sultan to him as he had last seen him in the garden, his looks severe, and his words menacing. "Go wretch," he thought he heard him cry, "go seek thy bread in a remote country, thou hast nothing to expect from me but contempt."

Nourjahad awoke in agonies: Oh heaven, cried he aloud, that I could now inherit the secret wish I was fool enough to disclose to thee, how little should I regard thy threats! And thou shalt, Oh Nourjahad, replied a voice, possess the utmost wishes of thy soul! Nourjahad started up in his bed, and rubbed his eyes, doubting whether he was really awake, or whether it was not his troubled imagination which cheated him with this delusive promise; when behold! to his unutterable astonishment, he saw a refulgent light in his chamber, and at his bed's side stood a youth of more than mortal beauty. The lustre of his white robes dazzled his eyes; his long and shining hair was incircled with a wreath of flowers that breathed the odours of paradise.

Nourjahad gazed at him, but had not power to open his mouth. Be not afraid, said the divine youth, with a voice of ineffable sweetness; I am thy guardian genius,[3] who have carefully watched over thee from thy infancy, though never till this hour have I been permitted to make myself visible to thee. I was present at thy conversation in the garden with Schemzeddin, I was a witness to thy unguarded declaration, but found thee afterwards awed by his frowns to retract what thou hadst said: I saw too the rigour of the sultan's looks as he departed from thee, and know that they proceeded from his doubting thy truth. I, though an immortal spirit, am not omniscient; to God only are the secrets of the heart revealed; speak boldly then, thou highly favoured of our prophet, and know that I have power from Mahomet to grant thy request, be it what it will. Wouldst thou be restored

[3] A genius (plural, *genii*), genie, ginn, or jinn signifies a fire spirit, familiar from the *Arabian Nights,* with the power to interfere (usually helpfully) in human affairs. Sometimes (as here) conflated in European texts with the guardian angel of Christian tradition.

to the favour and confidence of thy master, and receive from his friendship and generosity the reward of thy long attachment to him, or dost thou really desire the accomplishment of that extravagant wish, which thou didst in the openness of thy heart avow to him last night?

Nourjahad, a little recovered from his amazement, and encouraged by the condescension of his celestial visitant, bowed his head low in token of adoration.

Disguise to thee, Oh son of paradise, replied he, were vain and fruitless; if I dissembled to Schemzeddin it was in order to reinstate myself in his good opinion, the only means in my power to secure my future prospects: from thee I can have no reason to conceal my thoughts; and since the care of my happiness is consigned to thee my guardian angel; let me possess that wish, extravagant as it may seem, which I first declared.

Rash mortal, replied the shining vision, reflect once more, before you receive the fatal boon; for once granted, you will wish perhaps, and wish in vain, to have it recalled. What have I to fear, answered Nourjahad, possessed of endless riches and of immortality? Your own passions, said the heavenly youth. I will submit to all the evils arising from them, replied Nourjahad, give me but the power of gratifying them in their full extent. Take thy wish then, cried the genius, with a look of discontent. The contents of this viol will confer immortality on thee, and to-morrow's sun shall behold thee richer than all the kings of the East. Nourjahad stretched his hands out eagerly to receive a vessel of gold, enriched with precious stones, which the angel took from under his mantle. Stop, cried the aerial being, and hear the condition, with which thou must accept the wondrous gift I am now about to bestow. Know then, that your existence here shall equal the date of this sublunary globe, yet to enjoy life all that while, is not in my power to grant. Nourjahad was going to interrupt the celestial, to desire him to explain this, when he prevented him, by proceeding thus: Your life, said he, will be frequently interrupted by the temporary death of sleep. Doubtless, replied Nourjahad, nature would languish without that sovereign balm. Thou misunderstandest me, cried the genius; I do not mean that ordinary repose which nature requires: The sleep thou must be subject to, at certain periods, will last for months, years, nay, for a whole revolution of Saturn at a time, or perhaps for a century. Frightful! cried Nourjahad, with an emotion that made him forget the respect which was due to the presence of his guardian angel. He seemed suspended, while the radiant youth proceeded; It is worth considering, resolve not too hastily. If the

---

viol: vial (a small container).
sublunary globe: the earth. (*Sublunary* means "below the moon.")

frame of man, replied Nourjahad, in the usual course of things, requires for the support of that short span of life which is allotted to him, a constant and regular portion of sleep, which includes at least one third of his existence; my life, perhaps, stretched so much beyond its natural date, may require a still greater proportion of rest, to preserve my body in due health and vigour. If this be the case, I submit to the conditions; for what is thirty or fifty years out of eternity? Thou art mistaken, replied the genius; and though thy reasoning is not unphilosophical, yet is it far from reaching the true cause of these mysterious conditions which are offered thee; know that these are contingencies which depend entirely on thyself. Let me beseech you, said Nourjahad, to explain this. If thou walkest, said the genius, in the paths of virtue, thy days will be crowned with gladness, and the even tenor of thy life undisturbed by any evil; but if, on the contrary, thou pervertest the good which is in thy power, and settest thy heart on iniquity, thou wilt thus be occasionally punished by a total privation of thy faculties. If this be all, cried Nourjahad, then am I sure I shall never incur the penalty; for though I mean to enjoy all the pleasures that life can bestow, yet am I a stranger to my own heart, if it ever lead me to the wilful commission of a crime. The genius sighed. Vouchsafe then, proceeded Nourjahad, vouchsafe, I conjure you, most adorable and benign spirit, to fulfil your promise, and keep me not longer in suspence. Saying this, he again reached forth his hand for the golden vessel, which the genius no longer with-held from him. Hold thy nostrils over that viol, said he, and let the fumes of the liquor which it contains ascend to thy brain. Nourjahad opened the vessel, out of which a vapour issued of a most exquisite fragrance; it formed a thick atmosphere about his head, and sent out such volatile and sharp effluvia, as made his eyes smart exceedingly, and he was obliged to shut them whilst he snuffed up the essence. He remained not long in this situation, for the subtle spirit quickly evaporating, the effects instantly ceased, and he opened his eyes; but the apparition was vanished, and his apartment in total darkness. Had not he still found the viol in his hands, which contained the precious liquor, he would have looked on all this as a dream; but so substantial a proof of the reality of what had happened, leaving no room for doubts, he returned thanks to his guardian genius, whom he concluded, though invisible, to be still within hearing, and putting the golden vessel under his pillow, filled as he was with the most delightful ideas, composed himself to sleep.

The sun was at his meridian height when he awoke next day; and the vision of the preceding night immediately recurring to his memory, he sprung hastily from his bed; but how great was his surprize, how high his transports, at seeing the accomplishment of the genius's promise! His chamber was surrounded with several large urns of polished brass, some of which were filled with gold coin of different value and impressions; others with ingots of fine gold; and others with precious stones of prodigious size and lustre.

Amazed, enraptured at the sight, he greedily examined his treasures, and looking into each of the urns one after the other, in one of them he found a scroll of paper, with these words written on it.

'I have fulfilled my promise to thee, Oh Nourjahad. Thy days are without number, thy riches inexhaustible, yet cannot I exempt thee from the evils to which all the sons of Adam are subject. I cannot screen thee from the machinations of envy, nor the rapaciousness of power: thy own prudence must henceforth be thy guard. There is a subterraneous cave in thy garden where thou mayst conceal thy treasure: I have marked the place, and thou wilt easily find it. Farewel, my charge is at an end.'

And well hast thou acquitted thyself of this charge, most munificent and benevolent genius, cried Nourjahad; ten thousand thanks to thee for this last friendly warning; I should be a fool indeed if I had not sagacity enough to preserve myself against rapaciousness or envy; I will prevent the effects of the first, by concealing thee, my precious treasure, thou source of all felicity, where no mortal shall discover thee; and for the other, my bounty shall disarm it of its sting. Enjoy thyself, Nourjahad, riot in luxurious delights, and laugh at Schemzeddin's impotent resentment.

He hastened down into his garden, in order to find the cave, of which he was not long in search. In a remote corner, stood the ruins of a small temple, which in former days, before the true religion prevailed in Persia, had been dedicated to the worship of the Gentiles. The vestiges of this little building were so curious, that they were suffered to remain, as an ornament, where they stood. It was raised on a mount, and according to the custom of idolaters, surrounded with shady trees. On a branch of one of these, Nourjahad perceived hanging a scarf of fine white taffety, to which was suspended a large key of burnished steel.

Nourjahad's eager curiosity, soon rendered his diligence successful, in finding the door, to which this belonged; it was within-side the walls of the temple, and under what formerly seemed to have been the altar. He descended by a few steps into a pretty spacious cavern, and by groping about, for there was scarce any light, he judged it large enough to contain his treasures.

Whether his guardian genius had contrived it purely for his use, or whether it had been originally made for some other purpose, he did not

---

Gentiles: pre-Islamic worshippers; here, probably Zoroastrians.
taffety: taffeta (a fine silken fabric).

trouble himself to enquire; but glad to have found so safe a place, in which to deposite his wealth, he returned to his house; and having given orders that no visitors should approach him, he shut himself up in his chamber for the rest of the day, in order to contemplate his own happiness, and without interruption, to lay down plans of various pleasures and delights for ages to come.

Whilst Nourjahad was rich only in speculation, he really thought that he should be able to keep his word with the genius. That the employing his wealth to noble and generous purposes, would have constituted great part of his happiness; and that without plunging into guilt, he could have gratified the utmost of his wishes. But he soon found that his heart had deceived him, and that there is a wide difference between the fancied and actual possession of wealth. He was immediately absorbed in selfishness, and thought of nothing but the indulgence of his own appetites. My temper, said he, as he lay stretched at length on a sopha, does not much incline me to take any trouble; I shall therefore never aspire at high employments, nor would I be the sultan of Persia, if I might; for what addition would that make to my happiness? None at all; it would only disturb my breast with cares, from which I am now exempt. And which of the real, substantial delights of life, could I then possess, that are not now within my power? I will have a magnificent house in town, and others in the country, with delicious parks and gardens. What does it signify whether or not they are dignified with the names of palaces? or whether I am attended by princes or slaves? The latter will do my business as well, and be more subservient to my will. There are three particulars indeed, in which I will exceed my master. In the beauties of my seraglio; the delicacies of my table; and the excellence of my musicians. In the former of these especially, King Solomon himself shall be outdone.[4] All parts of the earth shall be explored for women of the most exquisite beauty; art and nature shall combine their utmost efforts, to furnish the boundless variety and elegance of my repasts; the sultan's frigid temperance shall not be a pattern to me. Then no fear of surfeits; I may riot to excess, and bid defiance to death. Here he started, on recollection that he had not requested the genius to secure him against the attacks of pain or sickness. I shall not however be impaired by age, said he, and this too perhaps is included in his gift. But no matter; since I cannot die, a little temporary pain will make me the more relish my returning health. Then, added he, I will enjoy the charms of music in its utmost perfection. I will have the

---

[4]In the Jewish and Christian scriptures, Solomon, King of Israel, built the Temple in Jerusalem and boasted 1,000 wives and concubines; he is revered as Sulayman in the Koran for his wisdom, secret knowledge, and mastery of the jinn or genii.

universe searched for performers of both sexes, whose exquisite skill both in instrumental and vocal harmony, shall ravish all hearts. I shall see the line of my posterity past numeration, and all the while enjoy a constant succession of new delights. What more is there wanting to consummate happiness, and who would ever wish to change such an existence, for one of which we are entirely ignorant? Here he paused. But are there not, he proceeded, some things called intellectual pleasures? Such as Schemzeddin used to talk of to me, and for which, when I was poor, I fancied I had a sort of relish. They may have their charms, and we will not leave them quite out of our plan. I will certainly do abundance of good; besides, I will retain in my family half a score of wise and learned men, to entertain my leisure hours with their discourse. Then when I am weary of living in this country, I will set out with some chosen companions to make a tour through the whole earth. There shall not be a spot of the habitable world, which contains any thing worthy of my curiosity, that I will not visit; residing longest in those places which I like best: and by this means I may pass through two or three centuries, even before I have exhausted the variety of my prospects: after that I must content myself with such local enjoyments, as may fall in my way.

With such thoughts as these he entertained himself, waiting for the hour when his slaves should be retired to rest, as he had resolved to take that opportunity of burying his treasure.

He had tried the weight of the urns one by one; those which contained the gold he found so extreamly heavy that it was impossible for him to lift them. Those which held the jewels, he could easily carry. Accordingly, when every one in his house was asleep, he loaded himself with his pleasing burdens; and having from each of the repositories which held the gold, filled several large purses for his immediate expences, he conveyed the rest by many journeys to and from the cave, all safe to his subterranean treasury; where having locked them up securely, he retired to his apartment, and went to bed.

For the three succeeding days his thoughts were so perplexed and divided, that he knew not which of his favourite schemes he should first enter upon. Satisfied with having the means in his power, he neglected those ends for which he was so desirous of them. Shall I, said he, purchase or set about building for myself a magnificent palace? Shall I dispatch emissaries in search of the most beautiful virgins that can be obtained? and others, at the same time, to procure for me the rarest musicians? My household, meanwhile, may be established, and put on a footing suitable to the grandeur in which I purpose to live. I will directly hire a number of domestics, amongst which shall be a dozen of the best cooks in Persia, that my table at least may be immediately better supplied than that of the sultan. I am bewildered with such a multiplicity of business, and must find out some person, who, without giving me any trouble, will undertake to regulate the economy of all my domestic concerns.

In these thoughts he was so immersed, that he entirely forgot to pay his court to Schemzeddin; and without any other enjoyment of his riches, than the pleasure of thinking of them, he sat for whole days alone, alternately improving on, or rejecting, such systems of happiness as arose in his mind.

The sultan, mean time, offended at his absenting himself, without offering any excuse for it, especially as their last parting had been a cold one; was so disgusted at his behaviour, that he sent one of his officers to forbid him his presence, and charge him never more to appear at court. Tell him, however, said he, that I have not so far forgot my former friendship for him, as to see him want a decent support; that house, therefore, in which he now lives, I freely bestow on him; and shall moreover allow him a pension of a thousand crowns yearly. Bid him remember that this is sufficient to supply him with all the sober enjoyments of life. These being his favourite's own words, the sultan thought proper to remind him of them.

Nourjahad received this message with the utmost indifference; but without daring to shew any mark of disrespect. Tell my lord the sultan, said he, that I would not have been thus long without prostrating myself at his feet, but that I was hastily sent for to visit a kinsman, whose dwelling was some leagues from Ormuz; and who in his last hours was desirous of seeing me. He died very rich, and has made me his heir. The thousand crowns a year therefore, my royal master may please to bestow on some one who wants them more, and is more deserving of his bounty, than I; wretch that I am, to have forfeited my prince's favour! The house that his goodness bestows on me, with all gratitude I thankfully accept, as it will daily remind me that Schemzeddin does not utterly detest his slave. Saying this, he presented the officer with a handsome diamond, which he took from his finger, and begged him to accept of it as a token of his respect for him, and submission to the sultan's pleasure.

Though Nourjahad had given such a turn to his acceptance of the house, his true reason was, that having his treasure buried in the garden, he thought he could not without great difficulty, and the hazard of a discovery, remove it. Thus had he already, in two instances, been obliged to depart from truth, in consequence of his ill judged and pernicious choice.

Ormuz: Hormuz, a major trading city on the Persian Gulf near the Strait of Hormuz in Persia (present-day Iran).

The house which the sultan had given him, was handsome and commodious; and he thought by enlarging and furnishing it magnificently, it would sufficiently answer the purpose of his town residence; besides, as it was a royal grant, he was sure of remaining unmolested in the possession of it.

He now bent his thoughts on nothing but in giving a loose to his appetites, and indulging without controul in every delight which his passions or imagination could suggest to him. As he was not of an active temper, he put the conduct of his pleasures into the hands of one, whom he had lately received into his service. This man, whose name was Hasem, he found had good sense, and a quickness of parts, which he thought qualified him for the trust he reposed in him. To him he committed the care of regulating his family, and appointed him the director of his household. In short, under Hasem's inspection, who on this occasion displayed an admirable taste, his house was soon furnished with every thing that could charm the senses, or captivate the fancy. Costly furniture, magnificent habits, sumptuous equipages, and a grand retinue, fully gratified his vanity. By Hasem's diligence his seraglio was soon adorned with a number of the most beautiful female slaves, of almost every nation, whom he purchased at a vast expence. By Hasem's care, his board was replenished with the most delicious products of every climate; and by Hasem's management he had a chosen band of the most skilful musicians of the age; and by Hasem's judgement and address, he had retained in his house some of the most learned and ingenious men of all Persia, skilled in every art and science. These were received into his family for the instruction and entertainment of his hours of reflection, if he should chance to be visited with any such.

Behold him now arrived at the height of human felicity; for, to render his happiness incapable of addition, he had distinguished amongst the beauties of his seraglio, a young maid, so exquisitely charming and accomplished, that he gave her the intire possession of his heart; and preferring her to the rest of his women, past whole days in her apartment. By Mandana he found himself equally beloved; a felicity very rare amongst Eastern husbands; and longing to unbosom himself to one, on whose tenderness and fidelity he could rely, to her he disclosed the marvellous story of his destiny. His mind thus disburthened of this important secret, which he had often longed to divulge, but could find none whom he dared to trust with the discovery, he had not one anxious thought remaining. He gave himself up to pleasures, he threw off all restraint, he plunged at once into a tide of luxurious enjoyments; he forgot his duty towards God, and neglected all the laws of his prophet. He grew lazy and effeminate; and had not his pride now and then urged him to display to the wondering eyes of the public, the magnificence of his state, he would seldom have been inclined to go out of his house.

Thus possessed of every thing that his soul could wish, he continued for the space of three moons, without any interruption, to wallow in voluptuousness: When one morning just as he was preparing to set out for a beautiful villa, which Hasem had recommended to him for his rural retirement, and which he purposed to buy if it answered his description, he was prevented by a messenger from the sultan. It was the same person who once before had been sent to him, to forbid him the court. I am sorry, my lord, said he, on entering Nourjahad's apartment, to be a second time the bearer of unwelcome tidings; but Schemzeddin, hearing of the extraordinary grandeur and magnificence in which you live, a magnificence indeed equal to that of the sultan himself, would needs know whence you derive your wealth, which seems so much to surpass that of any of his subjects; and has commanded me to conduct you to his presence, in order to give an account of it.

Nourjahad was exceedingly startled at this unexpected summons; but it was in vain to dispute the sultan's orders, and he was forced, though with great reluctance, to accompany the officer to the palace of Schemzeddin.

He entered it trembling, fearful to declare a falsehood to his sovereign, yet still more unwilling to confess the truth.

In this suspence the officer left him, to acquaint the sultan of his arrival. He waited not long before he was admitted to the royal presence.

Whence is it, Nourjahad, said the sultan, that thy imprudence hath drawn on thee the attention of my whole empire, insomuch that the representations made to me of thy pomp and luxury, now renders it necessary to enquire into thy riches. They seem indeed to be immense. Who was that relation that bequeathed them to thee, and wherein do they consist?

Though Nourjahad had endeavoured to prepare himself with proper answers to all those questions, which he naturally expected would be asked on the occasion, he was nevertheless confounded; he could not utter the lies he had framed with the unabashed look of sincerity; his speech faltered, and his colour changed. Schemzeddin saw his confusion. I perceive, said he, there is some mystery in this affair which thou hast no mind to discover; I pray heaven that thou hast used no sinister means to come at the great wealth which I am told thou possessest! Confess the truth, and beware of prevaricating with thy prince.

Nourjahad, frightened at the difficulties he found himself involved in, fell at the sultan's feet. If my lord, said he, will give me a patient hearing, and forgive the presumption of his servant, I will unfold such wonders as will amaze him, and at the same time utter nothing but the strictest truth. The sultan turned coldly towards him; but by seeming to attend to his explanation, encouraged him to proceed.

He then gave a faithful relation of the vision he had seen, with all the consequences of that miraculous event. Schemzeddin suffered him to conclude his narration without interruption; but instead of shewing any marks of surprize, or appearing to credit what he said, looking at him with the utmost indignation, Audacious wretch, cried he, how darest thou presume thus to abuse my patience, and affront my understanding with the relation of so ridiculous a forgery? Go tell thy incredible tales to fools and children, but dare not to insult thy sovereign with such outrageous falsehoods.

Though Nourjahad was terrified at the sultan's anger, he nevertheless persisted in his declaration, confirming all he had said by the most solemn oaths. The sultan commanded him to be silent. Thou art mad, said he: I perceive now that the riches thou hast acquired, let the means be what they may, have turned thy brain; and I am now more than ever convinced of the sordidness of thy mind, when the unexpected acquisition of a little wealth could thus pervert thy judgment, and teach thee to impose on thy master for truth, the monstrous chimeras of thy wild fancy. Thy folly be on thy head; for a little, a very little time must, with the unbounded extravagance of which thou art guilty, dissipate what thy friend hath left thee; and when thou art again reduced to thy former state, thou wilt be glad to sue to my bounty for that which thou didst lately with so much arrogance reject. Go, unhappy Nourjahad, continued he, (his voice a little softened) the remembrance of what thou once wert to me, will not permit me to see thee fall a victim to thy own desperate folly. Should it be publickly known that thou hast thus endeavoured by lies and profanation to abuse the credulity of thy prince, thou wouldst find that thy boasted immortality would not be proof against that death, which he should think himself obliged, in justice to his own honour and dignity, to inflict on so bold an impostor. Hence, miserable man, pursued he, retire to thy house; and if thou art not quite abandoned, endeavour by a sober and regular conduct to expiate thy offences against heaven and thy sovereign; but as a punishment for thy crime, presume not, without my leave, to stir beyond the limits of thy own habitation, on pain of a more rigorous and lasting confinement.

Nourjahad, thunder-struck at this unexpected sentence, was unable to reply; and the sultan having ordered the captain of his guards to be called, committed his prisoner to his hands; telling him if he suffered Nourjahad to escape, his head should answer it.

---

monstrous chimeras: strange delusions.

Filled with resentment and discontent, Nourjahad was conducted back to his own house; at all the avenues of which he had the mortification to see guards posted, agreeably to the charge given by the sultan.

He retired pensively to his closet, where, shutting himself up, he now for the first time repented of his indiscretion in the choice he had made.

Unfortunate that I am, cried he, what will riches or length of days avail me, if I am thus to be miserably immured within the walls of my own dwelling? Would it not have been better for me to have requested the genius to restore me to the favour of my prince? Schemzeddin always loved me, and would not fail to have promoted me to wealth and honours; mean while I should have enjoyed my liberty, which now methinks, as I am debarred of it, appears to me a greater blessing than any I possess. Unhappy Nourjahad, what is become of all thy schemes of felicity! He was even weak enough to shed tears, and gave himself up to vexation for the remainder of the day.

His mind, however, was by pleasure rendered too volatile to suffer any thing to make a lasting impression on him; and he had still too many resources of happiness in his power, to give himself up to despair. It is true, said he, I am debarred of my liberty, but have I not still a thousand delights in my possession? The incredulous sultan, satisfied with punishing me, will give himself no farther concern about me, provided I do not attempt to escape; and thus withdrawn from the public eye, envy will not endeavour to penetrate into the recesses of a private dwelling. I will secure the fidelity of my servants, by my liberality towards them. Schemzeddin's resentment will not last; or if it should, even as long as he lives, what is his life, the scanty portion of years allotted to common men, to my promised immortality?

Having thus reconciled his thoughts to his present situation, he resolved, in order to make himself amends for the restraint on his person, to indulge himself with an unbounded freedom in his most voluptuous wishes. He commanded a banquet to be prepared for him that night, which exceeded in luxury and profusion any of the preceding. He ordered all his women, of which he had a great number, adorned with jewels and dressed in their richest habits, to attend on him whilst he was at supper, permitting none but Mandana the favour to sit down with him. The magnificence of his apartments was heightened by a splendid illumination of a thousand torches, composed of odoriferous gums, which cast a blaze of light that vied with the glories of the sun. His musicians, both vocal and instrumental, were ordered to exert the utmost stretch of their art, and to sooth his mind with all the enchanting powers of harmony. Himself attired in robes, such as the kings of Persia were used to wear, was seated under a canopy of silver tissue, which he had put up for the purpose; and assuming the pomp of an Eastern monarch, suffered the illusion to take such possession of his mind, that if he were not before mad, he now seemed to be very near distraction.

Intoxicated with pleasure, the historian who writes his life, affirms that this night Nourjahad for the first time got drunk.[5]

Be that as it may, it is certain that having retired to rest, he slept sounder and longer than usual; for on his awaking, and missing Mandana from his side, whom he had made the partner of his bed, he called out to the slave who always attended in his antichamber, in order to enquire for her, resolving to chide her tenderly for leaving him.

He called loud and often, but nobody answering him, as he was naturally choleric, he jumped out of bed, and stepping hastily into the outer chamber, he found that none of the slaves were in waiting. Enraged at this neglect, he called several of his domestics by their names, one after another; when at length, after he was almost out of breath with passion, a female slave appeared, who was one of those appointed to wait on Mandana.

The damsel no sooner perceived him, than giving a loud shriek, she was about to run away; when Nourjahad, provoked at her behaviour, catching her roughly by the arm, Where is thy mistress, said he, and whence arises that terror and amazement in thy countenance? Alas! my lord, answered the slave, pardon my surprize, which is occasioned by my seeing you so unexpectedly. Nourjahad now perceiving that in his hurry he had forgot to put on his cloaths, concluded that it was that circumstance which had alarmed the damsel, and turning from her, Foolish woman, said he, go tell Mandana that I desire to see her. Ah, my lord, replied the maid, I would she were in a condition to come to you. Why, what is the matter, said Nourjahad, no ill I hope has befallen the dear light of my life? Is she sick? Methinks she went to bed last night in perfect health. Last night! my lord, replied the slave, and shook her head. Trifler, cried Nourjahad, what means that motion? Where is thy mistress? Speak! She is, I hope, said the slave, gone to receive the reward of her goodness! Here she began to weep. Oh Heaven, cried Nourjahad, is my dear Mandana dead? She is, answered the damsel, redoubling her tears, and I shall never have so kind a mistress.

Alas! replied Nourjahad, by what fatal accident am I thus suddenly deprived of the adorable creature?

It was not suddenly, my lord, replied the slave, Mandana died in childbed. Ah traitress, cried Nourjahad, how darest thou thus mock the sorrow of thy master, and traduce the chastity of my beloved. Thou knowest it is not

---

choleric: hot tempered.

[5] The drinking of wine and other alcoholic beverages is forbidden to followers of Islam by the Koran.

more than three moons since I received her a virgin to my arms, and doest thou presume to impose so ridiculous a story on me as that of her having died in childbed? My lord, answered the slave, it is more than three years since Mandana died. Audacious wretch, cried Nourjahad, wouldst thou persuade me out of my senses? With this he pinched the slave so hard by the arm, that she screamed out.

The noise she made brought several of the servants into the room, who, on seeing Nourjahad, all shewed manifest tokens of fear and surprize. What is the reason of all this, cried he out in a rage, are ye all leagued in combination against me? Be quick and explain to me the cause of this distraction which appears amongst you.

Hasem, who had run in amongst the other domestics, took upon him to answer for the rest. It is not to be wondered at, my lord, said he, that your slaves seem surprised at seeing you thus as it were raised from the dead; but if they are amazed, their joy doubtless is equal to their wonder; mine I am sure is unutterable, to behold my lord once more restored to his faithful servants, after we had almost despaired of your ever more unclosing your eyes.

You talk strangely, said Nourjahad, a little staggered at what he saw and heard. He just then recollected the terms on which he had received the important gift from the genius; and began to suspect that he had endured one of those preternatural slumbers, to which he had subjected himself. How long may I have slept, said he? Four years and twenty days exactly, answered Hasem; I have reason to know, for I counted the melancholy hours as they passed, and seldom quitted your bed-side. It may be so, said Nourjahad, I have been subject to these trances from a boy, but this has lasted rather longer than usual. He then commanded all his slaves to withdraw, retaining only Hasem, with whom he wanted to have some discourse.

Tell me now, said he, (when they were alone) and tell me truly, is all I have heard real, and is Mandana actually dead? Too true, my lord, replied Hasem, Mandana died in childbed, and dying left her infant son to my care. Is my child alive, said Nourjahad eagerly? He is, my lord, answered Hasem, and you shall see him presently: Mandana called me to her, continued he, when she found herself dying.

Hasem, said she, be careful of your lord; Heaven will one day restore him to you again. See that you manage his household with the same prudence and regularity that you would if he himself were to inspect into your conduct; for be assured he will sooner or later exact a just account of your proceedings. Here are the keys of his coffers. I ventured to take them from

---

three moons: three months.

under his pillow, where I knew he kept them. I have husbanded his fortune with economy, and have hitherto kept order and harmony in his family: On you it rests to preserve it in the same condition. Nourjahad will not fail to reward your diligence and fidelity. It is not expedient that any one should know the condition to which he is reduced. His life is governed by a strange fatality. You have nothing to do therefore, but to give out that he is seized with a lingering distemper, which confines him to his bed. Let no impertinent enquirers see him, and all curiosity about him will soon cease. These, proceeded Hasem, were almost the last words that my beloved mistress spoke. I have punctually complied with her orders. Your condition has been kept a profound secret from every one but your own family, and they all love you too well to betray their trust. Your women are all immured within the sacred walls of your seraglio, and though they murmur at their situation, they fail not to offer up their daily prayers that Heaven would restore you to them. I will now, continued he, present your son to you; it will be some consolation to you to see that charming pledge of Mandana's love. Saying this, he withdrew, but soon returned leading in the child, who was as beautiful as a little cherub.

Nourjahad melted into tears at the sight of him, and renewed his complaints for the loss of his adored Mandana. He saw that the child's age seemed to agree exactly with the account he had received; and now fully convinced of the truth of his misfortune, Oh Heaven, cried he, clasping the young boy to his bosom, what would I give that my dear Mandana were now here to partake of the pleasure I feel in this infant's caresses; gladly would I consent to have three ages cut off from the number of my years, to have her more precious life restored. But my felicity would then be too great, and I must submit to the destiny which I myself have chosen. Prudent Hasem, said he, observing he looked surprised, thou dost wonder at the words which thou hast heard me speak, but I will not conceal from thee the marvellous story of my life. Thy fidelity and zeal deserve this confidence; besides, it is requisite that I should trust some discreet person with my important secret, since Mandana, on whose tenderness and loyalty I could depend, is no more.

Nourjahad then acquainted Hasem with the wonderful mystery of his life. He did not, however, divulge the circumstance of his concealed treasure; he judged from his own heart, that it would not be altogether advisable to lay such a tempting bait in the way even of the most virtuous and steady mind; but contented himself with telling him that his genius constantly supplied him with riches, as his occasions required. Hasem listened to him with astonishment; but assured him, after what had already past, he doubted not a tittle of the truth of what he had been told, amazing and almost incredible as it appeared.

My lord, said he, you may securely rely on my zeal and diligence, so long as you are pleased to entertain me in your service. That I shall do during your life, interrupted Nourjahad: But, replied Hasem, what if one of those unmerciful long trances should continue for a length of time much beyond that from which you are but now awakened, and that I should happen to die before you recover your senses, who knows in that case what might be the consequences? It is an accident exceedingly to be dreaded, replied Nourjahad; Heaven knows to what indignities I might be exposed, perhaps to be buried alive, and condemned to pass a century or two in a dismal sepulchre. The thought makes me shudder, and I almost repent of having accepted life on such conditions. As I have no warning, continued he, when those fatal slumbers will overpower me, (for who can always be guarded against the starts of passion, or what man is so attentive to that impertinent monitor within, as to hear his whispers amidst the hurry of tumultuous pleasures?) As I know not, I say, when I am to be condemned to that state of insensibility, or how long I shall continue in it, I can only conjure thee if I should happen to be seized with another trance during thy life, (which, considering my disposition, is not impossible) that thou wilt observe the same conduct which thou hast lately done; and if the angel of death should summon thee away before my senses are loosed from their mysterious bands, that thou wilt with thy dying breath, commit the secret to some one faithful person of my family, whom thou thinkest most fit to be relied on, for a punctual discharge of their duty. As I shall never part with any of my servants, till the inevitable stroke of death separates them from me, and shall constantly supply their places with the worthiest persons that can be found, I think I cannot fail of a succession of people, from amongst whom, one at least may always be found, in whose secrecy and truth I may safely confide.

Without doubt, my lord, answered Hasem, you may by such wise measures as these, be always guarded against the worst that may befal you.

Though Nourjahad had, by thus providing against evil events, exceedingly relieved his mind from the fears by which it was agitated, lest any ill should happen to him during his slumbers; yet was his heart far from being at ease. The loss of Mandana preyed upon his spirits. He had no relish for the charms of his other women. Mandana's superior loveliness was always present to his eyes: The delicacies of his table grew tasteless; Mandana's sprightly wit was wanting to give a relish to the feast. The melodious concerts of music with which he was wont to be so delighted, now only served to overwhelm him with melancholy: Mandana's enchanting voice was not heard, which used to swell his heart to rapture.

In short, for a time he took pleasure in nothing but the caresses and innocent prattle of his little son, whom by his tenderness and endearments he had taught to love him.

I am unhappy, my dear Hasem, would he often say; the loss of Mandana imbitters all my joys, and methinks I begin to look forward with disgust.

My lord, said Hasem, there is nothing which has befallen you but what is common to all. Every one may naturally expect to see the death of some person or other whom they love; but you who are endowed with so miraculous a life must needs look to drop a tear over a thousand graves.

Melancholy reflection, said Nourjahad! it occurred not to me in this light when I made my choice. I knew indeed I must of necessity bury hundreds of succeeding generations; but said I to myself, I shall insensibly contract new amities, as I perceive the old ones are likely to be dissolved by the hand of time. My heart, said I, shall never feel a vacuity, for want of fit objects of desire. A new beauty will naturally take place of her whose charms begin to decline; thus the ardors of love will be supplied with perpetual fewel; and upon the same principle will the social joys of friendship be unremitting. I considered the world as a flower garden, the product of which was to delight my senses for a certain season. The bloom is not made to last, thought I, but it will be succeeded by a fresh blow, whose sweetness and variety will equal the former, and intirely obliterate them from my memory. I thought not, alas, that before the spring ended, a cruel blast might suddenly destroy my fairest flower.

Would you, my lord, said Hasem, if it were in your power, absolve your genius from his promise, seeing your life must be perpetually subject to such misfortunes?

Not so neither, answered Nourjahad; time is a never-failing remedy for grief; I shall get over this, and be better prepared against the next assault of evil.

In effect, Nourjahad kept his word, and soon returned to his former way of living.

He had the mortification, however, to find himself still a prisoner. Hasem told him that the sultan had not yet taken off the restraint, under which he had formerly laid him; and whether it was through forgetfulness or design, the guards still maintained their posts about his house. This Nourjahad was himself convinced of, by seeing them from his windows.

It is strange, said he, that Schemzeddin should retain his resentment against me for so long a time; especially as he might have been convinced of the truth of what I asserted, by the extraordinary state in which I have

---

blow: blossom.

lain all this while. You forget, my lord, said Hasem, that this was an absolute secret, no one from under your own roof knowing a word of the matter. Such were Mandana's last injunctions, and your faithful servants never divulged a tittle of it.

Did not my friends come to visit me, said Nourjahad, during that interval in which I slept? Those whom you called your friends, answered Hasem, came as usual, during the first month of your dormant state; but being refused admittance, under pretence that your health was so much declined, that you were not in a condition to receive them, they soon desisted from their visits; and finding they could no more be entertained with feasting and jollity, they have never since inquired after you.

Ungrateful wretches, said Nourjahad! I cast them off for ever. Yet it is an irksome thing to live without friends. You Hasem are a prudent and honest man, but still you are my servant; I cannot therefore consider you on that footing of equality which friendship requires. There is one man, said Hasem, who has shewn himself grateful and compassionate; and those two virtues never come alone, but are ever found attended with many others. Oh name him, said Nourjahad. It is Zamgrad, replied Hasem, that officer of the sultan's whom you once obliged by a trifling present of a ring; he never fails sending every day to enquire after your welfare. Nay, he has often called himself, and expressed an honest sorrow for the ill state of health to which I told him you were reduced; tenderly blaming the sultan for his rigorous confinement of you.

Worthy Zamgrad, said Nourjahad, thou, thou alone shalt be the chosen friend of my heart; the rest of my worthless acquaintance I from this minute discard.

I will write to Schemzeddin, pursued he; perhaps he may now relent and restore me to my liberty. I long to shift the scene, and remove to some place where Mandana's image may not be so often revived in my memory. Wert thou not, Hasem, about to procure for me a noble seat in the country, which I was going to take a view of that day on which the good Zamgrad came to carry me before the sultan? If I might but retire thither, I should think myself happy.

Alas, my lord, replied Hasem, that fine seat cannot now be yours. You may remember I made only a conditional agreement with the owner of it, depending on your approbation of the place after your having seen it. I recollect it, said Nourjahad, but may it not still be mine? By no means, answered Hasem; the owner has long since disposed of it to another.

That is unlucky, said Nourjahad; but we can easily find another. Be it your care to look out for one, whilst I endeavour to move the sultan in my favour.

Hasem was not slow in executing his master's orders. In three days he told him he had seen a villa, which seemed to him to surpass all the descriptions of Eden in its primary state of beauty. It is but at the distance of ten leagues from Ormuz, said he. The house and gardens are in compleat order, and you may purchase the whole for fifty thousand pieces of gold. The sultan himself hath not in his possession any thing more delightful. I will have it, said Nourjahad: Get the money ready, you have the keys of my coffers, and they contain more than that sum.

My lord, answered Hasem, when you last saw them they did contain much more; but you will be pleased to recollect that it is above four years since, and that your household has been maintained during that time; which, notwithstanding I have used the utmost economy, must needs have somewhat diminished your treasury. I had forgot, replied Nourjahad, but I will soon supply you with the gold you want.

Accordingly he paid a visit to the subterraneous cave that very night; where finding every thing as he had left it, he loaded himself with a quantity of gold, sufficient to prevent the necessity of drawing from his hidden store of wealth for a considerable time.

Intent now on the pursuit of his pleasures, he neglected not applying to the sultan for a repeal, or at least a mitigation of his sentence. He writ to Schemzeddin a letter in terms full of humility; thinking if he could remove his incredulity by convincing him that the extraordinary fact he had related, was nothing more than the truth, that the sultan would no longer deny him his liberty. He scrupled not to acquaint him, that he had been for more than four years in a profound sleep, for the confirmation of which fact, strange as it might seem to his majesty, he desired leave to appeal to every one of his own household, and conjured the sultan to take the trouble of informing himself more fully from some of his people, whom he might cause to be brought into his presence and privately examined, as he confessed he did not wish to have so uncommon an event divulged.

Nourjahad from this expedient had great hopes of obtaining his desire; but the event turned out contrary to his expectations.

Zamgrad two days after brought him an answer from the sultan in writing: Nourjahad laid the paper on his head, then kissing the seals, he broke them open, and read as follows.

"I have not been unmindful of thy motions, and I was pleased to hear from time to time, that for these four years past, order and decency have been preserved in thy dwelling. I flattered myself that this was owing to thy having returned to a sense of thy duty. But my hope deceived me, when I found that Nourjahad was by a violent malady which seized him (doubtless the effects of his intemperance) disqualified from indulging in those excesses in which he was wont to riot.

"This visitation from heaven, I thought would have produced salutary effects on thy mind, and hoped if the angel of health were again to revisit thy pillow, that thou wouldst make a different use of thy recovered strength. How must my indignation then be roused against thee, abandoned as thou art to perdition, to find thou persistest in thy enormous folly and wickedness; and continuest to abuse the patience of thy benefactor and sovereign master, with such unparalleled falsehoods. A prince less merciful than myself, would no longer delay to punish thee with death: But I give thee thy wretched life. Spend it if thou canst in penitence. Nay, I will so far indulge thee, as to permit thee, for the more perfect recovery of thy health, to retire to thy house in the country; but at the peril of thy head presume not to stir beyond the bounds of thy own habitation."

Nourjahad now too late found his error in endeavouring to force belief of a thing which appeared so incredible, and wished he had rather availed himself of the sultan's prepossessions in favour of the story propagated by his servants, as he found that would have been the wiser course.

What a world is this, said he to Zamgrad, (after having read the letter) where he who ought to be the rewarder of truth, and the dispenser of justice, shuts his ears against conviction, and condemns an innocent man for endeavouring to set him right? But I will not involve you in the punishment imposed on my imaginary guilt, by requiring your belief of what I have in vain endeavoured to convince the incredulous Schemzeddin.

I know not, my lord, replied Zamgrad, what has passed between the sultan and you; of this only I am certain, that he seems exceedingly enraged against you. I would it were in my power, from the respect I bear you, to mitigate his resentment.

I thank thee, gentle Zamgrad, said Nourjahad; I find thou, of all my numerous acquaintance, art the only man who has shewn any attachment to me. If the friendship of one labouring under the displeasure of his prince, be worth thy accepting, I offer thee mine, and conjure thee to grant me yours in return. The base ingratitude I have already experienced from the rest of my pretended friends, has determined me to disclaim all society with them: if thou wilt sometimes visit me in my retirement, thou wilt find Nourjahad not undeserving of thy kindness.

Zamgrad promised to see him as often as he could, and took his leave.

However vexed Nourjahad was at his disappointment, in finding himself, by being still debarred of his liberty, deprived for a time at least from executing one of his favourite purposes, that of travelling all over the world, he yet contented himself with the reflection, that this project was only postponed to another opportunity; and that he should have time enough for executing his design, after Schemzeddin, and many of his posterity were in their graves. I will not waste my hours, said he, in fruitless languishment for what I cannot at present attain, but make the most of the good which now offers itself to my acceptance.

He ordered Hasem to pay down the money forthwith, for that fine seat: I will remove thither, said he, immediately; and make myself some recompence by all the means that art can devise, for that cruel long trance, which over-powered me so unseasonably: I hope I shall not be visited by another for these fifty or sixty years at least.

Hasem's diligence kept pace with his lord's impatience: He got every thing in readiness for his reception at his rural mansion: and to avoid the notice which might be taken of so numerous a seraglio, and such a train of domestics, the prudent Hasem advised that they should set out and travel by night. This precaution, said he, will prevent the malice of your enemies from making ill-natured representations of your conduct to the sultan; and as you yourself are supposed by every body in Ormuz to have laboured under a long and painful illness, I think, to give colour to this report, it would be most advisable for you to be carried in a litter. As Nourjahad loved his ease, he readily enough consented to this proposal, and in this manner suffered himself to be conveyed to his new habitation.

On his arrival he found Hasem had not exaggerated in his description of this place. The house, or rather palace, for such it might be called, infinitely exceeded his expectations; but above all, the gardens were so delicious, that his senses were ravished with delight. He declared that those mansions of joy prepared for the reception of the faithful,[6] could not exceed them; and forgetting that this paradise was to be his prison, he ordered that a pavilion of light brocade should be reared for him in the midst of his garden, where he purposed to enjoy the cool hours of the evening, amidst the noise of falling waters, and the wild notes of innumerable birds, who had taken up their residence in this terrestrial paradise.

Behold him now once more, in the possession of every thing, for which the heart of man in the wildest wishes of Epicurean phrenzy, could pant. He gave the reins to his passions; he again became the slave of voluptuous appetites: He submitted a second time to the power of beauty; he invented new modes of luxury; and his delightful abode became the scene of every licentious pleasure.

The delicacies and profusion in which he himself wallowed, made him forget that there were wants or miseries amongst his fellow-creatures; and

---

Epicurean phrenzy: sensualist obsession.

[6]The Muslim paradise, *al-Jannah* (the garden), is described in the Koran as offering physical as well as spiritual rewards to the faithful.

as he had but little intercourse with mankind, except with those who flattered his follies, or administered to his loose pleasures, he became hardened to all the social affections. He ceased to relieve the poor, because they never came in his way; and with a heart naturally generous and benevolent, he lived only for himself.

Immersed in sensual gratifications, he lost all relish for any others. The poets and sages whom he entertained in his house, began to grow irksome to him. He derided the wisdom and philosophy of the latter; and if they attempted to entertain him with learned or grave discourses, he laughed at them; and at length thinking their company tedious, he turned them out of his house.

His bards would have shared the same fate, if they had not by a timely address rendered their art subservient to his depraved inclinations. They composed nothing but pieces filled with adulation on himself, or light verses in praise of one or other of his mistresses; these were set to melting airs, and sung accompanied by the lute.

Thus did Nourjahad pass his days. Every rising sun beheld some fresh outrage on the laws of temperance and decency; and the shades of every night descended on his unatoned offences.

The delightful season of the year, winged with pleasures, was now almost fled, when one of the most extravagant projects came into the head of Nourjahad, that ever entered the imagination of man.

As the gardens of his palace were exceedingly delicious, he vainly fancied that they must be very like the regions of paradise (where all good Mussulmen are received after death) and that in order to make the resemblance perfectly complete, he would cause the women of his seraglio to personate the Houriis;[7] those beautiful virgins who are given as a reward to all true believers. He himself would needs represent Mahomet; and one of his mistresses whom he loved best, and who was indeed the handsomest of them, he would have to appear under the name and character of Cadiga, the favourite wife of the great Prophet.[8]

The idea, wild and profane as it was, was notwithstanding readily adopted by all the people about him, no one presuming to dispute his will. Nor were the women on this occasion much inclined to do so, as it served them for a very agreeable amusement.

Some debates however arose amongst them on account of the dresses

---

[7]Female companions reserved for the faithful in al-Jannah, the houris are perpetual virgins.

[8]Cadiga (Khadija), Muhammad's first (and, during her lifetime, his only) wife, is highly revered in the Koran.

proper to be worn on this occasion; as none of them remembered to have read in the Koran what sort of habits the Houriis wore; and some of the ladies gave it as their opinion that those beauties went naked.

After many disputes on the subject, however, they struck a sort of medium, and agreed to be attired in loose robes of the thinnest Persian gauze, with chaplets of flowers on their heads.

Nourjahad approved of the invention, and gave orders to Hasem to prepare for this celestial masquerade, with all possible diligence; charging him to leave nothing out, that could render the entertainment worthy of Mahomet himself.

Neither art nor expence were spared on this extraordinary occasion. He gave commandment that the fountains which adorned his garden should be so contrived, that instead of water, they should pour forth milk and wine; that the seasons should be anticipated, and the early fragrance of the spring should be united with the more vivid colours of the glowing summer. In short, that fruits, blossoms, and flowers, should at once unite their various beauties to imbellish this terrestrial paradise.

The diligence of Hasem was so active, that every thing was got in readiness, even sooner than Nourjahad expected. He descended into his garden to take a survey of these wondrous preparations; and finding all exactly to his mind, he gave orders to his women to hold themselves prepared to act their parts; telling them that on that very evening he would give them a foretaste of the ravishing pleasures they were to enjoy, in the happy regions of light.

The weather was extremely hot, and Nourjahad, in order to take a view of the magnificent decorations, having fatigued himself with wandering through his elysium, retired to his apartment, and threw himself down on a sopha, with intent to take a short repose, the better to prepare himself for the excesses of the night: leaving orders with Hasem and Cadiga to awake him from sleep before sunset.

Nourjahad, however, opened his eyes without any one's having roused him from his slumbers; when perceiving that the day was almost closed, and finding that his commands had been neglected, he flew into a violent passion, suspecting that his women had prevailed on Hasem, to grant them this opportunity whilst he slept, of indulging themselves in liberties without that restraint to which they were accustomed in his presence.

Enraged at the thought, he resolved to have them called before him, and after severely reprimanding them, and punishing Hasem proportionally to his fault, to have his women all locked up, and postpone his festivity till he was in a better humour to relish it.

Impatient, and even furious at his disappointment, he stamped on the floor with his foot; when immediately a black eunuch presented himself at the door. Go, said he, his words almost choaked with indignation, go and bid my women one and all hasten directly into my presence.

The slave retired in respectful silence; and presently after all the ladies of his seraglio entered his apartment. They were, according to the custom, covered with vails, but on appearing in their lord's presence, they threw them off. But, Oh Heaven! what was Nourjahad's anger and astonishment, when instead of the beautiful Houriis whom he expected to see, to behold a train of wrinkled and deformed old hags.

Amazement and rage for a while suspended the power of speech: When the foremost of the old women approaching, and offering to embrace him, he thrust her rudely from him: Detestable fiend, said he, whence this presumption? where are my slaves? Where is Hasem? and the women of my seraglio? The traitoresses! they shall pay dearly for thus abusing my indulgence.

The old women at this all fell upon their faces to the ground; but the first who had advanced addressing herself to speak, Avaunt! cried Nourjahad, begone wretches, and rid my sight of such hideous aspects.

Alas, my lord, replied the old woman, have you intirely forgot me? has time left no traces to remind you of your once beloved Cadiga? Cadiga! thou Cadiga? do not provoke me, said Nourjahad, or by Allah I'll spurn thee with my foot.

The old women now all set up a lamentable cry, Miserable wretches that we are, said they, beating their withered breasts, it had been happy for us if we had all died in our youth, rather than have thus out-lived our lord's affections!

Evil betide ye, said Nourjahad, who in the name of deformity are ye all? Hereupon the beldames cried out with one voice, Your mistresses! the once admired and loved partners of your bed, but the relentless hand of time has made such cruel ravage on our charms, that we do not wonder thou shouldst find it impossible to recollect us.

Nourjahad now began to suspect that he had been over-powered by a second trance. Why, how long, in the devil's name, have I then slept, said he?

Forty years and eleven moons, answered the lady who called herself Cadiga. Thou liest, I am sure, said Nourjahad, for it appears to me but as yesterday since I ordered thee (if thou really art Cadiga) to awake me at a certain hour, that I might enjoy the glorious entertainment prepared for me in the gardens of the Houriis.

I do remember it, said Cadiga, and we your faithful slaves were to personate those beautiful virgins. Alas, alas, we are not now fit to represent

---

vails: veils.

those daughters of paradise! Thou art fitter, said Nourjahad, to represent the furies. I tell thee again, it cannot be many hours since I first fell into a slumber.

It may well seem so, answered Cadiga, buried as your senses have been in forgetfulness, and every faculty consigned to oblivion, that the interval of time so past must be quite annihilated; yet it is most certain that you have slept as long as I tell you.

Nourjahad upon this examined the faces of the old women one after the other, but finding them so totally different from what they once were, he swore that he did not believe a word they said. Thou Cadiga! said he, the black-browed Cadiga, whose enchanting smiles beguiled all hearts; thou art wonderously like her I confess!

Yet that I am that identical fair one, answered she, I shall be able to convince you, from a remarkable signature which I bear on my bosom, and which still remains, though the rest of my person is so entirely changed.

Saying this, she uncovered her breast, on which the figure of a rose-bud was delineated by the hand of nature. Nourjahad well remembered the mark; he had once thought it a beauty, and made it the subject of an amorous sonnet, when the bosom of the fair Cadiga was as white and as smooth as alabaster.

Convinced by this proof, that these women were really what they pretended to be, Nourjahad could not conceal his vexation. By the Temple of Mecca,[9] said he, this genius of mine is no better than he should be, and I begin to suspect he is little less than an evil spirit, or he could not thus take delight in persecuting me for nothing.

Ah, my lord, said Cadiga, I am not ignorant of the strange fate by which your life is governed. Hasem, your faithful Hasem, communicated the secret to me with his dying breath. Is Hasem dead, cried Nourjahad? He is, my lord, answered Cadiga, and so is the worthy Zamgrad. What is become of my son, said Nourjahad? I hope he has not shared the same fate. It were better that he had, replied Cadiga, for it is now some five and twenty years since he ran away from the governor in whose hands the wise Hasem had placed him for his education; and having in vain endeavoured to prevail on that honest man to bury you, that giving out you were deceased, he might take possession of all your wealth, finding he could not succeed in his unnatural design, he took an opportunity of breaking open your cabinet, and

---

furies: goddesses of vengeance in classical mythology, often represented as haglike in appearance.

[9]The temple or *Ka-ba* (cube) is an ancient and important sanctuary within the Great Mosque of Mecca, Islam's holiest city.

securing all the treasure he could find, stole secretly away, and has never been heard of since.

Ungrateful viper! exclaimed Nourjahad; and thou cruel genius, thus to imbitter a life, which was thy own voluntary gift; for thou camest to me unasked.

Had not, proceeded Cadiga, myself and the rest of your women consented to give up all our jewels to Hasem, who turned them into money, we must long ere this have been reduced to want; for your unworthy son stripped you of all your wealth; but Hasem conducted every thing with the same regularity and care as if you had been awake, discharging such of your domestics as he thought unnecessary, and replacing such as died in your service; and it is not many days since the good old man was himself summoned away by the angel of death.

Tell me, said Nourjahad, does Schemzeddin still live?

He does, replied Cadiga, but bending under the weight of age and infirmities, he is become so intolerably peevish that no one dares speak to him. Indeed he is at times so fantastical and perverse, that it is secretly whispered he is not perfectly in his senses. It may very well be, said Nourjahad, that he is doating by this time, for he cannot be much less than seventy years old. The genius has in this article been faithful to his promise; for I, though nearly of the same age, find myself as vigorous and healthy as ever, but I give him little thanks for this, seeing he has defrauded me of such an unconscionable portion of my life.

My lord, said Cadiga, there is one circumstance which may in some measure reconcile you to what has already happened. You know, by the severity of the sultan, you have been the greatest part of your days a prisoner; which condition, however it might have been alleviated by the pleasures which surrounded you, must nevertheless have by this time grown exceedingly irksome, had you all the while been sensible of your restraint; and you would not probably have been so palled with the repetition of the same enjoyments, that I know not whether your good genius, has not, instead of cruelty, shewn an extreme indulgence, in rendering you for such a number of years unconscious of your misfortune; especially as the sultan, by what I learnt from Hasem, has, notwithstanding the length of time since he first deprived you of your liberty, never reversed the barbarous sentence.

What thou hast said, has some colour, replied Nourjahad; and I am very much inclined to think thou hast hit upon the truth. Sage Cadiga, pursued he, what thou hast lost in beauty, thou hast gained in wisdom; and though I can no longer regard thee with tenderness, I will still retain thee in my service, and constitute thee governess over my female slaves; for I must have my seraglio supplied with a new race of beauties. For the rest of those hags, as I do not know of any thing they are now good for, I desire to see them no more. Be gone, said he to them, I shall give orders to Cadiga concerning you.

When Nourjahad was left alone, he began seriously to reflect on his condition. How unhappy I am, said he, thus to find myself at once deprived of every thing that was dear to me; my two faithful friends, Hasem and Zamgrad, all the blooming beauties of my seraglio, who used to delight my eyes; but above all, my son, whose ingratitude and cruelty pierces me more deeply than all my other losses; and that rigid spirit who presides over my life, to take advantage of those hours of insensibility, to deprive me of all my comforts! Yet why do I reproach my protector for that? the same ills might have befallen me, had the progress of my life been conducted by the common laws of nature. I must have seen the death of my friends, and they might possibly have been snatched from me in a manner equally sudden and surprising as their loss now appears.

My women, had I seen them every day, must necessarily by this time have grown old and disgustful to me; and I should certainly before now, have discarded two or three generations of beauties. My son too, would, in his heart, have been the same thankless and perfidious creature that he has now shewn himself, had the eye of watchful authority been constantly open on his conduct; and there is only this difference perhaps, between me and every other parent, that I have lived to see my offspring trampling on filial duty, riotously seizing on my wealth, leaving my family to poverty, and not so much as bestowing a grateful thought on him who gave him being, and by whose spoils he is enriched; whilst other fathers, deceived by a specious outside, in the full persuasion of the piety, justice, and affection of their children, have descended to the grave in peace, whilst their heirs, with as little remorse as my graceless child, have laughed at their memories.

I see it is in vain, proceeded he, to escape the miseries that are allotted to human life. Fool that I was to subject myself to them more by ten thousand fold than any other can possibly experience! But stop, Nourjahad, how weak are thy complaints? thou knowest the conditions of thy existence, and that thou must of necessity behold the decay and dissolution of every thing that is mortal; take comfort then, and do not imbitter thy days by melancholy reflections, but resolve for the future to let no events disturb thy peace, seize every fleeting joy as it passes, and let variety be thy heaven, for thou seest there is nothing permanent.

As Nourjahad was never used, but on occasions of distress, to make use of his reason or philosophy, he no sooner found an alleviation of the evil, than he put them both to flight, as impertinent intruders. He did not therefore long disturb himself with disagreeable reflections, but resolved as soon as possible to return to those pleasures which he thought constituted the felicity of man's life.

He gave himself but little concern about those treasures of which his son had robbed him, knowing he had an inexhaustible fund of wealth, of which, agreeably to the genius's promise, he could not be deprived.

From Cadiga he learnt that his house at Ormuz was in the same condition he had left it; Hasem having taken care to place a diligent and faithful servant there, on whom he might rely with equal security as on himself; and he had the farther precaution, added Cadiga, not long before his death, to solicit, through Zamgrad's means, the sultan's permission for your return thither. This, said he, may be necessary in case our lord awakes before Schemzeddin's decease, and should have a desire to quit this place, he may do it without the trouble of a fresh application.

And has the sultan granted this, cried Nourjahad?

He has, answered Cadiga, as a matter of great indulgence: for having, as he said, heard that your profusion was unbounded, finding there were no hopes of reclaiming you, he had determined to confine you for the remainder of your life, with this liberty however, that you might make choice either of this palace or your house at Ormuz for your prison.

Fool, cried Nourjahad, he little imagines how impotent are his threats, when he speaks of confining me for life! I would however *he* were dead, that I might be rid of this irksome restraint; but it cannot last much longer, for the days of Schemzeddin must needs draw towards a period. I will not, mean while, bestow any farther thought on him, but avail myself of that liberty which he has allowed me, and return to Ormuz; for I am weary of this solitude, seeing I have lost every thing that could render my retirement agreeable.

Do thou, said he, see that every thing is prepared for my reception. I would have my seraglio filled once more, otherwise my house, when I enter it, will appear a desert to me, and I shall be at a loss how to divert the tedious hours which may yet remain of my confinement. I will depend on thy experience and skill in beauty, to make choice of such virgins, as you think will well supply the place of those I have lost.

I have a friend, said Cadiga, a merchant, who deals in female slaves; and he has always such a number, that it will be easy to select from amongst them some whose charms cannot fail to please you. I will order him to repair to your house, and bring with him a collection of the rarest beauties he has in his possession; you may then chuse for yourself.

Be it so, said Nourjahad, I leave the conduct of every thing to thee; if I approve of the damsels, I shall not scruple at any price for their purchase.

The day being come for his return to Ormuz, full of pleasing eagerness to behold the divine creatures which he was told waited his arrival, he set out with a splendid equipage, but had the mortification to behold his chariot surrounded by a party of the sultan's guards, with drawn sabres in their hands, to repress the curiosity of those who might approach the chariot, to gaze at the person who was conducted in so unusual a manner.

I could well excuse this part of my retinue, said Nourjahad, as he passed along, but there is no resisting the commands of this whimsical old fellow Schemzeddin. Being thus conducted to his house, the guards as before posted themselves round it.

However chagrined Nourjahad was at this circumstance, he was resolved it should not interrupt his pleasures.

He found the young slaves whom Cadiga had prepared all waiting his arrival. They were richly cloathed, and standing together in a row, in a long gallery through which he was to pass. On his entering, the merchant to whom they belonged, ordered the women to unvail.

Nourjahad examined them one after the other, but none of them pleased him. One had features too large, and another's were too small; the complexion of this was not brilliant, and the air of that wanted softness; this damsel was too tall, and the next was ill proportioned.

Dost thou call these beauties, said Nourjahad, angrily? By my life they are a pack of as awkward damsels as ever I beheld.

Surely, my lord, cried the merchant, you do not speak as you think. These young maids are allowed by all good judges to be the most perfect beauties that ever were seen in Persia: The sultan himself has none equal to them in his seraglio.

I tell thee, man, said Nourjahad, they are not worthy even to wait on those of whom I myself was formerly master. I know not that, my lord, answered the merchant, but this I am sure of, that I can have any sum which I shall demand for their purchase. Then thou must carry them to some other market, cried Nourjahad, for to me they appear fit for nothing but slaves.

Cadiga, who was present, now taking Nourjahad aside, said, These, my lord, these damsels are less charming than those of which you were formerly possessed, but the taste for beauty is quite altered since that time: You may assure yourself that none will be offered to your acceptance that will exceed these. Were I and my companions, whom you once so much admired, to be restored to our youth again, we should not now be looked upon; such is the fantastic turn of the age.

If this be so, said Nourjahad, I shall be very unfashionable in my amours; for the present, however, I shall content myself with some of the most tolerable of these maidens, till I have time and opportunity of supplying myself with better.

Saying this, he selected half a dozen of those young slaves, whom he thought the most agreeable, and having paid the merchant what he demanded for them, dismissed the rest.

Nourjahad having now once more established his household, and perceiving that these damsels upon a longer acquaintance were really amiable, expected to find himself restored to his former contentment and alacrity of spirits. But in this he was deceived. He was seized with a lassitude that rendered his days tiresome. The vacancy he found in his heart was insupportable. Surrounded by new faces, he saw nobody for whom he could entertain either love or friendship. This is a comfortless life, would he exclaim to himself, yet how often, during the date of my existence, must this situation, melancholy as it is, recur to me. A friend shall no sooner be endeared to me by long experience of kindness and fidelity, without which it is impossible I should regard him; than death will deprive me of him, as it has already done of Hasem and Zamgrad; and how many bright eyes am I doomed to see for ever closed, or what is as mortifying to behold, their faded lustre. There is but one way, said he, to guard against those evils: I will no more contract friendships amongst men, nor ever again suffer my mind to be subdued by female charms. I will confound all distinction by variety, nor permit one woman to engross my heart; for I find by sad experience, even after such an amazing length of time, that the bare idea of my dear Mandana, inspires me with more tenderness, than ever I experienced from the fondest blandishments of all the beauties I have since possessed.

Nourjahad endeavoured to banish those melancholy thoughts by others more agreeable; but he had no resources within himself. He had nothing to reflect on, from which he could derive any satisfaction. My life, said he, appears like a dream of pleasure, that has passed away without leaving any substantial effects: and I am even already weary of it, though in fact, notwithstanding my advanced age, I have enjoyed it but a short time, dating from that period whence my immortality commenced.

He tried to read to divert his distempered thoughts; but from books he could receive no entertainment. If he turned over the pages of philosophers, moralists, or expounders of the mysteries of his religion, What have I to do with thy tedious lessons, or dry precepts, said he? Thou writest to men like thyself, subject to mortality; thou teachest them how to live, that they may learn how to die; but what is this to me? as I am not subject to the latter, thy advice can be of little use to me in regard to the former.

He had next recourse to the poets; but their works gave him as little pleasure as the others. Absorbed as he had been in the grosser pleasures of sense, he had lost those fine feelings, which constitute that delicate and pleasing perception we have, of such images, as are addressed to the heart. He knew the fallacy and even essence of all sensual enjoyments; and to the most warm descriptions of love, and the most pathetic pictures of grief he was equally insensible.

Poor wretches, said he, on reading a fine elegy written by a lover on the death of his mistress, doomed as thou wert to a short span of life, and a narrow circle of enjoyments, thou magnifiest every thing within thy confined sphere. One single object having engrossed thy whole heart, and inspired thee with transports, thou dost immortalize her charms. Her death (despairing to supply her place) filled thy eyes with tears, and taught thee to record thy own sorrows with her praises. I partake not of thy pleasures or thy pains; none but such as are liable to the same fate can be affected by thy sentiments.

When he read of the death of heroes and kings, and the destruction of cities, or the revolution of empires, How circumscribed, said he, is the knowledge of a paltry historian! Who is at the pains of collecting the scanty materials which a life of forty or fifty years perhaps affords him, and then he makes a mighty parade of learning, with the poor pittance for which he has been drudging all his days. How infinitely superior will my fund of information be, who shall myself be an eye-witness to events as extraordinary as these, and numbered a thousand times over; for doubtless the same things which have happened, will happen again. What curiosity can you incite in me, who shall infallibly see the same chain of causes and effects take place over and over again, in the vast round of eternity.

The accounts of travellers, descriptions of the manners and customs of various countries, and books of geography, afforded him a little more entertainment. All these places, said he, I shall visit in my own proper person, and shall then be able to judge whether these accounts are just.

Whilst he endeavoured to fill up the vacuity he found in his mind, his time was spent at best but in a sort of insipid tranquillity. The voluptuary has no taste for mental pleasures.

He every now and then returned to his former excesses, but he had not the same relish for them as before. Satiety succeeded every enjoyment. In vain did his slaves torture their invention to procure new delights for him. The powers of luxury were exhausted, and his appetites palled with abundance.

He grew peevish, morose, tyrannical; cruelty took possession of his breast; he abused his women and beat his slaves, and seemed to enjoy no satisfaction but that of tormenting others.

In vain did the prudent Cadiga, who had still some little influence over him, expostulate with him on the enormity of his behaviour.

How darest thou, said he, presume to dictate to thy master, or to censure his conduct! To whom am I accountable for my actions? To God and our prophet, answered Cadiga, with a boldness that provoked Nourjahad's wrath. Thou liest, said he, as I am exempt from death, I never can be brought to judgment, what then have I to fear from the resentment, or hope from the favour of the powers whom thou namest?

But hast thou no regard, said Cadiga, for the laws of society, nor pity for the sufferings of thy fellow creatures, whom thou makest to groan every day under thy cruelty?

Foolish woman, said Nourjahad, dost thou talk to me of laws, who think myself bound by none. Civil and religious laws are so interwoven, that you cannot pluck out a single thread without spoiling the whole texture, and if I cut the woof, thinkest thou that I will spare the weft, when I can do it with impunity? The privilege of immortality which I enjoy, would be bestowed on me to little purpose, if I were to suffer the weak prejudices of religion, in which I am no way concerned, to check me in any of my pursuits. And what can the feeble laws of man do? My life they cannot reach. Yet thou art a prisoner notwithstanding, answered Cadiga. True, replied Nourjahad, but even in my confinements I have surfeited with delights. Schemzeddin's death must soon give me that liberty, which considering the race of uncontrouled freedom I have before me, I do not now think worth attempting. I shall then expatiate freely all over the globe; mean while I tell thee, woman, I am weary of the dull round of reiterated enjoyments which are provided for me; my sensual appetites are cloyed, I have no taste for intellectual pleasures, and I must have recourse to those which gratify the malevolent passions.

Thou art not fit to live, cried Cadiga, with a warmth of which she had cause to repent; for Nourjahad, enraged at her reply, plucked a poniard from his girdle, Go tell thy prophet so, said he, and plunged it into the side of the unfortunate slave, who fell at his feet weltering in blood.

The brutal Nourjahad, so far from being moved with this spectacle, turned from her with indifference, and quitting the chamber, entered the apartments of his women, to whom with barbarous mirth he related what he had done.

Though he had now lost all relish for delicate pleasures, or even for the more gross enjoyments of sense, he nevertheless indulged himself in them to excess; and knowing he was not accountable to any one for the death of his slave, he thought no more of Cadiga; but after a day spent in extravagant debauchery sunk to repose.

But his eyes were opened to a different scene from that on which he had closed them. He no sooner awoke than he perceived a man sitting at his bed's-foot, who seemed to be plunged in sorrow; he leaned pensively on his arm, holding a handkerchief before his eyes.

What mockery is this, said Nourjahad, didst thou suppose me dead, and art thou come to mourn over me?

Not so, my lord, replied the man, I knew that you still lived; but the sultan is dead, the good Schemzeddin is no more! I am glad of it, replied Nourjahad, I shall now obtain my liberty. Who then is to reign in Ormuz? Doubtless, my lord, answered the man, the prince Schemerzad, the eldest son of Schemzeddin. Thou ravest, cried Nourjahad, Schemzeddin has no son. Pardon me, my lord, said the man, the sultana Nourmahal was delivered of this prince the very hour on which the unfortunate Cadiga died by your hand. Thou art insolent, replied Nourjahad, to mention that circumstance; but if so, we have indeed got a very young successor to the throne. My lord, answered the man, Schemerzad is allowed to be one of the most accomplished and wise young princes in all Persia. That is marvellous, cried Nourjahad, bursting into a fit of laughter, a sultan of four and twenty hours old must needs be wonderously wise and accomplished. Nay, my lord, replied the man, the prince is this day exactly twenty years of age.

(Nourjahad, on hearing this, looked in the face of the man, whom, from his dress, supposing he had been one of his slaves, he had not regarded before, but now perceived he was a stranger.) Twenty years old! cried he, starting up, thou dost not tell me so! Most certain, said the man. Schemzeddin was so far advanced in years before the birth of the prince, that he despaired of ever having a child; yet had the righteous monarch the satisfaction to see his beloved son arrive at manhood, and adorned with such virtues as made him worthy to fill his father's throne. When did the old sultan die, cried Nourjahad? His funeral obsequies were performed last night, answered the man, and the people of Ormuz have not yet wiped the tears from their eyes. It should seem then, said Nourjahad, that I have slept about twenty years! if so, prithee, who art thou? for I do not remember ever to have seen thy face before.

My name, answered the stranger, is Cozro, and I am the brother of Cadiga, that faithful creature whom thy ungoverned fury deprived of life. How darest thou mention her again, cried Nourjahad, art thou not afraid to share the same fate thyself for thy presumption?

I do not value my life, answered Cozro; having acquitted myself well of my duty here, I am sure of my reward in those blessed mansions, where avarice, luxury, cruelty and pride, can never enter. Strike then, Nourjahad, if thou darest; dismiss me to endless and uninterrupted joys, and live thyself a prey to remorse and disappointment, the slave of passions never to be gratified, and a sport to the vicissitudes of fortune.

Nourjahad was confounded at the undaunted air with which Cozro pronounced these words; he trembled with indignation, but had not courage to strike the unarmed man who thus insulted him; wherefore, dissembling his anger, I see, said he, that thou partakest of thy sister Cadiga's spirit; but answer me, How camest thou hither, and in what condition are the rest of my family? I will tell thee, answered Cozro. When Cadiga found herself dying, she sent for me: I was then a page to one of the emirs[10] of Schemzeddin's court. She made me kneel by her bed-side and take a solemn oath, to perform with fidelity and secrecy what she should enjoin me. She then told me the secret of your life, and conjured me to watch and attend you carefully. I have hitherto, said she, had the conduct of his house; do you supply my place, and do not let Nourjahad, when he awakes from his trance, be sensible of the loss of the unfortunate Cadiga.

She then called in your principal slaves, and delivering to me in their presence the keys with which you had entrusted her, she told them they were henceforth to obey me, as they had done her. Tell my lord, said she to me, that I forgive him the death which his cruelty inflicted on a woman who loved him to the latest minute of her life. In pronouncing these words, she expired.

I knew not till then, pursued Cozro, that thou hadst been the murderer of my sister; but she was no sooner dead, than the slaves informed me of the manner of her death. My resentment against thee was proportioned to the horror of thy guilt; and had I thrown myself at the feet of Schemzeddin, and implored justice on thy crimes, neither thy riches nor thy immortality would have availed thee, but thou wouldst have been condemned by a perpetual decree, to have languished out thy wretched existence in a vile dungeon.

And what hindered thee, cried Nourjahad, from pursuing thy revenge, seeing I was not in a condition to resist thee? My reverence for the oath I had taken, answered Cozro, and fear of offending the Almighty!

Nourjahad, at this reply, was struck with a secret awe which he could not repel; he remained silent whilst Cozro proceeded.

I obtained permission of the master whom I served, to leave him, and entered immediately on my new employment; but I found I had undertaken a difficult task. Thou hadst rendered thyself so odious to thy women, that not one of them retained the smallest degree of love or fidelity towards thee. In spite of my vigilance they made thy hated seraglio the scene of their unlawful pleasures; and at length having bribed the eunuchs who guarded them, they all in one night fled from thy detested walls, taking with them the slaves who had assisted them in their purpose. Pernicious spirit, exclaimed Nourjahad, are these the fruits I am to reap from thy fatal indulgence! The rest of your servants, pursued Cozro, I endeavoured to keep

[10] Emir is an Arabic title for a prince, ruler, or commander.

within the bounds of their duty. And how didst thou succeed, cried Nourjahad? But ill, replied Cozro; they all declared that nothing could have induced them to stay so long with a master of so capricious and tyrannical a humour, but the luxury and idleness in which thou permittedst them to live; and finding I managed your affairs with economy, they one after the other left your house; neither promises nor threats having power to prevent those who stayed longest in thy service, from following the example of the first who deserted thee; so that I alone of all thy numerous household have remained faithful to thee: I, who of all others, had the most reason to abhor thee! But I have now acquitted myself of the trust which was reposed in me, and I leave thee as one condemned to wander in an unknown land, where he is to seek out for new associates, and to endeavour by the power of gold, to bribe that regard from men, which his own worth cannot procure for him.

Unfortunate wretch that I am, cried Nourjahad, pierced to the quick with what he had just been told, what benefit have I hitherto received from my long life, but that of feeling by miserable experience, the ingratitude and frailty of man's nature. How transitory have been all my pleasures! the recollection of them dies on my memory, like the departing colours of the rainbow, which fades under the eye of the beholder, and leaves not a trace behind. Whilst on the other hand, every affliction with which I have been visited, has imprinted a deep and lasting wound on my heart, which not even the hand of time itself has been able to heal.

What have thy misfortunes been, said Cozro, that are not common to all the race of man? Oh, I have had innumerable griefs, said Nourjahad. After a short enjoyment (during my fatal slumbers) the grave robbed me of Mandana, whilst she was yet in the bloom of youth and beauty. I lamented her death, tears and heaviness of heart were my portion for many days. Yet remembering that sorrow would not recall the dead, I suffered myself to be comforted, and sought for consolation in the society of my other women, and the fond and innocent caresses of an infant son, whom Mandana left me. Joy and tranquillity revisited my dwelling, and new pleasures courted my acceptance; but they again eluded my grasp, and in one night (for so it appeared to me) my son like an unnatural viper, forgetting all my tenderness, plundered and deserted me. The two faithful friends in whom I most confided, had closed their eyes for ever; and the beauties of my seraglio, whom I had last beheld fresh and charming as the lillies of the field, I now saw deformed with wrinkles and bending under the infirmities of age.

Yet these afflictions I surmounted; and resolved once more to be happy. And wert thou so, interrupted Cozro? No, replied Nourjahad, the treacherous joys deceived me; yet I still looked forward with hope, but now awake to fresh disappointment. I find myself abandoned by those whose false professions of love had lulled me into security, and I rouse myself like a savage beast in the desart, whose paths are shunned by all the children of men.

Nourjahad could not conclude this speech without a groan, that seemed to rend his heart.

As thou art, said Cozro, exempt from punishment here-after, dost thou think also to escape the miseries of this life? Mistaken man, know, that the righteous Being, whose ordinances thou defyest, will even here take vengeance on thy crimes. And if thou wilt look back on thy past life, thou wilt find (for I have heard thy story) that every one of those several ills of which thou complainest, were sent as scourges to remind thee of thy duty, and inflicted immediately after the commission of some notorious breach of it.

The death of Mandana was preceded by a brutal fit of drunkenness, by which, contrary to the laws of our prophet, thou sufferedst thyself to be overtaken. Then it was thy good genius, to punish thee, plunged thee into that temporary death, from which thou didst awake to grief and disappointment: But thou madest no use of the admonition, but didst permit thyself to be again swallowed up by intemperance; and not content to tread the ordinary paths of vice, thou turnedst out of the road, to the commission of a crime, to which thou couldst have no temptation, but the pride and licentiousness of thy heart. Thy profanation of our holy religion, in presuming to personate our great prophet, and make thy concubines represent the virgins of paradise, was immediately chastised as it deserved, by a second time depriving thee of those faculties, which thou didst prostitute to such vile purposes.

The ills with which thou foundest thyself surrounded on awaking from thy trance, served to no other purpose than to stir up thy resentment against the power who governed thy life. And instead of reforming thy wickedness, thou soughtest out new ways of rendering thyself still more obnoxious to the wrath of Heaven. In the wantonness of thy cruelty, thou stainedst thy hand in blood; and that same night, were thy eyelids sealed up by the avenging hand of thy watchful genius, and thy depraved senses consigned for twenty years to oblivion! See then, continued Cozro, if a life which is to be a continued round of crimes and punishments in alternate succession, is a gift worthy to be desired by a wise man? for assure thyself, Oh Nourjahad, that by the immutable laws of heaven one is to be a constant concomitant of the other, and that either in this world or the next, vice will meet its just reward.

Alas, replied Nourjahad, thou hast awakened in me a remorse of which I was never sensible before; I look back with shame on the detested use I have made of those extraordinary gifts vouchsafed me by my guardian spirit.

What shall I do, Oh Cozro, to expiate the offences I have committed? For though I have no dread of punishment hereafter, yet does that etherial spark within, inspire me with such horror for my former crimes, that all the vain delights which this world can afford me, will not restore my mind to peace, till by a series of good actions I have atoned for my past offences.

If thou art sincere in thy resolutions, replied Cozro, the means, thou knowest, are amply in thy power. Thy riches will enable thee to diffuse blessings amongst mankind, and thou wilt find more true luxury in that, than in all the gratifications wherewith thou hast indulged thy appetites.

It shall be so, replied Nourjahad; my treasures shall be open to thee, thou venerable old man, and do thou make it thy business to find out proper objects, whereon charity and benevolence may exert their utmost powers.

Enquire out every family in Ormuz whom calamity hath overtaken, and provided they did not bring on their distresses by their own wilful misconduct, restore them to prosperity. Seek out the helpless and the innocent; and by a timely supply of their wants, secure them against the attacks of poverty, or temptations of vice. Search for such as you think have talents which will render them useful to society; but who, for want of the goods of fortune, are condemned to obscurity; relieve their necessities, and enable them to answer the purposes for which nature designed them. Find out merit wherever it lies concealed, whether with-held from the light by diffidence, chained down and clogged by adversity, obscured by malice, or overborn by power; lift it up from the dust, and let it shine conspicuous to the world.

Glorious talk! cried Cozro; happy am I in being the chosen instrument of Nourjahad's bounty, and still more happy shall he be in seeing the accomplishment of his good designs.

We must not stop here, said Nourjahad; I will have hospitals built for the reception of the aged and the sick; and my tables shall be spread for the refreshment of the weary traveller. No virtuous action shall pass by me unrewarded, and no breach of the laws of temperance, justice, or mercy, shall escape unreproved. My own example, so far as it can influence, shall henceforth countenance the one, and discourage the other.

Blessed be the purpose of thy heart, said Cozro, and prosperous be the days of thy life!

Nourjahad now found the anxiety under which he had but a little before laboured, exceedingly relieved. My mind, said he, is much more at ease than it was; let us not delay to put our design in execution. I will lead you to the place where my treasure is concealed, which I never yet discovered to any one. Saying this, he took Cozro by the hand, and conducted him to the cave.

Thou seest here, said he, riches which can never be exhausted; thou mayest perceive that I have not yet sunk a third part of one of these urns which contain my wealth; yet have I with monstrous profusion lavished away immense sums. Five more such urns as these are yet untouched. Those six which thou seest on the right hand, contain wedges of the finest gold, which must be equal in value to the others. These six, which are ranged on the left, are filled with precious stones, whose worth must be inestimable: The wealth of Ormuz would not purchase a single handful. Judge then, my friend, if I need be sparing in my liberality.

Cozro expressed his astonishment at the sight of these wonders. If thou wouldst be advised by me, said he, thou wouldst secretly remove from Ormuz, and carry thy treasures with thee. Thou mayest deposit part of them in each of the different countries through which thou passest in thy progress all over the earth. By this means thou mayest have it in thy power to distribute with more ease thy bounty wherever thou goest; and be always provided with riches in what part soever of the world thou shalt chuse for a time to take up thy residence. Thy long abode in this city will draw observations on thee sooner or later; and thy person's not having undergone any change from length of time, will bring on thee the suspicion of magic; for tradition will not fail to inform posterity of thy strange history.

You counsel well, replied Nourjahad; as I am now at liberty, I will retire from Ormuz. You, my dear Cozro, shall accompany me; your prudent counsel shall be my guide; and when I shall be deprived of you by death, I will still endeavour to follow your wise precepts.

Come, continued he, I am in haste to enter on my new course of life, let us both go into the city and try to find out proper objects on which to exert our charity. I shall pass without observation, and unknown, as few of my contemporaries can now be living, and I will not leave the country which gave me birth, without first making it feel the effects of that beneficence which thou hast awakened in my heart.

Deserving of praise as thou art, said Cozro, thou for the present must suppress thy ardor to do good; for though by the death of Schemzeddin thou art no longer a prisoner, thou art not nevertheless yet at liberty to leave thy house. Why not? answered Nourjahad, who is there now to prevent me?

The young sultan, replied Cozro, deeply afflicted for the death of his father, and out of a pious regard to his memory, has given strict commandment, that all his subjects should observe a solemn mourning for him, during the space of twenty days; in which time all the shops, and places of public resort (except the mosques) are to be shut up, and no business of any kind transacted; nor are any persons to be seen in the streets, excepting those who visit the sick, and the slaves who must necessarily be employed to carry provisions, on pain of the sultan's heavy displeasure.

This edict was published yesterday, and the people of Ormuz all love the memory of Schemzeddin, and the person of their present sultan too well, not to pay an exact obedience to it.

If so, said Nourjahad, I will not by my example encourage others to infringe their duty; yet as the relieving of the poor is in itself meritorious, I would not wish to be withheld from doing it so long as twenty days; How many virtuous people may be during that time pining for want! more especially as this prohibition must cut off all intercourse between man and man, and deprive many poor wretches of the charitable succour they might otherwise receive. I think therefore that thou, Cozro, in thy slave's habit, mayst go forth unsuspected; and by privately seeking out, and alleviating the miseries of our fellow citizens, do an act of more real benefit, than can result from the strictest conformity to this pageant of sorrow, which many in their hearts I am sure must condemn.

Cozro approving of these sentiments, readily agreed to the expedient, and taking a large purse of gold with him to distribute as occasion might serve, immediately set out in order to execute his lord's commands.

Nourjahad now entered on a total reformation in his way of living. He rose at day break, and spent the morning in study or meditation. Luxury and intemperance were banished from his board; his table was spread with the plainest dishes, and he wholly abstained from excess in wine. His slumbers were sweet, and he found his health more vigorous.

I will no more, said he, enslave myself to the power of beauty. I have lived to see the decay of a whole seraglio of the fairest faces in Persia, and have sighed for the ingratitude of the next generation that succeeded them. I will not then seek out for those destroyers of my quiet, for whose death or infidelity I must for ever complain. Mandana was the only woman who ever really deserved my love; could I recal her from the grave, and endue her with the same privilege of which I am myself possessed, I would confine myself to her arms alone; but since that is impossible, I will devote myself to the charms of virtue, which of all things she most resembled.

Whilst Nourjahad was thus resolving to correct the errors of his past life, his virtue was not merely in speculation. He never laid him down to rest, without the satisfaction of having made some one the better for him. Cozro, who constantly spent the day in enquiring out and relieving the distressed, failed not to return every night to give an account of his charitable mission, and to infuse into his master's bosom, the (till now unfelt) joy which springs from righteous deeds.

The heart of Nourjahad was expanded, and glowed with compassion for those sufferings which Cozro feelingly described as the lot of so many of his fellow creatures. As charity and benevolence rose in his breast, he found his pride subside. He was conscious of his own unworthiness. He kneeled, he prayed, he humbled himself before the Almighty, and returned thanks to God for enabling him to succour the unfortunate.

In this happy frame of mind he continued for eighteen days; there wanted but two more to the expiration of the mourning for the sultan, when Nourjahad was to be at full liberty to pursue in his own person the dictates of his reformed, and now truly generous and benevolent heart.

He was sitting alone in his apartment, waiting the arrival of Cozro, in the pleasing expectation of receiving some fresh opportunity of doing good. The hour of his usual return was already past, and Nourjahad began to fear some accident had happened to him; but he little knew that a black cloud hung over him, which was ready to pour down all its malignity on his own head.

As he mused on what might be the occasion of Cozro's long stay, he heard a loud knocking at his door. It was immediately opened by one of his slaves, and a man, who by his habit he knew to be one of the cady's officers, rudely entered his chamber.

How comes it, said the stranger, that thou hast had the temerity, in contempt of our sovereign lord's commands, to employ thy emissary about the city at a time when thou knowest that so strict an injunction has been laid on all people to keep within their houses, none being permitted to stir abroad but for the absolute necessities of life, or in cases of imminent danger?

Far be it from me, replied Nourjahad, to disobey our mighty sultan's orders; but I understood that slaves had permission to go unquestioned on their master's business. And what business, answered the man, can thy slave have from morning to night in so many different quarters of the city?

Nourjahad, who did not care to be himself the trumpeter of his own good deeds, hesitated to give an answer.

Ha, ha, cried the stranger, I see plainly there is something dangerous in thy mystery, and that the money which thy slave has been distributing amongst such a variety of people, is for a purpose very different from that which he pretends. A likely matter it is indeed that a private man should bestow in charity such sums as Cozro acknowledges he has within these few days distributed.

Yet nothing is more certain, replied Nourjahad, than that Cozro has

---

cady: qadi, here an officer of justice.

spoke the truth. We shall see that, replied the officer, in a tone of insolence; Cozro is already in prison, and my orders are to conduct thee to him.

Nourjahad, exceedingly troubled at hearing this, replied, He was ready to go with him; and the officer led him out of his house.

It was now late at night; they passed along the streets without meeting any one, and soon reached the place wherein Cozro was confined. It was the prison where such persons were shut up as were accused of treason against the state.

Here he found the unfortunate Cozro in a dungeon. Alas, cried he, as soon as his master entered, why do I see thee here? Say rather, my dear Cozro, replied Nourjahad, what strange fatality has brought *thee* to this dismal place?

I can give no other account, answered Cozro, but that in returning home this night, I was seized on in the street by some of those soldiers who were employed to patrol about the city, to see that the sultan's orders were punctually observed; and being questioned concerning my business, I told them that I had been relieving the wants of indigent people, and saving even from perishing, some poor wretches who had not wherewithal to buy food.

That is an idle errand, replied one of them, and might have been deferred till the term of mourning was expired; however, if you will give me a piece of gold, I will let you pass for this time, otherwise both you and your employer may happen to repent of having transgressed the sultan's commands. I made no scruple, pursued Cozro, to take out my purse, in which there were ten sequins left. I gave one of them to the soldier, but the rapacious wretches seeing I had more money, were not content with this, but insisted on my giving the whole amongst them. I refused; some angry words ensued; one of the miscreants struck me, and I returned the blow. Enraged at this, they hurried me before the cady, to whom they accused me of having disobeyed the edict, and assaulted the sultan's officers in the discharge of their duty. I was not heard in my defence, having four witnesses against me, but was immediately dragged to this horrid prison; and the sultan himself, they say, is to take cognizance of my offence.

Oh, Heaven, cried Nourjahad, to what mischiefs does not the love of gold expose us! See, my friend, into what misfortunes thou art plunged by the sordid avarice of those vile soldiers. But why, why didst thou hesitate to give up that paltry sum which thou hadst in thy purse, to obtain thy liberty? I do not repent what I have done, answered Cozro, and shall contentedly suffer the penalty I have incurred, since it was in so good a cause.

---

sequins: Venetian or Turkish coins.

If the sultan is just, replied Nourjahad, the punishment ought only to fall on me, who alone am guilty, since what thou didst was by my command.

Here the officer who had conducted Nourjahad to prison, and who was present at this discourse, interposed, and addressing himself to Nourjahad, Thou hast not as yet been accused to the sultan, said he, and it is not too late to extricate even thy slave from this troublesome affair; it is but making a handsome present to the cady, and I will undertake this matter will go no farther. I am willing to do so, replied Nourjahad, eagerly; name your demand, and you shall have it. Provided I am allowed to go home to my own house, I will fetch the money; and if you are afraid of my escaping, you yourself may bear me company.

I will not consent to it, replied Cozro; neither liberty nor life are worth purchasing on base conditions. I will submit my cause to Schemerzad's justice; the cause of uprightness and truth; my own innocence shall be my support, and I will dare the worst that fraud and malice can suggest against me.

In vain did Nourjahad urge him to accept the profered terms; he remained inflexible to all the arguments he could use to persuade him; wherefore, finding him determined, he was obliged to desist; and Cozro, after passing the remainder of the night in quiet and profound sleep, though without any other bed than the bare earth, was at dawn of day called forth to appear before the sultan.

The reflections Nourjahad made on the resolute behaviour of Cozro, served not a little to fortify his mind. How noble must this man's soul be, said he, which sets him thus above the reach of adversity? and with what contempt he looks down on the glorious prospects he has before him, when put in the balance with his integrity. Surely it is not in this life he places his happiness, since he is so ready to forego the pleasures he might enjoy with me, in that participation of wealth and liberty which I have promised him. How superior is my servant to me, who but for his example, should now sink under my fears; but he has resources which I have not. Alas, why did I barter my hopes of paradise for the vain, the transitory, the fallacious joys which this vile world bestows! Already I have tried them; what do they inspire but satiety and disgust. I never experienced true contentment, but during the time, short as it is, since I abjured those follies in which I once delighted: And I am now persuaded, that after having past a few, a very few years more in the enjoyment of such gratifications as I have not yet had an opportunity of tasting, that I shall grow even weary of the light, and wish to be dismissed to that place, where we are told no sorrows can approach.

Nourjahad was buried in these reflections, when he was roused by the return of Cozro. The glimmering light which a lamp afforded, struck full on the face of his friend (for he no longer considered him as a servant) and he rejoiced to see Cozro's chearful countenance, by which he judged that he had nothing to fear.

I am come, said Cozro, approaching Nourjahad, and kissing his hand, to bid thee adieu, for from this day, we are to be for ever divided! It is that thought only which makes our separation grievous: Had I hopes of ever beholding thy face in the mansions of light, I should go to death with the same alacrity with which I close my eyes in slumber.

Good Heaven, cried Nourjahad, doest thou talk of death? Can it be, is it possible that thy life is in danger?

What is the life, about which thou art anxious? replied Cozro; our being here is but a shadow; that only is real existence which the blessed enjoy after their short travel here. And know, Oh Nourjahad, I would not yield up my expectations of the humblest place in paradise for the sovereign rule of the whole earth, though my days were to be extended to the date of thy life, and every wish of my soul gratified to the utmost. Think then, with how little reluctance I shall leave a world, wherein I am sure of meeting nothing but oppression, treachery, and disappointment, where mercy is construed into treason, and charity is called sedition!

And art thou then doomed to die? said Nourjahad, pale and trembling at the thought, though convinced it was a predicament in which he could never stand.

I am, answered Cozro, my offence was found capital. Disobedience to the sultan's edict alone, incurred a heavy punishment; but my crime was, by the malice of my accusers, so highly aggravated, that the penalty became death. They charged me with having distributed money for evil purposes, amongst persons disaffected to the state, and with having beat and abused those officers who first detected me. In vain did I offer all the pleas that truth could suggest; my enemies, exasperated at losing the sum which they hoped to have extorted from you, swore to the facts of which I was accused, and the rigid sultan condemned me to death. What thy fate is to be, I know not; but since it is thy misfortune to be doomed to perpetual life, better purchase thy freedom on any terms, than be condemned to languish for years in a prison, for such probably will be thy lot.

Oh that I could die with thee! said Nourjahad, miserable that I am, thus to be deprived of thy counsel and friendship, at a time when I so much stood in need of them; but wherefore, my friend, why should we submit to the tyranny of the sultan? though thou art condemned, there may yet be found means to deliver thee. The keeper of the prison will gladly set a price on thy liberty; a hundred thousand pieces of gold shall be thy ransom; and

I shall think myself rich by the purchase! And what is to become of thee, replied Cozro? I will buy my own freedom at the same rate, answered Nourjahad, and we will both fly from Ormuz together. And leave your treasures behind you, cried Cozro, for it will be impossible to convey from hence such a vast mass of riches without discovery.

I value them no longer, said Nourjahad; they can never yield me any permanent enjoyment. The saving thy life is the only good turn I now expect from them. That once accomplished, I shall desire to retain no more of them than what will support me above want, and I will leave the rest to be for ever hid in the bosom of the earth, where they now lie, that they may never more become a snare to others as they have been to me.

Praised be our holy prophet, said Cozro, that has at length endued the heart of Nourjahad with wisdom. Pursue the purposes of thy soul; effect thy own freedom as soon as possible, since no comfort can visit thee in the gloom of this frightful prison; but tempt not Cozro back to a life which he despises. I tell thee again, there is nothing in this world to be put in competition with the glories I have in prospect in that state to which I am now hastening. Why then, Nourjahad, wouldst thou retard my felicity, or wish me to hazard, for the sake of delusive pleasures, those transcendent joys which await the virtuous.

The energy with which Cozro delivered himself, pierced Nourjahad to the inmost soul. A holy ardor was kindled in his breast, which he had never felt before; he found his faculties enlarged, his mind was transported above this world; he felt as it were unimbodied, and an involuntary adjuration burst from his lips. "Oh, holy prophet," said he, "take, take back the gift, that I in the ignorance and presumption of my heart so vainly sought, and which too late I find a punishment instead of a blessing! I contemn riches, and for ever cast them from me; suffer me then to yield up my life; for there can be no true happiness but in beholding thee, Oh Mahomet, face to face, in the never-fading fields of paradise!"

Saying this, he prostrated himself on the ground, and continued for some time in mental prayer.

Cozro observed an awful silence whilst he continued in this posture. When Nourjahad arose from the earth, May our great prophet, said Cozro, hear your prayers; and were he even now to grant them, all the favours he has already bestowed on you would be poor and contemptible to this last best boon. Farewel, said he, I must now leave thee, I was only permitted to come and bid thee adieu. May the Supreme grant thy petition, then shall we again meet in the mansions of happy spirits. Nourjahad embraced him, and Cozro withdrew.

Being now left at liberty to his own thoughts, he made bitter reflections on the strangeness of his fate. Fool, fool that I was, cried he aloud, beating his breast, to prefer so rash, so impious a petition to the prophet, as to desire the everlasting laws of nature to be overturned, to gratify my mad luxurious wishes. I thought the life of man too short for the enjoyment of those various and unbounded pleasures which wealth could procure; but it is long since I have found my error. Well did my guardian spirit say I should repent of the gift I had implored, when it should be too late. I do indeed repent; but Oh, thou benign intelligence, if thou hast remaining any favour for thy inconsiderate unhappy charge, descend once more to my relief, and if possible restore me to that state, for which I was designed by my creator; a poor mortal, liable to, and now longing for the friendly stroke of death.

He had scarce pronounced these words, when his prison doors flew open; a refulgent light flashed in, which illuminated the whole dungeon, and he beheld his guardian genius standing before him, exactly as he had appeared to him before. Thy prayers are heard, said he, Oh son of frailty, and thy penitence is accepted in the sight of the Most High. I am sent down again by our prophet to reassume that gift which thou art now satisfied must make thee miserable. Yet examine thy heart once more before I pronounce thy irrevocable doom; say, art thou willing again to become subject to the common lot of mortals?

Most willing, replied Nourjahad; yet I wonder not, my seraphic guide, that thou shouldst doubt the stability of my mind; but in this last purpose of it I am sure I shall remain unshaken.

If so, replied the shining vision, thy guardian angel consigns thee to the arms of death, with much more joy than he conferred on thee riches and immortality. Thou hast nothing more to do, than to prostrate thyself with thy face to the earth. Remain this evening in fervent prayer, and await what shall befal thee to-morrow.

Nourjahad made no reply, but falling with his face to the ground, he soon found the dungeon restored to its former gloom, the light and the guardian spirit vanishing together in an instant.

He continued in devout prayer till night; when the keeper of the prison entered his dungeon to bring him some refreshment.

The sultan, said he, purposes to examine you to-morrow, and much I fear you will have as rigorous a sentence passed on you, as that which has been already executed on Cozro. Is he then dead? cried Nourjahad, mournfully. He is, replied the keeper; it is but an hour since I saw him deprived of breath; but he received the blow with such an heroic firmness, that thou wouldst have thought he rather enjoyed a triumph, than suffered an ignominious death.

Happy, happy Cozro! cried Nourjahad; thou art now beyond the reach of misfortune, whilst I, perhaps, may be doomed to sustain for years a wretched life.

Thy life, said the keeper, may be nearer a period than thou art aware of. The sultan is covetous, and surrounded by needy favourites, whom the report of your immense wealth has made eager for your destruction; for you cannot be ignorant, that should you die, involved as it is said you are, in Cozro's guilt, your treasures would be confiscated to the sultan. From this circumstance I have heard it whispered, your head is already devoted; and this perhaps was the true cause of Cozro's death, and will give the better colour to yours. It is not, however, added he, even yet too late to prevent the danger; had not your slave been obstinate, he might now have been alive, and out of the reach of harm. You have the same means of preservation in regard to your own person, still in your power; and if you will make it worth my while to run the risque, I will this night set you at liberty.

And dost thou think, said Nourjahad, that I have profited so little by the example of my noble friend, as to accept of thy offer, sordid and treacherous as thou art? If thou art base enough to betray thy trust for gold, know that the mind of Nourjahad is above receiving a favour from such a wretch. As for my wealth, let the sultan take it; my only wish is to part with that and my life also.

That wish may speedily be accomplished, said the keeper, in an angry tone, and to-morrow perhaps you may repent of your folly, when you find yourself condemned to follow your noble friend to the other world. Nourjahad made no reply; and the keeper sullenly departed.

Nourjahad spent the night in prayers and meditation; he found peace and tranquillity restored to his breast, and perfectly resigned to the will of the prophet, he waited the event of the next day with the utmost composure.

In the morning the keeper of the prison entered to him. Follow me, said he; thou art going to appear before the sultan, who himself is to be thy judge; a rigorous one thou wilt find him, but thy folly be on thy own head, who didst proudly refuse the profer I made thee of liberty and life.

Lead on, said Nourjahad, it is not for such men as thou art, to censure a conduct, to which thou dost not know the motive.

He was now carried out of the dungeon, and ordered to ascend a chariot, in which the captain of the sultan's guards was already placed, to receive his prisoner. The chariot was surrounded by soldiers; and in this manner he was conducted to the presence of the sultan.

Schemerzad was seated on a throne, in the hall of his palace, wherein he was used to distribute justice. The emirs, and great officers of his court, were standing round him.

Nourjahad stood before him with his eyes bent to the ground; and however awed he might be at the presence of his royal master, and the august assembly which surrounded him, yet the dignity of conscious innocence, and the perfect reliance he had on the Supreme Judge of *his* judge, rendered him superior to every thing. His deportment was modest and respectful, yet did he discover no symptom of fear.

The sultan made a sign for every one present to withdraw, but one person who stood on the lower step of his throne, and whom Nourjahad judged to be his prime visier.

What hast thou to say, presumptuous man, said Schemerzad, in a stern voice, what excuse canst thou offer for daring, in contempt of my edict, to employ thy agent (during the time set apart for mourning) in going about the city from day to day; ostentatiously displaying thy ill-timed liberality amongst my subjects; endeavouring, as I am informed, to conciliate their affections, for purposes dangerous to me, and the safety of my crown. What hast thou to offer in answer to this charge?

Nourjahad prostrated himself to the ground. Mighty sultan, said he, I have nothing to offer in extenuation of my fault, with regard to the first part of the charge. I acknowledge that I distributed money amongst your majesty's subjects, and that at a time too when every act (but those of absolute necessity) was interdicted. I offer not to palliate this breach of my duty.—

Audacious wretch, interrupted the sultan, to what end was thy profusion employed?

To obtain a blessing from heaven, answered Nourjahad; and by relieving the wants and afflictions of others, to make some atonement for my own riotous and intemperate abuse of that wealth, which ought to have been employed to better purposes.

Wouldst thou persuade me then, cried Schemerzad, that charity was thy motive! It was, illustrious sultan, replied Nourjahad; I have spoke the truth, and to convince your majesty that I have no sinister designs against the ever sacred person of my sovereign, I will now voluntarily yield up that treasure to thee, which had I been vile enough to have so employed, would have bought the fidelity of more than half thy subjects, though every man of them had stood near the heart, and throne of Schemerzad.

The undaunted manner in which Nourjahad spoke these words, made Schemerzad shake on his imperial seat; but quickly reassuming the majesty of his station, Do then as thou hast spoken, said he, and I will believe thee.

If your majesty will permit me, said Nourjahad, to go to my house, and will send a proper person with me, I will deliver up into his hands all my

---

visier: vizier, from the Arabic *wazir,* the lieutenant or first minister of a king or sultan.

wealth, requesting no more than will supply my wants so long as heaven permits me to live.

I will not trust thee out of my sight, said Schemerzad; thou mayest as well instruct some one in my presence where to find the riches of which I hear thou art possessed, and I will send for them.

Nourjahad then informed the sultan of the subterraneous cave in his garden; and delivering him the key, told him he would there find all the wealth of which he was master.

Schemerzad immediately dispatched his visier, ordering him to have the riches he should find, immediately conveyed to his treasury. He then commanded Nourjahad to retire into a saloon, that was separated from the hall only by a curtain, and there wait the return of the visier; before whom, the sultan said he had some farther questions to put to him.

As the gardens of Nourjahad joined to those belonging to the royal palace, the visier was not long in going and returning. Nourjahad heard him talk to Schemerzad, and straight he was called on to come forth, and stand before the sultan: But Schemerzad now accosted him in a voice like thunder. Perfidious and insolent slave, said he, art thou not afraid of instant death falling on thee, for daring thus to falsify before thy sovereign lord and master? Say, before thou art cut off by torture from the face of the earth, where thou hast concealed thy wealth! for well thou knowest, there is nothing contained in that cave, which thou pretendest with so much care to lock up.

Nothing! replied Nourjahad, in amazement. By the head of our prophet, when I last was there, it contained more than would purchase thy whole empire a thousand times over. It was but the very day on which I was dragged to prison, that I saw it; the key has never since been out of my pocket; who then could possibly have conveyed away my treasure?

As Nourjahad applied himself to the visier whilst he spoke, that minister thinking himself reflected on by his words, replied scornfully, Thou thinkest perhaps it is I who have robbed thee, and that I have framed this story to deceive the sultan, and ruin thee. I do not say so, answered Nourjahad; but this I am sure of, that no human being but thyself knew where to find my treasure. Some daemon, perhaps, replied the visier, with an air of contempt, has removed it thence.

Nourjahad now recollecting suddenly, that his guardian spirit had probably reclaimed this, as well as the other gift, replied coolly, It is not at all unlikely; a certain genius, who watches over my motions, has undoubtedly carried away my wealth.

---

saloon: salon (reception room).

Do not think, said the sultan, that affecting to be out of thy senses, shall preserve thee from my wrath.

Your majesty, said the visier, had best order that his head be instantly struck off, for daring to impose on your credulity, and abuse your clemency in suffering him to out-live that slave, who obstinately persisted in refusing to discover his master's riches.

Did Cozro do so? cried Nourjahad: He did, answered the visier; but we will see whether thou wilt persevere in the denial, and to the latest minute of thy life preserve the firmness of thy slave.

And who is it that thou callest a slave, thou minister of cruelty? said Nourjahad boldly: The soul of Cozro raised him infinitely more above thee, than the rank of the sultan of Persia lifts him above the meanest of his subjects.—My lord, pursued he, throwing himself at Schemerzad's feet, I have no other plea to offer for my life; I call Heaven to witness I have spoken nothing but the truth; the severest tortures you can inflict on me will extort no more. I was willing to make a voluntary sacrifice of my riches: I am now as ready to yield my life.

Art thou not then afraid to die? said Schemerzad.

No, mighty sultan, answered Nourjahad, I look upon death to a virtuous man, as the greatest good the Almighty can bestow!

The sultan, instead of making any reply, clapped his hands; and Nourjahad supposing it was a signal to have him seized and carried to execution, rose up, and stood with an intrepidity in his looks, that shewed how little he was affected with the near prospect of death.

But instead of the slaves whom he expected to see coming to lay hold on him, he beheld standing close to the throne of Schemerzad, his guardian genius, just in the same celestial form in which he had twice before appeared to him!

Awed and amazed, Nourjahad started back, and gazed at the heavenly vision. Not daring to trust his senses, he remained mute, and motionless, for some minutes; but he was roused from his deep attention, by a loud burst of laughter, which broke at once from the sultan, the visier, and the guardian genius.

This new and extraordinary incident threw Nourjahad into fresh astonishment; when, without giving him time to recover himself, the angelic youth, snatching from his head a circlet of flowers intermixed with precious stones, which encompassed his brows, and shaded a great part of his forehead; and at the same time throwing off a head of artificial hair which flowed in golden ringlets down his shoulders; a fine fall of brown hair which was concealed under it succeeded, dropping in light curls on his neck and blushing cheeks; and Nourjahad, in the person of his seraphic guide, discovered his beloved and beautiful Mandana!

Whatever transports the sight of her would at another time have inspired in the breast of Nourjahad, his faculties were now too much absorbed in wonder, to leave room for any other passion. Wherefore, not daring to approach her, the sultan, willing to put an end to his suspence, cried out, Look up, Nourjahad, raise thy eyes to thy master's face, no longer the angry Schemerzad, thy offended prince, but the real Schemzeddin, thy friend and kind protector.

Nourjahad, who before, out of respect and awful distance, had not ventured to look in the sultan's face, now fixed his eyes earnestly upon him. By the life of Schemerzad, said he, if I were not certain that all this is illusion, and that thy illustrious father, my royal and once beloved master, is dead, thou art so very like him, that I should swear that thou wert the real sultan Schemzeddin himself; such at thy years was his countenance and features.

The sultan at this burst into a second fit of laughter. And for whom, said the visier, (who had by this time taken off his turban, and a false beard which he wore) for whom wouldst thou take me?

By Mahomet, cried Nourjahad, falling back a step or two, I should take thee for my old friend Hasem, if I were not convinced that the good man died above twenty years ago.

It is time, said the sultan, descending from his throne, and taking Nourjahad by the hand, it is now time to undeceive thee, and explain to thee the mystery of all those extraordinary events, which seem to have bewildered thy senses.

Know then, Nourjahad, that the adventure of thy guardian genius was all a deception, and a piece of machinery of my contrivance. You are now convinced, by the evidence of your own eyes, that your celestial intelligence was no other than this young damsel.

I had a mind to make trial of thy heart, and for this purpose made choice of this charming virgin, for whom I own I had entertained a passion, but found I could not gain her affections. She had seen you from the windows of the womens apartments, walking with me in the gardens of the seraglio, and had conceived a tenderness for you, which she frankly confessed to me, declaring at the same time, she would never give her love to any other. Though she was my slave, I would not put a constraint upon her inclinations; but told her, if she would assist me faithfully in a design I had formed, I would reward her, by bestowing her on you.

She readily assented to my proposal, and having previously prepared every thing for my purpose, I equipped her as you see.

It was not difficult for me to introduce her into your chamber, by a pri-

---

celestial intelligence: divine spirit.

vate door which you know communicates between your apartments, and certain lodgings in my palace.

I myself stood at the door, whilst she entered as you slept, and contrived to throw that light into your chamber, which disclosed to you the wonderful vision. I overheard all your discourse, and could scarce contain my laughter, when you so greedily received that marvellous essence from Mandana; which you supposed would confer immortality; but which was in reality nothing more than a soporific drug, of so potent a nature, that the fumes of it alone, were capable of throwing the person who smelt to them into a profound sleep. It had quickly this effect on you; and I took that opportunity of conveying into your chamber those coffers which you thought contained such immense treasures; but which in truth were as great counterfeits as your guardian angel. The supposed precious stones, were nothing more than false gems, which I procured from a skilful lapidary, who had given them such an extraordinary polish and lustre, that they might well pass for jewels of inestimable value, on one better skilled in those matters than you were.

The ingots of gold were all base metal, which I got from the same artist. Nothing, in short, was real, but the money, part of which I was very willing to sacrifice to my experiment; though, as I have managed it, the largest sums which thou in thy extravagance hast expended, were returned into my coffers.

As I naturally supposed, that so long as the money lasted you would not have recourse to the other treasures, I was not afraid of having the fraud detected. The cave, which was an accidental circumstance, but of which I had long known, was by my contrivance made the repository of thy riches.

When thou wert settled in the full possession of thy imaginary felicity, thou mayst remember that Hasem was first recommended to thy service; Mandana too was amongst other slaves presented to thy view. No wonder that her charms captivated thy heart. Her love to thee was as pure as it was fervent; but thy boundless wishes were not to be restrained; and forgetting all the rational principles that thou didst at first lay down to regulate thy conduct, thou gavest thyself up to all manner of vile excesses, and didst shew the depravity of the human heart, when unrestrained by divine laws.

It was now time, I thought, to punish thee, and to shew thee the vanity of all earthly enjoyments. By opiates infused into thy wine that night on which thou didst debase thyself by drunkenness, I threw thee into a sound sleep; and though it lasted not much longer than the usual term of ordinary repose, it yet gave me an opportunity of making such farther dispositions, as I thought necessary for the carrying on of my design.

I laid hold of this juncture to withdraw Mandana from thy arms, promising however to restore her to thee, if I found thee ever worthy of her.

I believe it is needless to inform you, that the confinement I laid you under was for no other end than to cut off all intercourse between you and any others than those of your own household, every one of whom were of my placing about you, even to the ladies of your seraglio, who were no others than the prettiest slaves I could find, amongst those who attended on my own women.

Every one entrusted with my secret, were tied down by the most solemn oaths to keep it inviolably; and this with a promise of reward, served, as the event has shewn, to secure their fidelity.

There was not an action of thy life but I was made acquainted with; and whilst thou didst triumph in the joys of my successful illusion, I sometimes pitied thy weakness, and sometimes laughed at thy extravagance.

That magnificent palace of which thou thoughtest thyself master, was one which I had borrowed for the purpose from an emir who was in my secret, and who was himself often present in disguise amongst your slaves, a witness to your extravagancies. I will not encrease thy confusion by reminding thee of the inordinate excesses thou wert guilty of in thy retirement. Thou canst not have forgot the project of creating for thyself an earthly paradise. This was the second crisis I laid hold on to punish thee; and by tearing thee from thy impious pleasures, to remind thee that crimes cannot be committed with impunity. A second sleep, procured as the former was, but of somewhat a longer duration, gave me full opportunity to make a total change in the face of thy affairs. Hasem (whom thou didst suppose to be dead) remained still secretly concealed in thy house, to be as it were the grand spring to move all the rest of thy domestics. The hags whom thou hadst imposed upon thee for the decayed beauties of thy seraglio, were really a set of notable old dames, whom he had tutored for the purpose: Thy former mistresses, who were insignificant slaves, were dismissed. She who personated the feigned Cadiga, acted her part to admiration, and with the artful contrivance of having a rose-bud painted on her breast, a mark which your young favourite really bore from nature, she had cunning and address enough to impose herself on you for the very Cadiga whom you formerly loved.

I believe, proceeded the sultan, you are by this time convinced, that there was nothing supernatural in the several events of your life, and that you were in reality nothing more than the dupe of your own folly and avarice.

Thou mayst remember after this period, that, sated with voluptuousness, thy licentious heart began to grow hardened; and from rioting without controul in pleasures, which, however criminal in themselves, carry at least with them the excuse of temptation, thou wantonly didst stir up, and indulge the latent cruelty of thy nature. Thy ungoverned passions led thee to an act of blood! thou piercedst with thy poniard the honest creature who remonstrated with thee on thy evil works; but Heaven did not, however, permit thee to deprive her of life.

See, Nourjahad, of what the heart of man is capable, when he shuts his eyes against the precepts of our holy prophet. Thou stoodst as it were alone in the creation, and self-dependent for thy own happiness or misery, thou lookedst not for rewards or punishments in that invisible world, from which thou thoughtest thyself by thy own voluntary act excluded.

This last barbarous deed, however, called aloud for chastisement; and thou wast for the third time deceived with a belief that thou hadst slept a number of years, in which many mortifying revolutions had happened in thy family.

I was now resolved to be myself an eye-witness of thy behaviour, and to try if there was any spark of virtue remaining in thy soul which could possibly be rekindled.

I disguised myself in the habit of a slave; and having altered my face, and my voice, I presented myself to thee under the name of Cozro. Thou knowest what passed between us on thy first awaking from thy compelled slumbers, and that I heard and saw with what indifference thou receivedst the news of my supposed death. But I will not reproach thee with ingratitude—let the memory of *that* be buried with the rest of thy errors.

I had soon the satisfaction to find that thou wast as it were a new man. The natural goodness of thy disposition, thy reason, thy experience of the deceitfulness of worldly enjoyments, joined to the remorse which thou couldst not help feeling, for a series of vice and folly, at length rouzed thee to a just sense of what thou owedst to the dignity of thy own nature, and to the duties incumbent on thee towards the rest of thy fellow-creatures.

I now discovered, with joy, that thou hadst intirely divested thyself of that insatiable love of pleasure, to which thou hadst before addicted thyself, and that thou no longer didst regard wealth, but as it enabled thee to do good. There was but one trial more remained. If, said I, his repentance be sincere, and he has that heroism of mind which is inseparable from the truly virtuous, he will not shrink at death; but, on the contrary, will look upon it as the only means by which he can obtain those refined enjoyments suited to the divine part of his nature, and which are as much superior in their essence, as they are in their duration to all the pleasures of sense.

I made the trial—The glorious victory, Oh Nourjahad, is thine! By thy contempt of riches, thou hast proved how well thou deservedst them; and thy readiness to die, shews how fit thou art to live.—

In the space of fourteen moons (for it is no longer since I first imposed on thy credulity the belief of thy miraculous state) thou hast had the experience of four times so many years. Such assuredly would be the vicissitudes of thy life, hadst thou in reality possessed what thou didst in imagination. Let this dream of existence then be a lesson to thee for the future, never to suppose that riches can ensure happiness; that the gratification of our passions can satisfy the human heart; or that the immortal part of our nature, will suffer us to taste unmixed felicity, in a world which was never meant for our final place of abode. Take thy amiable Mandana to thee for a wife, and receive the fixed confidence and love of Schemzeddin.

The history says that Nourjahad was from that minute raised to be the first man in power next to the sultan; that his wisdom and virtue proved an ornament and support to the throne of Persia during the course of a long and prosperous life; and that his name was famous throughout the Eastern world.

FINIS

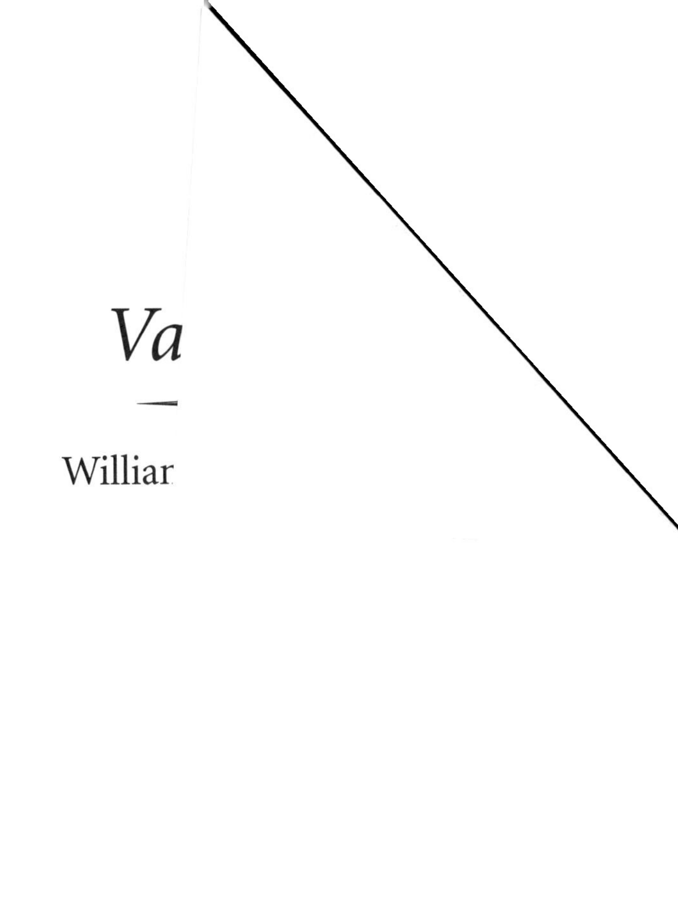

Va

Williar

Vathek, ninth Caliph of the race of the Abassides, was the son of Motassem, and the grandson of Haroun al Raschid.[1] From an early accession to the throne, and the talents he possessed to adorn it, his subjects were induced to expect that his reign would be long and happy. His figure was pleasing and majestic; but when he was angry, one of his eyes became so terrible, that no person could bear to behold it; and the wretch upon whom it was fixed, instantly fell backward, and sometimes expired. For fear, however, of depopulating his dominions and making his palace desolate, he but rarely gave way to his anger.

Being much addicted to women and the pleasures of the table, he sought by his affability, to procure agreeable companions; and he succeeded the better as his generosity was unbounded and his indulgencies unrestrained: for he did not think, with the Caliph Omar Ben Abdalaziz that it was necessary to make a hell of this world to enjoy paradise in the next.[2]

He surpassed in magnificence all his predecessors. The palace of Alkoremi, which his father, Motassem, had erected on the hill of Pied Horses, and which commanded the whole city of Samarah, was, in his idea far too scanty: he added, therefore, five wings, or rather other palaces, which he destined for the particular gratification of each of the senses.

3rd English ed. London: Clarke, 1816. (All footnotes to *Vathek* are provided by the volume editor of this New Riverside Edition. The original endnotes by William Beckford and Samuel Henley are reprinted with minor changes in format on pages 159–79 following the text of the tale.)

Samarah: Samarra, an ancient city north of Baghdad in what is now Iraq, established as al-Mu'tasim's palatial seat in A.D. 833.

[1] Harun al-Rashid (763–809) was caliph of Baghdad and is featured in numerous Arabian Nights tales. Vathek is loosely based on a later caliph, al-Wathik Bi-allah, son of the caliph al-Mu'tasim Bi'allah and grandson of Harun al-Rashid. The Abbasid dynasty of Muslim caliphs, based first in Damascus (in present-day Syria), then Baghdad (in present-day Iraq), lasted from 750 to 1258 and traced its descent to Muhammad's uncle, Al-Abbas.

[2] See the Beckford-Henley note (hereafter *B/H*), 159.

In the first of these were tables continually covered with the most exquisite dainties; which were supplied both by night and by day, according to their constant consumption; whilst the most delicious wines and the choicest cordials flowed forth from a hundred fountains that were never exhausted. This palace was called *The Eternal or unsatiating Banquet.*

The second was styled, *The Temple of Melody,* or *The Nectar of the Soul.* It was inhabited by the most skilful musicians and admired poets of the time; who not only displayed their talents within, but dispersing in bands without, caused every surrounding scene to reverberate their songs; which were continually varied in the most delightful succession.

The palace named *The Delight of the Eyes,* or *The Support of Memory,* was one entire enchantment. Rarities, collected from every corner of the earth were there found in such profusion as to dazzle and confound, but for the order in which they were arranged. One gallery exhibited the pictures of the celebrated Mani, and statues, that seemed to be alive. Here a well-managed perspective attracted the sight; there the magic of optics agreeably deceived it: whilst the naturalist on his part, exhibited in their several classes the various gifts that Heaven had bestowed on our globe. In a word, Vathek omitted nothing in this palace, that might gratify the curiosity of those who resorted to it, although he was not able to satisfy his own; for, of all men, he was the most curious.

The Palace of Perfumes, which was termed likewise *The Incentive to Pleasure,* consisted of various halls, where the different perfumes which the earth produces were kept perpetually burning in censers of gold. Flambeaux and aromatic lamps were here lighted in open day. But the too powerful effects of this agreeable delirium might be alleviated by descending into an immense garden, where an assemblage of every fragrant flower diffused through the air the purest odours.

The fifth palace, denominated *The Retreat of Mirth,* or *the Dangerous,* was frequented by troops of young females beautiful as the Houris, and not less seducing; who never failed to receive with caresses, all whom the Caliph allowed to approach them, and enjoy a few hours of their company.[3]

Notwithstanding the sensuality in which Vathek indulged, he experienced no abatement in the love of his people, who thought that a sovereign giving himself up to pleasure, was as able to govern, as one who declared

---

Mani: reputed to be a great Chinese painter of the time of Harun al-Rashid (see *B/H* 159).
Flambeaux: torches.

[3]For the Houris, see *Nourjahad* 46 n. 7 and *B/H* 159.

himself an enemy to it. But the unquiet and impetuous disposition of the Caliph would not allow him to rest there. He had studied so much for his amusement in the life-time of his father, as to acquire a great deal of knowledge, though not a sufficiency to satisfy himself; for he wished to know every thing; even sciences that did not exist. He was fond of engaging in disputes with the learned; but did not allow them to push their opposition with warmth. He stopped with presents the mouths of those whose mouths could be stopped; whilst others, whom his liberality was unable to subdue, he sent to prison to cool their blood; a remedy that often succeeded.

Vathek discovered also a predilection for theological controversy; but it was not with the orthodox that he usually held. By this means he induced the zealots to oppose him, and then persecuted them in return; for he resolved, at any rate, to have reason on his side.

The great prophet, Mahomet,[4] whose vicars the caliphs are, beheld with indignation from his abode in the seventh heaven, the irreligious conduct of such a vicegerent.[5] "Let us leave him to himself," said he to the Genii,[6] who are always ready to receive his commands: "let us see to what lengths his folly and impiety will carry him: if he run into excess, we shall know how to chastise him. Assist him, therefore, to complete the tower, which, in imitation of Nimrod,[7] he hath begun; not, like that great warrior, to escape being drowned, but from the insolent curiosity of penetrating the secrets of heaven:—he will not divine the fate that awaits him."

The Genii obeyed; and, when the workmen had raised their structure a cubit in the day time, two cubits more were added in the night. The expedition, with which the fabric arose, was not a little flattering to the vanity of Vathek: he fancied, that even insensible matter shewed a forwardness to subserve his designs; not considering, that the successes of the foolish and wicked form the first rod of their chastisement.

His pride arrived at its height, when having ascended, for the first time, the fifteen hundred stairs of his tower, he cast his eyes below, and beheld men not larger than pismires; mountains, than shells; and cities, than beehives. The idea, which such an elevation inspired of his own grandeur,

---

vicegerent: viceregent.
pismires: ants.

[4] See *Nourjahad* 25 n. 2. and *B/H* 160.
[5] As caliph and commander of the Muslim faithful, Vathek rules in the name of Muhammad.
[6] See *Nourjahad* 26 n. 3. and *B/H* 160.
[7] Nimrod was the biblical ruler of Babylon and presumed builder of the Tower of Babel (see Genesis 10.8–9 and 11.1–9). The ruins of Babylon are located south of Baghdad in modern Iraq. Beckford aligns Samarah with the site of the Tower of Babel (*B/H* 159).

completely bewildered him: he was almost ready to adore himself; till, lifting his eyes upward, he saw the stars as high above him as they appeared when he stood on the surface of the earth. He consoled himself, however, for this intruding and unwelcome perception of his littleness, with the thought of being great in the eyes of others; and flattered himself that the light of his mind would extend beyond the reach of his sight, and extort from the stars the decrees of his destiny.

With this view, the inquisitive Prince passed most of his nights on the summit of his tower, till becoming an adept in the mysteries of astrology, he imagined that the planets had disclosed to him the most marvellous adventures, which were to be accomplished by an extraordinary personage, from a country altogether unknown. Prompted by motives of curiosity, he had always been courteous to strangers; but, from this instant, he redoubled his attention, and ordered it to be announced, by sound of trumpet through all the streets of Samarah, that no one of his subjects, on peril of his displeasure, should either lodge or detain a traveller, but forthwith bring him to the palace.

Not long after this proclamation, arrived in his metropolis a man so abominably hideous that the very guards, who arrested him, were forced to shut their eyes, as they led him along: the Caliph himself appeared startled at so horrible a visage; but joy succeeded to this emotion of terror, when the stranger displayed to his view such rarities as he had never before seen, and of which he had no conception.

In reality, nothing was ever so extraordinary as the merchandize this stranger produced: most of his curiosities, which were not less admirable for their workmanship than splendour, had, besides, their several virtues described on a parchment fastened to each. There were slippers, which, by spontaneous springs, enabled the feet to walk; knives, that cut without motion of the hand; sabres, that dealt the blow at the person they were wished to strike; and the whole enriched with gems, that were hitherto unknown.

The sabres, especially, the blades of which, emitted a dazzling radiance, fixed, more than all the rest, the Caliph's attention; who promised himself to decipher, at his leisure, the uncouth characters engraven on their sides. Without, therefore, demanding their price, he ordered all the coined gold to be brought from his treasury, and commanded the merchant to take what he pleased. The stranger obeyed, took little, and remained silent.

Vathek, imagining that the merchant's taciturnity was occasioned by the awe which his presence inspired, encouraged him to advance; and asked

---

uncouth characters: strange letters.

him, with an air of condescension, who he was? whence he came? and where he obtained such beautiful commodities? The man, or rather monster, instead of making a reply, thrice rubbed his forehead, which, as well as his body, was blacker than ebony; four times clapped his paunch, the projection of which was enormous; opened wide his huge eyes, which glowed like firebrands; began to laugh with a hideous noise, and discovered his long amber-coloured teeth, bestreaked with green.

The Caliph, though a little startled, renewed his inquiries, but without being able to procure a reply. At which, beginning to be ruffled, he exclaimed:—"Knowest thou, wretch, who I am, and at whom thou art aiming thy gibes?"—Then, addressing his guards,—"Have ye heard him speak?—is he dumb?"—"He hath spoken," they replied, "but to no purpose." "Let him speak then again," said Vathek, "and tell me who he is, from whence he came, and where he procured these singular curiosities; or I swear, by the ass of Balaam, that I will make him rue his pertinacity."[8]

This menace was accompanied by one of the Caliph's angry and perilous glances, which the stranger sustained without the slightest emotion; although his eyes were fixed on the terrible eye of the Prince.

No words can describe the amazement of the courtiers, when they beheld this rude merchant withstand the encounter unshocked. They all fell prostrate with their faces on the ground, to avoid the risk of their lives; and would have continued in the same abject posture, had not the Caliph exclaimed in a furious tone—"Up, cowards! seize the miscreant! see that he be committed to prison, and guarded by the best of my soldiers! Let him, however, retain the money I gave him; it is not my intent to take from him his property; I only want him to speak."

No sooner had he uttered these words, than the stranger was surrounded, pinioned and bound with strong fetters, and hurried away to the prison of the great tower; which was encompassed by seven empalements of iron bars, and armed with spikes in every direction, longer and sharper than spits. The Caliph, nevertheless, remained in the most violent agitation. He sat down indeed to eat; but, of the three hundred dishes that were daily placed before him, he could taste of no more than thirty-two.

A diet, to which he had been so little accustomed, was sufficient of itself to prevent him from sleeping; what then must be its effect when joined to the anxiety that preyed upon his spirits? At the first glimpse of dawn he hastened to the prison, again to importune this intractable stranger; but the rage of Vathek exceeded all bounds on finding the prison empty; the grates

---

[8] In the Bible, Balaam is a Babylonian diviner who becomes an inadvertent prophet of the God of Israel; in a comic interlude, he is reproached by the ass he rides (see Numbers 22.21–35).

burst asunder, and his guards lying lifeless around him. In the paroxism of his passion he fell furiously on the poor carcases, and kicked them till evening without intermission. His courtiers and vizirs[9] exerted their efforts to soothe his extravagance; but, finding every expedient ineffectual, they all united in one vociferation—"The Caliph is gone mad! the Caliph is out of his senses!"

This outcry, which soon resounded through the streets of Samarah, at length reached the ears of Carathis, his mother, who flew in the utmost consternation to try her ascendancy on the mind of her son. Her tears and caresses called off his attention; and he was prevailed upon, by her intreaties, to be brought back to the palace.

Carathis, apprehensive of leaving Vathek to himself, had him put to bed; and, seating herself by him, endeavoured by her conversation to appease and compose him. Nor could any one have attempted it with better success; for the Caliph not only loved her as a mother, but respected her as a person of superior genius. It was she who had induced him, being a Greek herself, to adopt the sciences and systems of her country which all good Mussulmans hold in such thorough abhorrence.

Judiciary astrology was one of those sciences, in which Carathis was a perfect adept. She began, therefore, with reminding her son of the promise which the stars had made him; and intimated an intention of consulting them again. "Alas!" said the Caliph as soon as he could speak, "what a fool I have been! not for having bestowed forty thousand kicks on my guards, who so tamely submitted to death; but for never considering that this extraordinary man was the same that the planets had foretold; whom, instead of ill-treating, I should have conciliated by all the arts of persuasion."

"The past," said Carathis, "cannot be recalled; but it behoves us to think of the future: perhaps, you may again see the object you so much regret: it is possible the inscriptions on the sabres will afford information. Eat, therefore, and take thy repose, my dear son. We will consider, to-morrow, in what manner to act."

Vathek yielded to her counsel as well as he could, and arose in the morning with a mind more at ease. The sabres he commanded to be instantly brought; and, poring upon them, through a coloured glass, that their glittering might not dazzle, he set himself in earnest to decipher the inscriptions; but his reiterated attempts were all of them nugatory: in vain did he beat his head, and bite his nails; not a letter of the whole was he able to

---

Mussulmans: Muslims.

[9] Viziers. See *Nourjahad* 71.

ascertain. So unlucky a disappointment would have undone him again, had not Carathis, by good fortune, entered the apartment.

"Have patience, my son!" said she:—"you certainly are possessed of every important science; but the knowledge of languages is a trifle at best; and the accomplishment of none but a pedant. Issue a proclamation, that you will confer such rewards as become your greatness, upon any one that shall interpret what you do not understand, and what is beneath you to learn; you will soon find your curiosity gratified."

"That may be," said the Caliph; "but, in the mean time, I shall be horribly disgusted by a crowd of smatterers, who will come to the trial as much for the pleasure of retailing their jargon, as from the hope of gaining the reward. To avoid this evil, it will be proper to add, that I will put every candidate to death, who shall fail to give satisfaction: for, thank Heaven! I have skill enough to distinguish, whether one translates or invents."

"Of that I have no doubt," replied Carathis; "but, to put the ignorant to death is somewhat severe, and may be productive of dangerous effects. Content yourself with commanding their beards to be burnt:—beards in a state, are not quite so essential as men."

The Caliph submitted to the reasons of his mother; and, sending for Morakanabad, his prime vizir, said,—"Let the common criers proclaim, not only in Samarah, but throughout every city in my empire, that whosoever will repair hither and decipher certain characters which appear to be inexplicable, shall experience that liberality for which I am renowned; but, that all who fail upon trial shall have their beards burnt off to the last hair. Let them add, also, that I will bestow fifty beautiful slaves, and as many jars of apricots from the Isle of Kirmith, upon any man that shall bring me intelligence of the stranger."

The subjects of the Caliph, like their sovereign, being great admirers of women and apricots from Kirmith, felt their mouths water at these promises, but were totally unable to gratify their hankering; for no one knew what had become of the stranger.

As to the Caliph's other requisition, the result was different. The learned, the half learned, and those who were neither, but fancied themselves equal to both, came boldly to hazard their beards, and all shamefully lost them. The exaction of these forfeitures, which found sufficient employment for the eunuchs, gave them such a smell of singed hair, as greatly to disgust the ladies of the seraglio,[10] and to make it necessary that this new occupation of their guardians should be transferred to other hands.

---

[10] See *Nourjahad* 80 n. 1.

At length, however, an old man presented himself, whose beard was a cubit and a half longer than any that had appeared before him. The officers of the palace whispered to each other, as they ushered him in—"What a pity, oh! what a great pity that such a beard should be burnt!" Even the Caliph, when he saw it, concurred with them in opinion; but his concern was entirely needless. This venerable personage read the characters with facility, and explained them verbatim as follows: "We were made where every thing is well made: we are the least of the wonders of a place where all is wonderful and deserving the sight of the first potentate on earth."

"You translate admirably!" cried Vathek; "I know to what these marvellous characters allude. Let him receive as many robes of honour and thousands of sequins of gold as he hath spoken words. I am in some measure relieved from the perplexity that embarrassed me!" Vathek invited the old man to dine, and even to remain some days in the palace.

Unluckily for him, he accepted the offer; for the Caliph having ordered him next morning to be called, said—"Read again to me what you have read already; I cannot hear too often the promise that is made me—the completion of which I languish to obtain." The old man forthwith put on his green spectacles, but they instantly dropped from his nose, on perceiving that the characters he had read the day preceding, had given place to others of different import. "What ails you?" asked the Caliph; "and why these symptoms of wonder?"—"Sovereign of the world!" replied the old man, "these sabres hold another language to-day from that they yesterday held."—"How say you?" returned Vathek:—"but it matters not; tell me, if you can, what they mean."—"It is this, my lord," rejoined the old man: "Woe to the rash mortal who seeks to know that of which he should remain ignorant; and to undertake that which surpasseth his power!"—"And woe to thee!" cried the Caliph, in a burst of indignation, "to-day thou art void of understanding: begone from my presence, they shall burn but the half of thy beard, because thou wert yesterday fortunate in guessing:—my gifts I never resume." The old man, wise enough to perceive he had luckily escaped, considering the folly of disclosing so disgusting a truth, immediately withdrew and appeared not again.

But it was not long before Vathek discovered abundant reason to regret his precipitation; for, though he could not decipher the characters himself, yet, by constantly poring upon them, he plainly perceived that they every day changed; and, unfortunately, no other candidate offered to explain

---

sequins: Venetian or Turkish coins.
precipitation: haste.

them. This perplexing occupation inflamed his blood, dazzled his sight, and brought on such a giddiness and debility that he could hardly support himself. He failed not, however, though in so reduced a condition, to be often carried to his tower, as he flattered himself that he might there read in the stars, which he went to consult, something more congruous to his wishes; but in this his hopes were deluded: for his eyes, dimmed by the vapours of his head, began to subserve his curiosity so ill, that he beheld nothing but a thick, dun cloud, which he took for the most direful of omens.

Agitated with so much anxiety, Vathek entirely lost all firmness; a fever seized him, and his appetite failed. Instead of being one of the greatest eaters, he became as distinguished for drinking. So insatiable was the thirst which tormented him, that his mouth, like a funnel, was always open to receive the various liquors that might be poured into it, and especially cold water, which calmed him more than any other.

This unhappy prince, being thus incapacitated for the enjoyment of any pleasure, commanded the palaces of the five senses to be shut up; forebore to appear in public, either to display his magnificence, or administer justice, and retired to the inmost apartment of his harem. As he had ever been an excellent husband, his wives, overwhelmed with grief at his deplorable situation, incessantly supplied him with prayers for his health, and water for his thirst.

In the mean time the Princess Carathis, whose affliction no words can describe, instead of confining herself to sobbing and tears, was closetted daily with the vizir Morakanabad, to find out some cure, or mitigation, of the Caliph's disease. Under the persuasion that it was caused by enchantment, they turned over together, leaf by leaf, all the books of magic that might point out a remedy; and caused the horrible stranger, whom they accused as the enchanter, to be every where sought for, with the strictest diligence.

At the distance of a few miles from Samarah stood a high mountain, whose sides where swarded with wild thyme and basil, and its summit overspread with so delightful a plain, that it might have been taken for the Paradise destined for the faithful.[11] Upon it grew a hundred thickets of eglantine and other fragrant shrubs; a hundred arbours of roses, entwined with jessamine and honey-suckle; as many clumps of orange trees, cedar, and citron; whose branches, interwoven with the palm, the pomegranate, and the vine, presented every luxury that could regale the eye or the taste. The ground was strewed with violets, hare-bells, and pansies; in the midst

---

[11] See *Nourjahad* 45 n. 6.

of which numerous tufts of jonquils, hyacinths, and carnations perfumed the air. Four fountains, not less clear than deep, and so abundant as to slake the thirst of ten armies, seemed purposely placed here, to make the scene more resemble the garden of Eden watered by four sacred rivers.[12] Here, the nightingale sang the birth of the rose, her well-beloved, and, at the same time, lamented its short-lived beauty;[13] whilst the dove deplored the loss of more substantial pleasures; and the wakeful lark hailed the rising light that re-animates the whole creation. Here, more than any where, the mingled melodies of birds expressed the various passions which inspired them; and the exquisite fruits, which they pecked at pleasure, seemed to have given them a double energy.

To this mountain Vathek was sometimes brought, for the sake of breathing a purer air; and, especially, to drink at will of the four fountains. His attendants were his mother, his wives, and some eunuchs, who assiduously employed themselves in filling capacious bowls of rock crystal, and emulously presenting them to him. But it frequently happened, that his avidity exceeded their zeal, insomuch, that he would prostrate himself upon the ground to lap the water, of which he could never have enough.

One day, when this unhappy Prince had been long lying in so debasing a posture, a voice, hoarse but strong, thus addressed him: "Why dost thou assimilate thyself to a dog, O Caliph, proud as thou art of thy dignity and power?" At this apostrophe, he raised up his head, and beheld the stranger that had caused him so much affliction. Inflamed with anger at the sight, he exclaimed: — "Accursed Giaour![14] what comest thou hither to do? — is it not enough to have transformed a prince, remarkable for his agility, into a water budget? Perceivest thou not, that I may perish by drinking to excess, as well as by thirst?

"Drink then this draught," said the stranger, as he presented to him a phial of a red and yellow mixture: "and, to satiate the thirst of thy soul, as well as of thy body, know, that I am an Indian; but, from a region of India, which is wholly unknown."

The Caliph, delighted to see his desires accomplished in part, and flattering himself with the hope of obtaining their entire fulfilment, without a moment's hesitation swallowed the potion, and instantaneously found his health restored, his thirst appeased, and his limbs as agile as ever. In the

---

[12] See the biblical account in Genesis 2.10–14. The third and fourth rivers, the Tigris and Euphrates, form the basin where Babylon stood and where Baghdad is located.

[13] On the nightingale and rose, see *B/H* 170.

[14] Pronounced with a soft *g* to rhyme with *bower,* Giaour signifies an infidel or unbeliever (in the creed of Islam). Often used pejoratively to describe Christians, as in Byron's *Giaour,* the term here refers to a non-Muslim, allegedly from India.

transports of his joy, Vathek leaped upon the neck of the frightful Indian, and kissed his horrid mouth and hollow cheeks, as though they had been the coral lips and the lilies and roses of his most beautiful wives.

Nor would these transports have ceased, had not the eloquence of Carathis repressed them. Having prevailed upon him to return to Samarah, she caused a herald to proclaim as loudly as possible—"The wonderful stranger hath appeared again; he hath healed the Caliph;—he hath spoken! he hath spoken!"

Forthwith, all the inhabitants of this vast city quitted their habitations, and ran together in crowds to see the procession of Vathek and the Indian, whom they now blessed as much as they had before execrated, incessantly shouting—"He hath healed our sovereign;—he hath spoken! he hath spoken!" Nor were these words forgotten in the public festivals, which were celebrated the same evening, to testify the general joy; for the poets applied them as a chorus to all the songs they composed on this interesting subject.

The Caliph, in the meanwhile, caused the palaces of the senses to be again set open; and, as he found himself naturally prompted to visit that of Taste in preference to the rest, immediately ordered a splendid entertainment, to which his great officers and favourite courtiers were all invited. The Indian, who was placed near the Prince, seemed to think that, as a proper acknowledgment of so distinguished a privilege, he could neither eat, drink, nor talk too much. The various dainties were no sooner served up than they vanished, to the great mortification of Vathek, who piqued himself on being the greatest eater alive; and, at this time in particular, was blessed with an excellent appetite.

The rest of the company looked round at each other in amazement; but the Indian, without appearing to observe it, quaffed large bumpers to the health of each of them; sung in a style altogether extravagant; related stories, at which he laughed immoderately; and poured forth extemporaneous verses, which would not have been thought bad, but for the strange grimaces with which they were uttered. In a word, his loquacity was equal to that of a hundred astrologers; he ate as much as a hundred porters, and caroused in proportion.

The Caliph, notwithstanding the table had been thirty-two times covered, found himself incommoded by the voraciousness of his guest, who was now considerably declined in the Prince's esteem. Vathek, however, being unwilling to betray the chagrin he could hardly disguise, said in a whisper to Bababalouk, the chief of his eunuchs, "You see how enormous his performances are in every way; what would be the consequence should

---

eunuchs: castrated slaves whose duty was to guard and supervise the harem (see n. 15).

he get at my wives!—Go! redouble your vigilance, and be sure look well to my Circassians, who would be more to his taste than all of the rest."

The bird of the morning had thrice renewed his song, when the hour of the Divan was announced. Vathek, in gratitude to his subjects, having promised to attend, immediately arose from table, and repaired thither, leaning upon his vizir who could scarcely support him: so disordered was the poor Prince by the wine he had drunk, and still more by the extravagant vagaries of his boisterous guest.

The vizirs, the officers of the crown and of the law, arranged themselves in a semicircle about their sovereign, and preserved a respectful silence; whilst the Indian, who looked as cool as if he had been fasting, sat down without ceremony on one of the steps of the throne, laughing in his sleeve at the indignation with which his temerity had filled the spectators.

The Caliph, however, whose ideas were confused, and whose head was embarrassed, went on administering justice at haphazard; till at length the prime vizir, perceiving his situation, hit upon a sudden expedient to interrupt the audience and rescue the honour of his master, to whom he said in a whisper:—"My lord, the Princess Carathis, who hath passed the night in consulting the planets, informs you, that they portend you evil, and the danger is urgent. Beware, lest this stranger, whom you have so lavishly recompensed for his magical gewgaws, should make some attempt on your life: his liquor, which at first had the appearance of effecting your cure, may be no more than a poison, the operation of which will be sudden.—Slight not this surmise: ask him, at least, of what it was compounded, whence he procured it; and mention the sabres, which you seem to have forgotten."

Vathek, to whom the insolent airs of the stranger became every moment less supportable, intimated to his vizir, by a wink of acquiescence, that he would adopt his advice; and, at once turning towards the Indian, said—"Get up, and declare in full Divan of what drugs was compounded the liquor you enjoined me to take, for it is suspected to be poison: give also, that explanation I have so earnestly desired, concerning the sabres you sold me, and thus shew your gratitude for the favours heaped on you."

Having pronounced these words, in as moderate a tone as he well could, he waited in silent expectation for an answer. But the Indian, still keeping his seat, began to renew his loud shouts of laughter, and exhibit the same horrid grimaces he had shewn them before, without vouchsafing a word in

---

my Circassians: a group of Vathek's wives from Circassia, a region in the northern Caucasus, above Georgia, famed in Orientalist writing for its beautiful, fair-skinned women.
Divan: from the Arabic *diwan,* a ruler's council hall or assembly room and, by extension, the judicial assemblies held there.
gewgaws: gaudy, useless toys or trinkets.

reply. Vathek, no longer able to brook such insolence, immediately kicked him from the steps; instantly descending, repeated his blow; and persisted, with such assiduity, as incited all who were present to follow his example. Every foot was up and aimed at the Indian, and no sooner had any one given him a kick, than he felt himself constrained to reiterate the stroke.

The stranger afforded them no small entertainment: for, being both short and plump, he collected himself into a ball, and rolled round on all sides, at the blows of his assailants, who pressed after him, wherever he turned, with an eagerness beyond conception, whilst their numbers were every moment increasing. The ball indeed, in passing from one apartment to another, drew every person after it that came in its way; insomuch, that the whole palace was thrown into confusion and resounded with a tremendous clamour. The women of the harem,[15] amazed at the uproar, flew to their blinds to discover the cause; but, no sooner did they catch a glimpse of the ball, than, feeling themselves unable to refrain, they broke from the clutches of their eunuchs, who, to stop their flight, pinched them till they bled; but, in vain: whilst themselves, though trembling with terror at the escape of their charge, were as incapable of resisting the attraction.

After having traversed the halls, galleries, chambers, kitchens, gardens, and stables of the palace, the Indian at last took his course through the courts; whilst the Caliph, pursuing him closer than the rest, bestowed as many kicks as he possibly could; yet, not without receiving now and then a few which his competitors, in their eagerness, designed for the ball.

Carathis, Morakanabad, and two or three old vizirs, whose wisdom had hitherto withstood the attraction, wishing to prevent Vathek from exposing himself in the presence of his subjects, fell down in his way to impede the pursuit: but he, regardless of their obstruction, leaped over their heads, and went on as before. They then ordered the Muezins to call the people to prayers;[16] both for the sake of getting them out of the way, and of endeavouring, by their petitions, to avert the calamity; but neither of these expedients was a whit more successful. The sight of this fatal ball was alone sufficient to draw after it every beholder. The Muezins themselves, though they saw it but at a distance, hastened down from their minarets, and mixed with the crowd; which continued to increase in so surprising a man-

---

[15]The harem (from the Arabic *haram*) signifies a sacred or forbidden precinct, including the interior part of a Muslim house or seraglio forbidden to all but the women (wives and concubines) and members of the immediate family. In Orientalist writing, the harem is often associated with the excessive sexual license of an Oriental tyrant and can refer (like seraglio) to the collective women of the harem as well as to their apartments.

[16]The muezzin calls the Muslim faithful to prayer at appointed hours, five times daily, often from a minaret or high tower attached to a mosque (see *B/H* 161).

ner, that scarce an inhabitant was left in Samarah, except the aged; the sick, confined to their beds; and infants at the breast, whose nurses could run more nimbly without them. Even Carathis, Morakanabad, and the rest, were all become of the party. The shrill screams of the females, who had broken from their apartments, and were unable to extricate themselves from the pressure of the crowd, together with those of the eunuchs jostling after them, and terrified lest their charge should escape from their sight; the execrations of husbands, urging forward and menacing each other; kicks given and received; stumblings and overthrows at every step; in a word, the confusion that universally prevailed, rendered Samarah like a city taken by storm, and devoted to absolute plunder. At last, the cursed Indian, who still preserved his rotundity of figure, after passing through all the streets and public places, and leaving them empty, rolled onwards to the plain of Catoul, and entered the valley at the foot of the mountain of the four fountains.

As a continual fall of water had excavated an immense gulph in the valley whose opposite side was closed in by a steep acclivity, the Caliph and his attendants were apprehensive, lest the ball should bound into the chasm, and, to prevent it, redoubled their efforts, but in vain. The Indian persevered in his onward direction; and, as had been apprehended, glancing from the precipice with the rapidity of lightning, was lost in the gulph below.

Vathek would have followed the perfidious Giaour, had not an invisible agency arrested his progress. The multitude that pressed after him were at once checked in the same manner, and a calm instantaneously ensued. They all gazed at each other with an air of astonishment, and notwithstanding that the loss of veils and turbans, together with torn habits, and dust blended with sweat, presented a most laughable spectacle, yet there was not one smile to be seen. On the contrary, all with looks of confusion and sadness returned in silence to Samarah, and retired to their inmost apartments, without ever reflecting, that they had been impelled by an invisible power into the extravagance, for which they reproached themselves: for it is but just that men, who so often arrogate to their own merit the good of which they are but instruments, should also attribute to themselves absurdities which they could not prevent.

The Caliph was the only person who refused to leave the valley. He commanded his tents to be pitched there, and stationed himself on the very edge of the precipice, in spite of the representations of Carathis and Morakanabad, who pointed out the hazard of its brink giving way, and the vicinity to the magician, that had so cruelly tormented him. Vathek derided all their remonstrances; and, having ordered a thousand flambeaux to be lighted, and directed his attendants to proceed in lighting more, lay down on the slippery margin, and attempted, by the help of this artificial splendour, to look through that gloom, which all the fires of the empyrean had been insufficient to pervade. One while he fancied to himself voices arising from the depth of the gulph; at another, he seemed to distinguish the accents of the Indian; but all was no more than the hollow murmur of waters, and the din of the cataracts that rushed from steep to steep down the sides of the mountain.

Having passed the night in this cruel perturbation, the Caliph, at daybreak, retired to his tent; where, without taking the least sustenance, he continued to doze till the dusk of evening began again to come on. He then resumed his vigils as before, and persevered in observing them for many nights together. At length, fatigued with so fruitless an employment, he sought relief from change. To this end, he sometimes paced with hasty strides across the plain; and, as he wildly gazed at the stars, reproached them with having deceived him; but, lo! on a sudden, the clear blue sky appeared streaked over with streams of blood, which reached from the valley even to the city of Samarah. As this awful phenomenon seemed to touch his tower, Vathek at first thought of repairing thither to view it more distinctly; but, feeling himself unable to advance, and being overcome with apprehension, he muffled up his face in the folds of his robe.

Terrifying as these prodigies were, this impression upon him was no more than momentary, and served only to stimulate his love of the marvellous. Instead, therefore, of returning to his palace, he persisted in the resolution of abiding where the Indian had vanished from his view. One night, however, while he was walking as usual on the plain, the moon and stars were eclipsed at once, and a total darkness ensued. The earth trembled beneath him, and a voice came forth, the voice of the Giaour, who, in accents more sonorous than thunder, thus addressed him: "Wouldest thou devote thyself to me? adore the terrestrial influences, and abjure Mahomet? On these conditions I will bring thee to the Palace of Subterranean Fire. There shalt thou behold, in immense depositories, the treasures which the stars have promised thee; and which will be conferred by those intelligences, whom thou shalt thus render propitious. It was from thence I brought my sabres, and it is there that Soliman Ben Daoud[17] reposes, surrounded by the talismans that control the world."

The astonished Caliph trembled as he answered, yet he answered in a style that shewed him to be no novice in preternatural adventures: "Where art thou? be present to my eyes; dissipate the gloom that perplexes

---

empyrean: the highest heaven in ancient cosmography, made up of pure fire or light.

[17] Solomon, son of David: see *Nourjahad* 30 n. 4 and *B/H* 161.

me, and of which I deem thee the cause. After the many flambeaux I have burnt to discover thee, thou mayest, at least, grant a glimpse of thy horrible visage."—"Abjure then Mahomet!" replied the Indian, "and promise me full proofs of thy sincerity: otherwise, thou shalt never behold me again."

The unhappy Caliph, instigated by insatiable curiosity, lavished his promises in the utmost profusion. The sky immediately brightened; and, by the light of the planets, which seemed almost to blaze, Vathek beheld the earth open; and, at the extremity of a vast black chasm, a portal of ebony, before which stood the Indian, holding in his hand a golden key, which he sounded against the lock.

"How," cried Vathek, "can I descend to thee;—Come, take me, and instantly open the portal."—"Not so fast," replied the Indian, "impatient Caliph!—Know that I am parched with thirst, and cannot open this door, till my thirst be thoroughly appeased; I require the blood of fifty children. Take them from among the most beautiful sons of thy vizirs and great men; or, neither can my thirst nor thy curiosity be satisfied. Return to Samarah; procure for me this necessary libation; come back hither; throw it thyself into this chasm, and then shalt thou see!"

Having thus spoken, the Indian turned his back on the Caliph, who, incited by the suggestions of demons, resolved on the direful sacrifice.—He now pretended to have regained his tranquillity, and set out for Samarah amidst the acclamations of a people who still loved him, and forbore not to rejoice, when they believed him to have recovered his reason. So successfully did he conceal the emotion of his heart, that even Carathis and Morakanabad were equally deceived with the rest. Nothing was heard of but festivals and rejoicings. The fatal ball, which no tongue had hitherto ventured to mention, was brought on the tapis. A general laugh went round, though many, still smarting under the hands of the surgeon, from the hurts received in that memorable adventure, had no great reason for mirth.

The prevalence of this gay humour was not a little grateful to Vathek, who perceived how much it conduced to his project. He put on the appearance of affability to every one; but especially to his vizirs, and the grandees of his court, whom he failed not to regale with a sumptuous banquet; during which, he insensibly directed the conversation to the children of his guests. Having asked, with a good-natured air, which of them were blessed with the handsomest boys, every father at once asserted the pretensions of his own; and the contest imperceptibly grew so warm, that nothing could have withholden them from coming to blows, but their

---

on the tapis: literally, on the carpet; that is, into discussion.

profound reverence for the person of the Caliph. Under the pretence, therefore, of reconciling the disputants, Vathek took upon him to decide; and, with this view, commanded the boys to be brought.

It was not long before a troop of these poor children made their appearance, all equipped by their fond mothers with such ornaments, as might give the greatest relief to their beauty, or most advantageously display the graces of their age. But, whilst this brilliant assemblage attracted the eyes and hearts of every one besides, the Caliph scrutinized each, in his turn, with a malignant avidity that passed for attention, and selected from their number the fifty whom he judged the Giaour would prefer.

With an equal shew of kindness as before, he proposed to celebrate a festival on the plain, for the entertainment of his young favourites, who, he said, ought to rejoice still more than all, at the restoration of his health, on account of the favours he intended for them.

The Caliph's proposal was received with the greatest delight, and soon published through Samarah. Litters, camels, and horses were prepared. Women and children, old men and young, every one placed himself as he chose. The cavalcade set forward, attended by all the confectioners in the city and its precincts; the populace, following on foot, composed an amazing crowd, and occasioned no little noise. All was joy; nor did any one call to mind, what most of them had suffered, when they lately travelled the road they were now passing so gaily.

The evening was serene, the air refreshing, the sky clear, and the flowers exhaled their fragrance. The beams of the declining sun, whose mild splendour reposed on the summit of the mountain, shed a glow of ruddy light over its green declivity, and the white flocks sporting upon it. No sounds were heard, save the murmurs of the four fountains; and the reeds and voices of shepherds calling to each other from different eminences.

The lovely innocents destined for the sacrifice, added not a little to the hilarity of the scene. They approached the plain full of sportiveness, some coursing butterflies, others culling flowers, or picking up the shining little pebbles that attracted their notice. At intervals they nimbly started from each other for the sake of being caught again, and mutually imparting a thousand caresses.

The dreadful chasm, at whose bottom the portal of ebony was placed, began to appear at a distance. It looked like a black streak that divided the plain. Morakanabad and his companions, took it for some work which the Caliph had ordered. Unhappy men! little did they surmise for what it was destined. Vathek unwilling that they should examine it too nearly, stopped

---

eminences: heights.

the procession, and ordered a spacious circle to be formed on this side, at some distance from the accursed chasm. The body-guard of eunuchs was detached, to measure out the lists intended for the games; and prepare the rings for the arrows of the young archers. The fifty competitors were soon stripped, and presented to the admiration of the spectators the suppleness and grace of their delicate limbs. Their eyes sparkled with a joy, which those of their fond parents reflected. Every one offered wishes for the little candidate nearest his heart, and doubted not of his being victorious. A breathless suspence awaited the contest of these amiable and innocent victims.

The Caliph, availing himself of the first moment to retire from the crowd, advanced towards the chasm; and there heard, yet not without shuddering, the voice of the Indian; who, gnashing his teeth, eagerly demanded: "Where are they?—Where are they?—perceivest thou not how my mouth waters?"—"Relentless Giaour!" answered Vathek, with emotion; "can nothing content thee but the massacre of these lovely victims? Ah! wert thou to behold their beauty, it must certainly move thy compassion."—"Perdition on thy compassion, babbler!" cried the Indian: "give them me; instantly give them, or, my portal shall be closed against thee for ever!"—"Not so loudly," replied the Caliph, blushing.—"I understand thee," returned the Giaour with the grin of an Ogre; "thou wantest no presence of mind: I will, for a moment, forbear."

During this exquisite dialogue, the games went forward with all alacrity, and at length concluded, just as the twilight began to overcast the mountains. Vathek, who was still standing on the edge of the chasm, called out, with all his might:—"Let my fifty little favourites approach me, separately; and let them come in the order of their success. To the first, I will give my diamond bracelet; to the second, my collar of emeralds; to the third, my aigret of rubies; to the fourth, my girdle of topazes; and to the rest, each a part of my dress, even down to my slippers."

This declaration was received with reiterated acclamations; and all extolled the liberality of a prince, who would thus strip himself, for the amusement of his subjects, and the encouragement of the rising generation. The Caliph, in the meanwhile, undressed himself by degrees; and, raising his arm as high as he was able, made each of the prizes glitter in the air; but, whilst he delivered it, with one hand, to the child, who sprung forward to receive it; he, with the other, pushed the poor innocent into the gulph; where the Giaour, with a sullen muttering, incessantly repeated; "more! more!"

---

aigret: plume-shaped jeweled ornament.
girdle: belt, sash, or cord worn around the waist.

This dreadful device was executed with so much dexterity, that the boy who was approaching him, remained unconscious of the fate of his forerunner; and, as to the spectators, the shades of evening, together with their distance, precluded them from perceiving any object distinctly. Vathek, having in this manner thrown in the last of the fifty; and, expecting that the Giaour, on receiving him, would have presented the key; already fancied himself, as great as Soliman, and, consequently, above being amenable for what he had done:—when, to his utter amazement, the chasm closed, and the ground became as entire as the rest of the plain.

No language could express his rage and despair. He execrated the perfidy of the Indian; loaded him with the most infamous invectives; and stamped with his foot, as resolving to be heard. He persisted in this till his strength failed him; and, then, fell on the earth like one void of sense. His vizirs and grandees, who were nearer than the rest, supposed him, at first, to be sitting on the grass, at play with their amiable children; but, at length, prompted by doubt, they advanced towards the spot, and found the Caliph alone, who wildly demanded what they wanted? "Our children! our children!" cried they. "It is, assuredly, pleasant," said he, "to make me accountable for accidents. Your children, while at play, fell from the precipice, and I should have experienced their fate, had I not suddenly started back."

At these words, the fathers of the fifty boys cried out aloud; the mothers repeated their exclamations an octave higher; whilst the rest, without knowing the cause, soon drowned the voices of both, with still louder lamentations of their own. "Our Caliph," said they, and the report soon circulated, "our Caliph has played us this trick, to gratify his accursed Giaour. Let us punish him for perfidy! let us avenge ourselves! let us avenge the blood of the innocent! let us throw this cruel prince into the gulph that is near, and let his name be mentioned no more!"

At this rumour and these menaces, Carathis, full of consternation, hastened to Morakanabad, and said: "Vizir, you have lost two beautiful boys, and must necessarily be the most afflicted of fathers; but you are virtuous; save your master."—"I will brave every hazard," replied the vizir, "to rescue him from his present danger; but, afterwards, will abandon him to his fate. Bababalouk," continued he, "put yourself at the head of your eunuchs: disperse the mob, and, if possible, bring back this unhappy prince to his palace." Bababalouk and his fraternity, felicitating each other in a low voice on their having been spared the cares as well as the honour of paternity, obeyed the mandate of the vizir; who, seconding their exertions, to the utmost of his power, at length, accomplished his generous enterprize; and retired, as he resolved, to lament at his leisure.

No sooner had the Caliph re-entered his palace, than Carathis commanded the doors to be fastened; but, perceiving the tumult to be still violent, and hearing the imprecations which resounded from all quarters, she said to her son: "Whether the populace be right or wrong, it behoves you to provide for your safety; let us retire to your own apartment, and, from thence, through the subterranean passage, known only to ourselves, into your tower: there, with the assistance of the mutes who never leave it, we may be able to make a powerful resistance. Bababalouk, supposing us to be still in the palace, will guard its avenues, for his own sake; and we shall soon find, without the counsels of that blubberer Morakanabad, what expedient may be the best to adopt."

Vathek, without making the least reply, acquiesced in his mother's proposal, and repeated as he went: "Nefarious Giaour! where art thou? hast thou not yet devoured those poor children? where are thy sabres? thy golden key? thy talismans?"—Carathis, who guessed from these interrogations a part of the truth, had no difficulty to apprehend, in getting at the whole as soon as he should be a little composed in his tower. This Princess was so far from being influenced by scruples, that she was as wicked, as woman could be; which is not saying a little; for the sex pique themselves on their superiority, in every competition. The recital of the Caliph, therefore, occasioned neither terror nor surprize to his mother: she felt no emotion but from the promises of the Giaour, and said to her son: "This Giaour, it must be confessed, is somewhat sanguinary in his taste; but, the terrestrial powers are always terrible; nevertheless, what the one hath promised, and the others can confer, will prove a sufficient indemnification. No crimes should be thought too dear for such a reward: forbear, then, to revile the Indian; you have not fulfilled the conditions to which his services are annexed: for instance; is not a sacrifice to the subterranean Genii[18] required? and should we not be prepared to offer it as soon as the tumult is subsided? This charge I will take on myself, and have no doubt of succeeding, by means of your treasures, which as there are now so many others in store, may, without fear, be exhausted." Accordingly, the Princess, who possessed the most consummate skill in the art of persuasion, went immediately back through the subterranean passage; and, presenting herself to the populace, from a window of the palace, began to harangue them with all the address of which she was mistress; whilst Bababalouk, showered money from both hands amongst the crowd, who by these united means were soon appeased. Every person retired to his home, and Carathis returned to the tower.

---

terrestrial: earthly, here with the sense of subterranean or demonic.

[18] In Muslim tradition, there are evil genii (jinn), as well as friendly ones.

Prayer at break of day was announced, when Carathis and Vathek ascended the steps, which led to the summit of the tower; where they remained for some time though the weather was lowering and wet. This impending gloom corresponded with their malignant dispositions; but when the sun began to break through the clouds, they ordered a pavilion to be raised, as a screen against the intrusion of his beams. The Caliph, overcome with fatigue, sought refreshment from repose; at the same time, hoping that significant dreams might attend on his slumbers; whilst the indefatigable Carathis, followed by a party of her mutes, descended to prepare whatever she judged proper, for the oblation of the approaching night.

By secret stairs, contrived within the thickness of the wall, and known only to herself and her son, she first repaired to the mysterious recesses in which were deposited the mummies that had been wrested from the catacombs of the ancient Pharaohs. Of these she ordered several to be taken. From thence, she resorted to a gallery; where, under the guard of fifty female negroes mute and blind of the right eye, were preserved the oil of the most venomous serpents; rhinoceros' horns; and woods of a subtile and penetrating odour, procured from the interior of the Indies, together with a thousand other horrible rarities. This collection had been formed for a purpose like the present, by Carathis herself; from a presentiment, that she might one day, enjoy some intercourse with the infernal powers: to whom she had ever been passionately attached, and to whose taste she was no stranger.

To familiarize herself the better with the horrors in view, the Princess remained in the company of her negresses, who squinted in the most amiable manner from the only eye they had; and leered with exquisite delight, at the sculls and skeletons which Carathis had drawn forth from her cabinets; all of them making the most frightful contortions and uttering such shrill chatterings, that the Princess stunned by them and suffocated by the potency of the exhalations, was forced to quit the gallery, after stripping it of a part of its abominable treasures.

Whilst she was thus occupied, the Caliph, who instead of the visions he expected, had acquired in these unsubstantial regions a voracious appetite, was greatly provoked at the mutes. For having totally forgotten their deafness, he had impatiently asked them for food; and seeing them regardless of his demand, he began to cuff, pinch, and bite them, till Carathis arrived to terminate a scene so indecent, to the great content of these miserable creatures: "Son! what means all this?" said she, panting for breath. "I thought I heard as I came up, the shrieks of a thousand bats, torn from their crannies in the recesses of a cavern; and it was the outcry only of these poor mutes, whom you were so unmercifully abusing. In truth, you but ill deserve the admirable provision I have brought you."—"Give it me instantly," exclaimed the Caliph; "I am perishing for hunger!"—"As to that," answered she, "you must have an excellent stomach if it can digest what I have brought."—"Be quick," replied the Caliph;—"but, oh heavens! what horrors! what do you intend?" "Come; come;" returned Carathis, "be not so squeamish; but help me to arrange every thing properly; and you shall see that, what you reject with such symptoms of disgust, will soon complete your felicity. Let us get ready the pile, for the sacrifice of to-night; and think not of eating, till that is performed: know you not, that all solemn rites ought to be preceded by a rigorous abstinence?"

The Caliph, not daring to object, abandoned himself to grief and the wind that ravaged his entrails, whilst his mother went forward with the requisite operations. Phials of serpents' oil, mummies, and bones, were soon set in order on the balustrade of the tower. The pile began to rise; and in three hours was twenty cubits high. At length darkness approached, and Carathis, having stripped herself to her inmost garment, clapped her hands in an impulse of ecstacy; the mutes followed her example; but Vathek, extenuated with hunger and impatience, was unable to support himself, and fell down in a swoon. The sparks had already kindled the dry wood; the venomous oil burst into a thousand blue flames; the mummies, dissolving, emitted a thick dun vapour; and the rhinoceros' horns, beginning to consume; all together diffused such a stench, that the Caliph, recovering, started from his trance, and gazed wildly on the scene in full blaze around him. The oil gushed forth in a plenitude of streams; and the negresses, who supplied it without intermission, united their cries to those of the Princess. At last, the fire became so violent, and the flames reflected from the polished marble so dazzling, that the Caliph, unable to withstand the heat and the blaze, effected his escape; and took shelter under the imperial standard.

In the mean time, the inhabitants of Samarah, scared at the light which shone over the city, arose in haste; ascended their roofs; beheld the tower on fire, and hurried, half naked to the square. Their love for their sovereign immediately awoke; and, apprehending him in danger of perishing in his tower, their whole thoughts were occupied with the means of his safety. Morakanabad flew from his retirement, wiped away his tears, and cried out for water like the rest. Bababalouk, whose olfactory nerves were more familiarized to magical odours, readily conjecturing, that Carathis was engaged in her favourite amusements, strenuously exhorted them not to be alarmed. Him, however, they treated as an old poltroon, and styled him a rascally traitor. The camels and dromedaries were advancing with water; but, no one knew by which way to enter the tower. Whilst the populace was

---

extenuated: thinned, emaciated.
poltroon: worthless coward.

obstinate in forcing the doors, a violent north-east wind drove an immense volume of flame against them. At first, they recoiled, but soon came back with redoubled zeal. At the same time, the stench of the horns and mummies increasing, most of the crowd fell backward in a state of suffocation. Those that kept their feet, mutually wondered at the cause of the smell; and admonished each other to retire. Morakanabad, more sick than the rest, remained in a piteous condition. Holding his nose with one hand, every one persisted in his efforts with the other to burst open the doors and obtain admission. A hundred and forty of the strongest and most resolute, at length accomplished their purpose. Having gained the stair-case, by their violent exertions, they attained a great height in a quarter of an hour.

Carathis, alarmed at the signs of her mutes, advanced to the stair-case; went down a few steps, and heard several voices calling out from below: "You shall, in a moment have water!" Being rather alert, considering her age, she presently regained the top of the tower; and bade her son suspend the sacrifice for some minutes; adding,—"We shall soon be enabled to render it more grateful. Certain dolts of your subjects, imagining no doubt that we were on fire, have been rash enough to break through those doors, which had hitherto remained inviolate; for the sake of bringing up water. They are very kind, you must allow, so soon to forget the wrongs you have done them; but that is of little moment. Let us offer them to the Giaour,—let them come up; our mutes, who neither want strength nor experience, will soon dispatch them; exhausted as they are, with fatigue."—"Be it so," answered the Caliph, "provided we finish, and I dine." In fact, these good people, out of breath from ascending fifteen hundred stairs in such haste; and chagrined, at having spilt by the way, the water they had taken, were no sooner arrived at the top, than the blaze of the flames, and the fumes of the mummies, at once overpowered their senses. It was a pity! for they beheld not the agreeable smile, with which the mutes and negresses adjusted the cord to their necks: these amiable personages rejoiced, however, no less at the scene. Never before had the ceremony of strangling been performed with so much facility. They all fell, without the least resistance or struggle: so that Vathek, in the space of a few moments, found himself surrounded by the dead bodies of the most faithful of his subjects; all which were thrown on the top of the pile. Carathis, whose presence of mind never forsook her, perceiving that she had carcasses sufficient to complete her oblation, commanded the chains to be stretched across the stair-case, and the iron doors barricadoed, that no more might come up.

No sooner were these orders obeyed, than the tower shook; the dead bodies vanished in the flames; which, at once, changed from a swarthy crimson, to a bright rose colour: an ambient vapour emitted the most exquisite fragrance; the marble columns rang with harmonious sounds, and the liquified horns diffused a delicious perfume. Carathis, in transports, anticipated the success of her enterprize; whilst her mutes and negresses, to whom these sweets had given the cholic, retired grumbling to their cells.

Scarcely were they gone, when, instead of the pile, horns, mummies and ashes, the Caliph both saw and felt, with a degree of pleasure which he could not express, a table, covered with the most magnificent repast: flaggons of wine, and vases of exquisite sherbet reposing on snow. He availed himself, without scruple, of such an entertainment; and had already laid hands on a lamb stuffed with pistachios, whilst Carathis was privately drawing from a fillagreen urn, a parchment that seemed to be endless; and which had escaped the notice of her son. Totally occupied in gratifying an importunate appetitite, he left her to peruse it without interruption; which having finished, she said to him, in an authoritative tone, "Put an end to your gluttony, and hear the splendid promises with which you are favoured!" She then read, as follows: "Vathek, my well-beloved, thou hast surpassed my hopes: my nostrils have been regaled by the savour of thy mummies, thy horns; and, still more by the lives, devoted on the pile. At the full of the moon, cause the bands of thy musicians, and thy tymbals, to be heard; depart from thy palace, surrounded by all the pageants of majesty; thy most faithful slaves, thy best beloved wives; thy most magnificent litters; thy richest loaden camels; and set forward on thy way to Istakhar. There, I await thy coming: that is the region of wonders: there shalt thou receive the diadem of Gian Ben Gian; the talismans of Soliman; and the treasures of the pre-adamite sultans: there shalt thou be solaced with all kinds of delight.[19]—But, beware how thou enterest any dwelling on thy route; or thou shalt feel the effects of my anger."

The Caliph, notwithstanding his habitual luxury, had never before dined with so much satisfaction. He gave full scope to the joy of these golden tidings; and betook himself to drinking anew. Carathis, whose antipathy to wine was by no means insuperable, failed not to pledge him at every bumper he ironically quaffed to the health of Mahomet.[20] This infernal liquor completed their impious temerity, and prompted them to utter a profusion of blasphemies. They gave a loose to their wit, at the expense

---

sherbet: drink made with fruit juices and sugared water, often cooled with snow.
tymbals: kettledrums.
Istakhar: Istakhr or Persepolis, ancient capital of Persia; its ruins are located north of Shiraz in what is now Iran.

[19] See *B/H* 162.
[20] See *Nourjahad* 37 n. 5.

of the ass of Balaam, the dog of the seven sleepers, and the other animals admitted into the paradise of Mahomet.[21] In this sprightly humour, they descended the fifteen hundred stairs, diverting themselves as they went, at the anxious faces they saw on the square, through the barbacans and loop-holes of the tower; and, at length, arrived at the royal apartments, by the subterranean passage. Bababalouk was parading to and fro, and issuing his mandates, with great pomp to the eunuchs; who were snuffing the lights and painting the eyes of the Circassians. No sooner did he catch sight of the Caliph and his mother, than he exclaimed, "Hah! you have, then, I perceive, escaped from the flames: I was not, however, altogether out of doubt."—"Of what moment is it to us what you thought, or think?" cried Carathis: "go; speed; tell Morakanabad that we immediately want him: and take care, not to stop by the way, to make your insipid reflections."

Morakanabad delayed not to obey the summons; and was received by Vathek and his mother, with great solemnity. They told him, with an air of composure and commiseration, that the fire at the top of the tower was extinguished; but that it had cost the lives of the brave people who sought to assist them.

"Still more misfortunes!" cried Morakanabad, with a sigh. "Ah, commander of the faithful, our holy prophet is certainly irritated against us! it behoves you to appease him."—"We will appease him, hereafter!" replied the Caliph, with a smile, that augured nothing of good. "You will have leisure sufficient for your supplications, during my absence: for this country is the banc of my health. I am disgusted with the mountain of the four fountains, and am resolved to go and drink of the stream of Rocnabad.[22] I long to refresh myself, in the delightful vallies which it waters. Do you, with the advice of my mother, govern my dominions, and take care to supply whatever her experiments may demand: for, you well know, that our tower abounds in materials for the advancement of science."

The tower but ill suited Morakanabad's taste. Immense treasures had been lavished upon it; and nothing had he ever seen carried thither but female negroes, mutes and abominable drugs. Nor did he know well what to think of Carathis, who, like a cameleon, could assume all possible colours. Her cursed eloquence had often driven the poor mussulman to his last shifts. He considered, however, that if she possessed but few good qualities, her son had still fewer; and that the alternative, on the whole, would be in her favour. Consoled, therefore, with this reflection; he went, in good spir-

---

barbicans: outworks.

[21] See 84 n. 8. and *B/H* 163.
[22] See *B/H* 163.

its, to soothe the populace, and make the proper arrangements for his master's journey.

Vathek, to conciliate the Spirits of the subterranean palace, resolved that his expedition should be uncommonly splendid. With this view he confiscated, on all sides, the property of his subjects; whilst his worthy mother stripped the seraglios she visited, of the gems they contained. She collected all the sempstresses and embroiderers of Samarah and other cities, to the distance of sixty leagues; to prepare pavilions, palanquins, sofas, canopies, and litters for the train of the monarch. There was not left, in Masulipatan, a single piece of chintz; and so much muslin had been brought up to dress out Bababalouk and the other black eunuchs, that there remained not an ell of it in the whole Irak of Babylon.

During these preparations, Carathis, who never lost sight of her great object, which was to obtain favour with the powers of darkness, made select parties of the fairest and most delicate ladies of the city: but in the midst of their gaiety, she contrived to introduce vipers amongst them, and to break pots of scorpions under the table. They all bit to a wonder, and Carathis would have left her friends to die, were it not that, to fill up the time, she now and then amused herself in curing their wounds, with an excellent anodyne of her own invention: for this good Princess abhorred being indolent.

Vathek, who was not altogether so active as his mother, devoted his time to the sole gratification of his senses, in the palaces which were severally dedicated to them. He disgusted himself no more with the divan, or the mosque. One half of Samarah followed his example, whilst the other lamented the progress of corruption.

In the midst of these transactions, the embassy returned, which had been sent, in pious times, to Mecca. It consisted of the most reverend Moullahs[23] who had fulfilled their commission, and brought back one of those precious besoms which are used to sweep the sacred Cahaba:[24] a present truly worthy of the greatest potentate on earth!

The Caliph happened at this instant to be engaged in an apartment by no means adapted to the reception of embassies. He heard the voice of Bababalouk, calling out from between the door and the tapestry that hung before it: "Here are the excellent Edris al Shafei, and the seraphic Al Mouhateddin, who have brought the besom from Mecca, and, with tears

---

ell: a measure equal to forty-five inches.
besoms: brooms made of bundled twigs.

[23] *Mullah* is a title of respect for religious scholars and jurists.
[24] The *Ka-ba* in Mecca; see 49 n. 8. and *B/H* 164.

of joy, entreat they may present it to your majesty in person."—"Let them bring the besom hither, it may be of use," said Vathek. "How!" answered Bababalouk, half aloud and amazed. "Obey," replied the Caliph, "for it is my sovereign will; go instantly, vanish! for here will I receive the good folk who have thus filled thee with joy."

The eunuch departed muttering, and bade the venerable train attend him. A sacred rapture was diffused amongst these reverend old men. Though fatigued with the length of their expedition, they followed Bababalouk with an alertness almost miraculous, and felt themselves highly flattered, as they swept along the stately porticos, that the Caliph would not receive them like ambassadors in ordinary in his hall of audience. Soon reaching the interior of the harem (where, through blinds of Persian, they perceived large soft eyes, dark and blue, that came and went like lightning) penetrated with respect and wonder, and full of their celestial mission, they advanced in procession towards the small corridors that appeared to terminate in nothing, but, nevertheless, led to the cell where the Caliph expected their coming.

"What! is the commander of the faithful sick?" said Edris al Shafei, in a low voice to his companion.—"I rather think he is in his oratory," answered Al Mouhateddin. Vathek, who heard the dialogue, cried out:—"What imports it you, how I am employed? approach without delay." They advanced, whilst the Caliph, without shewing himself, put forth his hand from behind the tapestry that hung before the door, and demanded of them the besom. Having prostrated themselves as well as the corridor would permit, and, even in a tolerable semicircle, the venerable Al Shafei, drawing forth the besom from the embroidered and perfumed scarves, in which it had been enveloped, and secured from the profane gaze of vulgar eyes, arose from his associates, and advanced, with an air of the most awful solemnity towards the supposed oratory; but, with what astonishment! with what horror was he seized!——Vathek, bursting out into a villainous laugh, snatched the besom from his trembling hand, and, fixing upon some cobwebs, that hung from the ceiling, gravely brushed them away till not a single one remained. The old men, overpowered with amazement, were unable to lift their beards from the ground: for, as Vathek had carelessly left the tapestry between them half drawn, they were witnesses of the whole transaction. Their tears bedewed the marble. Al Mouhateddin swooned through mortification and fatigue, whilst the Caliph, throwing himself backward on his seat, shouted, and clapped his hands without mercy. At last, addressing himself to Bababalouk!—"My dear black," said he, "go, re-

---

blinds of Persian: Persian blinds (or persiennes), similar to Venetian blinds.

gale these pious poor souls, with my good wine from Shiraz,[25] since they can boast of having seen more of my palace than any one besides." Having said this, he threw the besom in their face, and went to enjoy the laugh with Carathis. Bababalouk did all in his power to console the ambassadors; but the two most infirm expired on the spot: the rest were carried to their beds, from whence, being heart-broken with sorrow and shame, they never arose.

The succeeding night, Vathek, attended by his mother, ascended the tower to see if every thing were ready for his journey: for, he had great faith in the influence of the stars. The planets appeared in their most favourable aspects. The Caliph, to enjoy so flattering a sight, supped gaily on the roof; and fancied that he heard, during his repast, loud shouts of laughter resound through the sky, in a manner, that inspired the fullest assurance.

All was in motion at the palace; lights were kept burning through the whole of the night: the sound of implements, and of artizans finishing their work; the voices of women, and their guardians, who sung at their embroidery: all conspired to interrupt the stillness of nature, and infinitely delighted the heart of Vathek who imagined himself going in triumph to sit upon the throne of Soliman. The people were not less satisfied than himself: all assisted to accelerate the moment, which should rescue them from the wayward caprices of so extravagant a master.

The day preceding the departure of this infatuated Prince, was employed by Carathis, in repeating to him the decrees of the mysterious parchment; which she had thoroughly gotten by heart; and, in recommending him, not to enter the habitation of any one by the way: "for, well thou knowest," added she, "how liquorish thy taste is after good dishes and young damsels; let me, therefore, enjoin thee, to be content with thy old cooks, who are the best in the world: and not to forget that, in thy ambulatory seraglio, there are at least three dozen of pretty faces which Bababalouk hath not yet unveiled. I myself have a great desire to watch over thy conduct, and visit the subterranean palace, which, no doubt, contains whatever can interest persons, like us. There is nothing so pleasing as retiring to caverns: my taste for dead bodies, and every thing like mummy is decided: and, I am confident, thou wilt see the most exquisite of their kind. Forget me not then, but the moment thou art in possession of the talismans which are to open the way to the mineral kingdoms and the centre of the earth itself, fail not to dispatch some trusty genius to take me and my cabinet: for the oil of the serpents I have pinched to death will be a pretty present to the Giaour who cannot but be charmed with such dainties."

---

liquorish: lustful.

[25] See *Nourjahad* 37 n. 12 and *B/H* 164.

Scarcely had Carathis ended this edifying discourse, when the sun, setting behind the mountain of the four fountains, gave place to the rising moon. This planet, being that evening at full, appeared of unusual beauty and magnitude, in the eyes of the women, the eunuchs and the pages who were all impatient to set forward. The city re-echoed with shouts of joy, and flourishing of trumpets. Nothing was visible, but plumes, nodding on pavilions, and aigrets shining in the mild lustre of the moon. The spacious square resembled an immense parterre variegated with the most stately tulips of the east.

Arrayed in the robes which were only worn at the most distinguished ceremonials, and supported by his vizir and Bababalouk, the Caliph descended the great staircase of the tower in the sight of all his people. He could not forbear pausing, at intervals, to admire the superb appearance which every where courted his view: whilst the whole multitude, even to the camels with their sumptuous burthens, knelt down before him. For some time a general stillness prevailed, which nothing happened to disturb, but the shrill screams of some eunuchs in the rear. These vigilant guards, having remarked certain cages of the ladies swagging somewhat awry, and discovered that a few adventurous gallants had contrived to get in, soon dislodged the enraptured culprits and consigned them, with good commendations, to the surgeons of the serail.[26] The majesty of so magnificent a spectacle, was not, however, violated by incidents like these. Vathek, meanwhile, saluted the moon with an idolatrous air, that neither pleased Morakanabad, nor the doctors of the law, any more than the vizirs and grandees of his court, who were all assembled to enjoy the last view of their sovereign.

At length, the clarions and trumpets from the top of the tower, announced the prelude of departure. Though the instruments were in unison with each other, yet a singular dissonance was blended with their sounds. This proceeded from Carathis who was singing her direful orisons to the Giaour, whilst the negresses and mutes supplied thorough base, without articulating a word. The good Mussulmans fancied that they heard the sullen hum of those nocturnal insects, which presage evil; and importuned Vathek to beware how he ventured his sacred person.

On a given signal, the great standard of the Califat was displayed; twenty thousand lances shone around it; and the Caliph, treading royally on the cloth of gold, which had been spread for his feet, ascended his litter, amidst the general acclamations of his subjects.

---

[26] Serail (*serai*) is the original form of the Italianized *seraglio* (see *Nourjahad* 24 n. 1); its surgeons would presumably be expert at castration.

The expedition commenced with the utmost order and so entire a silence, that, even the locusts were heard from the thickets on the plain of Catoul. Gaiety and good humour prevailing, they made full six leagues before the dawn; and the morning star was still glittering in the firmament, when the whole of this numerous train had halted on the banks of the Tigris, where they encamped to repose for the rest of the day.

The three days that followed were spent in the same manner; but, on the fourth, the heavens looked angry; lightnings broke forth, in frequent flashes; re-echoing peals of thunder succeeded; and the trembling Circassians clung with all their might, to their ugly guardians. The Caliph himself, was greatly inclined to take shelter in the large town of Ghulchissar, the governor of which, came forth to meet him, and tendered every kind of refreshment the place could supply. But, having examined his tablets, he suffered the rain to soak him, almost to the bone, notwithstanding the importunity of his first favourites. Though he began to regret the palace of the senses; yet, he lost not sight of his enterprize, and his sanguine expectation confirmed his resolution. His geographers were ordered to attend him; but, the weather proved so terrible that these poor people exhibited a lamentable appearance: and their maps of the different countries spoiled by the rain, were in a still worse plight than themselves. As no long journey had been undertaken since the time of Haroun al Raschid, every one was ignorant which way to turn; and Vathek, though well versed in the course of the heavens, no longer knew his situation on earth. He thundered even louder than the elements; and muttered forth certain hints of the bow-string which were not very soothing to literary ears. Disgusted at the toilsome weariness of the way, he determined to cross over the craggy heights and follow the guidance of a peasant, who undertook to bring him, in four days, to Rocnabad. Remonstrances were all to no purpose; his resolution was fixed.

The females and eunuchs uttered shrill wailings at the sight of the precipices below them, and the dreary prospects that opened, in the vast gorges of the mountains. Before they could reach the ascent of the steepest rock, night overtook them, and a boisterous tempest arose, which, having rent the awnings of the palanquins and cages, exposed to the raw gusts the poor ladies within, who had never before felt so piercing a cold. The dark clouds that overcast the face of the sky deepened the horrors of this disastrous night, insomuch that nothing could be heard distinctly, but the mewling of pages and lamentations of sultanas.

To increase the general misfortune, the frightful uproar of wild beasts resounded at a distance; and there were soon perceived in the forest they were skirting, the glaring of eyes, which could belong only to devils or tigers. The pioneers, who, as well as they could, had marked out a track;

and a part of the advanced guard, were devoured, before they had been in the least apprized of their danger. The confusion that prevailed was extreme. Wolves, tigers, and other carnivorous animals, invited by the howling of their companions, flocked together from every quarter. The crashing of bones was heard on all sides, and a fearful rush of wings over head; for now vultures also began to be of the party.

The terror at length reached the main body of the troops which surrounded the monarch and his harem at the distance of two leagues from the scene. Vathek (voluptuously reposed in his capacious litter upon cushions of silk, with two little pages beside him of complexions more fair than the enamel of Franguistan, who were occupied in keeping off flies) was soundly asleep, and contemplating in his dreams the treasures of Soliman. The shrieks however of his wives, awoke him with a start; and, instead of the Giaour with his key of gold, he beheld Bababalouk full of consternation. "Sire," exclaimed this good servant of the most potent of monarchs, "misfortune is arrived at its height, wild beasts, who entertain no more reverence for your sacred person, than for a dead ass, have beset your camels and their drivers; thirty of the most richly laden are already become their prey, as well as your confectioners, your cooks, and purveyors: and, unless our holy Prophet should protect us, we shall have all eaten our last meal." At the mention of eating, the Caliph lost all patience. He began to bellow, and even beat himself (for there was no seeing in the dark). The rumour every instant increased; and Bababalouk, finding no good could be done with his master, stopped both his ears against the hurlyburly of the harem, and called out aloud: "Come, ladies, and brothers! all hands to work: strike light in a moment! never shall it be said, that the commander of the faithful served to regale these infidel brutes." Though there wanted not in this bevy of beauties, a sufficient number of capricious and wayward; yet, on the present occasion, they were all compliance. Fires were visible, in a twinkling, in all their cages. Ten thousand torches were lighted at once. The Caliph, himself, seized a large one of wax: every person followed his example; and, by kindling ropes ends, dipped in oil and fastened on poles, an amazing blaze was spread. The rocks were covered with the splendour of sun-shine. The trails of sparks, wafted by the wind, communicated to the dry fern, of which there was plenty. Serpents were observed to crawl forth from their retreats, with amazement and hissings; whilst the horses snorted, stamped the ground, tossed their noses in the air, and plunged about, without mercy.

---

holy Prophet: Muhammad (see *Nourjahad* 25 n. 2).

One of the forests of cedar that bordered their way, took fire; and the branches that overhung the path, extending their flames to the muslins and chintzes, which covered the cages of the ladies obliged them to jump out, at the peril of their necks. Vathek, who vented on the occasion a thousand blasphemies, was himself compelled to touch, with his sacred feet, the naked earth.

Never had such an incident happened before. Full of mortification, shame, and despondence, and not knowing how to walk, the ladies fell into the dirt. "Must I go on foot!" said one: "Must I wet my feet!" cried another: "Must I soil my dress!" asked a third: "Execrable Bababalouk!" exclaimed all: "Outcast of hell! what hast thou to do with torches! Better were it to be eaten by tigers, than to fall into our present condition! we are for ever undone! Not a porter is there in the army nor a currier of camels; but hath seen some part of our bodies; and, what is worse, our very faces!" On saying this, the most bashful amongst them hid their foreheads on the ground, whilst such as had more boldness flew at Bababalouk; but he, well apprized of their humour and not wanting in shrewdness, betook himself to his heels along with his comrades, all dropping their torches and striking their tymbals.

It was not less light than in the brightest of the dog-days, and the weather was hot in proportion; but how degrading was the spectacle, to behold the Caliph bespattered, like an ordinary mortal! As the exercise of his faculties seemed to be suspended, one of his Ethiopian wives (for he delighted in variety) clasped him in her arms; threw him upon her shoulder, like a sack of dates, and, finding that the fire was hemming them in, set off, with no small expedition, considering the weight of her burden. The other ladies, who had just learnt the use of their feet, followed her; their guards galloped after; and the camel-drivers brought up the rear, as fast as their charge would permit.

They soon reached the spot, where the wild beasts had commenced the carnage, but which they had too much good sense not to leave at the approaching of the tumult, having made besides a most luxurious supper. Bababalouk, nevertheless, seized on a few of the plumpest, which were unable to budge from the place, and began to flea them with admirable adroitness. The cavalcade having proceeded so far from the conflagration, that the heat felt rather grateful than violent, it was, immediately, resolved on to halt. The tattered chintzes were picked up; the scraps, left by the wolves and tigers, interred; and vengeance was taken on some dozens of

---

flea: flay or skin, preparatory to cooking.

vultures, that were too much glutted to rise on the wing. The camels, which had been left unmolested to make sal ammoniac, being numbered; and the ladies once more inclosed in their cages; the imperial tent was pitched on the levellest ground they could find.

Vathek, reposing upon a mattress of down, and tolerably recovered from the jolting of the Ethiopian, who, to his feelings, seemed the roughest trotting jade he had hitherto mounted, called out for something to eat. But, alas! those delicate cakes, which had been baked in silver ovens, for his royal mouth; those rich manchets; amber comfits; flaggons of Schiraz wine; porcelain vases of snow; and grapes from the banks of the Tigris; were all irremediably lost!—And nothing had Bababalouk to present in their stead, but a roasted wolf; vultures à la daube; aromatic herbs of the most acrid poignancy; rotten truffles; boiled thistles: and such other wild plants, as must ulcerate the throat and parch up the tongue. Nor was he better provided, in the article of drink: for he could procure nothing to accompany these irritating viands, but a few phials of abominable brandy which had been secreted by the scullions in their slippers. Vathek made wry faces at so savage a repast; and Bababalouk answered them, with shrugs and contortions. The Caliph, however, eat with tolerable appetite; and fell into a nap, that lasted six hours.

The splendour of the sun, reflected from the white cliffs of the mountains, in spite of the curtains that inclosed Vathek, at length disturbed his repose. He awoke, terrified; and stung to the quick by wormwood-colour flies, which emitted from their wings a suffocating stench. The miserable monarch was perplexed how to act; though his wits were not idle, in seeking expedients, whilst Bababalouk lay snoring, amidst a swarm of those insects that busily thronged, to pay court to his nose. The little pages, famished with hunger, had dropped their fans on the ground; and exerted their dying voices, in bitter reproaches on the Caliph; who now, for the first time, heard the language of truth.

Thus stimulated, he renewed his imprecations against the Giaour; and bestowed upon Mahomet some soothing expressions. "Where am I?" cried he: "What are these dreadful rocks? these valleys of darkness! are we arrived at the horrible Kaf! is the Simurgh coming to pluck out my eyes, as a punishment for undertaking this impious enterprize!"[27] Having said this he turned himself towards an outlet in the side of his pavilion, but, alas! what objects occurred to his view? on one side, a plain of black sand that

---

manchets: bread made from the finest white flour.
comfits: candy-covered nuts or fruits.

[27] For the Kaf and Simurgh, see *B/H* 166–67.

appeared to be unbounded; and, on the other, perpendicular crags, bristled over with those abominable thistles, which had, so severely, lacerated his tongue. He fancied, however, that he perceived, amongst the brambles and briars, some gigantic flowers but was mistaken: for, these were only the dangling palampores and variegated tatters of his gay retinue. As there were several clefts in the rock from whence water seemed to have flowed, Vathek applied his ear with the hope of catching the sound of some latent torrent; but could only distinguish the low murmurs of his people who were repining at their journey, and complaining for the want of water. "To what purpose," asked they, "have we been brought hither? hath our Caliph another tower to build? or have the relentless afrits, whom Carathis so much loves, fixed their abode in this place?"

At the name of Carathis, Vathek recollected the tablets he had received from his mother; who assured him, they were fraught with preternatural qualities, and advised him to consult them, as emergencies might require. Whilst he was engaged in turning them over, he heard a shout of joy, and a loud clapping of hands. The curtains of his pavilion were soon drawn back and he beheld Bababalouk, followed by a troop of his favourites, conducting two dwarfs each a cubit high; who brought between them a large basket of melons, oranges, and pomegranates. They were singing in the sweetest tones the words that follow: "We dwell on the top of these rocks, in a cabin of rushes and canes; the eagles envy us our nest: a small spring supplies us with water for the Abdest, and we daily repeat prayers, which the Prophet approves. We love you, O commander of the faithful! our master, the good Emir Fakreddin, loves you also: he reveres, in your person, the vicegerent of Mahomet. Little as we are, in us he confides: he knows our hearts to be as good, as our bodies are contemptible; and hath placed us here to aid those who are bewildered on these dreary mountains. Last night, whilst we were occupied within our cell in reading the holy Koran, a sudden hurricane blew out our lights, and rocked our habitation. For two whole hours, a palpable darkness prevailed; but we heard sounds at a distance, which we conjectured to proceed from the bells of a Cafila, passing over the rocks. Our ears were soon filled with deplorable shrieks, frightful roarings, and the sound of tymbals. Chilled with terror, we concluded that the Deggial, with his exterminating angels, had sent forth his plagues on the earth.[28] In the midst of these melancholy reflections, we perceived

---

palampores: Indian cotton prints used for canopies and clothing.
afrits: evil genii (jinn) or demons.
Cafila: caravan (see *B/H* 168).

[28] See *B/H* 168.

flames of the deepest red, glow in the horizon; and found ourselves, in a few moments, covered with flakes of fire. Amazed at so strange an appearance, we took up the volume dictated by the blessed intelligence, and, kneeling, by the light of the fire that surrounded us, we recited the verse which says: 'Put no trust in any thing but the mercy of Heaven: there is no help, save in the holy Prophet: the mountain of Kaf, itself, may tremble; it is the power of Alla only, that cannot be moved.' After having pronounced these words, we felt consolation, and our minds were hushed into a sacred repose. Silence ensued, and our ears clearly distinguished a voice in the air, saying: 'Servants of my faithful servant! go down to the happy valley of Fakreddin: tell him that an illustrious opportunity now offers to satiate the thirst of his hospitable heart. The commander of true believers is, this day, bewildered amongst these mountains and stands in need of thy aid.'—We obeyed, with joy, the angelic mission; and our master, filled with pious zeal, hath culled, with his own hands, these melons, oranges, and pomegranates. He is following us, with a hundred dromedaries, laden with the purest waters of his fountains; and is coming to kiss the fringe of your consecrated robe, and implore you to enter his humble habitation which, placed amidst these barren wilds, resembles an emerald set in lead." The dwarfs, having ended their address, remained still standing, and, with hands crossed upon their bosoms, preserved a respectful silence.

Vathek, in the midst of this curious harangue, seized the basket; and, long before it was finished, the fruits had dissolved in his mouth. As he continued to eat, his piety increased; and, in the same breath, he recited his prayers and called for the Koran and sugar.

Such was the state of his mind, when the tablets, which were thrown by, at the approach of the dwarfs, again attracted his eye. He took them up; but was ready to drop on the ground, when he beheld in large red characters inscribed by Carathis, these words; which were, indeed, enough to make him tremble; "Beware of old doctors and their puny messengers of but one cubit high: distrust their pious frauds; and, instead of eating their melons, empale on a spit the bearers of them. Shouldest thou be such a fool as to visit them, the portal of the subterranean palace will shut in thy face with such force, as shall shake thee asunder: thy body shall be spit upon, and bats will nestle in thy belly."

"To what tends this ominous rhapsody?" cries the Caliph: "and must I then perish in these deserts, with thirst; whilst I may refresh myself in the delicious valley of melons and cucumbers?—Accursed be the Giaour with his portal of ebony! he hath made me dance attendance, too long already. Besides, who shall prescribe laws to me?—I, forsooth, must not enter any one's habitation! Be it so: but, what one can I enter, that is not my own!"

Bababalouk, who lost not a syllable of this soliloquy, applauded it with all his heart; and the ladies, for the first time, agreed with him in opinion.

The dwarfs were entertained, caressed, and seated, with great ceremony, on little cushions of satin. The symmetry of their persons was a subject of admiration; not an inch of them was suffered to pass unexamined. Knick-nacks and dainties were offered in profusion; but all were declined, with respectful gravity. They climbed up the sides of the Caliph's seat; and, placing themselves each on one of his shoulders, began to whisper prayers in his ears. Their tongues quivered, like aspen leaves; and the patience of Vathek was almost exhausted, when the acclamations of the troops announced the approach of Fakreddin, who was come with a hundred old grey-beards, and as many Korans and dromedaries. They instantly set about their ablutions, and began to repeat the Bismillah.[29] Vathek, to get rid of these officious monitors, followed their example; for his hands were burning.

The good emir, who was punctiliously religious, and likewise a great dealer in compliments, made an harangue five times more prolix and insipid than his little harbingers had already delivered. The Caliph, unable any longer to refrain, exclaimed: "For the love of Mahomet, my dear Fakreddin, have done! let us proceed to your valley, and enjoy the fruits that Heaven hath vouchsafed you." The hint of proceeding, put all into motion. The venerable attendants of the emir set forward, somewhat slowly; but Vathek, having ordered his little pages, in private, to goad on the dromedaries, loud fits of laughter broke forth from the cages; for, the unwieldy curvetting of these poor beasts, and the ridiculous distress of their superannuated riders, afforded the ladies no small entertainment.

They descended, however, unhurt into the valley, by the easy slopes which the emir had ordered to be cut in the rock; and already, the murmuring of streams and the rustling of leaves began to catch their attention. The cavalcade soon entered a path, which was skirted by flowering shrubs, and extended to a vast wood of palm trees, whose branches overspread a vast building of free stone. This edifice was crowned with nine domes, and adorned with as many portals of bronze, on which was engraven the following inscription: "This is the asylum of pilgrims, the refuge of travellers, and the depositary of secrets from all parts of the world."

Nine pages, beautiful as the day, and decently clothed in robes of Egyptian linen, were standing at each door. They received the whole retinue with

---

emir: Arabic title for a prince, ruler, or commander.

[29] Muslims begin their prayers with the phrase "Bismillah al-Ruhman al-Raheem" ("In the name of Allah [God], the good, the merciful"); see also *B/H* 169.

an easy and inviting air. Four of the most amiable placed the Caliph on a magnificent tecthtrevan: four others, somewhat less graceful, took charge of Bababalouk, who capered for joy at the snug little cabin that fell to his share; the pages that remained waited on the rest of the train.

Every man being gone out of sight, the gate of a large inclosure, on the right, turned on its harmonious hinges; and a young female, of a slender form, came forth. Her light brown hair floated in the hazy breeze of the twilight. A troop of young maidens, like the Pleiades, attended her on tiptoe. They hastened to the pavilions that contained the sultanas: and the young lady, gracefully bending, said to them: "Charming princesses, every thing is ready: we have prepared beds for your repose, and strewed your apartments with jasmine: no insects will keep off slumber from visiting your eye-lids; we will dispel them with a thousand plumes. Come then, amiable ladies, refresh your delicate feet, and your ivory limbs, in baths of rose water; and, by the light of perfumed lamps, your servants will amuse you with tales." The sultanas accepted, with pleasure, these obliging offers; and followed the young lady to the emir's harem; where we must, for a moment, leave them, and return to the Caliph.

Vathek found himself beneath a vast dome, illuminated by a thousand lamps of rock crystal: as many vases of the same material, filled with excellent sherbet, sparkled on a large table, where a profusion of viands were spread. Amongst others, were rice boiled in milk of almonds, saffron soups, and lamb à la crême; of all which the Caliph was amazingly fond. He took of each, as much as he was able, testified his sense of the emir's friendship, by the gaiety of his heart; and made the dwarfs dance, against their will: for these little devotees durst not refuse the commander of the faithful. At last, he spread himself on the sopha, and slept sounder than he ever had before.

Beneath this dome, a general silence prevailed; for there was nothing to disturb it but the jaws of Bababalouk, who had untrussed himself to eat with greater advantage; being anxious to make amends for his fast, in the mountains. As his spirits were too high to admit of his sleeping; and hating to be idle, he proposed with himself to visit the harem and repair to his charge of the ladies: to examine if they had been properly lubricated with the balm of Mecca,[30] if their eye-brows, and tresses, were in order; and, in a word, to perform all the little offices they might need. He sought for a

---

tecthtrevan: portable throne; see *B/H* 169.
Pleiades: the seven daughters of Atlas and Pleione in Greek mythology, who became the seven-star constellation of the same name.

[30] See *B/H* 170.

long time together but without being able to find out the door. He durst not speak aloud for fear of disturbing the Caliph; and not a soul was stirring in the precincts of the palace. He almost despaired of effecting his purpose, when a low whispering just reached his ear. It came from the dwarfs, who were returned to their old occupation, and, for the nine hundred and ninety-ninth time in their lives, were reading over the Koran. They very politely invited Bababalouk to be of their party; but his head was full of other concerns. The dwarfs, though not a little scandalized at his dissolute morals, directed him to the apartments he wanted to find. His way thither lay through a hundred dark corridors, along which he groped as he went; and at last, began to catch, from the extremity of a passage, the charming gossiping of the women which not a little delighted his heart. "Ah, ha! what not yet asleep?" cried he; and, taking long strides as he spoke, "did you not suspect me of abjuring my charge?" Two of the black eunuchs, on hearing a voice so loud, left their party in haste, sabre in hand, to discover the cause: but, presently, was repeated on all sides: " 'Tis only Bababalouk! no one but Bababalouk!" This circumspect guardian, having gone up to a thin veil of carnation-colour silk that hung before the door-way, distinguished, by means of the softened splendor that shone through it, an oval bath of dark porphyry surrounded by curtains, festooned in large folds. Through the apertures between them, as they were not drawn close, groups of young slaves were visible; amongst whom, Bababalouk perceived his pupils, indulgingly expanding their arms, as if to embrace the perfumed water, and refresh themselves after their fatigues. The looks of tender languor; their confidential whispers; and the enchanting smiles with which they were imparted; the exquisite fragrance of the roses: all combined to inspire a voluptuousness, which even Bababalouk himself was scarce able to withstand.

He summoned up, however, his usual solemnity, and in the peremptory tone of authority, commanded the ladies, instantly, to leave the bath. Whilst he was issuing these mandates, the young Nouronihar, daughter of the emir, who was as sprightly as an antelope, and full of wanton gaiety, beckoned one of her slaves to let down the great swing which was suspended to the ceiling by cords of silk: and whilst this was doing, winked to her companions in the bath: who, chagrined to be forced from so soothing a state of indolence, began to twist and entangle their hair to plague and detain Bababalouk; and teased him besides with a thousand vagaries.

Nouronihar perceiving that he was nearly out of patience accosted him, with an arch air of respectful concern, and said: "My lord! it is not, by any means decent, that the chief eunuch of the Caliph our sovereign should thus continue standing: deign but to recline your graceful person upon this sofa which will burst with vexation, if it have not the honour to receive you." Caught by these flattering accents, Bababalouk gallantly replied:

"Delight of the apple of my eye! I accept the invitation of your honied lips; and, to say truth, my senses are dazzled with the radiance that beams from your charms."—"Repose, then, at your ease," replied the beauty; as she placed him on the pretended sofa which, quicker than lightning, flew up all at once. The rest of the women, having aptly conceived her design, sprang naked from the bath, and plied the swing, with such unmerciful jerks, that it swept through the whole compass of a very lofty dome, and took from the poor victim all power of respiration. Sometimes, his feet rased the surface of the water; and, at others, the skylight almost flattened his nose. In vain did he fill the air with the cries of a voice that resembled the ringing of a cracked jar; their peals of laughter were still predominant.

Nouronihar, in the inebriety of youthful spirits, being used only to eunuchs of ordinary harems; and having never seen any thing so eminently disgusting, was far more diverted than all of the rest. She began to parody some Persian verses and sang with an accent most demurely piquant: "Oh gentle white dove, as thou soar'st through the air, vouchsafe one kind glance on the mate of thy love: melodious Philomel, I am thy rose; warble some couplet to ravish my heart!"

The sultanas and their slaves, stimulated by these pleasantries, persevered at the swing, with such unremitted assiduity, that at length, the cord which had secured it, snapt suddenly asunder; and Bababalouk fell, floundering like a turtle, to the bottom of the bath. This accident occasioned an universal shout. Twelve little doors, till now unobserved, flew open at once; and the ladies, in an instant, made their escape; but not before having heaped all the towels on his head and put out the lights that remained.

The deplorable animal, in water to the chin, overwhelmed with darkness, and unable to extricate himself from the wrappers that embarrassed him, was still doomed to hear, for his further consolation, the fresh bursts of merriment his disaster occasioned. He bustled, but in vain, to get from the bath; for, the margin was become so slippery, with the oil spilt in breaking the lamps, that, at every effort, he slid back with a plunge which resounded aloud through the hollow of the dome. These cursed peals of laughter, were redoubled at every relapse, and he, who thought the place infested rather by devils than women, resolved to cease groping, and abide in the bath; where he amused himself with soliloquies, interspersed with imprecations, of which his malicious neighbours, reclining on down, suffered not an accent to escape. In this delectable plight, the morning sur-

---

Philomel: nightingale, from the classical myth of Tereus, Procne, and Philomela (transformed into a nightingale in some versions); see also *B/H* 170.

prised him. The Caliph, wondering at his absence, had caused him to be sought for every where. At last, he was drawn forth almost smothered from under the wisp of linen, and wet even to the marrow. Limping, and his teeth chattering with cold, he approached his master; who inquired what was the matter, and how he came soused in so strange a pickle?—"And why did you enter this cursed lodge?" answered Bababalouk, gruffly.—"Ought a monarch like you to visit with his harem, the abode of a grey-bearded emir, who knows nothing of life?—And, with what gracious damsels doth the place too abound! Fancy to yourself how they have soaked me like a burnt crust; and made me dance like a jack-pudding, the live-long night through, on their damnable swing. What an excellent lesson for your sultanas, into whom I had instilled such reserve and decorum!" Vathek, comprehending not a syllable of all this invective, obliged him to relate minutely the transaction: but, instead of sympathizing with the miserable sufferer, he laughed immoderately at the device of the swing and the figure of Bababalouk, mounted upon it. The stung eunuch could scarcely preserve the semblance of respect. "Aye, laugh, my lord! laugh," said he; "but I wish this Nouronihar would play some trick on you; she is too wicked to spare even majesty itself." These words made, for the present, but a slight impression on the Caliph; but they, not long after, recurred to his mind.

This conversation was cut short by Fakreddin, who came to request that Vathek would join in the prayers and ablutions, to be solemnized on a spacious meadow watered by innumerable streams. The Caliph found the waters refreshing, but the prayers abominably irksome. He diverted himself, however, with the multitude of calenders, santons, and derviches, who were continually coming and going; but especially with the bramins, faquirs, and other enthusiasts, who had travelled from the heart of India, and halted on their way with the emir.[31] These latter had each of them some mummery peculiar to himself. One dragged a huge chain wherever he went; another an ouran-outang; whilst a third, was furnished with scourges; and all performed to a charm. Some would climb up trees, holding one foot in the air; others poise themselves over a fire, and, without mercy, fillip

---

jack-pudding: clown or buffoon.

[31] Beckford's mixed group of holy men and "enthusiasts" (here signifying religious fanatics) includes "calendars" (qalandars), a Muslim order of wandering dervishes who live on alms; santons, a European term for Muslim monks or hermits; "derviches" (dervishes), Muslim ascetics and mystics (such as Sufis) who sometimes practice ecstatic religious observances like dancing or chanting; "bramins" (Brahmins), the highest, priestly caste among Hindu societies; and faquirs, religious ascetics (such as dervishes) and others who live on alms. See also *B/H* 170–71.

their noses. There were some amongst them that cherished vermin, which were not ungrateful in requiting their caresses. These rambling fanatics revolted the hearts of the derviches, the calenders, and santons; however, the vehemence of their aversion soon subsided, under the hope that the presence of the Caliph would cure their folly, and convert them to the mussulman faith. But, alas! how great was their disappointment! for Vathek, instead of preaching to them, treated them as buffoons, bade them present his compliments to Visnow and Ixhora, and discovered a predilection for a squat old man from the Isle of Serendib, who was more ridiculous than any of the rest. "Come!" said he, "for the love of your gods, bestow a few slaps on your chops to amuse me." The old fellow, offended at such an address, began loudly to weep; but, as he betrayed a villainous drivelling in shedding tears, the Caliph turned his back and listened to Bababalouk, who whispered, whilst he held the umbrella over him: "Your majesty should be cautious of this odd assembly; which hath been collected, I know not for what. Is it necessary to exhibit such spectacles to a mighty potentate, with interludes of talapoins more mangy than dogs? Were I you, I would command a fire to be kindled, and at once rid the estates of the emir, of his harem, and all his menagerie."—"Tush, dolt," answered Vathek; "and know, that all this infinitely charms me. Nor shall I leave the meadow, till I have visited every hive of these pious mendicants."

Wherever the Caliph directed his course, objects of pity were sure to swarm round him; the blind, the purblind, smarts without noses, damsels without ears, each to extol the munificence of Fakreddin, who, as well as his attendant grey-beards, dealt about, gratis, plasters and cataplasms to all that applied. At noon, a superb corps of cripples made its appearance; and soon after advanced, by platoons, on the plain, the completest association of invalids that had ever been embodied till then. The blind went groping with the blind, the lame limped on together, and the maimed made gestures to each other with the only arm that remained. The sides of a considerable water-fall were crowded by the deaf; amongst whom were some from Pegû, with ears uncommonly handsome and large, but who were still less able to hear than the rest. Nor were there wanting others in abundance with hump-backs; wenny necks; and even horns of an exquisite polish.

The emir, to aggrandize the solemnity of the festival, in honour of his

---

Visnow and Ixhora: Vishnu and Isvara, major Hindu deities.
Isle of Serendib: Arabic name for Sri Lanka (formerly called Ceylon).
talapoins: an order of Buddhist monks.
plasters and cataplasms: bandages and poultices.
Pegû: city and district in southern Burma (present-day Myanmar).

illustrious visitant, ordered the turf to be spread, on all sides, with skins and table-cloths; upon which were served up for the good Mussulmans, pilaus of every hue, with other orthodox dishes; and, by the express order of Vathek, who was shamefully tolerant, small plates of abominations were prepared, to the great scandal of the faithful. The holy assembly began to fall to. The Caliph, in spite of every remonstrance from the chief of his eunuchs, resolved to have a dinner dressed on the spot. The complaisant emir immediately gave orders for a table to be placed in the shade of the willows. The first service consisted of fish, which they drew from a river, flowing over sands of gold at the foot of a lofty hill. These were broiled as fast as taken, and served up with a sauce of vinegar, and small herbs that grew on mount Sinai: for every thing with the emir was excellent and pious.

The desert was not quite set on, when the sound of lutes, from the hill, was repeated by the echoes of the neighbouring mountains. The Caliph, with an emotion of pleasure and surprize, had no sooner raised up his head, than a handful of jasmine dropped on his face. An abundance of tittering succeeded the frolic, and instantly appeared, through the bushes, the elegant forms of several young females, skipping and bounding like roes. The fragrance diffused from their hair, struck the sense of Vathek, who, in an ecstacy, suspending his repast, said to Bababalouk: "Are the peries come down from their spheres? Note her, in particular, whose form is so perfect; venturously running on the brink of the precipice, and turning back her head, as regardless of nothing but the graceful flow of her robe. With what captivating impatience doth she contend with the bushes for her veil? could it be her who threw the jasmine at me!"—"Aye! she it was; and you too would she throw, from the top of the rock," answered Bababalouk; "for that is my good friend Nouronihar, who so kindly lent me her swing. My dear lord and master," added he, wresting a twig from a willow, "let me correct her for her want of respect: the emir will have no reason to complain; since (bating what I owe to his piety) he is much to be blamed for keeping a troop of girls on the mountains, where the sharpness of the air gives their blood too brisk a circulation."

"Peace! blasphemer," said the Caliph; "speak not thus of her, who, over these mountains, leads my heart a willing captive. Contrive, rather, that my eyes may be fixed upon hers: that I may respire her sweet breath as she bounds panting along these delightful wilds!" On saying these words, Vathek extended his arms towards the hill, and directing his eyes, with an

---

pilaus: pilafs, dishes of sautéed seasoned rice cooked in bouillon.
peries: beautiful fairylike beings in Persian mythology.

anxiety unknown to him before, endeavoured to keep within view the object that enthralled his soul: but her course was as difficult to follow, as the flight of one of those beautiful blue butterflies of Cachemire, which are, at once, so volatile and rare.

The Caliph, not satisfied with seeing, wished also to hear Nouronihar, and eagerly turned to catch the sound of her voice. At last, he distinguished her whispering to one of her companions behind the thicket from whence she had thrown the jasmine: "A Caliph, it must be owned, is a fine thing to see; but my little Gulchenrouz is much more amiable: one lock of his hair is of more value to me than the richest embroidery of the Indies. I had rather that his teeth should mischievously press my finger, than the richest ring of the imperial treasure. Where have you left him, Sutlememe? and why is he not here?"

The agitated Caliph still wished to hear more; but she immediately retired with all her attendants. The fond monarch pursued her with his eyes till she was gone out of sight; and then continued like a bewildered and benighted traveller, from whom the clouds had obscured the constellation that guided his way. The curtain of night seemed dropped before him: every thing appeared discoloured. The falling waters filled his soul with dejection, and his tears trickled down the jasmines he had caught from Nouronihar, and placed in his inflamed bosom. He snatched up a few shining pebbles, to remind him of the scene where he felt the first tumults of love. Two hours were elapsed, and evening drew on, before he could resolve to depart from the place. He often, but in vain, attempted to go: a soft languor enervated the powers of his mind. Extending himself on the brink of the stream, he turned his eyes towards the blue summits of the mountain, and exclaimed, "What concealest thou behind thee, pitiless rock? what is passing in thy solitudes? Whither is she gone? O heaven! perhaps she is now wandering in thy grottoes with her happy Gulchenrouz!"

In the mean time, the damps began to descend; and the emir, solicitous for the health of the Caliph, ordered the imperial litter to be brought. Vathek, absorbed in his reveries, was imperceptibly removed and conveyed back to the saloon, that received him the evening before. But, let us leave the Caliph immersed in his new passion: and attend Nouronihar beyond the rocks where she had again joined her beloved Gulchenrouz.

This Gulchenrouz was the son of Ali Hassan, brother to the emir: and the most delicate and lovely creature in the world. Ali Hassan, who had been absent ten years, on a voyage to the unknown seas, committed, at his

---

Cachemire: Kashmir, former princely state in the northern Indian peninsula.
saloon: salon (reception room).

departure, this child, the only survivor of many, to the care and protection of his brother. Gulchenrouz could write in various characters with precision, and paint upon vellum the most elegant arabesques that fancy could devise. His sweet voice accompanied the lute in the most enchanting manner; and, when he sang the loves of Megnoun and Leilah, or some unfortunate lovers of ancient days, tears insensibly overflowed the cheeks of his auditors. The verses he composed (for, like Megnoun, he, too, was a poet) inspired that unresisting languor, so frequently fatal to the female heart. The women all doated upon him; and, though he had passed his thirteenth year, they still detained him in the harem. His dancing was light as the gossamer waved by the zephyrs of spring; but his arms, which twined so gracefully with those of the young girls in the dance, could neither dart the lance in the chace, nor curb the steeds that pastured in his uncle's domains. The bow, however, he drew with a certain aim, and would have excelled his competitors in the race, could he have broken the ties that bound him to Nouronihar.

The two brothers had mutually engaged their children to each other; and Nouronihar loved her cousin, more than her own beautiful eyes. Both had the same tastes and amusements; the same long, languishing looks; the same tresses; the same fair complexions; and, when Gulchenrouz appeared in the dress of his cousin, he seemed to be more feminine than even herself. If, at any time, he left the harem, to visit Fakreddin; it was with all the bashfulness of a fawn, that consciously ventures from the lair of its dam: he was, however, wanton enough to mock the solemn old grey-beards, though sure to be rated without mercy in return. Whenever this happened, he would hastily plunge into the recesses of the harem; and, sobbing, take refuge in the fond arms of Nouronihar who loved even his faults beyond the virtues of others.

It fell out this evening, that, after leaving the Caliph in the meadow, she ran with Gulchenrouz over the green sward of the mountain, that sheltered the vale where Fakreddin had chosen to reside. The sun was dilated on the edge of the horizon; and the young people, whose fancies were lively and inventive, imagined they beheld, in the gorgeous clouds of the west, the domes of Shaddukian and Ambreabad, where the Peries have fixed their abode.[32] Nouronihar, sitting on the slope of the hill, supported on

---

Megnoun and Leilah: Mejnoun and Leila, legendary figures analogous to Romeo and Juliet, celebrated in Arabic and other Asian literatures (see *B/H* 172).
zephyrs: gentle breezes (from Zephyrus, Greek god of the west wind).
dam: mother.

[32] See *B/H* 173.

her knees the perfumed head of Gulchenrouz. The unexpected arrival of the Caliph and the splendour that marked his appearance, had already filled with emotion the ardent soul of Nouronihar. Her vanity irresistibly prompted her to pique the prince's attention; and this, she before took good care to effect, whilst he picked up the jasmine she had thrown upon him. But, when Gulchenrouz asked after the flowers he had culled for her bosom, Nouronihar was all in confusion. She hastily kissed his forehead; arose in a flutter; and walked, with unequal steps, on the border of the precipice. Night advanced, and the pure gold of the setting sun had yielded to a sanguine red; the glow of which, like the reflection of a burning furnace, flushed Nouronihar's animated countenance. Gulchenrouz, alarmed at the agitation of his cousin, said to her, with a supplicating accent—"Let us begone; the sky looks portentous; the tamarisks tremble more than common; and the raw wind chills my very heart. Come! let us begone; 'tis a melancholy night!" Then, taking hold of her hand, he drew it towards the path he besought her to go. Nouronihar, unconsciously followed the attraction; for, a thousand strange imaginations occupied her spirits. She passed the large round of honey-suckles, her favourite resort, without ever vouchsafing it a glance; yet Gulchenrouz could not help snatching off a few shoots in his way, though he ran as if a wild beast were behind.

The young females seeing them approach in such haste, and, according to custom, expecting a dance, instantly assembled in a circle and took each other by the hand: but, Gulchenrouz coming up out of breath, fell down at once on the grass. This accident struck with consternation the whole of this frolicsome party; whilst Nouronihar, half distracted and overcome, both by the violence of her exercise, and the tumult of her thoughts, sunk feebly down at his side; cherished his cold hands in her bosom, and chafed his temples with a fragrant perfume. At length, he came to himself; and, wrapping up his head in the robe of his cousin, intreated that she would not return to the harem. He was afraid of being snapped at by Shaban his tutor; a wrinkled old eunuch of a surly disposition; for, having interrupted the wonted walk of Nouronihar, he dreaded lest the churl should take it amiss. The whole of this sprightly group, sitting round upon a mossy knoll, began to entertain themselves with various pastimes; whilst their superintendants, the eunuchs, were gravely conversing at a distance. The nurse of the emir's daughter, observing her pupil sit ruminating with her eyes on the ground, endeavoured to amuse her with diverting tales; to which Gulchenrouz, who had already forgotten his inquietudes, listened with a breathless attention. He laughed; he clapped his hands; and passed a hundred little tricks on the whole of the company, without omitting the eunuchs whom he provoked to run after him, in spite of their age and decrepitude.

During these occurrences, the moon arose, the wind subsided, and the evening became so serene and inviting, that a resolution was taken to sup on the spot. One of the eunuchs ran to fetch melons whilst others were employed in showering down almonds from the branches that overhung this amiable party. Sutlememe, who excelled in dressing a salad, having filled large bowls of porcelain with eggs of small birds, curds turned with citron juice, slices of cucumber, and the inmost leaves of delicate herbs, handed it round from one to another and gave each their shares with a large spoon of cocknos.[33] Gulchenrouz, nestling, as usual, in the bosom of Nouronihar, pouted out his vermillion little lips against the offer of Sutlememe; and would take it, only, from the hand of his cousin, on whose mouth he hung, like a bee inebriated with the nectar of flowers.

In the midst of this festive scene, there appeared a light on the top of the highest mountain, which attracted the notice of every eye. This light was not less bright than the moon when at full, and might have been taken for her, had not the moon already risen. The phenomenon occasioned a general surprize and no one could conjecture the cause. It could not be a fire, for the light was clear and bluish: nor had meteors ever been seen of that magnitude or splendour. This strange light faded, for a moment; and immediately renewed its brightness. It first appeared motionless, at the foot of the rock; whence it darted in an instant, to sparkle in a thicket of palm-trees: from thence it glided along the torrent; and at last fixed in a glen that was narrow and dark. The moment it had taken its direction, Gulchenrouz, whose heart always trembled at any thing sudden or rare, drew Nouronihar by the robe and anxiously requested her to return to the harem. The women were importunate in seconding the intreaty; but the curiosity of the emir's daughter prevailed. She not only refused to go back, but resolved, at all hazards, to pursue the appearance.

Whilst they were debating what was best to be done, the light shot forth so dazzling a blaze that they all fled away shrieking. Nouronihar followed them a few steps; but, coming to the turn of a little bye path, stopped, and went back alone. As she ran with an alertness peculiar to herself, it was not long before she came to the place, where they had just been supping. The globe of fire now appeared stationary in the glen, and burned in majestic stillness. Nouronihar, pressing her hands upon her bosom, hesitated, for some moments, to advance. The solitude of her situation was new; the silence of the night, awful; and every object inspired sensations, which, till then, she never had felt. The affright of Gulchenrouz recurred to her mind, and she, a thousand times turned to go back; but this luminous appearance

[33] See *B/H* 173.

was always before her. Urged on by an irresistible impulse, she continued to approach it, in defiance of every obstacle that opposed her progress.

At length she arrived at the opening of the glen; but, instead of coming up to the light, she found herself surrounded by darkness; excepting that, at a considerable distance, a faint spark glimmered by fits. She stopped, a second time: the sound of water-falls mingling their murmurs; the hollow rustlings among the palm-branches; and the funereal screams of the birds from their rifted trunks: all conspired to fill her soul with terror. She imagined, every moment, that she trod on some venomous reptile. All the stories of malignant Dives and dismal Goules thronged into her memory:[34] but, her curiosity was, notwithstanding, more predominant than her fears. She, therefore, firmly entered a winding track that led towards the spark; but, being a stranger to the path, she had not gone far, till she began to repent of her rashness. "Alas!" said she, "that I were but in those secure and illuminated apartments, where my evenings glided on with Gulchenrouz! Dear child! how would thy heart flutter with terror, wert thou wandering in these wild solitudes, like me!" Thus speaking, she advanced, and, coming up to steps hewn in the rock, ascended them undismayed. The light, which was now gradually enlarging, appeared above her on the summit of the mountain, and as if proceeding from a cavern. At length, she distinguished a plaintive and melodious union of voices, that resembled the dirges which are sung over tombs. A sound, like that which arises from the filling of baths, struck her ear at the same time. She continued ascending, and discovered large wax torches in full blaze, planted here and there in the fissures of the rock. This appearance filled her with fear, whilst the subtle and potent odour, which the torches exhaled, caused her to sink, almost lifeless, at the entrance of the grot.

Casting her eyes within, in this kind of trance, she beheld a large cistern of gold, filled with a water, the vapour of which distilled on her face a dew of the essence of roses. A soft symphony resounded through the grot. On the sides of the cistern, she noticed appendages of royalty, diadems and feathers of the heron, all sparkling with carbuncles. Whilst her attention was fixed on this display of magnificence, the music ceased, and a voice instantly demanded: "For what monarch are these torches kindled, this bath prepared, and these habiliments which belong, not only to the sovereigns of the earth, but even to the talismanick powers!" To which a second voice answered: "They are for the charming daughter of the emir Fakreddin."—

---

habiliments: clothes.

[34] A dive (or div) is an evil spirit or demon in Persian mythology; a goul (from the Arabic *ghul*) is a demon that haunts wildernesses, cemeteries, and other deserted places.

"What," replied the first, "for that trifler, who consumes her time with a giddy child, immersed in softness, and who, at best, can make but a pitiful husband?"—"And can she," rejoined the other voice, "be amused with such empty toys, whilst the Caliph, the sovereign of the world, he who is destined to enjoy the treasures of the pre-adamite sultans; a prince six feet high; and whose eyes pervade the inmost soul of a female, is inflamed with love for her. No! she will be wise enough to answer that passion alone, that can aggrandize her glory. No doubt she will; and despise the puppet of her fancy. Then all the riches this place contains, as well as the carbuncle of Giamschid, shall be hers."[35]—"You judge right," returned the first voice; "and I haste to Istakhar, to prepare the palace of subterranean fire for the reception of the bridal pair."

The voices ceased; the torches were extinguished, the most entire darkness succeeded; and Nouronihar recovering, with a start, found herself reclined on a sofa, in the harem of her father. She clapped her hands, and immediately came together, Gulchenrouz and her women; who, in despair at having lost her, had dispatched eunuchs to seek her, in every direction. Shaban appeared with the rest, and began to reprimand her, with an air of consequence: "Little impertinent," said he, "have you false keys, or are you beloved of some genius, that hath given you a picklock? I will try the extent of your power: come to the dark chamber, and expect not the company of Gulchenrouz:—be expeditious! I will shut you up, and turn the key twice upon you!" At these menaces, Nouronihar indignantly raised her head, opened on Shaban her black eyes, which, since the important dialogue of the enchanted grot, were considerably enlarged, and said: "Go, speak thus to slaves; but learn to reverence her who is born to give laws and subject all to her power."

Proceeding in the same style, she was interrupted by a sudden exclamation of, "The Caliph! the Caliph!" All the curtains were thrown open, the slaves prostrated themselves in double rows, and poor little Gulchenrouz went to hide beneath the couch of a sofa. At first appeared a file of black eunuchs trailing after them long trains of muslin embroidered with gold, and holding in their hands censers, which dispensed, as they passed, the grateful perfume of the wood of aloes. Next marched Bababalouk with a solemn strut, and tossing his head, as not overpleased at the visit. Vathek came close after, superbly robed: his gait was unembarrassed and noble; and his presence would have engaged admiration, though he had not been the sovereign of the world. He approached Nouronihar with a throbbing heart, and seemed enraptured at the full effulgence of her radiant eyes, of which

[35] See *B/H* 173.

he had before caught but a few glimpses: but she instantly depressed them, and her confusion augmented her beauty.

Bababalouk, who was a thorough adept in coincidences of this nature, and knew that the worst game should be played with the best face, immediately made a signal for all to retire; and no sooner did he perceive beneath the sofa the little one's feet, than he drew him forth without ceremony, set him upon his shoulders, and lavished on him, as he went off, a thousand unwelcome caresses. Gulchenrouz cried out, and resisted till his cheeks became the colour of the blossom of pomegranates, and his tearful eyes sparkled with indignation. He cast a significant glance at Nouronihar, which the Caliph noticing, asked, "Is that, then, your Gulchenrouz?"—"Sovereign of the world!" answered she, "spare my cousin, whose innocence and gentleness deserve not your anger!"—"Take comfort," said Vathek, with a smile; "he is in good hands. Bababalouk is fond of children; and never goes without sweetmeats and comfits." The daughter of Fakreddin was abashed, and suffered Gulchenrouz to be borne away without adding a word. The tumult of her bosom betrayed her confusion, and Vathek becoming still more impassioned, gave a loose to his frenzy; which had only not subdued the last faint strugglings of reluctance, when the emir suddenly bursting in, threw his face upon the ground, at the feet of the Caliph, and said: "Commander of the faithful! abase not yourself to the meanness of your slave."—"No, emir," replied Vathek, "I raise her to an equality with myself: I declare her my wife; and the glory of your race shall extend from one generation to another."—"Alas! my lord," said Fakreddin, as he plucked off a few grey hairs of his beard; "cut short the days of your faithful servant, rather than force him to depart from his word. Nouronihar is solemnly promised to Gulchenrouz, the son of my brother Ali Hassan: they are united, also, in heart; their faith is mutually plighted; and affiances, so sacred, cannot be broken."—"What then!" replied the Caliph, bluntly, "would you surrender this divine beauty to a husband more womanish than herself; and can you imagine, that I will suffer her charms to decay in hands so inefficient and nerveless? No! she is destined to live out her life within my embraces: such is my will: retire; and disturb not the night I devote to the worship of her charms."

The irritated emir drew forth his sabre, presented it to Vathek, and, stretching out his neck, said, in a firm tone of voice: "Strike your unhappy host, my lord! he has lived long enough, since he hath seen the prophet's vicegerent violate the rights of hospitality." At his uttering these words, Nouronihar, unable to support any longer the conflict of her passions, sunk down in a swoon. Vathek, both terrified for her life, and furious at an opposition to his will, bade Fakreddin assist his daughter, and withdrew;

darting his terrible look at the unfortunate emir, who suddenly fell backward, bathed in a sweat as cold as the damp of death.

Gulchenrouz, who had escaped from the hands of Bababalouk and was, that instant, returned, called out for help, as loudly as he could, not having strength to afford it himself. Pale and panting, the poor child attempted to revive Nouronihar by caresses; and it happened, that the thrilling warmth of his lips restored her to life. Fakreddin beginning also to recover from the look of the Caliph, with difficulty tottered to a seat; and, after warily casting round his eye, to see if this dangerous Prince were gone, sent for Shaban and Sutlememe; and said to them apart: "My friends! violent evils require violent remedies: the Caliph has brought desolation and horror into my family; and, how, shall we resist his power? Another of his looks will send me to the grave. Fetch, then, that narcotick powder which a dervish brought me from Aracan. A dose of it, the effect of which will continue three days, must be administered to each of these children. The Caliph will believe them to be dead; for, they will have all the appearance of death. We shall go, as if to inter them in the cave of Meimoune, at the entrance of the great desert of sand and near the bower of my dwarfs. When all the spectators shall be withdrawn, you, Shaban, and four select eunuchs, shall convey them to the lake; where provision shall be ready to support them a month: for, one day allotted to the surprize this event will occasion; five, to the tears; a fortnight to reflection; and the rest, to prepare for renewing his progress; will, according to my calculation, fill up the whole time that Vathek will tarry; and I shall, then, be freed from his intrusion."

"Your plan is good," said Sutlememe, "if it can but be effected. I have remarked, that Nouronihar is well able to support the glances of the Caliph: and, that he is far from being sparing of them to her: be assured, therefore, that notwithstanding her fondness for Gulchenrouz, she will never remain quiet, while she knows him to be here. Let us persuade her, that both herself and Gulchenrouz are really dead; and, that they were conveyed to those rocks, for a limited season, to expiate the little faults, of which their love was the cause. We will add, that we killed ourselves in despair; and that your dwarfs, whom they never yet saw, will preach to them delectable sermons. I will engage that every thing shall succeed to the bent of your wishes."—"Be it so!" said Fakreddin, "I approve your proposal: let us lose not a moment to give it effect."

They hastened to seek for the powder which, being mixed in a sherbet, was immediately administered to Gulchenrouz and Nouronihar. Within

---

Aracan: northern coastal region of Burma (present-day Myanmar).

the space of an hour, both were seized with violent palpitations; and a general numbness gradually ensued. They arose from the floor where they had remained ever since the Caliph's departure; and, ascending to the sofa, reclined themselves upon it, clasped in each other's embraces. "Cherish me, my dear Nouronihar!" said Gulchenrouz: "put thy hand upon my heart; it feels as if it were frozen. Alas! thou art as cold as myself! hath the Caliph murdered us both, with his terrible look?"—"I am dying!" cried she, in a faultering voice: "Press me closer; I am ready to expire!"—"Let us die then, together," answered the little Gulchenrouz; whilst his breast laboured with a convulsive sigh: "let me, at least, breathe forth my soul on thy lips!" They spoke no more, and became as dead.

Immediately, the most piercing cries were heard through the harem; whilst Shaban and Sutlememe personated with great adroitness, the parts of persons in despair. The emir, who was sufficiently mortified, to be forced into such untoward expedients; and had now, for the first time, made a trial of his powder, was under no necessity of counterfeiting grief. The slaves, who had flocked together from all quarters, stood motionless, at the spectacle before them. All lights were extinguished, save two lamps; which shed a wan glimmering over the faces of these lovely flowers that seemed to be faded in the spring-time of life. Funeral vestments were prepared; their bodies were washed, with rose-water; their beautiful tresses were braided and incensed; and they were wrapped in symars whiter than alabaster.

At the moment, that their attendants were placing two wreaths of their favourite jasmines, on their brows, the Caliph, who had just heard the tragical catastrophe, arrived. He looked not less pale and haggard than the goules that wander, at night, among the graves. Forgetful of himself and every one else, he broke through the midst of the slaves; fell prostrate at the foot of the sofa; beat his bosom; called himself "atrocious murderer!" and invoked upon his head, a thousand imprecations. With a trembling hand he raised the veil that covered the countenance of Nouronihar, and uttering a loud shriek, fell lifeless on the floor. The chief of the eunuchs dragged him off, with horrible grimaces, and repeated as he went, "Aye, I foresaw she would play you some ungracious turn!"

No sooner was the Caliph gone, than the emir commanded biers to be brought, and forbad that any one should enter the harem. Every window was fastened; all instruments of music were broken; and the Imans[36] began

---

symars: loose, light robes or jackets worn by women (also spelled "cymars") and here used as shrouds.

[36] Iman (from the Arabic *imam*) can designate a prayer leader or serve more generally as a title of respect.

to recite their prayers. Towards the close of this melancholy day, Vathek sobbed in silence; for they had been forced to compose, with anodynes, his convulsions of rage and desperation.

At the dawn of the succeeding morning, the wide folding doors of the palace were set open, and the funeral procession moved forward for the mountain. The wailful cries of "La Ilah illa Alla!"[37] reached the Caliph, who was eager to cicatrize himself, and attend the ceremonial: nor could he have been dissuaded, had not his excessive weakness disabled him from walking. At the few first steps he fell on the ground, and his people were obliged to lay him on a bed, where he remained many days in such a state of insensibility as excited compassion in the emir himself.

When the procession was arrived at the grot of Meimoune, Shaban and Sutlememe dismissed the whole of the train, excepting the four confidential eunuchs who were appointed to remain. After resting some moments near the biers, which had been left in the open air; they caused them to be carried to the brink of a small lake, whose banks were overgrown with a hoary moss. This was the great resort of herons and storks which preyed continually on little blue fishes. The dwarfs, instructed by the emir, soon repaired thither; and, with the help of the eunuchs, began to construct cabins of rushes and reeds, a work in which they had admirable skill. A magazine also was contrived for provisions, with a small oratory for themselves, and a pyramid of wood, neatly piled to furnish the necessary fuel: for the air was bleak in the hollows of the mountains.

At evening two fires were kindled on the brink of the lake, and the two lovely bodies, taken from their biers, were carefully deposited upon a bed of dried leaves, within the same cabin. The dwarfs began to recite the Koran, with their clear, shrill voices; and Shaban and Sutlememe stood at some distance, anxiously waiting the effects of the powder. At length Nouronihar and Gulchenrouz faintly stretched out their arms; and, gradually opening their eyes, began to survey, with looks of increasing amazement, every object around them. They even attempted to rise; but, for want of strength, fell back again. Sutlememe, on this, administered a cordial, which the emir had taken care to provide.

Gulchenrouz, thoroughly aroused, sneezed out aloud: and, raising himself with an effort that expressed his surprize, left the cabin and inhaled the fresh air, with the greatest avidity. "Yes," said he, "I breathe again! again do I exist! I hear sounds! I behold a firmament, spangled over with stars!"—

---

cicatrize: ritually scar.

[37] "*La Ilaha illa Allah*" ("there is no God but Allah [God]") is part of the Muslim call to prayer.

Nouronihar, catching these beloved accents, extricated herself from the leaves and ran to clasp Gulchenrouz to her bosom. The first objects she remarked, were their long simars, their garlands of flowers, and their naked feet: she hid her face in her hands to reflect. The vision of the enchanted bath, the despair of her father, and, more vividly than both, the majestic figure of Vathek, recurred to her memory. She recollected also, that herself and Gulchenrouz had been sick and dying; but all these images bewildered her mind. Not knowing where she was, she turned her eyes on all sides, as if to recognize the surrounding scene. This singular lake, those flames reflected from its glassy surface, the pale hues of its banks, the romantic cabins, the bullrushes, that sadly waved their drooping heads; the storks, whose melancholy cries blended with the shrill voices of the dwarfs, every thing conspired to persuade her, that the angel of death had opened the portal of some other world.[38]

Gulchenrouz, on his part, lost in wonder, clung to the neck of his cousin. He believed himself in the region of phantoms; and was terrified at the silence she preserved. At length addressing her; "Speak," said he, "where are we? do you not see those spectres that are stirring the burning coals? Are they Monker and Nekir who are come to throw us into them?[39] Does the fatal bridge cross this lake, whose solemn stillness, perhaps, conceals from us an abyss, in which, for whole ages, we shall be doomed incessantly to sink."

"No, my children," said Sutlememe, going towards them, "take comfort! the exterminating angel, who conducted our souls hither after yours, hath assured us, that the chastisement of your indolent and voluptuous life, shall be restricted to a certain series of years, which you must pass in this dreary abode; where the sun is scarcely visible, and where the soil yields neither fruits nor flowers. These," continued she, pointing to the dwarfs, "will provide for our wants; for souls, so mundane as ours, retain too strong a tincture of their earthly extraction. Instead of meats, your food will be nothing but rice; and your bread shall be moistened in the fogs that brood over the surface of the lake."

At this desolating prospect, the poor children burst into tears, and prostrated themselves before the dwarfs; who perfectly supported their characters, and delivered an excellent discourse, of a customary length, upon the sacred camel; which, after a thousand years, was to convey them to the paradise of the faithful.

---

[38] Azrael (from the Arabic *Izra'il*) is the primary angel of death, separating souls from bodies, in Islamic tradition.

[39] In Islamic tradition, Monkir and Nekir are angels who judge and punish the dead (see *B/H* 174).

The sermon being ended, and ablutions performed, they praised Alla and the Prophet; supped very indifferently; and retired to their withered leaves. Nouronihar and her little cousin, consoled themselves on finding that the dead might lay in one cabin. Having slept well before, the remainder of the night was spent in conversation on what had befallen them; and both, from a dread of apparitions, betook themselves for protection to one another's arms.

In the morning, which was lowering and rainy, the dwarfs mounted high poles, like minarets, and called them to prayers. The whole congregation, which consisted of Sutlememe, Shaban, the four eunuchs, and a few storks that were tired of fishing, was already assembled. The two children came forth from their cabin with a slow and dejected pace. As their minds were in a tender and melancholy mood, their devotions were performed with fervour. No sooner were they finished than Gulchenrouz demanded of Sutlememe, and the rest, "how they happened to die so opportunely for his cousin and himself?"—"We killed ourselves," returned Sutlememe, "in despair at your death." On this, Nouronihar who, notwithstanding what had past, had not yet forgotten her vision said—"And the Caliph! is he also dead of his grief? and will he likewise come hither?" The dwarfs, who were prepared with an answer, most demurely replied: "Vathek is damned beyond all redemption!"—"I readily believe so," said Gulchenrouz; "and am glad, from my heart, to hear it; for I am convinced it was his horrible look that sent us hither, to listen to sermons, and mess upon rice." One week passed away, on the side of the lake, unmarked by any variety: Nouronihar ruminating on the grandeur of which death had deprived her; and Gulchenrouz applying to prayers and basket-making with the dwarfs, who infinitely pleased him.

Whilst this scene of innocence was exhibiting in the mountains, the Caliph presented himself to the emir in a new light. The instant he recovered the use of his senses, with a voice that made Bababalouk quake, he thundered out: "Perfidious Giaour! I renounce thee for ever! it is thou who hast slain my beloved Nouronihar! and I supplicate the pardon of Mahomet; who would have preserved her to me, had I been more wise. Let water be brought, to perform my ablutions, and let the pious Fakreddin be called to offer up his prayers with mine, and reconcile me to him. Afterwards, we will go together and visit the sepulchre of the unfortunate Nouronihar. I am resolved to become a hermit, and consume the residue of my days on this mountain, in hope of expiating my crimes."—"And what do you intend to live upon there?" inquired Bababalouk: "I hardly know," replied

---

mess: dine.

Vathek, "but I will tell you when I feel hungry—which, I believe, will not soon be the case."

The arrival of Fakreddin put a stop to this conversation. As soon as Vathek saw him, he threw his arms around his neck, bedewed his face with a torrent of tears, and uttered things so affecting, so pious, that the emir, crying for joy, congratulated himself, in his heart upon having performed so admirable and unexpected a conversion. As for the pilgrimage to the mountain, Fakreddin had his reasons not to oppose it; therefore, each ascending his own litter, they started.

Notwithstanding the vigilance with which his attendants watched the Caliph, they could not prevent his harrowing his cheeks with a few scratches, when on the place where he was told Nouronihar had been buried; they were even obliged to drag him away, by force of hands, from the melancholy spot. However he swore, with a solemn oath, that he would return thither every day. This resolution did not exactly please the emir—yet he flattered himself that the Caliph might not proceed farther, and would merely perform his devotions in the cavern of Meimouné. Besides, the lake was so completely concealed within the solitary bosom of those tremendous rocks, that he thought it utterly impossible any one could ever find it. This security of Fakreddin was also considerably strengthened by the conduct of Vathek, who performed his vow most scrupulously, and returned daily from the hill so devout, and so contrite, that all the grey-beards were in a state of ecstasy on account of it.

Nouronihar was not altogether so content; for though she felt a fondness for Gulchenrouz, who, to augment the attachment, had been left at full liberty with her, yet she still regarded him as but a bauble that bore no competition with the carbuncle of Giamschid. At times, she indulged doubts on the mode of her being; and scarcely could believe that the dead had all the wants and the whims of the living. To gain satisfaction, however, on so perplexing a topic; one morning, whilst all were asleep, she arose with a breathless caution from the side of Gulchenrouz: and, after having given him a soft kiss, began to follow the windings of the lake, till it terminated with a rock, the top of which was accessible, though lofty. This she climbed with considerable toil; and, having reached the summit, set forward in a run, like a doe before the hunter. Though she skipped with the alertness of an antelope, yet, at intervals, she was forced to desist, and rest beneath the tamarisks to recover her breath. Whilst she, thus reclined, was occupied with her little reflections on the apprehension that she had some knowledge of the place; Vathek, who, finding himself that morning but ill at ease, had gone forth before the dawn, presented himself, on a sudden, to her view. Motionless with surprise, he durst not approach the figure before him trembling and pale, but yet lovely to behold. At length, Nouronihar, with a mixture of pleasure and affliction, raising her fine eyes to him, said: "My lord! are you then come hither to eat rice and hear sermons with me?" — "Beloved phantom!" cried Vathek, "thou dost speak; thou hast the same graceful form; the same radiant features: art thou palpable likewise?" and, eagerly embracing her, added: "Here are limbs and a bosom, animated with a gentle warmth! — What can such a prodigy mean?"

Nouronihar, with indifference answered: "You know, my lord, that I died on the very night you honoured me with your visit. My cousin maintains it was from one of your glances; but I cannot believe him: for, to me, they seem not so dreadful. Gulchenrouz died with me, and we were both brought into a region of desolation, where we are fed with a wretched diet. If you be dead also, and are come hither to join us, I pity your lot: for, you will be stunned with the clang of the dwarfs and the storks. Besides, it is mortifying in the extreme, that you, as well as myself, should have lost the treasures of the subterranean palace."

At the mention of the subterranean palace, the Caliph suspended his caresses, (which indeed had proceeded pretty far) to seek from Nouronihar an explanation of her meaning. She then recapitulated her vision; what immediately followed; and the history of her pretended death; adding, also, a description of the place of expiation, from whence she had fled; and all, in a manner, that would have extorted his laughter, had not the thoughts of Vathek been too deeply engaged. No sooner, however, had she ended, than he again clasped her to his bosom and said: "Light of my eyes! the mystery is unravelled; we both are alive! Your father is a cheat, who, for the sake of dividing us, hath deluded us both: and the Giaour, whose design, as far as I can discover, is, that we shall proceed together, seems scarce a whit better. It shall be some time, at least, before he finds us in his palace of fire. Your lovely little person, in my estimation, is far more precious than all the treasures of the pre-adamite sultans; and I wish to possess it at pleasure, and, in open day, for many a moon, before I go to burrow under ground, like a mole. Forget this little trifler, Gulchenrouz; and" — "Ah! my lord!" interposed Nouronihar, "let me intreat that you do him no evil." — "No, no!" replied Vathek, "I have already bid you forbear to alarm yourself for him. He has been brought up too much on milk and sugar to stimulate my jealousy. We will leave him with the dwarfs; who, by the bye, are my old acquaintances: their company will suit him far better than yours. As to other matters; I will return no more to your father's. I want not to have my ears dinned by him and his dotards with the violation of the rights of hospitality: as if it were less an honour for you to espouse the sovereign of the world, than a girl dressed up like a boy!"

Nouronihar could find nothing to oppose, in a discourse so eloquent. She only wished the amorous monarch had discovered more ardour for the carbuncle of Giamschid: but flattered herself it would gradually increase; and, therefore, yielded to his will, with the most bewitching submission.

When the Caliph judged it proper, he called for Bababalouk, who was asleep in the cave of Meimouné, and dreaming that the phantom of Nouronihar, having mounted him once more on her swing, had just given him such a jerk, that he, one moment, soared above the mountains, and the next, sunk into the abyss. Starting from his sleep at the sound of his master, he ran, gasping for breath, and had nearly fallen backward at the sight, as he believed, of the spectre, by whom he had, so lately, been haunted in his dream. "Ah, my lord!" cried he, recoiling ten steps, and covering his eyes with both hands, "do you then perform the office of a goul! have you dug up the dead? yet hope not to make her your prey: for, after all she hath caused me to suffer, she is wicked enough to prey even upon you."

"Cease to play the fool," said Vathek, "and thou shalt soon be convinced that it is Nouronihar herself, alive and well, whom I clasp to my breast. Go and pitch my tents in the neighbouring valley. There will I fix my abode, with this beautiful tulip, whose colours I soon shall restore. There exert thy best endeavours to procure whatever can augment the enjoyments of life, till I shall disclose to thee more of my will."

The news of so unlucky an event soon reached the ears of the emir, who abandoned himself to grief and despair, and began, as did his old greybeards, to begrime his visage with ashes. A total supineness ensued; travellers were no longer entertained; no more plasters were spread; and, instead of the charitable activity that had distinguished this asylum, the whole of its inhabitants exhibited only faces of half a cubit long, and uttered groans that accorded with their forlorn situation.

Though Fakreddin bewailed his daughter, as lost to him for ever, yet Gulchenrouz was not forgotten. He dispatched immediate instruction to Sutlememe, Shaban, and the dwarfs, enjoining them not to undeceive the child, in respect to his state; but, under some pretence, to convey him far from the lofty rock, at the extremity of the lake, to a place which he should appoint, as safer from danger, for he suspected that Vathek intended him evil.

Gulchenrouz, in the meanwhile, was filled with amazement, at not finding his cousin; nor were the dwarfs less surprised; but Sutlememe, who had more penetration, immediately guessed what had happened. Gulchenrouz was amused with the delusive hope of once more embracing Nouronihar, in the interior recesses of the mountains, where the ground, strewed over with orange blossoms and jasmines, offered beds much more inviting than the withered leaves in their cabin; where they might accompany, with their voices, the sounds of their lutes, and chase butterflies. Sutlememe was far gone in this sort of description, when one of the four eunuchs beckoned her aside, to apprize her of the arrival of a messenger from their fraternity, who had explained the secret of the flight of Nouronihar, and brought the commands of the emir. A council with Shaban and the dwarfs was immediately held. Their baggage being stowed in consequence of it, they embarked in a shallop, and quietly sailed with the little one, who acquiesced in all their proposals. Their voyage proceeded in the same manner, till they came to the place where the lake sinks beneath the hollow of a rock; but, as soon as the bark had entered it and Gulchenrouz found himself surrounded with darkness, he was seized with a dreadful consternation, and incessantly uttered the most piercing outcries; for he now was persuaded he should actually be damned for having taken too many little freedoms, in his life-time, with his cousin.

But let us return to the Caliph, and her who ruled over his heart. Bababalouk had pitched the tents, and closed up the extremities of the valley, with magnificent screens of India cloth, which were guarded by Ethiopian slaves with their drawn sabres. To preserve the verdure of this beautiful inclosure in its natural freshness, white eunuchs went continually round it with gilt water vessels. The waving of fans was heard near the imperial pavilion; where, by the voluptuous light that glowed through the muslins, the Caliph enjoyed, at full view, all the attractions of Nouronihar. Inebriated with delight, he was all ear to her charming voice, which accompanied the lute: while she was not less captivated with his descriptions of Samarah, and the tower full of wonders; but especially with his relation of the adventure of the ball, and the chasm of the Giaour, with its ebony portal.

In this manner they conversed the whole day, and at night they bathed together, in a basin of black marble, which admirably set off the fairness of Nouronihar. Bababalouk, whose good graces this beauty had regained, spared no attention, that their repasts might be served up with the minutest exactness: some exquisite rarity was ever placed before them; and he sent even to Schiraz, for that fragrant and delicious wine, which had been hoarded up in bottles, prior to the birth of Mahomet. He had excavated little ovens in the rock, to bake the nice manchets which were prepared by the hands of Nouronihar, from whence they had derived a flavour so grateful to Vathek, that he regarded the ragouts of his other wives as entirely maukish: whilst they would have died of chagrin at the emir's, at finding themselves so neglected, if Fakreddin, notwithstanding his resentment, had not taken pity upon them.

The sultana Dilara, who, till then, had been the favourite, took this dereliction of the Caliph to heart, with a vehemence natural to her character:

---

shallop: boat designed for shallow waters.

for, during her continuance in favour, she had imbibed from Vathek many of his extravagant fancies, and was fired with impatience to behold the superb tombs of Istakar, and the palace of forty columns; besides, having been brought up amongst the magi, she had fondly cherished the idea of the Caliph's devoting himself to the worship of fire:[40] thus, his voluptuous and desultory life with her rival, was to her a double source of affliction. The transient piety of Vathek had occasioned her some serious alarms; but the present was an evil of far greater magnitude. She resolved, therefore, without hesitation, to write to Carathis, and acquaint her that all things went ill; that they had eaten, slept, and revelled at an old emir's, whose sanctity was very formidable; and that, after all, the prospect of possessing the treasures of the pre-adamite sultans, was no less remote than before. This letter was entrusted to the care of two woodmen, who were at work in one of the great forests of the mountains; and who, being acquainted with the shortest cuts, arrived in ten days at Samarah.

The Princess Carathis was engaged at chess with Morakanabad, when the arrival of these wood-fellers was announced. She, after some weeks of Vathek's absence, had forsaken the upper regions of her tower, because every thing appeared in confusion among the stars, which she consulted, relative to the fate of her son. In vain did she renew her fumigations, and extend herself on the roof, to obtain mystic visions; nothing more could she see in her dreams, than pieces of brocade, nose-gays of flowers, and other unmeaning gew-gaws. These disappointments had thrown her into a state of dejection, which no drug in her power was sufficient to remove. Her only resource was in Morakanabad, who was a good man, and endowed with a decent share of confidence; yet, whilst in her company, he never thought himself on roses.

No person knew aught of Vathek, and, of course, a thousand ridiculous stories were propagated at his expense. The eagerness of Carathis may be easily guessed at receiving the letter, as well as her rage at reading the dissolute conduct of her son. "Is it so!" said she: "either I will perish, or Vathek shall enter the palace of fire. Let me expire in flames, provided he may reign on the throne of Soliman!" Having said this, and whirled herself round in a magical manner, which struck Morakanabad with such terror as caused him to recoil, she ordered her great camel Alboufaki to be brought, and the hideous Nerkes, with the unrelenting Cafour, to attend. "I require no other retinue," said she to Morakanabad: "I am going on affairs of emer-

---

[40]The magi were priests of Zoroastrianism, the religion of the Persian Empire displaced by Islam in the seventh century but long lingering as an often-persecuted minority creed, vulgarly seen as a form of fire worship.

gency; a truce, therefore, to parade! Take you care of the people; fleece them well in my absence, for we shall expend large sums, and one knows not what may betide."

The night was uncommonly dark, and a pestilential blast blew from the plain of Catoul, that would have deterred any other traveller however urgent the call: but Carathis enjoyed most whatever filled others with dread. Nerkes concurred in opinion with her; and Cafour had a particular predilection for a pestilence. In the morning this accomplished caravan, with the woodfellers, who directed their route, halted on the edge of an extensive marsh, from whence so noxious a vapour arose, as would have destroyed any animal but Alboufaki, who naturally inhaled these malignant fogs with delight. The peasants entreated their convoy not to sleep in this place. "To sleep," cried Carathis, "what an excellent thought! I never sleep, but for visions; and, as to my attendants, their occupations are too many, to close the only eye they have." The poor peasants, who were not overpleased with their party, remained openmouthed with surprise.

Carathis alighted, as well as her negresses; and, severally stripping off their outer garments, they all ran to cull from those spots, where the sun shone fiercest, the venomous plants that grew on the marsh. This provision was made for the family of the emir; and whoever might retard the expedition to Istakar. The woodmen were overcome with fear, when they beheld these three horrible phantoms run; and, not much relishing the company of Alboufaki, stood aghast at the command of Carathis to set forward; notwithstanding it was noon, and the heat fierce enough to calcine even rocks. In spite however, of every remonstrance, they were forced implicitly to submit.

Alboufaki, who delighted in solitude, constantly snorted whenever he perceived himself near a habitation; and Carathis, who was apt to spoil him with indulgence, as constantly turned him aside: so that the peasants were precluded from procuring subsistence; for, the milch goats and ewes, which Providence had sent towards the district they traversed to refresh travellers with their milk, all fled at the sight of the hideous animal and his strange riders. As to Carathis, she needed no common aliment; for, her invention had previously furnished her with an opiate, to stay her stomach; some of which she imparted to her mutes.

At dusk, Alboufaki making a sudden stop, stampt with his foot; which, to Carathis, who knew his ways, was a certain indication, that she was near the confines of some cemetery. The moon shed a bright light on the spot, which served to discover a long wall with a large door in it, standing a-jar;

---

milch goats and ewes: dairy goats and sheep.

and so high that Alboufaki might easily enter. The miserable guides, who perceived their end approaching, humbly implored Carathis, as she had now so good an opportunity, to inter them; and immediately gave up the ghost. Nerkes and Cafour, whose wit was of a style peculiar to themselves, were by no means parsimonious of it on the folly of these poor people; nor could any thing have been found more suited to their taste, than the site of the burying ground, and the sepulchres which its precincts contained. There were, at least, two thousand of them on the declivity of a hill. Carathis was too eager to execute her plan, to stop at the view, charming as it appeared in her eyes. Pondering the advantages that might accrue from her present situation, she said to herself, "So beautiful a cemetery must be haunted by gouls! they never want for intelligence: having heedlessly suffered my stupid guides to expire, I will apply for directions to them; and, as an inducement, will invite them to regale on these fresh corpses." After this wise soliloquy, she beckoned to Nerkes and Cafour, and made signs with her fingers, as much as to say: "Go; knock against the sides of the tombs and strike up your delightful warblings."

The negresses, full of joy at the behests of their mistress; and promising themselves much pleasure from the society of the gouls, went, with an air of conquest, and began their knockings at the tombs. As their strokes were repeated, a hollow noise was heard in the earth; the surface hove up into heaps; and the gouls, on all sides, protruded their noses to inhale the effluvia, which the carcases of the woodmen began to emit. They assembled before a sarcophagus of white marble, where Carathis was seated between the bodies of her miserable guides. The Princess received her visitants with distinguished politeness; and, supper being ended, they talked of business. Carathis soon learnt from them every thing she wanted to discover; and, without loss of time, prepared to set forward on her journey. Her negresses, who were forming tender connexions with the gouls, importuned her, with all their fingers, to wait at least till the dawn. But Carathis, being chastity in the abstract, and an implacable enemy to love intrigues and sloth, at once rejected their prayer; mounted Alboufaki, and commanded them to take their seats instantly. Four days and four nights, she continued her route without interruption. On the fifth, she traversed craggy mountains, and half-burnt forests; and arrived on the sixth, before the beautiful screens which concealed from all eyes the voluptuous wanderings of her son.

It was day-break, and the guards were snoring on their posts in careless security, when the rough trot of Alboufaki awoke them in consternation. Imagining that a group of spectres, ascended from the abyss, was approaching, they all, without ceremony, took to their heels. Vathek was, at that instant, with Nouronihar in the bath; hearing tales, and laughing at

Bababalouk, who related them: but, no sooner did the outcry of his guards reach him, than he flounced from the water like a carp; and as soon threw himself back at the sight of Carathis; who, advancing with her negresses, upon Alboufaki, broke through the muslin awnings and veils of the pavilion. At this sudden apparition, Nouronihar (for she was not, at all times, free from remorse) fancied, that the moment of celestial vengeance was come; and clung about the Caliph, in amorous despondence.

Carathis, still seated on her camel, foamed with indignation, at the spectacle which obtruded itself on her chaste view. She thundered forth without check or mercy: "Thou double-headed and four-legged monster! what means all this winding and writhing? art thou not ashamed to be seen grasping this limber sapling; in preference to the sceptre of the pre-adamite sultans? Is it then, for this paltry doxy, that thou hast violated the conditions in the parchment of our Giaour! Is it on her, thou hast lavished thy precious moments! Is this the fruit of the knowledge I have taught thee! Is this the end of thy journey? Tear thyself from the arms of this little simpleton; drown her, in the water before me; and, instantly follow my guidance."

In the first ebullition of his fury, Vathek had resolved to rip open the body of Alboufaki and to stuff it with those of the negresses and of Carathis herself, but the remembrance of the Giaour, the palace of Istakar, the sabres, and the talismans, flashing before his imagination, with the simultaneousness of lightning, he became more moderate, and said to his mother, in a civil, but decisive tone; "Dread lady! you shall be obeyed; but I will not drown Nouronihar. She is sweeter to me than a Myrabolan comfit; and is enamoured of carbuncles; especially that, of Giamschid; which hath also been promised to be conferred upon her: she, therefore, shall go along with us; for, I intend to repose with her upon the sofas of Soliman: I can sleep no more without her."—"Be it so!" replied Carathis, alighting; and, at the same time, committing Alboufaki to the charge of her black women.

Nouronihar, who had not yet quitted her hold, began to take courage; and said, with an accent of fondness, to the Caliph: "Dear sovereign of my soul! I will follow thee, if it be thy will, beyond the Kaf, in the land of the afrits. I will not hesitate to climb, for thee, the nest of the Simurgh; who, this lady excepted, is the most awful of created beings."—"We have here then," subjoined Carathis, "a girl, both of courage and science!"[41]

---

doxy: abusive term for a mistress or prostitute.
ebullition: overflowing or outburst.
Myrabolan comfit: a kind of candy made from the plumlike myrobalan fruit (see *B/H* 175).

[41] In the eighteenth century, "science" still connoted general knowledge.

Nouronihar had certainly both; but, notwithstanding all her firmness, she could not help casting back a thought of regret upon the graces of her little Gulchenrouz; and the days of tender endearments she had participated with him. She, even, dropped a few tears; which, the Caliph observed; and inadvertently breathed out with a sigh: "Alas! my gentle cousin! what will become of thee!"—Vathek, at this apostrophe, knitted up his brows; and Carathis inquired what it could mean? "She is preposterously sighing after a stripling with languishing eyes and soft hair, who loves her," said the Caliph. "Where is he?" asked Carathis. "I must be acquainted with this pretty child: for," added she, lowering her voice, "I design, before I depart, to regain the favour of the Giaour. There is nothing so delicious, in his estimation, as the heart of a delicate boy palpitating with the first tumults of love."

Vathek, as he came from the bath, commanded Bababalouk to collect the women, and other moveables of his harem; embody his troops; and hold himself in readiness to march within three days: whilst Carathis, retired alone to a tent, where the Giaour solaced her with encouraging visions; but, at length, waking, she found at her feet, Nerkes and Cafour, who informed her, by their signs, that having led Alboufaki to the borders of a lake; to browse on some grey moss, that looked tolerably venomous; they had discovered certain blue fishes, of the same kind with those in the reservoir on the top of the tower. "Ah! ha!" said she, "I will go thither to them. These fish are past doubt of a species that, by a small operation, I can render oracular. They may tell me, where this little Gulchenrouz is; whom I am bent upon sacrificing." Having thus spoken, she immediately set out, with her swarthy retinue.

It being but seldom that time is lost, in the accomplishment of a wicked enterprize, Carathis and her negresses soon arrived at the lake; where, after burning the magical drugs, with which they were always provided; they stripped themselves naked, and waded to their chins; Nerkes and Cafour waving torches around them, and Carathis pronouncing her barbarous incantations. The fishes, with one accord, thrust forth their heads from the water; which was violently rippled by the flutter of their fins: and, at length, finding themselves constrained, by the potency of the charm, they opened their piteous mouths, and said: "From gills to tail, we are yours; what seek ye to know?"—"Fishes," answered she, "I conjure you, by your glittering scales; tell me where now is Gulchenrouz?"—"Beyond the rock," replied the shoal, in full chorus: "will this content you? for we do not delight in expanding our mouths."—"It will," returned the Princess: "I am not to learn, that you are not used to long conversations: I will leave you therefore to repose, though I had other questions to propound." The instant she had spoken, the water became smooth; and the fishes, at once, disappeared.

Carathis, inflated with the venom of her projects, strode hastily over the rock; and found the amiable Gulchenrouz, asleep, in an arbour; whilst the two dwarfs were watching at his side, and ruminating their accustomed prayers. These diminutive personages possessed the gift of divining, whenever an enemy to good Mussulmans approached: thus, they anticipated the arrival of Carathis; who, stopping short, said to herself: "How placidly doth he recline his lovely little head! how pale, and languishing, are his looks! it is just the very child of my wishes!" The dwarfs interrupted this delectable soliloquy, by leaping, instantly, upon her; and scratching her face, with their utmost zeal. But Nerkes and Cafour, betaking themselves to the succour of their mistress, pinched the dwarfs so severely, in return, that they both gave up the ghost; imploring Mahomet to inflict his sorest vengeance upon this wicked woman, and all her household.

At the noise which this strange conflict occasioned in the valley, Gulchenrouz awoke; and, bewildered with terror, sprung impetuously and climbed an old fig-tree that rose against the acclivity of the rocks; from thence he gained their summits, and ran for two hours without once looking back. At last, exhausted with fatigue, he fell senseless into the arms of a good old genius, whose fondness for the company of children, had made it his sole occupation to protect them. Whilst performing his wonted rounds through the air, he had pounced on the cruel Giaour, at the instant of his growling in the horrible chasm, and had rescued the fifty little victims which the impiety of Vathek had devoted to his voracity. These the genius brought up in nests still higher than the clouds, and himself fixed his abode, in a nest more capacious than the rest, from which he had expelled the Rocs that had built it.

These inviolable asylums were defended against the dives and the afrits, by waving streamers; on which were inscribed in characters of gold, that flashed like lightning, the names of Alla and the Prophet. It was there that Gulchenrouz, who, as yet remained undeceived with respect to his pretended death, thought himself in the mansions of eternal peace. He admitted without fear the congratulations of his little friends, who were all assembled in the nest of the venerable genius, and vied with each other in kissing his serene forehead and beautiful eye-lids.—Remote from the inquietudes of the world; the impertinence of harems, the brutality of eunuchs, and the inconstancy of women; there he found a place truly congenial to the delights of his soul. In this peaceable society his days, months, and years glided on; nor was he less happy than the rest of his

---

genius: a *jinn* or genie (see *Nourjahad* 26 n. 3).
Rocs: enormous condorlike birds in Arabic mythology.

companions: for the genius, instead of burthening his pupils with perishable riches and vain sciences, conferred upon them the boon of perpetual childhood.

Carathis, unaccustomed to the loss of her prey, vented a thousand execrations on her negresses, for not seizing the child, instead of amusing themselves with pinching to death two insignificant dwarfs from which they could gain no advantage. She returned into the valley murmuring; and, finding that her son was not risen from the arms of Nouronihar, discharged her ill-humour upon both. The idea, however, of departing next day for Istakar, and of cultivating, through the good offices of the Giaour, an intimacy with Eblis himself, at length consoled her chagrin. But fate had ordained it otherwise.

In the evening as Carathis was conversing with Dilara, who, through her contrivance had become of the party, and whose taste resembled her own, Bababalouk came to acquaint her that the sky towards Samarah looked of a fiery red, and seemed to portend some alarming disaster. Immediately recurring to her astrolabes[42] and instruments of magic, she took the altitude of the planets, and discovered, by her calculations, to her great mortification, that a formidable revolt had taken place at Samarah, that Motavakel, availing himself of the disgust, which was inveterate against his brother, had incited commotions amongst the populace, made himself master of the palace, and actually invested the great tower, to which Morakanabad had retired, with a handful of the few that still remained faithful to Vathek.

"What!" exclaimed she; "must I lose, then, my tower! my mutes! my negresses! my mummies! and, worse than all, the laboratory, the favourite resort of my nightly lucubrations, without knowing, at least, if my hair-brained son will complete his adventure? No! I will not be dupe! immediately will I speed to support Morakanabad. By my formidable art, the clouds shall pour grape-shot in the faces of the assailants and shafts of red-hot iron on their heads. I will let loose my stores of hungry serpents and torpedos,[43] from beneath them; and we shall soon see the stand they will make against such an explosion!"

Having thus spoken, Carathis hasted to her son who was tranquilly banqueting with Nouronihar, in his superb carnation-coloured tent. "Glutton,

---

Eblis: (in Arabic, *Iblis*), the chief devil in the Muslim tradition, similar to Satan (and sometimes called *al-Shaytan,* "the adversary").
lucubrations: studies.

[42] In early astronomy (and, as here, astrology), astrolabes were instruments used to measure the altitude of the sun, the stars and other celestial bodies.
[43] *Torpedo* originally referred to an electric ray or other fish capable of stunning its enemies and prey.

that thou art!" cried she, "were it not for me, thou wouldst soon find thyself the mere commander of savoury pies. Thy faithful subjects have abjured the faith they swore to thee. Motavakel, thy brother, now reigns on the hill of Pied Horses: and, had I not some slight resources in the tower, would not be easily persuaded to abdicate. But, that time may not be lost, I shall only add a few words: — Strike tent to-night; set forward; and beware how thou loiterest again by the way. Though, thou hast forfeited the conditions of the parchment, I am not yet without hope: for, it cannot be denied, that thou hast violated, to admiration, the laws of hospitality by seducing the daughter of the emir, after having partaken of his bread and his salt. Such a conduct cannot but be delightful to the Giaour; and if, on thy march, thou canst signalize thyself, by an additional crime; all will still go well, and thou shalt enter the palace of Soliman, in triumph. Adieu! Alboufaki and my negresses are waiting at the door."

The Caliph had nothing to offer in reply: he wished his mother a prosperous journey, and ate on till he had finished his supper. At midnight, the camp broke up, amidst the flourishing of trumpets and other martial instruments; but loud indeed must have been the sound of the tymbals, to overpower the blubbering of the emir, and his grey-beards; who, by an excessive profusion of tears, had so far exhausted the radical moisture, that their eyes shrivelled up in their sockets, and their hairs dropped off by the roots. Nouronihar, to whom such a symphony was painful, did not grieve to get out of hearing. She accompanied the Caliph in the imperial litter; where they amused themselves, with imagining the splendour which was soon to surround them. The other women, overcome with dejection were dolefully rocked in their cages; whilst Dilara consoled herself, with anticipating the joy of celebrating the rites of fire, on the stately terraces of Istakar.

In four days, they reached the spacious valley of Rocnabad. The season of spring was in all its vigour, and the grotesque branches of the almond trees, in full blossom, fantastically chequered with hyacinths and jonquils, breathed forth a delightful fragrance. Myriads of bees, and scarce fewer of santons, had there taken up their abode. On the banks of the stream, hives and oratories were alternately ranged; and their neatness and whiteness were set off, by the deep green of the cypresses, that spired up amongst them. These pious personages amused themselves, with cultivating little gardens, that abounded with flowers and fruits; especially, musk-melons, of the best flavour that Persia could boast. Sometimes dispersed over the meadow, they entertained themselves with feeding peacocks, whiter than snow; and turtles, more blue than the sapphire.[44] In this manner were they occupied,

[44] *Turtles* in this context most likely refers not to the familiar reptiles but to turtledoves.

when the harbingers of the imperial procession began to proclaim: "Inhabitants of Rocnabad! prostrate yourselves on the brink of your pure waters; and tender your thanksgivings to heaven, that vouchsafeth to shew you a ray of its glory: for, lo! the commander of the faithful draws near."

The poor santons, filled with holy energy, having bustled to light up wax torches in their oratories, and expand the Koran on their ebony desks, went forth to meet the Caliph with baskets of honeycomb, dates, and melons. But, whilst they were advancing in solemn procession and with measured steps, the horses, camels, and guards, wantoned over their tulips and other flowers, and made a terrible havoc amongst them. The santons could not help casting from one eye a look of pity on the ravages committing around them; whilst, the other was fixed upon the Caliph and heaven. Nouronihar, enraptured with the scenery of a place which brought back to her remembrance the pleasing solitudes where her infancy had passed, intreated Vathek to stop: but he, suspecting that these oratories might be deemed, by the Giaour, an habitation, commanded his pioneers to level them all. The santons stood motionless with horror, at the barbarous mandate; and, at last, broke out into lamentations; but these were uttered with so ill a grace, that Vathek bade his eunuchs to kick them from his presence. He then descended from the litter, with Nouronihar. They sauntered together in the meadow; and amused themselves with culling flowers, and passing a thousand pleasantries on each other. But the bees, who were staunch Mussulmans, thinking it their duty to revenge the insult offered to their dear masters, the santons, assembled so zealously to do it with good effect, that the Caliph and Nouronihar were glad to find their tents prepared to receive them.

Bababalouk, who, in capacity of purveyor, had acquitted himself with applause, as to peacocks and turtles; lost no time in consigning some dozens to the spit; and as many more to be fricasseed. Whilst they were feasting, laughing, carousing, and blaspheming at pleasure, on the banquet so liberally furnished; the moullahs, the sheiks, the cadis, and imans of Schiraz (who seemed not to have met the santons) arrived;[45] leading by bridles of riband, inscribed from the Koran, a train of asses which were loaded with the choicest fruits the country could boast. Having presented their offerings to the Caliph; they petitioned him, to honour their city and mosques, with his presence. "Fancy not," said Vathek, "that you can detain me. Your presents I condescend to accept; but beg you will let me be quiet; for, I am not over-fond of resisting temptation. Retire then:—Yet, as it is

[45] Sheik (from the Arabic *shaykh*) is a title of respect used for Islamic religious leaders and chiefs; cadis, here as in *Nourjahad*, are officers of justice.

not decent, for personages so reverend, to return on foot; and, as you have not the appearance of expert riders, my eunuchs shall tie you on your asses with the precaution that your backs be not turned towards me: for, they understand etiquette."—In this deputation, were some high-stomached sheiks who, taking Vathek for a fool, scrupled not to speak their opinion. These, Bababalouk girded with double cords; and having well disciplined their asses with nettles behind, they all started, with a preternatural alertness; plunging, kicking, and running foul of one another, in the most ludicrous manner imaginable.

Nouronihar and the Caliph mutually contended who should most enjoy so degrading a sight. They burst out in peals of laughter, to see the old men and their asses fall into the stream. The leg of one was fractured; the shoulder of another, dislocated; the teeth of a third, dashed out; and the rest suffered still worse.

Two days more, undisturbed by fresh embassies, having been devoted to the pleasures of Rocnabad, the expedition proceeded; leaving Schiraz on the right, and verging towards a large plain; from whence were discernible, on the edge of the horizon, the dark summits of the mountains of Istakar.

At this prospect, the Caliph and Nouronihar were unable to repress their transports. They bounded from their litter to the ground; and broke forth into such wild exclamations, as amazed all within hearing. Interrogating each other, they shouted, "Are we not approaching the radiant palace of light? or gardens, more delightful than those of Sheddad?"—Infatuated mortals! they thus indulged delusive conjecture, unable to fathom the decrees of the Most High!

The good Genii, who had not totally relinquished the superintendence of Vathek; repairing to Mahomet, in the seventh heaven; said: "Merciful Prophet! stretch forth thy propitious arms, towards thy vicegerent; who is ready to fall, irretrievably, into the snare, which his enemies, the dives, have prepared to destroy him. The Giaour is awaiting his arrival, in the abominable palace of fire; where, if he once set his foot, his perdition will be inevitable." Mahomet answered, with an air of indignation: "He hath too well deserved to be resigned to himself; but I permit you to try if one effort more will be effectual to divert him from pursuing his ruin."

One of these beneficent Genii, assuming, without delay, the exterior of a shepherd, more renowned for his piety than all the derviches and santons of the region, took his station near a flock of white sheep, on the slope of a hill; and began to pour forth, from his flute, such airs of pathetic melody, as subdued the very soul; and, wakening remorse, drove, far from it, every frivolous fancy. At these energetic sounds, the sun hid himself beneath a gloomy cloud; and the waters of two little lakes, that were naturally clearer than crystal, became of a colour like blood. The whole of this superb assembly was involuntarily drawn towards the declivity of the hill. With downcast eyes, they all stood abashed; each upbraiding himself with the evil he had done. The heart of Dilara palpitated; and the chief of the eunuchs, with a sigh of contrition, implored pardon of the women, whom, for his own satisfaction, he had so often tormented.

Vathek and Nouronihar turned pale in their litter; and, regarding each other with haggard looks, reproached themselves—the one with a thousand of the blackest crimes; a thousand projects of impious ambition;—the other, with the desolation of her family; and the perdition of the amiable Gulchenrouz. Nouronihar persuaded herself that she heard, in the fatal music, the groans of her dying father; and Vathek, the sobs of the fifty children he had sacrificed to the Giaour. Amidst these complicated pangs of anguish, they perceived themselves impelled towards the shepherd, whose countenance was so commanding that Vathek, for the first time, felt overawed; whilst Nouronihar concealed her face with her hands. The music paused; and the Genius, addressing the Caliph, said: "Deluded prince! to whom Providence hath confided the care of innumerable subjects; is it thus that thou fulfillest thy mission? Thy crimes are already completed; and, art thou now hastening towards thy punishment? Thou knowest that, beyond these mountains, Eblis and his accursed dives hold their infernal empire; and seduced by a malignant phantom, thou art proceeding to surrender thyself to them! This moment is the last of grace allowed thee: abandon thy atrocious purpose: return: give back Nouronihar to her father, who still retains a few sparks of life: destroy thy tower, with all its abominations: drive Carathis from thy councils: be just to thy subjects: respect the ministers of the Prophet; compensate for thy impieties, by an exemplary life: and, instead of squandering thy days in voluptuous indulgence, lament thy crimes on the sepulchres of thy ancestors. Thou beholdest the clouds that obscure the sun: at the instant he recovers his splendour, if thy heart be not changed, the time of mercy assigned thee will be past for ever."

Vathek, depressed with fear, was on the point of prostrating himself at the feet of the shepherd; whom he perceived to be of a nature superior to man: but, his pride prevailing, he audaciously lifted his head, and, glancing at him one of his terrible looks, said: "Whoever thou art, withhold thy useless admonitions: thou wouldst either delude me, or art thyself deceived. If what I have done be so criminal, as thou pretendest, there remains not for me a moment of grace. I have traversed a sea of blood, to acquire a power, which will make thy equals tremble: deem not that I shall retire, when in view of the port; or, that I will relinquish her, who is dearer to me than either my life, or thy mercy. Let the sun appear! let him illume my career! it matters not where it may end." On uttering these words, which made even the Genius shudder, Vathek threw himself into the arms of Nouronihar; and commanded that his horses should be forced back to the road.

There was no difficulty in obeying these orders: for, the attraction had ceased: the sun shone forth in all his glory, and the shepherd vanished with a lamentable scream.

The fatal impression of the music of the Genius, remained, notwithstanding, in the heart of Vathek's attendants. They viewed each other with looks of consternation. At the approach of night, almost all of them escaped; and, of this numerous assemblage, there only remained the chief of the eunuchs, some idolatrous slaves, Dilara, and a few other women; who, like herself, were votaries of the religion of the Magi.

The Caliph, fired with the ambition of prescribing laws to the powers of darkness, was but little embarrassed at this dereliction. The impetuosity of his blood prevented him from sleeping; nor did he encamp any more, as before. Nouronihar, whose impatience, if possible exceeded his own, importuned him to hasten his march, and lavished on him a thousand caresses, to beguile all reflection. She fancied herself already more potent than Balkis, and pictured to her imagination the Genii falling prostrate at the foot of her throne. In this manner they advanced by moon-light, till they came within view of the two towering rocks that form a kind of portal to the valley, at the extremity of which, rose the vast ruins of Istakar. Aloft, on the mountain, glimmered the fronts of various royal mausoleums, the horror of which was deepened by the shadows of night. They passed through two villages, almost deserted; the only inhabitants remaining being a few feeble old men: who, at the sight of horses and litters, fell upon their knees, and cried out: "O Heaven! is it then by these phantoms that we have been, for six months tormented! Alas! it was from the terror of these spectres and the noise beneath the mountains, that our people have fled, and left us at the mercy of the malificent spirits!" The Caliph, to whom these complaints were but unpromising auguries, drove over the bodies of these wretched old men; and, at length, arrived at the foot of the terrace of black marble. There he descended from his litter, handing down Nouronihar; both with beating hearts, stared wildly around them, and expected, with an apprehensive shudder, the approach of the Giaour. But nothing as yet announced his appearance.

A death-like stillness reigned over the mountain and through the air. The moon dilated on a vast platform, the shades of the lofty columns which

---

Balkis: *Bilqis,* the Arabic name for the Queen of Sheba, consort of Solomon (see also *B/H* 176).

reached from the terrace almost to the clouds. The gloomy watch-towers, whose number could not be counted, were covered by no roof; and their capitals, of an architecture unknown in the records of the earth, served as an asylum for the birds of night, which, alarmed at the approach of such visitants, fled away croaking.

The chief of the eunuchs, trembling with fear, besought Vathek that a fire might be kindled. "No!" replied he, "there is no time left to think of such trifles; abide where thou art, and expect my commands." Having thus spoken, he presented his hand to Nouronihar; and, ascending the steps of a vast staircase, reached the terrace, which was flagged with squares of marble, and resembled a smooth expanse of water, upon whose surface not a blade of grass ever dared to vegetate. On the right rose the watch-towers, ranged before the ruins of an immense palace, whose walls were embossed with various figures. In front stood forth the colossal forms of four creatures, composed of the leopard and the griffin, and though but of stone, inspired emotions of terror. Near these were distinguished by the splendour of the moon, which streamed full on the place, characters like those on the sabres of the Giaour, and which possessed the same virtue of changing every moment. These, after vacillating for some time, fixed at last in Arabic letters, and prescribed to the Caliph the following words:—"Vathek! thou hast violated the conditions of my parchment, and deservest to be sent back, but in favour to thy companion, and, as the meed for what thou hast done to obtain it; Eblis permitteth that the portal of his palace shall be opened; and the subterranean fire will receive thee into the number of its adorers."

He scarcely had read these words, before the mountain, against which the terrace was reared, trembled; and the watch-towers were ready to topple headlong upon them. The rock yawned, and disclosed within it a staircase of polished marble, that seemed to approach the abyss. Upon each stair were planted two large torches, like those Nouronihar had seen in her vision; the camphorated vapour of which ascended and gathered itself into a cloud under the hollow of the vault.

This appearance, instead of terrifying, gave new courage to the daughter of Fakreddin. Scarcely deigning to bid adieu to the moon, and the firmament; she abandoned, without hesitation, the pure atmosphere, to plunge into these infernal exhalations. The gait of those impious personages was haughty, and determined. As they descended, by the effulgence of the torches, they gazed on each other with mutual admiration; and both appeared so resplendent, that they already esteemed themselves spiritual

---

meed: reward.

intelligences. The only circumstance that perplexed them, was their not arriving at the bottom of the stairs. On hastening their descent, with an ardent impetuosity, they felt their steps accelerated to such a degree, that they seemed not walking but falling from a precipice. Their progress, however, was at length impeded, by a vast portal of ebony which the Caliph, without difficulty, recognized. Here, the Giaour awaited them, with the key in his hand. "Ye are welcome!" said he to them, with a ghastly smile, "in spite of Mahomet, and all his dependents. I will now usher you into that palace, where you have so highly merited a place." Whilst he was uttering these words, he touched the enameled lock with his key; and the doors, at once, flew open with a noise still louder than the thunder of the dog days, and as suddenly recoiled, the moment they had entered.

The Caliph and Nouronihar beheld each other with amazement, at finding themselves in a place, which, though roofed with a vaulted ceiling, was so spacious and lofty, that, at first, they took it for an immeasurable plain. But their eyes, at length, growing familiar to the grandeur of the surrounding objects, they extended their view to those at a distance; and discovered rows of columns and arcades, which gradually diminished, till they terminated in a point radiant as the sun, when he darts his last beams athwart the ocean. The pavement, strewed over with gold dust and saffron, exhaled so subtile an odour, as almost overpowered them. They, however, went on; and observed an infinity of censers, in which, ambergrise and the wood of aloes, were continually burning. Between the several columns, were placed tables; each, spread with a profusion of viands; and wines, of every species, sparkling in vases of crystal. A throng of Genii, and other fantastic spirits, of either sex, danced lasciviously, at the sound of music, which issued from beneath.

In the midst of this immense hall, a vast multitude was incessantly passing; who severally kept their right hands on their hearts; without once regarding any thing around them. They had all, the livid paleness of death. Their eyes, deep sunk in their sockets, resembled those phosphoric meteors, that glimmer by night, in places of interment. Some stalked slowly on; absorbed in profound reverie: some shrieking with agony, ran furiously about like tigers, wounded with poisoned arrows; whilst others, grinding their teeth in rage, foamed along more frantic than the wildest maniac. They all avoided each other; and, though surrounded by a multitude that no one could number, each wandered at random, unheedful of the rest, as if alone on a desert where no foot had trodden.

---

ambergrise: ambergris, an aromatic, precious, waxy substance derived from sperm whales and used in perfumes.

Vathek and Nouronihar, frozen with terror, at a sight so baleful, demanded of the Giaour what these appearances might mean; and, why these ambulating spectres never withdrew their hands from their hearts? "Perplex not yourselves, with so much at once," replied he bluntly; "you will soon be acquainted with all: let us haste, and present you to Eblis." They continued their way, through the multitude; but, notwithstanding their confidence at first, they were not sufficiently composed to examine, with attention, the various perspective of halls and of galleries, that opened on the right hand and left; which were all illuminated by torches and braziers, whose flames rose in pyramids to the centre of the vault. At length they came to a place, where long curtains brocaded with crimson and gold, fell from all parts in solemn confusion. Here, the choirs and dances were heard no longer. The light which glimmered, came from afar.

After some time, Vathek and Nouronihar perceived a gleam brightening through the drapery, and entered a vast tabernacle hung around with the skins of leopards. An infinity of elders with streaming beards, and afrits in complete armour, had prostrated themselves before the ascent of a lofty eminence; on the top of which, upon a globe of fire, sat the formidable Eblis. His person was that of a young man, whose noble and regular features seemed to have been tarnished by malignant vapours. In his large eyes appeared both pride and despair: his flowing hair retained some resemblance to that of an angel of light. In his hand, which thunder had blasted, he swayed the iron sceptre, that causes the monster Ouranbad,[46] the afrits, and all the powers of the abyss to tremble. At his presence, the heart of the Caliph sunk within him; and he fell prostrate on his face. Nouronihar, however, though greatly dismayed, could not help admiring the person of Eblis: for, she expected to have seen some stupendous giant. Eblis, with a voice more mild than might be imagined, but such as penetrated the soul and filled it with the deepest melancholy, said: "Creatures of clay, I receive you into mine empire: ye are numbered amongst my adorers: enjoy whatever this palace affords; the treasures of the pre-adamite sultans; their fulminating sabres; and those talismans, that compel the dives to open the subterranean expanses of the mountain of Kaf, which communicate with these. There, insatiable as your curiosity may be, shall you find sufficient objects to gratify it. You shall possess the exclusive privilege of entering the fortresses of Aherman, and the halls of Argenk,[47] where are pourtrayed all creatures endowed with intelligence; and the various animals that inhab-

---

Aherman: Ahriman (Angra Mainyu), the devil or destructive principle in Zoroastrianism.

[46] See *B/H* 177.
[47] See *B/H* 177.

ited the earth prior to the creation of that contemptible being whom ye denominate the father of mankind."

Vathek and Nouronihar feeling themselves revived and encouraged by this harangue, eagerly said to the Giaour; "Bring us instantly to the place which contains these precious talismans."—"Come," answered this wicked dive, with his malignant grin, "come and possess all that my sovereign hath promised; and more." He then conducted them into a long aisle adjoining the tabernacle; preceding them with hasty steps, and followed by his disciples with the utmost alacrity. They reached, at length, a hall of great extent, and covered with a lofty dome; around which appeared fifty portals of bronze, secured with as many fastenings of iron. A funereal gloom prevailed over the whole scene. Here, upon two beds of incorruptible cedar, lay recumbent the fleshless forms of the pre-adamite kings, who had been monarchs of the whole earth. They still possessed enough of life to be conscious of their deplorable condition. Their eyes retained a melancholy motion: they regarded one another with looks of the deepest dejection; each holding his right hand, motionless, on his heart. At their feet were inscribed the events of their several reigns, their power, their pride, and their crimes; Soliman Daki; and Soliman, called Gian Ben Gian, who, after having chained up the dives in the dark caverns of Kaf, became so presumptuous as to doubt of the Supreme Power. All these maintained great state; though not to be compared with the eminence of Soliman Ben Daoud.

This king, so renowned for his wisdom, was on the loftiest elevation; and placed immediately under the dome.[48] He appeared to possess more animation than the rest. Though, from time to time, he laboured with profound sighs; and, like his companions, kept his right hand on his heart; yet his countenance was more composed, and he seemed to be listening to the sullen roar of a cataract visible in part through one of the grated portals. This was the only sound that intruded on the silence of these doleful mansions. A range of brazen vases surrounded the elevation. "Remove the covers from these cabalistic depositaries," said the Giaour to Vathek; "and avail thyself of the talismans which will break asunder all these gates of bronze; and not only render thee master of the treasures contained within them, but also of the spirits by which they are guarded."

---

cabalistic: from Caballa (derived from Hebrew *qabbalah,* "tradition"), a mystic tradition of interpretation within Judaism.

[48] Somewhat confusingly, Beckford identifies Soliman Ben Daoud (Solomon son of David) with the biblical (and koranic) king of Israel known for his wisdom, for building the Temple, and for being misled into idolatry by his concubines, yet also places him among the "pre-adamite kings" said to have ruled the earth before the creation of humanity.

The Caliph, whom this ominous preliminary had entirely disconcerted, approached the vases with faltering footsteps; and was ready to sink with terror when he heard the groans of Soliman. As he proceeded, a voice from the livid lips of the prophet articulated these words: "In my life-time, I filled a magnificent throne; having, on my right hand, twelve thousand seats of gold, where the patriarchs and the prophets heard my doctrines; on my left, the sages and doctors, upon as many thrones of silver, were present at all my decisions. Whilst I thus administered justice to innumerable multitudes, the birds of the air, hovering over me, served as a canopy against the rays of the sun. My people flourished; and my palace rose to the clouds. I erected a temple to the Most High, which was the wonder of the universe: but, I basely suffered myself to be seduced by the love of women, and a curiosity that could not be restrained by sublunary things. I listened to the counsels of Aherman, and the daughter of Pharaoh; and adored fire, and the hosts of heaven. I forsook the holy city, and commanded the Genii to rear the stupendous palace of Istakar, and the terrace of the watch towers; each of which was consecrated to a star. There, for a while, I enjoyed myself in the zenith of glory and pleasure. Not only men, but supernatural beings were subject also to my will. I began to think, as these unhappy monarchs around had already thought, that the vengeance of Heaven was asleep; when, at once, the thunder burst my structures asunder, and precipitated me hither: where, however, I do not remain, like the other inhabitants, totally destitute of hope; for, an angel of light hath revealed that in consideration of the piety of my early youth, my woes shall come to an end, when this cataract shall for ever cease to flow. Till then I am in torments, ineffable torments! an unrelenting fire preys on my heart."

Having uttered this exclamation, Soliman raised his hands towards heaven, in token of supplication; and the Caliph discerned through his bosom, which was transparent as crystal, his heart enveloped in flames. At a sight so full of horror, Nouronihar fell back, like one petrified, into the arms of Vathek, who cried out with a convulsive sob; "O Giaour! whither hast thou brought us! Allow us to depart, and I will relinquish all thou hast promised. O Mahomet! remains there no more mercy!"—"None! none!" replied the malicious dive. "Know, miserable prince! thou art now in the abode of vengeance and despair. Thy heart, also, will be kindled like those of the other votaries of Eblis. A few days are allotted thee previous to this fatal period: employ them as thou wilt; recline on these heaps of gold; command the infernal potentates; range, at thy pleasure, through these immense subterranean domains: no barrier shall be shut against thee. As for me, I have fulfilled my mission: I now leave thee to thyself." At these words he vanished.

The Caliph and Nouronihar remained in the most abject affliction. Their tears were unable to flow, and scarcely could they support themselves. At length, taking each other, despondingly, by the hand, they went faltering from this fatal hall; indifferent which way they turned their steps. Every portal opened at their approach. The dives fell prostrate before them. Every reservoir of riches was disclosed to their view: but they no longer felt the incentives of curiosity, of pride, or avarice. With like apathy they heard the chorus of Genii, and saw the stately banquets prepared to regale them. They went wandering on, from chamber to chamber; hall to hall; and gallery to gallery; all without bounds or limit; all distinguishable by the same louring gloom; all adorned with the same awful grandeur; all traversed by persons in search of repose and consolation; but, who sought them in vain; for every one carried within him a heart tormented in flames. Shunned by these various sufferers, who seemed by their looks to be upbraiding the partners of their guilt, they withdrew from them to wait, in direful suspense, the moment which should render them to each other the like objects of terror.

"What!" exclaimed Nouronihar; "will the time come when I shall snatch my hand from thine!"—"Ah!" said Vathek, "and shall my eyes ever cease to drink from thine long draughts of enjoyment! Shall the moments of our reciprocal ecstasies be reflected on with horror! It was not thou that broughtest me hither; the principles by which Carathis perverted my youth, have been the sole cause of my perdition! it is but right she should have her share of it." Having given vent to these painful expressions, he called to an afrit, who was stirring up one of the braziers, and bade him fetch the Princess Carathis from the palace of Samarah.

After issuing these orders, the Caliph and Nouronihar continued walking amidst the silent croud, till they heard voices at the end of the gallery. Presuming them to proceed from some unhappy beings, who, like themselves, were awaiting their final doom; they followed the sound, and found it to come from a small square chamber, where they discovered, sitting on sofas, four young men, of goodly figure, and a lovely female, who were holding a melancholy conversation by the glimmering of a lonely lamp. Each had a gloomy and forlorn air; and two of them were embracing each other with great tenderness. On seeing the Caliph and the daughter of Fakreddin enter, they arose, saluted, and made room for them. Then he who appeared the most considerable of the group, addressed himself thus to Vathek:—"Strangers! who doubtless are in the same state of suspense with ourselves, as you do not yet bear your hand on your heart, if you are come hither to pass the interval allotted, previous to the infliction of our common punishment, condescend to relate the adventures that have brought you to this fatal place; and we, in return, will acquaint you with ours, which deserve but too well to be heard. To trace back our crimes to their source, though we are not permitted to repent, is the only employment suited to wretches like us!"

The Caliph and Nouronihar assented to the proposal; and Vathek began, not without tears and lamentations, a sincere recital of every circumstance that had passed. When the afflicting narrative was closed, the young man entered on his own. Each person proceeded in order; and, when the third prince had reached the midst of his adventures, a sudden noise interrupted him, which caused the vault to tremble and to open.[49]

Immediately a cloud descended, which gradually dissipating, discovered Carathis on the back of an afrit, who grievously complained of his burden. She, instantly springing to the ground, advanced towards her son, and said, "What dost thou here, in this little square chamber? As the dives are become subject to thy beck, I expected to have found thee on the throne of the pre-adamite kings."

"Execrable woman!" answered the Caliph; "cursed be the day thou gavest me birth! Go, follow this afrit; let him conduct thee to the hall of the Prophet Soliman: there thou wilt learn to what these palaces are destined, and how much I ought to abhor the impious knowledge thou hast taught me."

"Has the height of power, to which thou art arrived, turned thy brain?" answered Carathis: "but I ask no more than permission to shew my respect for Soliman the prophet. It is, however, proper thou shouldest know that (as the afrit has informed me neither of us shall return to Samarah) I requested his permission to arrange my affairs; and he politely consented. Availing myself, therefore, of the few moments allowed me, I set fire to the tower, and consumed in it the mutes, negresses, and serpents, which have rendered me so much good service: nor should I have been less kind to Morakanabad, had he not prevented me, by deserting at last to thy brother. As for Bababalouk, who had the folly to return to Samarah, to provide husbands for thy wives, I undoubtedly would have put him to the torture; but being in a hurry, I only hung him, after having decoyed him in a snare, with thy wives: whom I buried alive by the help of my negresses; who thus spent their last moments greatly to their satisfaction. With respect to Dilara, who ever stood high in my favour, she hath evinced the greatness of her mind,

[49] Beckford had written, in French, a series of "Episodes" to *Vathek* that he often intended but never managed to publish; they are referred to more explicitly in an earlier issue of the 1816 edition as the histories of Alasi and Firouz, of Prince Barkiarokh, and of Prince Kalilah and Princess Zulkais (a fourth "episode" goes unmentioned).

by fixing herself near, in the service of one of the magi; and, I think, will soon be one of our society."

Vathek, too much cast down to express the indignation excited by such a discourse, ordered the afrit to remove Carathis from his presence, and continued immersed in thoughts which his companions durst not disturb.

Carathis, however, eagerly entered the dome of Soliman, and, without regarding in the least the groans of the prophet, undauntedly removed the covers of the vases, and violently seized on the talismans. Then, with a voice more loud than had hitherto been heard within these mansions, she compelled the dives to disclose to her the most secret treasures, the most profound stores, which the afrit himself had not seen. She passed, by rapid descents, known only to Eblis and his most favoured potentates; and thus penetrated the very entrails of the earth, where breathes the sansar, or the icy wind of death. Nothing appalled her dauntless soul. She perceived, however, in all the inmates who bore their hands on their heart, a little singularity, not much to her taste.

As she was emerging from one of the abysses, Eblis stood forth to her view; but, notwithstanding he displayed the full effulgence of his infernal majesty, she preserved her countenance unaltered; and even paid her compliments with considerable firmness.

This superb monarch thus answered: "Princess, whose knowledge, and whose crimes, have merited a conspicuous rank in my empire; thou dost well to avail thyself of the leisure that remains: for, the flames and torments, which are ready to sieze on thy heart, will not fail to provide thee soon with full employment." He said, and was lost in the curtains of his tabernacle.

Carathis paused for a moment with surprise; but resolved to follow the advice of Eblis, she assembled all the choirs of genii, and all the dives, to pay her homage. Thus marched she, in triumph, through a vapour of perfumes, amidst the acclamations of all the malignant spirits; with most of whom she had formed a previous acquaintance. She even attempted to dethrone one of the Solimans, for the purpose of usurping his place; when a voice, proceeding from the abyss of death, proclaimed: "All is accomplished!" Instantaneously, the haughty forehead of the intrepid princess became corrugated with agony: she uttered a tremendous yell; and fixed, no more to be withdrawn, her right hand upon her heart, which was become a receptacle of eternal fire.

In this delirium, forgetting all ambitious projects, and her thirst for that knowledge which should ever be hidden from mortals, she overturned the offerings of the genii; and, having execrated the hour she was begotten and the womb that had borne her, glanced off in a rapid whirl that rendered her invisible, and continued to revolve without intermission.

Almost at the same instant, the same voice announced to the Caliph, Nouronihar, the four princes, and the princess, the awful, and irrevocable decree. Their hearts immediately took fire, and they, at once, lost the most precious gift of heaven: —Hope. These unhappy beings recoiled, with looks of the most furious distraction. Vathek beheld in the eyes of Nouronihar nothing but rage and vengeance; nor could she discern ought in his, but aversion and despair. The two princes who were friends, and, till that moment, had preserved their attachment, shrunk back, gnashing their teeth with mutual and unchangeable hatred. Kalilah and his sister made reciprocal gestures of imprecation; all testified their horror for each other by the most ghastly convulsions, and screams that could not be smothered. All severally plunged themselves into the accursed multitude, there to wander in an eternity of unabating anguish.

Such was, and such should be, the punishment of unrestrained passions and atrocious deeds! Such shall be, the chastisement of that blind curiosity, which would transgress those bounds the wisdom of the Creator has prescribed to human knowledge; and such the dreadful disappointment of that restless ambition, which, aiming at discoveries reserved for beings of a supernatural order, perceives not, through its infatuated pride, that the condition of man upon earth is to be—humble and ignorant.

Thus the Caliph Vathek, who, for the sake of empty pomp and forbidden power, had sullied himself with a thousand crimes, became a prey to grief without end, and remorse without mitigation: whilst the humble, the despised Gulchenrouz passed whole ages in undisturbed tranquillity, and in the pure happiness of childhood.

ORIGINAL NOTES TO *VATHEK*

William Beckford and Samuel Henley

PAGE 80—*Caliph*. This title amongst the Mahometans implies the three characters of Prophet, Priest, and King: it signifies, in the Arabic, *Successor*, or *Vicar*; and, by appropriation, the *Vicar of God on Earth*. It is, at this day, one of the titles of the Grand Signior, as successor of Mahomet; and of the Sophi of Persia, as successor of Ali. *Habesci's State of the Ottoman Empire*, p. 9. *D'Herbelot*, p. 985. [Elias Habesci, *The Present State of the Ottoman Empire*, trans. Alexander Ghiga (London: Baldwin, 1784); Barthélemy d'Herbelot de Molainville, *Bibliothèque Orientale* (Paris: Compagnie des Libraries, 1697). Only the principal sources cited by Henley and Beckford are identified here; for fuller information, see Roger Lonsdale's edition of *Vathek*, listed in the Works Cited. ED.]

PAGE 80—*one of his eyes became so terrible*. The author of Nighiaristan hath preserved a fact that supports this account; and there is no history of Vathek, in which his *terrible eye* is not mentioned.

PAGE 80—*Omar Ben Abdalaziz*. This Caliph was eminent above all others for temperance and self-denial; insomuch, that, according to the Mahometan faith, he was raised to Mahomet's bosom, as a reward for his abstinence in an age of corruption. *D'Herbelot*, p. 690.

PAGE 80—*Samarah*. A city of the Babylonian Irak; supposed to have stood on the site where Nimrod erected his tower. Khondemir relates, in his life of Motassem, that this prince, to terminate the disputes which were perpetually happening between the inhabitants of Bagdat and his Turkish slaves, withdrew from thence, and, having fixed on a situation in the plain of Catoul, there founded Samarah. He is said to have had in the stables of this city, a hundred and thirty thousand *pied horses*; each of which carried, by his order, a sack of earth to a place he had chosen. By this accumulation, an elevation was formed that commanded a view of all Samarah, and served for the foundation of his magnificent palace. *D'Herbelot*, p. 752, 808, 985. *Anecdotes Arabes*, p. 413.

PAGE 81—*in the most delightful succession*. The great men of the East have been always fond of music. Though forbidden by the Mahometan religion, it commonly makes a part of every entertainment. *Nitimur in vetitum semper*. ["We always reach for what is forbidden." Ovid, *Amores* 3.4.17. ED.] Female slaves are generally kept to amuse them, and the ladies of their harems.

PAGE 81—*Mani*. This artist, whom Inatulla of Delhi styles *the far-famed*, lived in the reign of Schabur, or Sapor, the son of Ardschir Babegan; and was, by profession, a painter and sculptor. It appears, from the Arabian Nights, that Haroun al Raschid, Vathek's grandfather, had adorned his palace and furnished his magnificent pavilion, with the most capital performances of the Persian artists.

PAGE 81—*Houris*. The virgins of Paradise, called, from their large black eyes, *Hur al oyun*. An intercourse with these, according to the institution of

Mahomet, is to constitute the principal felicity of the faithful. Not formed of clay, like mortal women, they are adorned with unfading charms, and deemed to possess the celestial privilege of an eternal youth. *Al Koran; passim.*

PAGE 82—*Mahomet in the seventh heaven.* In this heaven, the paradise of Mahomet is supposed to be placed contiguous to the throne of Alla. Hagi Khalfah relates, that Ben Iatmaiah, a celebrated doctor of Damascus, had the temerity to assert, that, when the Most High erected his throne, he reserved a vacant place for Mahomet upon it.

PAGE 82—*Genii.* It is asserted, and not without plausible reasons, that the words *Genn, Ginn—Genius, Genie, Gian, Gigas, Giant, Geant* proceed from the same themes, *viz. Γὴ, the earth,* and *Γὰω, to produce*; as if these supernatural agents had been an early production of the earth, long before Adam was modelled out from a lump of it. The *Ωντες* and *Εωντες* of Plato, bear a close analogy to these supposed intermediate creatures between God and man. From these premises arose the consequence that, boasting a higher order, formed of more subtile matter and possessed of much greater knowledge than man, they lorded over this planet and invisibly governed it with superior intellect. From this last circumstance, they obtained in Greece, the title of *Δὰιμονες*, Demons, from Δὰημων, *Sciens*, knowing. The Hebrew word נפלים Nephilim. (Gen. Chap. vi. 4.) translated by *Gigantes*, giants, claiming the same etymon with Νεφελη a cloud, seems also to indicate that these intellectual beings inhabited the void expanse of the terrestrial atmosphere. Hence the very ancient fable of men of enormous strength and size revolting against the Gods, and all the mythological lore relating to that mighty conflict; unless we trace the origin of this important event to the ambition of Satan, his revolt against the Almighty and his fall with the angels.

PAGE 82—*Assist him to complete the tower.* The genii were famous for their architectural skill. The pyramids of Egypt have been ascribed to Gian Ben Gian their chief, most likely, because they could not, from records, be attributed to any one else. According to the Koran, ch. 34, the genii were employed by Solomon in the erection of his temple.

The reign of Gian Ben Gian, over the Peris, is said to have continued for two thousand years; after which, Eblis was sent by the Deity to exile them, on account of their disorders, and confine them in the remotest region of the earth. *D'Herbelot*, p. 396. *Bailly sur l'Atlantide*, p. 147.

PAGE 83—*the stranger displayed such rarities as he had never before seen.* That such curiosities were much sought after in the days of Vathek, may be concluded from the encouragement which Haroun al Raschid gave to the mechanic arts, and the present he sent, by his ambassadors, to Charlemagne. This consisted of a clock, which, when put into motion, by means of a clepsydra, not only pointed out the hours, but also, by dropping small balls on a bell, struck them; and, at the same instant, threw open as many little doors, to let out an equal number of horsemen. *Ann. Reg. Franc. Pip. Caroli, &c. ad ann.* 807. *Weidler*, p. 205.

PAGE 86—*their beards to be burnt.* The loss of the beard, from the earliest ages, was accounted highly disgraceful. An instance occurs, in the Tales of Inatulla, of one being *singed off*, as a mulct [penalty] on the owner, for having failed to explain a question propounded; and, in the Arabian Nights, a proclamation may be seen similar to this of Vathek. Vol. I. p. 268. Vol. II. p. 228. [In-ayat Allah, *Tales, Translated from the Persian of Inatulla of Delhi,* trans. Alexander Dow (London: Becket and de Hondt, 1768). ED.]

PAGE 89—*Giaour* means *infidel.*

PAGE 91—*the Divan.* This was both the supreme council and court of justice, at which the caliphs of the race of the Abassides assisted in person, to redress the injuries of every appellant. *D'Herbelot*, p. 298.

PAGE 91—*the prime vizir.* Vazir, vezir, or as we express it, vizir, literally signifies a *porter*; and, by metaphor, the minister who bears the principal burthen of the state, generally called the sublime Porte.

PAGE 92—*The Meuzins and their minarets.* Valid, the son of Abdalmalek, was the first who erected a *minaret*, or turret; and this he placed on the grand mosque at Damascus; for the *meuzin*, or crier, to announce from it, the hour of prayer. This practice has constantly been kept to this day. *D'Herbelot*, p. 576.

PAGE 94—*Soliman Ben Daoud.* The name of *David* in Hebrew is composed of the letter ו *Vau* between two ד *Daleths* דוד; and according to the Massoretic points ought to be pronounced *David.* Having no *v* consonant in their tongue, the Septuagint substituted the letter *b* for *v*, and wrote *Δαβιδ*, *Dabid.* The Syriac reads *Dad* or *Dod*; and the Arabs articulate *Daoud.*

PAGE 97—*with the grin of an ogre.* Thus, in the history of the punished vizir:—"The prince heard enough to convince him of his danger, and then perceived that the lady, who called herself the daughter of an *Indian* king, was an *ogress*; wife to one of those *savage demons*, called ogre, who stay in remote places, and make use of a thousand wiles to surprize and devour passengers." *Arab. Nights*, vol. I. p. 56. [The notes refer to the four-volume 1783 edition of the "Grub Street" translation of Galland's *Arabian Nights Entertainments.* ED.]

PAGE 99—*mutes.* It has been usual, in eastern courts, from time immemorial, to retain a number of mutes. These are not only employed to amuse the monarch, but also to instruct his pages, in an art to us little known, that of communicating their thoughts by signs, lest the sounds of their voices should disturb the sovereign.—*Habesci's State of the Ottoman Empire*, p. 164.—The mutes are also the secret instruments of his private vengeance, in carrying the fatal string.

PAGE 100—*Prayer announced at break of day.* The stated seasons of public prayer, in the twenty-four hours, were five: day-break, noon, mid-time between noon and sun-set, immediately as the sun leaves the horizon, and an hour and half after it is down.

PAGE 100—*mummies. Moumia* (from *moum*, wax and tallow) signifies the flesh of the human body preserved in the sand, after having been embalmed and wrapt in cerements. They are frequently found in the sepulchres of Egypt; but most of the Oriental mummies are brought from a cavern near Abin, in Persia. *D'Herbelot*, p. 647.

PAGE 103—*a parchment.* Parchments of the like mysterious import are frequently mentioned in the works of the Eastern writers. One in particular, amongst the Arabians, is held in high veneration. It was written by Ali, and Giafar Sadek, in mystic characters, and is said to contain the destiny of the Mahometan religion, and the great events which are to happen previous to the end of the world. This parchment is of *camel's skin.*

PAGE 103—*Istakhar.* This city was the ancient Persepolis and capital of Persia, under the kings of the three first races. The author of Lebtarikh writes, that Kischtab there established his abode, erected several temples to the element of fire, and hewed out, for himself and his successors, sepulchres in the rocks of the mountain contiguous to the city. The ruins of columns and broken figures which still remain, defaced as they were by Alexander, and mutilated by time, plainly evince that those ancient potentates had chosen it for the place of their interment.

PAGE 103—*the talismans of Soliman.* The most famous *talisman* of the East, and which could control even the arms and magic of the dives, or giants, was *Mohur Solimani*, the seal or ring of Soliman Jared, fifth monarch of the world after Adam. By means of it, the possessor had the entire command, not only of the elements, but also of demons, and every created being. *Richardson's Dissertat.* p. 272 [John Richardson, *A Dissertation on the Languages, Literatures, and Manners of the Eastern Nations*, 2nd ed. (London: Murray, 1778).] *D'Herbelot*, p. 820.

PAGE 103—*pre-adamite sultans.* These monarchs, which were seventy-two in number, are said to have governed each a distinct species of rational beings, prior to the existence of Adam.

PAGE 103—*beware how thou enterest any dwelling.* Strange as this injunction may seem, it is by no means incongruous to the customs of the country. Dr. Pocock[e] mentions his travelling with the train of the Governor of Faiume, who, instead of lodging in a village that was near, preferred to pass the night in a grove of palm-trees. *Travels*, vol. I. p. 56. [Richard Pococke, *A Description of the East*, 2 vols. (London: Bowyer, 1743–45). ED.]

PAGE 103—*every bumper he ironically quaffed to the health of Mahomet.* There are innumerable proofs that the Grecian custom, *ονμπιειν κναθιζόμενδς*, [ladling out and drinking together] prevailed amongst the Arabs; but had these been wanted, Carathis could not be supposed a stranger to it. The practice was to hail the gods, in the first place; and then, those who were held in the highest veneration.

PAGE 104—*the ass of Balaam, the dog of the seven sleepers, and the other animals admitted into the paradise of Mahomet.* It was a tenet of the Mussulman creed, that all animals would be raised again, and many of them honoured with admission to paradise. The story of the seven sleepers, borrowed from Christian legends, was this:—In the days of the Emperor Decius, there were certain Ephesian youths of a good family, who, to avoid the flames of persecution, fled to a secret cavern, and there slept for a number of years. In their flight towards the cave, they were followed by a dog, which, when they attempted to drive him back, said: "*I love those who are dear unto God; go sleep, therefore, and I will guard you.*"—For this dog the Mahometans retain so profound a reverence, that their harshest sarcasm against a covetous person, is, "He would not throw a bone to the dog of the seven sleepers." It is even said, that their superstition induces them to write his name upon the letters they send to a distance, as a kind of talisman to secure them a safe conveyance. *Religious Ceremonies*, vol. VII. p. 74, n. *Sale's Koran*, ch. xviii. and notes. [Jean Frédéric Bernard, *The Ceremonies and Religious Customs of the Various Nations of the Known World*, 7 vols. (London: du Bosc, 1773–79); George Sale, *The Koran, Commonly Called The Alcoran of Mohammed, Translated into English Immediately from the Original Arabic . . . to Which Is Prefixed a Preliminary Discourse* (London: Wilcox, 1734). ED.]

PAGE 104—*painting the eyes of the Circassians.* It was an ancient custom in the East, which still continues, to tinge the eyes of women, particularly those of a fair complexion, with an impalpable powder, prepared chiefly from crude antimony, and called *surmeh.* Ebni'l Motezz, in a passage translated by Sir W[illiam] Jones, hath not only ascertained its *purple* colour, but also likened the *violet* to it.

> Viola collegit folia sua, similia
> Collyrionigro, quod bibit lachrymas die discessus,
> Velut si esset super vasa in quibus fulgent
> Primae ignis flammulae in sulphuris extremis partibus.

> [The violet has gathered up its petals, like
> The Collyrionigro (dark eyeshadow), that drinks up tears on
> the day of parting,
> As though it were over the braziers in which gleam
> The first points of flame along the edges of brimstone. ED.]

This pigment, when applied to the inner surface of the lids, communicates to the eye (especially if seen by the light of lamps) so tender and fascinating a languor, as no language is competent to express. Hence the epithet *Ιοβλεφαρος*, violet-colour eye-lids, attributed by the Greeks to the goddess of beauty.

PAGE 104—*Rocnabad.* The stream thus denominated, flows near the city of Schiraz. Its waters are uncommonly pure and limpid, and its banks swarded with the finest verdure. Its praises are celebrated by Hafez, in an animated song, which Sir W. Jones has admirably translated:—

> Boy, let yon liquid ruby flow,
> And bid thy pensive heart be glad,
> Whate'er the frowning zealots say:
> Tell them, their Eden cannot shew
> A stream so clear as Rocnabad,
> A bower so sweet as Mosella.

[William Jones, "A Persian Song of Hafiz," in *Poems Consisting Chiefly of Translations from the Asiatick Languages* (London: Elmsly, 1772). Ed.]

Mosella was an oratory on the banks of Rocnabad.

Page 105—*Moullahs.* Those amongst the Mahometans who were bred to the law, had this title; and the judges of cities and provinces were taken from their order.

Page 105—*the sacred Cahaba.* That part of the temple at Mecca which is chiefly revered, and, indeed, gives a sanctity to the rest, is a square stone building, the length of which, from north to south, is twenty-four cubits; and its breadth, from east to west, twenty-three. The door is on the east side, and stands about four cubits from the ground, the floor being level with the threshold. The Cahaba has a double roof, supported internally by three octangular pillars of aloes-wood; between which, on a bar of iron, hangs a row of silver lamps. The outside is covered with rich black damask, adorned with an embroidered band of gold. This hanging, which is changed every year, was formerly sent by the caliphs. *Sale's Preliminary Discourse*, p. 152.

Page 107—*regale these pious poor souls with my good wine from Schiraz.* The prohibition of wine in the Koran is so rigidly observed by the conscientious, especially if they have performed the pilgrimage to Mecca, that they deem it sinful to press grapes for the purpose of making it, and even to use the money arising from its sale. *Chardin*, *Voy. de Perse*, tom. II. p. 212.—*Schiraz* was famous in the East, for its wines of different sorts, but particularly for its red, which was esteemed more highly than even the white wine of *Kismische.*

Page 108—*the most stately tulips of the East.* The tulip is a flower of eastern growth, and there held in great estimation. Thus, in an ode of Mesihi: "The edge of the bower is filled with the light of Ahmed: among the plants, the fortunate *tulips* represent his companions."

Page 108—*certain cages of ladies.* There are many passages of the Moallakat in which these *cages* are fully described. Thus, in the poem of Lebeid:—

> How were thy tender affections raised, when the damsels of the tribe departed; when they hid themselves in carriages of cotton, like antelopes in their lair, and the tents as they were struck gave piercing sound!
>
> They were concealed in vehicles, whose sides were well covered with awnings and carpets, with fine-spun curtains and pictured veils.

Again, Zohair:—

> They are mounted in carriages covered with costly awnings, and with rose-coloured veils, the lining of which have the hue of crimson andem-wood.
> —*Moallakat, by Sir W. Jones*, p. 46. 35.

[William Jones, *The Moallakat* (London: Elmsly, 1782). Ed.]

See also Lady M. W. Montague, Let. xxvi.[a] [Lady Mary Wortley Montagu's "Turkish Embassy Letters" were first printed in *Letters . . . Written during Her Travels in Europe, Asia, and Africa* (London: Becket and de Hondt, 1763). Ed.]

Page 109—*the locusts were heard from the thickets, on the plain of Catoul.* These insects are of the same species with the τεττιζ of the Greeks, and the *cicada* of the Latins. The locusts are mentioned in Pliny, b. II. 29. They were so called from *loco usto*, because the havoc they made wherever they passed left behind the appearance of a place desolated by fire. How could then the commentators of Vathek say that they are called *locusts*, from their having been so denominated by the first English settlers in America?

Page 110 — *Vathek—with two little pages.*

> All the pages of the seraglio are sons of Christians made slaves in time of war, in their most tender age. The incursions of robbers in the confines of Circassia, afford the means of supplying the seraglio, even in times of peace.
> —*Habesci's State of the Ottoman Empire*, p. 157.

That the pages here mentioned were *Circassians*, appears from the description of their complexion:—*more fair than the enamel of Franguistan.*

Page 110—*Confectioners and cooks.* What their precise number might have been in Vathek's establishment, it is not now easy to determine; but, in the household of the present Grand Seignor, there are not fewer than a hundred and ninety. *Habesci's State*, p. 145.

Page 110—*torches were lighted, &c.* Mr. Marsden relates, in his *History of Sumatra*, that tigers prove most fatal and destructive enemies to the inhabitants, particularly in their journies; and adds, that the numbers annually slain by those rapacious tyrants of the woods, is almost incredible. As these tremendous enemies are alarmed at the appearance of fire, it is usual for the natives to carry a splendid kind of torch, chiefly to frighten them; and, also, to make a blaze with wood, in different parts, round their villages, p. 149.

Page 111—*One of the forests of cedar, that bordered their way, took fire.* Accidents of this kind, in Persia, are not unfrequent.

> It was an ancient practice with the kings and great men to set fire to large bunches of dry combustibles, fastened round wild beasts and birds, which being then let loose, naturally fled to the woods for shelter, and caused destructive conflagrations.
> —*Richardson's Dissertation*, p. 185.

Page 111—*hath seen some part of our bodies; and, what is worse, our very faces.* "I was informed," writes Dr. Cooke, "that the Persian women, in general, would sooner expose to public view any part of their bodies than their faces." *Voyages and Travels*, vol. II. p. 443.

PAGE 112—*cakes baked in silver ovens for his royal mouth*. Portable ovens were a part of the furniture of eastern travellers. St. Jerom[e] (on Lament. v. 10) hath particularly described them. The Caliph's were of the same kind, only substituting silver for brass. Dr. Pocock[e] mentions his having been entertained in an Arabian camp with cakes baked for him. In what the peculiarity of the royal bread consisted, it is not easy to determine; but, in one of the Arabian Tales, a woman, to gratify her utmost desire, wishes to become the wife of the sultan's baker; assigning for the reason, that she might have her fill of that bread, which is called the sultan's. Vol. IV. p. 269.

PAGE 112—*vases of snow; and grapes from the banks of the Tigris*. It was customary in eastern climates, and especially in the sultry season, to carry, when journeying, supplies of snow. These *aestivae nives* (as Mamertinus styles them) being put into separate vases, were, by that means, better kept from the air, as no more was opened at once than might suffice for immediate use. To preserve the whole from solution, the vessels that contained it were secured in packages of straw. *Gesta Dei*, p. 1098.—Vathek's ancestor, the Caliph Mahadi, in the pilgrimage to Mecca, which he undertook from ostentation rather than devotion, loaded upon camels so prodigious a quantity as was not only sufficient for himself and his attendants, amidst the burning sands of Arabia; but, also, to preserve, in their natural freshness, the various fruits he took with him, and to ice all their drink whilst he staid at Mecca: the greater part of whose inhabitants had never seen snow till then. *Anecdotes Arabes*, p. 326.

PAGE 112—*horrible Kaf*. This mountain, which, in reality, is no other than Caucasus, was supposed to surround the earth, like a ring encompassing a finger. The sun was believed to rise from one of its eminences, (as over Oeta, by the Latin poets) and to set on the opposite; whence, *from Kaf to Kaf*, signified from one extremity of the earth to the other. The fabulous historians of the East affirm, that this mountain was founded upon a stone, called *sakhrat*, one grain of which, according to Lokman, would enable the possessor to work wonders. This stone is further described as the pivot of the earth; and said to be one vast emerald, from the refraction of whose beams, the heavens derive their azure. It is added, that whenever God would excite an earthquake, he commands the stone to move one of its fibres, (which supply in it the office of nerves) and, that being moved, the part of the earth connected with it, quakes, is convulsed, and sometimes expands. Such is the philosophy of the Koran!—

The Tarikh Tabari, written in Persian, analagous to the same tradition, relates, that, were it not for this emerald, the earth would be liable to perpetual commotions and unfit for the abode of mankind.

To arrive at the Kaf, a vast region,

> Far from the sun and summer-gale, must be traversed. Over this dark and cheerless desart, the way is inextricable, without the direction of su-

pernatural guidance. Here the dives or giants were confined after their defeat by the first heroes of the human race; and here, also, the peries, or faeries, are supposed in ordinary to reside. Sukrage, the giant, was King of Kaf, and had Rucail, one of the children of Adam, for his prime minister. The giant Argenk, likewise, from the time that Tahamurah made war upon him, reigned here, and reared a superb palace in the city of Aherman, with galleries, on whose walls were painted the creatures that inhabited the world prior to the formation of Adam. *D'Herbelot*, p. 230, &c. &c.

PAGE 112—*the simurgh*. That wonderful bird of the East, concerning which so many marvels are told, was not only endowed with reason, but possessed also the knowledge of every language. Hence it may be concluded to have been a dive in a borrowed form. This creature relates of itself that it had seen the great revolution of seven thousand years, twelve times commence and close; and that, in its duration, the world had been seven times void of inhabitants, and as often replenished. The simurgh is represented as a great friend to the race of Adam, and not less inimical to the dives. Tahamurath and Aherman were apprised by its predictions of all that was destined to befal them, and from it they obtained the promise of assistance in every undertaking. Armed with the buckler of Gian Ben Gian, Tahamurath was borne by it through the air, over the dark desart, to Kaf. From its bosom his helmet was crested with plumes, which the most renowned warriors have ever since worn. In every conflict the simurgh was invulnerable, and the heroes it favoured never failed of success. Though possessed of power sufficient to exterminate its foes, yet the exertion of that power was supposed to be forbidden.—Sadi, a serious author, gives it as an instance of the universality of Providence, that the simurgh, notwithstanding its immense bulk, is at no loss for sustenance on the mountain of Kaf.

PAGE 113—*afrits*. These were a kind of Medusae, or Lamiae, supposed to be the most terrible and cruel of all the orders of the dives. *D'Herbelot*, p. 66.

PAGE 113—*Tablets fraught with preternatural qualities.* Mr. Richardson observes, "that in the East, men of rank in general carried with them pocket astronomical tables, which they consulted on every affair of moment." These tablets, however, were of the *magical* kind; and such as often occur in works of romance. Thus, in Boiardo, Orlando receives, from the father of the youth he had rescued, "a book that would solve all doubts:" and, in Ariosto, Logistilla bestows upon Astolpho a similar directory. [Refers to two Italian epic romances, Matteo Maria Boiardo's *Orlando Innamorato* (1487) and Ludovico Ariosto's *Orlando Furioso* (1532). ED.]

PAGE 113—*dwarfs*. Such unfortunate beings, as are thus "curtailed of fair proportion," have been, for ages, an appendage of Eastern grandeur. One part of their office consists in the instruction of the pages, but their principal duty is the amusement of their master. If a dwarf happen to be a mute, he is much esteemed; but if he be also an eunuch, he is regarded as a prodigy; and no pains or expense are spared to obtain him. Habesci's State of the Ottoman Empire, p. 164, &c.

PAGE 113—*A small spring supplies us with water for the abdest, and we daily repeat prayers, &c.* Amongst the indispensable rules of the Mahometan faith, ablution is one of the chief. This rite is divided into three kinds. The first, performed before prayers, is called *abdest.* It begins with washing both hands, and repeating these words:—"Praised be Alla, who created clean water, and gave it the virtue to purify: he also hath rendered our faith conspicuous." This done, water is taken in the right hand thrice, and the mouth being washed, the worshipper subjoins:—"I pray thee, O Lord, to let me taste of that water, which thou hast given to thy Prophet Mahomet in paradise, more fragrant than musk, whiter than milk, sweeter than honey: and which has the power to quench for ever, the thirst of him that drinks it." This petition is accompanied with sniffing a little water into the nose; the face is then three times washed, and behind the ears; after which, water is taken with both hands, beginning with the right, and thrown to the elbow. The washing of the crown next follows, and the apertures of the ear with the thumbs: afterward the neck with all the fingers; and, finally, the feet. In this last operation, it is held sufficient to wet the sandal only. At each ceremonial a suitable petition is offered, and the whole concludes with this: "Hold me up firmly, O Lord! and suffer not my foot to slip, that I may not fall from the bridge into hell." Nothing can be more exemplary than the attention with which these rites are performed. If an involuntary cough or sneeze interrupt them, the whole service is begun anew, and that as often as it happens. *Habesci*, p. 91, &c.

PAGE 113—*the bells of a cafila.* A cafila, or caravan, according to Pitts, is divided into distinct companies, at the head of which an officer, or person of distinction, is carried in a kind of horse litter, and followed by a sumpter camel, loaded with his treasure. This camel hath a bell fastened to either side, the sound of which may be heard at a considerable distance. Others have bells on their necks and their legs, to solace them when drooping with heat and fatigue.—Inatulla also, in his tales, hath a similar reference:—"the bells of the cafila may be rung in the thirsty desart." vol. II. p. 15. These small bells were known at Rome from the earliest times, and called from their sounds *tintinnabulum.* Phaedrus gives us a lively description of the mule carrying the fiscal monies; *clarumque collo jactans tintinnabulum.* Book II. fabl. vii. ["And jingles the clear-toned bell on his neck," Phaedrus, *Fables* 2.7. ED.]

PAGE 113—*Deggial.* This word signifies properly a liar and impostor, but is applied, by Mahometan writers, to their *Antichrist.* He is described as having but one eye and eye-brow, and on his forehead the radicals of *cafer* or *infidel* are said to be impressed. According to the traditions of the faithful, his first appearance will be between Irak and Syria, mounted on an ass. Seventy thousand Jews from Ispahan are expected to follow him. His continuance on earth is to be forty days. All places are to be destroyed by him and his emissaries, except *Mecca* or *Medina*; which will be protected by angels from the general overthrow. At last, however, he will be slain by Jesus, who is to encounter him at the gate of Lud. *D'Herbelot*, p. 282. *Sale's Prelim. Disc.* p. 106.

PAGE 114—*sugar*. Dr. Pocock[e] mentions the sugar-cane as a great des[s]ert in Egypt; and adds, that, besides coarse loaf sugar and sugar candy, it yields a third sort, remarkably fine, which is sent to the Grand Seignor, and prepared only for himself. *Travels*, vol. 1. p. 183. 204. The jeweller's son, in the story of the third Calender, desires the prince to fetch some *melon* and *sugar*, that he might refresh himself with them. *Arab. Nights*, vol. I. p. 159.

PAGE 114—*red characters*. The laws of Draco are recorded by Plutarch, in his life of Solon, to have been written in blood. If more were meant by this expression, than that those laws were of a sanguinary nature, they will furnish the earliest instance of the use of *red characters*; which were afterwards considered as appropriate to supreme authority, and employed to denounce some requisition or threatening designed to strike terror.

PAGE 114—*thy body shall be spit upon*. There was no mark of contempt amongst the Easterns so ignominious as this. *Arab. Nights* vol. I. p. 115. Vol. IV. p. 275.

PAGE 114—*bats will nestle in thy belly*. Bats, in those countries, were very abundant; and, both from their numbers and size, held in abhorrence. See what is related of them by Thevenot, Part I. p. 132, 3. *Egmont and Hayman*, vol. II. p. 87, and other travellers in the East.

PAGE 115—*the Bismillah*. This word (which is prefixed to every chapter of the Koran, except the ninth) signifies, "in the name of the most merciful God."—It became not the initiatory formula of prayer, till the time of Moez the Fatimite. *D'Herbelot*, p. 326.

PAGE 116—*a magnificent tecth*. This kind of *moving throne*, though more common, at present, than in the days of Vathek, is still confined to persons of the highest rank.

PAGE 116—*baths of rose water*. The use of perfumed waters for the purpose of bathing is of an early origin in the East, where every odoriferous plant breathes a richer fragrance than is known to our more humid climates. The rose which yields this lotion is, according to Hasselquist, of a beautiful pale bluish colour, double, large as a man's fist, and more exquisite in scent than any other species. The quantities of this water distilled annually at Fajhum, and carried to distant countries, is immense. The mode of conveying it is in vessels of copper, coated with wax. *Voyag*. p. 248.

PAGE 116—*lamb à la crême*. No dish amongst the Easterns was more generally admired. The Caliph Abdolmelek, at a splendid entertainment, to which whoever came was welcome, asked Amrou, the son of Hareth, what kind of meat he preferred to all others. The old man answered: "An ass's neck, well seasoned and roasted."—"But what say you," replied the Caliph, "to the leg or shoulder of a LAMB *à la crême*?" and added, "How sweetly we live if a shadow would last!" *M. S. Laud. Numb. 161. A. Ockley's Hist. of the Saracens*, vol. II. p. 277.

PAGE 116—*made the dwarfs dance against their will.* Ali Chelebi al Moufti, in a treatise on the subject, held that dancing, after the example of the derviches, who made it a part of their devotion, was allowable. But in this opinion he was deemed to be heterodox; for Mahometans, in general, place dancing amongst the things that are forbidden. *D'Herbelot,* p.98.

PAGE 116—*durst not refuse the commander of the faithful.* The mandates of Oriental potentates have ever been accounted irresistible. Hence the submission of these devotees to the will of the Caliph. *Esther* i. 19. *Daniel* vi. 8. *Ludeke Expos. brevis,* p. 60.

PAGE 116—*properly lubricated with the balm of Mecca.* Unguents, for reasons sufficiently obvious, have been of general use in hot climates. According to Pliny, "at the time of the Trojan war, they consisted of oils perfumed with the odours of flowers, and, chiefly, of roses."—Hasselquist speaks of oil, impregnated with the tuberose and jessamine; but the unguent here mentioned was preferred to every other. Lady M. W. Montagu, desirous to try its effects, seems to have suffered materially from having improperly applied it.

PAGE 117—*black eunuchs, sabre in hand.* In this manner the apartments of the ladies were constantly guarded. Thus, in the story of the enchanted horse, Firouz Schah, traversing a strange palace by night, entered a room, "and, by the light of a lanthorn, saw that the persons he had heard snoring, were black eunuchs with naked sabres by them; which was enough to inform him that this was the guard-chamber of some queen or princess." *Arabian Nights,* vol. IV. p. 189.

PAGE 117—*to let down the great swing.* The swing was an exercise much used in the apartments of the Eastern ladies, and not only contributed to their amusement, but also to their health. *Tales of Inatulla,* vol. I. p. 259.

PAGE 118—*melodious Philomel, I am thy rose.* The passion of the nightingale for the rose is celebrated over all the East. Thus, Meshii, as translated by Sir W. Jones: [Jones, "A Turkish Ode of Mesihi," in *Poems Consisting Chiefly of Translations.* ED.]

> Come, charming maid, and hear thy poet sing,
> Thyself the rose, and he the bird of Spring:
> Love bids him sing, and Love will be obey'd,
> Be gay: too soon the flowers of Spring will fade.

PAGE 118—*oil spilt in breaking the lamps.* It appears from Thevenot, that illuminations were usual on the arrival of a stranger, and he mentions, on an occasion of this sort, two hundred lamps being lighted. The quantity of oil, therefore, spilt on the margin of the bath, may be easily accounted for, from this custom.

PAGE 119—*calenders.* These were a sort of men amongst the Mahometans, who abandoned father and mother, wife and children, relations and possessions, to wander through the world, under a pretence of religion, entirely subsisting on the fortuitous bounty of those they had the address to dupe. *D'Herbelot, Suppl.* p. 204. [*Bibliothèque Orientale . . . Par Messieurs C. Visdelou et A. Galand* (Maastricht: Defour, 1780), published as a supplement to D'Herbelot. Ed.]

Page 119—*santons.* A body of religionists who were also called *abdals,* and pretended to be inspired with the most enthusiastic raptures of divine love. They were regarded by the vulgar as *saints. Olearius,* tom. I. p. 971. *D'Herbelot,* p. 5.

Page 119—*derviches.* The term *dervich* signifies a *poor man,* and is the general appellation by which a Mahometan monk is named. There are, however, discriminations that distinguish this class from the others already mentioned. They are bound by no vow of poverty, they abstained not from marriage, and, whenever disposed, they may relinquish both their blue shirt and profession. *D'Herbelot, Suppl.* 214.—It is observable that these different orders, though not established till the reign of Nasser al Samani, are not withstanding mentioned by our author as coeval with Vathek, and by the author of the Arabian Nights, as existing in the days of Haroun al Raschid: so that the Arabian fabulists appear as inattentive to chronological exactness in points of this sort, as our immortal dramatist himself.

Page 119—*Bramins.* These constitute the principal caste of the Indians, according to whose doctrine *Brahma,* from whom they are called, is the first of the three created beings, by whom the world was made. This Brahma is said to have communicated to the Indians four books, in which all the sciences and ceremonies of their religion are comprized. The word Brahma, in the Indian language, signifies *pervading all things:* The Brahmins lead a life of most rigid abstinence, refraining not only from the use, but even the touch, of animal food; and are equally exemplary for their contempt of pleasures and devotion to philosophy and religion. *D'Herbelot,* p. 212. *Bruckeri Hist. Philosoph.* tom. I. p. 194.

Page 119—*faquirs.* This sect are a kind of religious anchorets, who spend their whole lives in the severest austerities and mortification. It is almost impossible for the imagination to form an extravagance that has not been practised by some of them, to torment themselves. As their reputation for sanctity rises in proportion to their sufferings, those amongst them are reverenced the most, who are most ingenious in the invention of tortures, and persevering in enduring them. Hence some have persisted in sitting or standing for years together in one unvaried posture; supporting an almost intolerable burden; dragging the most cumbrous chains; exposing their naked bodies to the scorching sun, and hanging with the head downward before the fiercest fires. *Relig. Ceremon.* vol. III. p. 264, &c. *White's Sermons,* p. 504.

Page 120—*some that cherished vermin.* In this attachment they were not singular. The Emperor Julian not only discovered the same partiality, but celebrated, with visible complacency, the shaggy and *populous* beard, which he fondly cherished; and even "The Historian of the Roman Empire," affirms "that the little animal is a beast familiar to man, and signifies love." Vol. II. p. 343.

PAGE 120—*Visnow and Ixhora.* Two deities of the Hindoos. The traditions of their votaries are, probably, allegorical; but without a key to disclose their mystic import, they are little better than senseless jargon; and, with the key, downright nonsense.

PAGE 120—*talapoins.* This order, which abounds in Siam, Laos, Pegu, and other countries, consists of different classes, and both sexes, but chiefly of men. *Relig. Ceremon.* vol. IV. p. 62, &c.

PAGE 120—*objects of pity were sure to swarm around him.* Ludeke mentions the practice of bringing those who were suffering under any calamity, or had lost the use of their limbs, &c. into public, for the purpose of exciting compassion. On an occasion, therefore, of this sort, when Fakreddin, like a pious Mussulman, was publicly to distribute his alms, and the commander of the faithful to make his appearance, such an assemblage might well be expected. The Eastern custom of regaling a convention of this kind is of great antiquity, as is evident from the parable of the king, in the Gospels, who entertained the maimed, the lame, and the blind; nor was it discontinued when Dr. Pocock[e] visited the East. Vol. I. p. 182.

PAGE 121—*small plates of abominations.* The Koran hath established several distinctions relative to different kinds of food, in imitation of the Jewish prescriptions; and many Mahometans are so scrupulous as not to touch the flesh of any animal over which, *in articulo mortis* [at the moment of death] the butcher had omitted to pronounce the *Bismillah. Relig. Cerem.* vol. VII. p. 110.

PAGE 121—*Sinai.* This mountain is deemed by Mahometans the noblest of all others, and even regarded with the highest veneration, because the divine law was promulgated from it. *D'Herbelot*, p. 812.

PAGE 121—*Peries.* The word *Peri*, in the Persian language, signifies that beautiful race of creatures which constitutes the link between angels and men.—*See note to page* 160.

PAGE 122—*butterflies of Cachemire.* The same insects are celebrated in an unpublished poem of Mesihi. Sir Anthony Shirley relates, that it was customary in Persia "to hawke after butterflies with sparrows, made to that use, and stares."—It is, perhaps, to this amusement that our Author alludes in the context.

PAGE 123—*Megnoun and Leilah.* These personages are esteemed amongst the Arabians as the most beautiful, chaste, and impassioned of lovers; and their amours have been celebrated with all the charms of verse in every Oriental language. The Mahometans regard them, and the poetical records of their love, in the same light as the Bridegroom and Spouse, and the Song of Songs are regarded by the Jews. *D'Herbelot*, p. 573.

PAGE 123—*dart the lance in the chace.* Throwing the lance was a favourite pastime with the young Arabians; and so expert were they in this practice (which prepared them for the mightier conflicts, both of the chace and war) that they could bear off a ring on the points of their javelins. *Richardson's Dissertat.* p. 198, 281.

PAGE 123—*The two brothers had mutually engaged their children to each other.* Contracts of this nature were frequent amongst the Arabians. Another instance occurs in the Story of Noureddin Ali and Benreddin Hassan.

PAGE 123—*Nouronihar loved her cousin, more than her own beautiful eyes.* This mode of expression not only occurs in the sacred writers, but also in the Greek and Roman. Thus Catullus says:

Quem plus illa oculis suis amabat.

[Whom she loved more than her own eyes
—Catullus, *Poems* 3.5.]

PAGE 123—*the same long languishing looks.* So Ariosto:

———negri occhi,———
Pietosi a riguardare, a mover parchi.

[———dark eyes,———
Merciful in looking, sparing in movement.
—Ludovico Ariosto, *Orlando Furioso* 7 st. 12.]

PAGE 123—*Shaddukian and Ambreabad.* These were two cities of the Peries, in the imaginary region of *Ginnistan*, the former signifies *pleasure* and *desire*, the latter *the city of Ambergris. See Richardson's Dissertat*, p. 169.

PAGE 125—*a spoon of cocknos.* The cocknos is a bird whose beak is much esteemed for its beautiful polish, and sometimes used as a spoon. Thus, in the History of Atalmulck and Zelica Begum, it was employed for a similar purpose:—"Zelica having called for refreshment, six old slaves instantly brought in and distributed *Mahramas*, and then served about in a great bason of Martabam, a salad *made of herbs of various kinds, citron juice, and the pith of cucumbers.* They served it first to the Princess in a *cocknos' beak*: she took a beak of the salad, eat it, and gave another to the next slave that sat by her on her right hand; which slave did as her mistress had done."

PAGE 126—*Goules.* Goul, or *ghul*, in Arabic, signifies any terrifying object, which deprives people of the use of their senses. Hence it became the appellative of that species of monster which was supposed to haunt forests, cemeteries, and other lonely places; and believed not only to tear in pieces the living, but to dig up and devour the dead. *Richardson's Dissert.* p. 174. 274.

PAGE 126—*feathers of the heron, all sparkling with carbuncles.* Panaches of this kind are amongst the attributes of Eastern royalty. *Tales of Inatulla*, vol. ii. p. 205.

PAGE 127—*the carbuncle of Giamschid.* This mighty potentate was the fourth sovereign of the dynasty of the Pischadians, and brother or nephew to Tahamurath. His proper name was *giam* or *gem*, and *sched*, which in the language of the ancient Persians denominated the sun: an addition, ascribed by some to the majesty of his person, and by others to the splendour of his actions. One of the most magnificent monuments of his reign was the city of Istakhar, of which Tahamurath had laid the foundations. This city, at present called *Gihil-*, or *Tchil-minar*, from the forty columns reared in it by Homai, or (according to our author and others) by Soliman Ben Daoud, was known to the Greeks by the name of Persepolis: and there is still extant in the East a tradition, that, when Alexander burnt the edifices of the Persian kings, seven stupendous structures of Giamschid were consumed with his palace.

PAGE 127—*the torches were extinguished.* To the union here prefigured, the following lines may be applied:

> Non *Hymenaeus* adest illi, non gratia lecto;
> Eumenides tenuere faces de funere raptas:
> Eumenides stravere torum.

> [Hymen was not present, nor the Graces at that wedding:
> The Eumenides (Furies) held torches stolen from a funeral,
> The Eumenides spread the bridal couch.
> —Ovid, *Metamorphoses* 6.429–31.]

PAGE 127—*She clapped her hands.* This was the ordinary method in the East of calling the attendants in waiting. See Arabian Nights, vol. I. p. 5. 106. 193, &c.

PAGE 130—*Funeral vestments were prepared; their bodies washed, &c.* The rites here practised had obtained from the earliest ages. Most of them may be found in Homer and the other poets of Greece. Lucian describes the dead in his time as washed, perfumed, vested, and crowned, with the flowers most in season; or, according to other writers, those in particular which the deceased were wont to prefer.

PAGE 130—*all instruments of music were broken.* Thus, in the Arabian Nights: "Haroun al Raschid wept over Schemselnihar, and, before he left the room, ordered all the musical instruments to be broken." Vol. II. p. 196.

PAGE 130—*Imans began to recite their prayers.* An iman is the principal priest of a mosque. It was the office of the imans to precede the bier, praying as the procession moved on. *Relig. Ceremon.* vol. VII. p. 117.

PAGE 132—*the angel of death had opened the portal of some other world.* The name of this exterminating angel is *Azrael*, and his office is to conduct the dead to the abode assigned them; which is said by some to be near the place of their interment. Such was the office of Mercury in the Grecian Mythology. *Sale's Prelim. Disc.* p. 101. *Hyde in notis ad Bobov.* p. 19. *R. Elias, in Tishbi. Buxtorf Synag. Jud. et Lexic. Talmud. Homer. Odyss.*

PAGE 132—*Monker and Nekir.* These are two black angels of a tremendous appearance, who examine the departed on the subject of his faith: by whom, if he give not a satisfactory account, he is sure to be cudgelled with maces of red-hot iron, and tormented more variously than words can describe. *Relig. Ceremon.* vol. VII. p. 59. 68. 118. vol. V. p. 290. *Sale's Prelim. Disc.* p. 101.

PAGE 132—*the fatal bridge.* This bridge, called in Arabick *al Siral*, and said to extend over the infernal gulph, is represented as narrower than a spider's web, and sharper than the edge of a sword. Yet the paradise of Mahomet can be entered by no other avenue. Those indeed who have behaved well need not be alarmed; mixed characters will find it difficult; but the wicked soon miss their standing, and plunge headlong into the abyss. *Pocock in Port. Mos.* p. 282, &c.

PAGE 132—*a certain series of years.* According to the tradition from the Prophet, not less than nine hundred, nor more than seven thousand.

PAGE 132—*the sacred camel.* It was an article of the Mahometan creed, that all animals would be raised again, and some of them admitted into paradise. The animal here mentioned appears to have been one of those *white-winged* camels *caparisoned with gold*, which Ali affirmed would be provided to convey the faithful. *Relig. Ceremon.* vol. VII. p. 70. *Sale's Prelim. Disc.* p. 112. *Al Janheri. Ebno'l Athir*, &c.

PAGE 133—*the Caliph presented himself to the emir in a new light.* The propensity of a vicious person, in affliction, to seek consolation from the ceremonies of religion, is an exquisite trait in the character of Vathek.

PAGE 137—*wine hoarded up in bottles, prior to the birth of Mahomet.* The prohibition of wine by the Prophet materially diminished its consumption, within the limits of his own dominions. Hence a reserve of it might be expected, of the age here specified. The custom of hoarding wine was not unknown to the Persians, though not so often practised by them, as by the Greeks and the Romans.

"I purchase" (says Lebeid) "the old liquor, at a dear rate, in dark leathern bottles, long reposited; or in casks black with pitch, whose seals I break, and then fill the cheerful goblet." *Moallakat*, p. 53.

PAGE 137—*excavated ovens in the rock.* As substitutes for the portable ovens, which were lost.

PAGE 139—*the confines of some cemetery.* Places of interment in the East were commonly situated in scenes of solitude. We read of one in the history of the first calender, abounding with so many monuments, that four days were successively spent in it without the inquirer being able to find the tomb he looked for: and, from the story of Ganem, it appears that the doors of these cemeteries were often left open. *Arabian Nights*, vol. II. p. 112.

PAGE 141—*a Myrabolan comfit.* The invention of this confection is attributed by M. Cardonne to Avicenna, but there is abundant reason, exclusive of our author's authority, to suppose it of a much earlier origin. Both the Latins and Greeks were acquainted with the balsam, and the tree that produced it was indigenous in various parts of Arabia.

PAGE 142—*blue fishes.* Fishes of the same colour are mentioned in the Arabian Nights; and, like these, were endowed with the gift of speech.

PAGE 144—*astrolabes.* The mention of the astrolabe may be deemed incompatible, at first view, with chronological exactness, as there is no instance of any being constructed by a Mussulman, till after the time of Vathek. It may, however, be remarked, to go no higher, that Sinesius, bishop of Ptolemais, invented one in the fifth century; and that Carathis was not only herself a Greek, but also cultivated those sciences which the good Mussulmans of her time all held in abhorrence. *Bailly, Hist. de l' Astronom. Moderne,* tom. I. p. 563. 573.

PAGE 145—*On the banks of the stream, hives and oratories.* The bee is an insect held in high veneration amongst the Mahometans, it being pointed out in the Koran, "for a sign unto the people that understand." It has been said, in the same sense: "Go to the ant, thou sluggard," *Prov.* vi. 6. The santons, therefore, who inhabit the fertile banks of Rocnabad, are not less famous for their hives than their oratories. *D'Herbelot,* p. 717.

PAGE 146—*Shieks, cadis.* Shieks are the chiefs of the societies of derviches: cadis are the magistrates of a town or city.

PAGE 146—*Asses in bridles of riband inscribed from the Koran.* As the judges of Israel in ancient days rode on white asses, so amongst the Mahometans, those that affect an extraordinary sanctity, use the same animal in preference to the horse. Sir John Chardin observed in various parts of the East, that their reins, as here represented, were of silk, with the name of God, or other inscriptions upon them. *Ludeke Expos. brevis,* p. 49. *Chardin's MS.* cited by Harmer.

PAGE 148—*Eblis.* D'Herbelot supposes this title to have been a corruption of the Greek *Διαβολος diabolos.* It was the appellation conferred by the Arabians upon the prince of the apostate angels, and appears more likely to originate from the Hebrew הבר, *hebel,* vanity, pride.—*See below the note* 152, *"creatures of clay."*

PAGE 148—*compensate for thy impieties by an exemplary life.* It is an established article of the Mussulman creed, that the actions of mankind are all weighed in a vast unerring balance, and the future condition of the agents determined according to the preponderance of evil or good. This fiction, which seems to have been borrowed from the Jews, had probably its origin in the figurative language of scripture. Thus, Psalm lxii. 9. Surely men of low degree are vanity, and men of high degree are a lie: to be laid in the balance, they are altogether lighter than vanity:—and, in Daniel, the sentence against the King of Babylon, inscribed on the wall: Thou art weighed in the balance, and found wanting.

PAGE 149—*Balkis.* This was the Arabian name of the Queen of Sheba, who went from the south to hear the wisdom and admire the glory of Solomon. The Koran represents her as a worshipper of fire. Solomon is said not only to have entertained her with the greatest magnificence, but also to have raised her to his bed and his throne. *Al Koran,* ch. XXVII. and *Sale's notes. D'Herbelot,* p. 182.

Page 152—*Ouranbad.* This monster is represented as a fierce flying hydra, and belongs to the same class with the *rakshe* whose ordinary food was serpents and dragons; the *soham*, which had the head of a horse, with four eyes, and the body of a flame-coloured dragon; the *syl*, a basilisk with a face resembling the human, but so tremendous that no mortal could bear to behold it; the *ejder*, and others. See these respective titles in Richardson's Persian, Arabic, and English Dictionary.

Page 152—*Creatures of clay.* Nothing could have been more appositely imagined than this compellation. Eblis, according to Arabian mythology, had suffered a degradation from his primeval rank, and was consigned to these regions, for having refused to worship Adam, in obedience to the supreme command: alledging in justification of his refusal, that himself had been formed of etherial fire, whilst Adam was only a creature of clay. *Al Koran*, c. 55, &c.

Page 152—*the fortress of Aherman.* In the mythology of the easterns, Aherman was accounted *the Demon of Discord.* The ancient Persian romances abound in descriptions of this fortress, in which the inferior demons assemble to receive the behests of their prince; and from whom they proceed to exercise their malice in every part of the world. *D'Herbelot*, p. 71.

Page 152—*the halls of Argenk.* The halls of this mighty dive, who reigned in the mountains of Kaf, contained the statues of the seventy-two Solimans, and the portraits of the various creatures subject to them; not one of which bore the slightest similitude to man. Some had many heads; others, many arms; and some consisted of many bodies. Their heads were all very extraordinary, some resembling the elephant's, the buffalo's and the boar's; whilst others were still more monstrous. *D'Herbelot*, p. 820. Some of the idols worshipped to this day in the Hindostan answer to this description.

Ariosto, who owes more to Arabian fable than his commentators have hitherto supposed, seems to have been no stranger to the halls of Argenk, when he described one of the fountains of Merlin:—

Era una delle fonti di Merlino
Delle quattro di Francia da lui fatte;
D'intorno cinta di bel marmo fino,
Lucido, e terso, e bianco piû che latte.
Quivi d' intaglio con lavor divino
Avea Merlino immagini ritratte.
Direste che spiravano, e se prive
Non fossero di voce, ch' eran vive.

Quivi una Bestia uscir della foresta
Parea di crudel vista, odiosa, e brutta,
Che avea le orecchie d'asino, e la testa
Di lupo, e i denti, e per gran fame asciutta;
Branche avea di leon; l'altro, che resta,
Tutto era volpe.

[It was one of the fountains of those four
That Merlin had constructed in France
Within a girdle of finest marble,
Lucid, and bright, and whiter than milk.
There, etched with divine skill,
Merlin had created images
That one would say could breathe,
And, were they not voiceless, had life.

There, a Beast emerged from the forest,
Looking wild in appearance, hateful and ugly:
It had the ears of an ass, and the head
And teeth of a wolf, lean and famished;
It had the claws of a lion; in all the rest besides
It was pure fox.
—Ariosto, *Orlando Furioso* 26 st. 30–31]

PAGE 153—*holding his right hand motionless on his heart.* Sandys observes, that the application of the right hand to the heart is the customary mode of eastern salutation; but the perseverance of the votaries of Eblis in this attitude, was intended to express their devotion to him both heart and hand.

PAGE 154—*In my life-time, I filled, &c.* This recital agrees perfectly with those in the Koran, and other Arabian legends.

PAGE 156—*Carathis on the back of an afrit.* The expedition of the afrit in fetching Carathis, is characteristic of this order of dives. We read in the Koran that another of the fraternity offered to bring the Queen of Saba's [Sheba's] throne to Solomon, before he could rise from his place, c. 27.

PAGE 157—*Glanced off in a whirl that rendered her invisible.* It was extremely proper to punish Carathis by a rite, and one of the principal characteristics of that science in which she so much delighted, and which was the primary cause of Vathek's perdition and of her own. The circle, the emblem of eternity, and the symbol of the sun, was held sacred in the most ancient ceremonies of incantations; and the whirling round deemed as a necessary operation in magical mysteries. Was not the name of the greatest enchantress in fabulous antiquity, Circe, derived from Κιϱκος, a circle, on account of her magical revolutions and of the circular appearance and motion of the sun her father? The fairies and elves used to arrange themselves in a ring on the grass; and even the augur, in the liturgy of the Romans, whirled round, to encompass the four cardinal points of the world. It is remarkable, that a derivative of the Arabic word (which corresponds to the Hebrew סהר and is interpreted *scindere secare se in orbem, inde notio circinandi, mox gyrandi et hinc à motu versatili, fascinavit, incantavit*) signifies, in the Koran, *the glimmering of twilight*; a sense deducible from the shapeless glimpses of objects, when hurried round with the velocity here described, and very applicable to the sudden disappearance of Carathis, who, like the stone in a sling, by the progressive and rapid increase of the circular motion, soon ceased to be perceptible. [The Latin phrase describes a process of meaning extension from the root word: "to rend (or) cut itself in a circle, thence the notion of forming into (or flying about in) a circle, then gyrating [or wheeling] and hence, from the revolving motion, (comes to signify) bewitched, enchanted." Ed.] Nothing can impress a greater awe upon the mind than does this passage in the original.

Page 158—*They at once lost the most precious gift of heaven—Hope.* It is a soothing reflection to the bulk of mankind, that the commonness of any blessing is the true test of its value. Hence, Hope is justly styled "the most precious of the gifts of heaven," because, as Thales long since observed—*όις αλλο μηδεν, αυτη παϱεςιν* [To whom nothing else (is present), she is present.]—it abides with those who are destitute of every other. Dante's inscription over the gate of hell was written in the same sense, and perhaps in allusion to the saying of the Grecian sage:—

Per me si va nella città dolente:
Per me si va nell' eterno dolore:
Per me si va tra la perduta gente.
Giustizia mosse 'l mio alto fattore:
Fecemi la divina potestate,
La somma sapienza, e 'l primo amore.
Dinanzi a me non fur cose create,
Se non eterne, ed io eterno duro:
Lasciate ogni speranza, voi che 'ntrate.
Canto III

[Through me one passes to the woeful city:
Through me one passes to eternal pain:
Through me one passes among the lost people.
Justice moved my great creator:
The divine power made me,
The highest wisdom, and the primal love.
Before me, nothing was created
Save eternal things, and eternally I last:
Abandon every hope, you who enter here.
—Dante Alighieri, *Inferno* 3.109]

Strongly impressed with this idea, and in order to complete his description of the infernal dungeon, Milton says,

——where——
———hope never comes
That comes to all.
—*Paradise L.* 1. 66

[John Milton, *Paradise Lost* 1.65–67; Milton's portrayal of Satan is echoed in Beckford's descriptions of both Vathek and Eblis, as well as in Byron's characterization of the Giaour. Ed.]

THE END

The Giaour

A Fragment of a Turkish Tale

George Gordon, Lord Byron

One fatal remembrance—one sorrow that throws
Its bleak shade alike o'er our joys and our woes—
To which Life nothing darker nor brighter can bring,
For which joy hath no balm—and affliction no sting.
—Moore[1]

[1]Thomas Moore, "As a beam o'er the face of the waters may glow" st. 2 (from *Irish Melodies*). [ED.]

TO

SAMUEL ROGERS, ESQ.

AS A SLIGHT BUT MOST SINCERE TOKEN

OF ADMIRATION OF HIS GENIUS;

RESPECT FOR HIS CHARACTER,

AND GRATITUDE FOR HIS FRIENDSHIP;

THIS PRODUCTION IS INSCRIBED BY

HIS OBLIGED AND AFFECTIONATE SERVANT,

BYRON

ADVERTISEMENT[2]

The tale which these disjointed fragments present, is founded upon circumstances now less common in the East than formerly; either because the ladies are more circumspect than in the "olden time"; or because the Christians have better fortune, or less enterprize. The story, when entire, contained the adventures of a female slave, who was thrown, in the Mussulman manner, into the sea for infidelity,[3] and avenged by a young Venetian, her lover, at the time the Seven Islands were possessed by the Republic of Venice, and soon after the Arnauts were beaten back from the Morea, which they had ravaged for some time subsequent to the Russian invasion. The desertion of the Mainotes, on being refused the plunder of Misitra, led to the abandonment of that enterprize, and to the desolation of the Morea, during which the cruelty exercised on all sides was unparalleled even in the annals of the faithful.

12th ed. London: Murray, 1814. (All footnotes to *The Giaour* are provided by the volume editor of this New Riverside Edition. Byron's original endnotes are reprinted with minor changes in format on pages 220–26 following the text of the poem. Lines of asterisks are Byron's, indicating gaps between the "disjointed fragments" that make up the poem.)

[2]Byron's Advertisement sets the action of the poem at a time of political and social turmoil in Greece and the Balkans. The Venetian Empire was virtually extinct, though Venice remained in possession of the Ionian Seven Islands (off the west coast of Greece) until 1797. Russia invaded the Morea or Peloponnesus (the peninsula that forms southern Greece) in 1770 but left it in 1794 to be "ravaged" by the Arnauts, that is, the Albanians. The Ottoman Empire was in decline, and local military chieftans like Hassan Pacha—perhaps the model for Byron's Hassan—had a good deal of autonomy, though nominally subordinate to the Ottoman Turks.

[3]Byron himself seems to have been involved in saving a "Turkish girl" from such a fate in Athens (see Byron, *Letters* 3:230).

No breath of air to break the wave
That rolls below the Athenian's grave,
That tomb[4a] which, gleaming o'er the cliff,
First greets the homeward-veering skiff,
High o'er the land he saved in vain—
When shall such hero live again?[5]

*　*　*　*　*

Fair clime! where every season smiles
Benignant o'er those blessed isles,
Which seen from far Colonna's height,
Make glad the heart that hails the sight,
And lend to loneliness delight.
There mildly dimpling—Ocean's cheek
Reflects the tints of many a peak
Caught by the laughing tides that lave
These Edens of the eastern wave;
And if at times a transient breeze
Break the blue chrystal of the seas,
Or sweep one blossom from the trees,
How welcome is each gentle air,
That wakes and wafts the odours there!
For there—the Rose o'er crag or vale,
Sultana of the Nightingale,[b]
The maid for whom his melody—
His thousand songs are heard on high,
Blooms blushing to her lover's tale;
His queen, the garden queen, his Rose,
Unbent by winds, unchill'd by snows,
Far from the winters of the west
By every breeze and season blest,
Returns the sweets by nature given
In softest incense back to heaven;
And grateful yields that smiling sky
Her fairest hue and fragrant sigh.
And many a summer flower is there,
And many a shade that love might share,

---

[4]To preserve their integrity, Byron's original notes (signalled by superscript letters rather than numerals) are included after the text, as they were in early editions of the poem.
[5]The hero is Themistocles, leader of the Athenian resistance to the Persian invasion of Greece led by Xerxes in 480–479 B.C., mentioned in Byron's note (a).

And many a grotto, meant for rest,
That holds the pirate for a guest;
Whose bark in sheltering cove below
Lurks for the passing peaceful prow,
Till the gay mariner's guitar[c]
Is heard, and seen the evening star;
Then stealing with the muffled oar,
Far shaded by the rocky shore,
Rush the night-prowlers on the prey,
And turn to groans his roundelay.
Strange—that where Nature lov'd to trace,
As if for Gods, a dwelling-place,
And every charm and grace hath mixed
Within the paradise she fixed—
There man, enamour'd of distress,
Should mar it into wilderness,
And trample, brute-like, o'er each flower
That tasks not one laborious hour;
Nor claims the culture of his hand
To bloom along the fairy land,
But springs as to preclude his care,
And sweetly woos him—but to spare!
Strange—that where all is peace beside
There passion riots in her pride,
And lust and rapine wildly reign,
To darken o'er the fair domain.
It is as though the fiends prevail'd
Against the seraphs they assail'd,
And fixed, on heavenly thrones, should dwell
The freed inheritors of hell—
So soft the scene, so form'd for joy,
So curst the tyrants that destroy!

He who hath bent him o'er the dead,
Ere the first day of death is fled;
The first dark day of nothingness,
The last of danger and distress;

---

bark: boat.
roundelay: song with a recurring refrain.
as though the fiends prevailed . . . : as though the devils (fallen angels) had won the War in Heaven depicted in John Milton's epic poem, *Paradise Lost* (1667).

(Before Decay's effacing fingers
Have swept the lines where beauty lingers)
And mark'd the mild angelic air—
The rapture of repose that's there—
The fixed yet tender traits that streak
The languor of the placid cheek,
And—but for that sad shrouded eye,
 That fires not—wins not—weeps not—now—
 And but for that chill changeless brow,
Where cold Obstruction's apathy[d]
 Appals the gazing mourner's heart,
 As if to him it could impart
 The doom he dreads, yet dwells upon—
 Yes—but for these and these alone,
 Some moments—ay—one treacherous hour,
 He still might doubt the tyrant's power,
 So fair—so calm—so softly seal'd
 The first—last look—by death reveal'd![e]
 Such is the aspect of this shore—
 'Tis Greece—but living Greece no more!
 So coldly sweet, so deadly fair,
 We start—for soul is wanting there.
 Hers is the loveliness in death,
 That parts not quite with parting breath;
 But beauty with that fearful bloom,
 That hue which haunts it to the tomb—
 Expression's last receding ray,
 A gilded halo hovering round decay,
 The farewell beam of Feeling past away!
Spark of that flame—perchance of heavenly birth—
Which gleams—but warms no more its cherish'd earth!

  Clime of the unforgotten brave!—
 Whose land from plain to mountain-cave
 Was Freedom's home or Glory's grave—
 Shrine of the mighty! can it be,
 That this is all remains of thee?
 Approach thou craven crouching slave—
 Say, is not this Thermopylae?

Thermopylae: site of heroic Greek resistance, under King Leonidas of Sparta, to the Persian invasion of Greece led by Xerxes. (See note 5.)

These waters blue that round you lave,
Oh servile offspring of the free—
Pronounce what sea, what shore is this?
The gulf, the rock of Salamis!
These scenes—their story not unknown—
Arise, and make again your own;
Snatch from the ashes of your sires
The embers of their former fires,
And he who in the strife expires
Will add to theirs a name of fear,
That Tyranny shall quake to hear,
And leave his sons a hope, a fame,
They too will rather die than shame;
For Freedom's battle once begun,
Bequeathed by bleeding Sire to Son,
Though baffled oft is ever won.
Bear witness, Greece, thy living page,
Attest it many a deathless age!
While kings in dusty darkness hid,
Have left a nameless pyramid,
Thy heroes—though the general doom
Hath swept the column from their tomb,
A mightier monument command,
The mountains of their native land!
There points thy Muse to stranger's eye,
The graves of those that cannot die!
'Twere long to tell, and sad to trace,
Each step from splendour to disgrace,
Enough—no foreign foe could quell
Thy soul, till from itself it fell,
Yes! Self-abasement pav'd the way
To vilain-bonds and despot-sway.

What can he tell who treads thy shore?
  No legend of thine olden time,
No theme on which the muse might soar,
High as thine own in days of yore,

Salamis: site of the great sea battle in which the Greeks defeated Xerxes's Persian fleet (480 B.C.).

When man was worthy of thy clime.
The hearts within thy valleys bred,
The fiery souls that might have led
Thy sons to deeds sublime;
Now crawl from cradle to the grave,
Slaves—nay, the bondsmen of a slave,[f]
And callous, save to crime;
Stain'd with each evil that pollutes
Mankind, where least above the brutes;
Without even savage virtue blest,
Without one free or valiant breast.
Still to the neighbouring ports they waft
Proverbial wiles, and ancient craft,
In this the subtle Greek is found,
For this, and this alone, renown'd.
In vain might Liberty invoke
The spirit to its bondage broke,
Or raise the neck that courts the yoke:
No more her sorrows I bewail,
Yet this will be a mournful tale,
And they who listen may believe,
Who heard it first had cause to grieve.

* * * * *

Far, dark, along the blue sea glancing,
The shadows of the rocks advancing,
Start on the fisher's eye like boat
Of island-pirate or Mainote,[6]
And fearful for his light caique
He shuns the near but doubtful creek,
Though worn and weary with his toil,
And cumber'd with his scaly spoil,
Slowly, yet strongly, plies the oar,
Till Port Leone's safer shore
Receives him by the lovely light
That best becomes an Eastern night.

* * * * *

---

caique: small boat.

[6]The Mainotes, from the peninsula of Maina (Mani) in southern Greece, were a fierce, warlike people known for piracy.

Who thundering comes on blackest steed?
With slacken'd bit and hoof of speed,
Beneath the clattering iron's sound
The cavern'd echoes wake around
In lash for lash, and bound for bound;
The foam that streaks the courser's side
Seems gather'd from the ocean-tide:
Though weary waves are sunk to rest,
There's none within his rider's breast,
And though to-morrow's tempest lower,
'Tis calmer than thy heart, young Giaour![g][7]
I know thee not, I loathe thy race,
But in thy lineaments I trace
What time shall strengthen, not efface;
Though young and pale, that sallow front
Is scath'd by fiery passion's brunt,
Though bent on earth thine evil eye
As meteor like thou glidest by,
Right well I view, and deem thee one
Whom Othman's sons[8] should slay or shun.

On—on he hastened—and he drew
My gaze of wonder as he flew:
Though like a demon of the night
He passed and vanished from my sight;
His aspect and his air impressed
A troubled memory on my breast;
And long upon my startled ear
Rung his dark courser's hoofs of fear.
He spurs his steed—he nears the steep,
That jutting shadows o'er the deep—
He winds around—he hurries by—
The rock relieves him from mine eye—
For well I ween unwelcome he
Whose glance is fixed on those that flee;

---

[7] Giaour, pronounced with a soft *g* to rhyme with *bower,* connotes an infidel or non-Muslim, here a Christian-born Venetian.

[8] Descendants of Osman, founder of the Ottoman Empire, that is, Turks. In contrast to the European narrator of lines 1–167, who laments the "sorrows" of Greece under Turkish "bondage," the speaker of lines 180–287, an internal narrator, brings a Muslim perspective to bear on the events he observes.

And not a star but shines too bright
On him who takes such timeless flight.
He wound along—but ere he passed
One glance he snatched—as if his last—
A moment checked his wheeling steed—
A moment breathed him from his speed—
A moment on his stirrup stood—
Why looks he o'er the olive wood?—
The crescent glimmers on the hill,
The Mosque's high lamps are quivering still;
Though too remote for sound to wake
In echoes of the far tophaike,[h]
The flashes of each joyous peal
Are seen to prove the Moslem's zeal.
To-night—set Rhamazani's sun—
To-night—the Bairam feast's begun—[9]
To-night—but who and what art thou
Of foreign garb and fearful brow?
And what are these to thine or thee,
That thou should'st either pause or flee?
He stood—some dread was on his face—
Soon Hatred settled in its place—
It rose not with the hasty flush
Of transient Anger's darkening blush,[10]
But pale as marble o'er the tomb,
Whose ghastly whiteness aids its gloom.
His brow was bent—his eye was glazed—
He raised his arm, and fiercely raised;
And sternly shook his hand on high,
As doubting to return or fly;—
Impatient of his flight delayed,
Here loud his raven charger neighed—
Down glanced that hand, and grasped his blade—
That sound had burst his waking dream,
As Slumber starts at owlet's scream.—
The spur hath lanced his courser's sides—
Away—away—for life he rides—

---

[9] Ramadan, a holy month of fasting and prayer in the Muslim calendar, ends with a day of feasting (Bairam) at the appearance of the new moon.

[10] In earlier editions, these lines read: "It rose not with the reddening flush / Of transient Anger's hasty blush."

Swift as the hurled on high jerreed,[i]
Springs to the touch his startled steed,
The rock is doubled—and the shore
Shakes with the clattering tramp no more—
The crag is won—no more is seen
His Christian crest and haughty mien.—
'Twas but an instant—he, restrained
That fiery barb so sternly reined—
'Twas but a moment that he stood,
Then sped as if by death pursued;
But in that instant, o'er his soul
Winters of Memory seemed to roll;
And gather in that drop of time
A life of pain, an age of crime.
O'er him who loves, or hates, or fears,
Such moment pours the grief of years—
What felt *he* then—at once opprest
By all that most distracts the breast?
That pause—which pondered o'er his fate,
Oh, who its dreary length shall date!
Though in Time's record nearly nought,
It was Eternity to Thought!
For infinite as boundless space
The thought that Conscience must embrace,
Which in itself can comprehend
Woe without name—or hope—or end.—

The hour is past, the Giaour is gone,
And did he fly or fall alone?
Woe to that hour he came or went,
The curse for Hassan's sin was sent
To turn a palace to a tomb;
He came, he went, like the Simoom,[j]
That harbinger of fate and gloom,
Beneath whose widely-wasting breath
The very cypress droops to death—
Dark tree—still sad, when others' grief is fled,
The only constant mourner o'er the dead!

---

mien: expression, air.
barb: horse of the Barbary breed.

The steed is vanished from the stall,
No serf is seen in Hassan's hall,
The lonely Spider's thin grey pall
Waves slowly widening o'er the wall;
The Bat builds in his Haram bower;
And in the fortress of his power
The Owl usurps the beacon-tower;
The wild-dog howls o'er the fountain's brim,
With baffled thirst, and famine, grim,
For the stream has shrunk from its marble bed,
Where the weeds and the desolate dust are spread.
'Twas sweet of yore to see it play
And chase the sultriness of day—
As springing high the silver dew
In whirls fantastically flew,
And flung luxurious coolness round
The air, and verdure o'er the ground.—
'Twas sweet, when cloudless stars were bright,
To view the wave of watery light,
And hear its melody by night.—
And oft had Hassan's Childhood played
Around the verge of that cascade;
And oft upon his mother's breast
That sound had harmonized his rest;
And oft had Hassan's Youth along
Its bank been sooth'd by Beauty's song;
And softer seemed each melting tone
Of Music mingled with its own.—
But ne'er shall Hassan's Age repose
Along the brink at Twilight's close—
The stream that filled that font is fled—
The blood that warmed his heart is shed!—
And here no more shall human voice
Be heard to rage—regret—rejoice—
The last sad note that swelled the gale
Was woman's wildest funeral wail—
That quenched in silence—all is still,
But the lattice that flaps when the wind is shrill—
Though raves the gust, and floods the rain,

Haram: harem (see *Vathek* 92 n. 15.)

No hand shall close its clasp again.
On desart sands 'twere joy to scan
The rudest steps of fellow man,
So here the very voice of Grief
Might wake an Echo like relief—
At least 'twould say, "all are not gone;
There lingers Life, though but in one—"
For many a gilded chamber's there,
Which Solitude might well forbear;
Within that dome as yet Decay
Hath slowly worked her cankering way—
But Gloom is gathered o'er the gate,
Nor there the Fakir's self will wait;
Nor there will wandering Dervise stay,[11]
For Bounty cheers not his delay;
Nor there will weary stranger halt
To bless the sacred "bread and salt."[k]
Alike must Wealth and Poverty
Pass heedless and unheeded by,
For Courtesy and Pity died
With Hassan on the mountain side.—
His roof—that refuge unto men—
Is Desolation's hungry den.—
The guest flies the hall, and the vassal from labour,
Since his turban was cleft by the infidel's sabre![l]

* * * * *

I hear the sound of coming feet,[12]
But not a voice mine ear to greet—
More near—each turban I can scan,
And silver-sheathed ataghan;[m]
The foremost of the band is seen
An Emir by his garb of green:[n]
"Ho! who art thou?"—"this low salam[o]
Replies of Moslem faith I am."
"The burthen ye so gently bear,
Seems one that claims your utmost care,

Emir: Arabic title for a prince, ruler, or commander.

[11] *Fakir* and *dervise* are alternate spellings of *faquir* and *dervish*. See Vathek 119 n. 31.
[12] Lines 352–87 are related by a Muslim boatman.

And, doubtless, holds some precious freight,
My humble bark would gladly wait."

"Thou speakest sooth, thy skiff unmoor,
And waft us from the silent shore;
Nay, leave the sail still furl'd, and ply
The nearest oar that's scatter'd by,
And midway to those rocks where sleep
The channel'd waters dark and deep.—
Rest from your task—so—bravely done,
Our course has been right swiftly run,
Yet 'tis the longest voyage, I trow,
That one of—" * * *

* * * * *

Sullen it plunged, and slowly sank,
The calm wave rippled to the bank;
I watch'd it as it sank, methought
Some motion from the current caught
Bestirr'd it more,—'twas but the beam
That chequer'd o'er the living stream—
I gaz'd, till vanishing from view,
Like lessening pebble it withdrew;
Still less and less, a speck of white
That gemm'd the tide, then mock'd the sight;
And all its hidden secrets sleep,
Known but to Genii of the deep,
Which, trembling in their coral caves,
They dare not whisper to the waves.

* * * * *

As rising on its purple wing
The insect-queen[p] of eastern spring,
O'er emerald meadows of Kashmeer
Invites the young pursuer near,
And leads him on from flower to flower
A weary chase and wasted hour,
Then leaves him, as it soars on high,
With panting heart and tearful eye:
So Beauty lures the full-grown child

Genii: the plural of *genius* (fire spirit). See *Nourjahad* 26 n.3.

With hue as bright, and wing as wild;
A chase of idle hopes and fears,
Begun in folly, closed in tears.
If won, to equal ills betrayed,
Woe waits the insect and the maid,
A life of pain, the loss of peace,
From infant's play, or man's caprice:
The lovely toy so fiercely sought
Has lost its charm by being caught,
For every touch that wooed its stay
Has brush'd the brightest hues away,
Till charm, and hue, and beauty gone,
'Tis left to fly or fall alone.
With wounded wing, or bleeding breast,
Ah! where shall either victim rest?
Can this with faded pinion soar
From rose to tulip as before?
Or Beauty, blighted in an hour,
Find joy within her broken bower?
No: gayer insects fluttering by
Ne'er droop the wing o'er those that die,
And lovelier things have mercy shewn
To every failing but their own,
And every woe a tear can claim
Except an erring sister's shame.

* * * * *

The Mind, that broods o'er guilty woes,
  Is like the Scorpion girt by fire,
In circle narrowing as it glows
The flames around their captive close,
Till inly search'd by thousand throes,
  And maddening in her ire,
One sad and sole relief she knows,
The sting she nourish'd for her foes,
Whose venom never yet was vain,
Gives but one pang, and cures all pain,
And darts into her desperate brain.—
So do the dark in soul expire,
Or live like Scorpion girt by fire;[q]
So writhes the mind Remorse hath riven,
Unfit for earth, undoom'd for heaven,

Darkness above, despair beneath,
Around it flame, within it death!—

* * * * *

Black Hassan from the Haram flies,
Nor bends on woman's form his eyes,
The unwonted chase each hour employs,
Yet shares he not the hunter's joys.
Not thus was Hassan wont to fly
When Leila dwelt in his Serai.
Doth Leila there no longer dwell?
That tale can only Hassan tell:
Strange rumours in our city say
Upon that eve she fled away;
When Rhamazan's[r] last sun was set,
And flashing from each minaret
Millions of lamps proclaim'd the feast
Of Bairam through the boundless East.
'Twas then she went as to the bath,
Which Hassan vainly search'd in wrath,
But she was flown her master's rage
In likeness of a Georgian page;
And far beyond the Moslem's power
Had wrong'd him with the faithless Giaour.
Somewhat of this had Hassan deem'd,
But still so fond, so fair she seem'd,
Too well he trusted to the slave
Whose treachery deserv'd a grave:
And on that eve had gone to mosque,
And thence to feast in his kiosk.
Such is the tale his Nubians tell,
Who did not watch their charge too well;
But others say, that on that night,
By pale Phingari's[s] trembling light,
The Giaour upon his jet black steed
Was seen—but seen alone to speed

Serai: harem. See *Nourjahad* 24 n. 1.
kiosk: a kind of summer house often found in palace gardens.
Nubians: black slaves of African origin, said in Orientalist writing to be preferred as guardians of the serai or harem.

With bloody spur along the shore,
Nor maid nor page behind him bore.

* * * * *

Her eye's dark charm 'twere vain to tell,
But gaze on that of the Gazelle,
It will assist thy fancy well,
As large, as languishingly dark,
But Soul beam'd forth in every spark
That darted from beneath the lid,
Bright as the jewel of Giamschid.[t]
Yea, *Soul,* and should our prophet say
That form was nought but breathing clay,
By Alla! I would answer nay;
Though on Al-Sirat's[u] arch I stood,
Which totters o'er the fiery flood,
With Paradise within my view,
And all his Houris beckoning through.[13]
Oh! who young Leila's glance could read
And keep that portion of his creed[v]
Which saith, that woman is but dust,
A soulless toy for tyrant's lust?
On her might Muftis gaze, and own
That through her eye the Immortal shone—
On her fair cheek's unfading hue
The young pomegranate's[w] blossoms strew
Their bloom in blushes ever new—
Her hair in hyacinthine[x] flow
When left to roll its folds below,
As midst her handmaids in the hall
She stood superior to them all,
Hath swept the marble where her feet
Gleamed whiter than the mountain sleet
Ere from the cloud that gave it birth
It fell, and caught one stain of earth.
The cygnet nobly walks the water—

---

our prophet: Muhammad; see *Nourjahad* 25 n. 2.
Muftis: religious judges, interpreters of Muslim religious law.

[13]For the Muslim Paradise and the Houris, see *Nourjahad* 45 n. 6 and 46 n. 7.

So moved on earth Circassia's daughter—
The loveliest bird of Franguestan![y]
As rears her crest the ruffled Swan,
  And spurns the wave with wings of pride,
When pass the steps of stranger man
  Along the banks that bound her tide;
Thus rose fair Leila's whiter neck:—
Thus armed with beauty would she check
Intrusion's glance, till Folly's gaze
Shrunk from the charms it meant to praise.
Thus high and graceful was her gait;
Her heart as tender to her mate—
Her mate—stern Hassan, who was he?
Alas! that name was not for thee!

* * * * *

  Stern Hassan hath a journey ta'en
With twenty vassals in his train,
Each arm'd as best becomes a man
With arquebuss and ataghan;
The chief before, as deck'd for war
Bears in his belt the scimitar
Stain'd with the best of Arnaut blood,
When in the pass the rebels stood,
And few return'd to tell the tale
Of what befell in Parne's vale.
The pistols which his girdle bore
Were those that once a pasha wore,
Which still, though gemm'd and boss'd with gold,
Even robbers tremble to behold.—
'Tis said he goes to woo a bride
More true than her who left his side;

Circassia's daughter: a woman of Circassia (or Franguestan), a region in the northern Caucasus, above Georgia, famed in Orientalist writing for its beautiful, fair-skinned women.
arquebuss and ataghan: long gun (operated by a matchlock) and dagger.
scimitar: curved sword.
Arnaut blood: Albanian blood.
Parne's vale: the valley of Parnassus, highest section of the mountain range above Delphi in central Greece.
pasha: governor or lord of an Ottoman province.

The faithless slave that broke her bower,
And, worse than faithless, for a Giaour!—

* * * * *

The sun's last rays are on the hill,
And sparkle in the fountain rill,
Whose welcome waters cool and clear,
Draw blessings from the mountaineer;
Here may the loitering merchant Greek
Find that repose 'twere vain to seek
In cities lodg'd too near his lord,
And trembling for his secret hoard—
Here may he rest where none can see,
In crowds a slave, in deserts free;
And with forbidden wine[14] may stain
The bowl a Moslem must not drain.—

* * * * *

The foremost Tartar's[15] in the gap,
Conspicuous by his yellow cap,
The rest in lengthening line the while
Wind slowly through the long defile;
Above, the mountain rears a peak,
Where vultures whet the thirsty beak,
And theirs may be a feast to-night,
Shall tempt them down ere morrow's light.
Beneath, a river's wintry stream
Has shrunk before the summer beam,
And left a channel bleak and bare,
Save shrubs that spring to perish there.
Each side the midway path there lay
Small broken crags of granite gray,
By time or mountain lightning riven,
From summits clad in mists of heaven;
For where is he that hath beheld
The peak of Liakura unveil'd?

* * * * *

Liakura: Lycorea, one of the two highest summits of Parnassus.

[14]The drinking of wine and other alcoholic beverages is forbidden to followers of Islam by the Koran.

[15]Tartars are members of various Central Asian Mongol tribes of Muslim faith, known for horsemanship and military skill.

They reach the grove of pine at last,
"Bismillah![z] now the peril's past;
For yonder view the opening plain,
And there we'll prick our steeds amain:"
The Chiaus spake, and as he said,
A bullet whistled o'er his head;
The foremost Tartar bites the ground!
   Scarce had they time to check the rein
Swift from their steeds the riders bound,
   But three shall never mount again,
Unseen the foes that gave the wound,
   The dying ask revenge in vain.
With steel unsheath'd, and carbine bent,
Some o'er their courser's harness leant,
   Half shelter'd by the steed,
Some fly behind the nearest rock,
And there await the coming shock,
   Nor tamely stand to bleed
Beneath the shaft of foes unseen,
Who dare not quit their craggy screen.
Stern Hassan only from his horse
Disdains to light, and keeps his course,
Till fiery flashes in the van
Proclaim too sure the robber-clan
Have well secur'd the only way
Could now avail the promis'd prey;
Then curl'd his very beard[A] with ire,
And glared his eye with fiercer fire.
"Though far and near the bullets hiss,
I've scaped a bloodier hour than this."
And now the foe their covert quit,
And call his vassals to submit;
But Hassan's frown and furious word
Are dreaded more than hostile sword,
Nor of his little band a man
Resign'd carbine or ataghan—
Nor rais'd the craven cry, Amaun![B]
In fuller sight, more near and near,
The lately ambush'd foes appear,

Chiaus: Turkish uniformed attendant, here a sergeant or aide-de-camp.

And issuing from the grove advance,
Some who on battle-charger prance.—
Who leads them on with foreign brand,
Far flashing in his red right hand?
"'Tis he—'tis he—I know him now,
I know him by his pallid brow;
I know him by the evil eye[C]
That aids his envious treachery;
I know him by his jet-black barb,
Though now array'd in Arnaut garb,
Apostate from his own vile faith,[16]
It shall not save him from the death;
'Tis he, well met in any hour,
Lost Leila's love—accursed Giaour!"

As rolls the river into ocean,
In sable torrent wildly streaming;
  As the sea-tide's opposing motion
In azure column proudly gleaming,
Beats back the current many a rood,
In curling foam and mingling flood;
While eddying whirl, and breaking wave,
Roused by the blast of winter rave;
Through sparkling spray in thundering clash,
The lightnings of the waters flash
In aweful whiteness o'er the shore,
That shines and shakes beneath the roar;
Thus—as the stream and ocean greet,
With waves that madden as they meet—
Thus join the bands whom mutual wrong,
And fate and fury drive along.
The bickering sabres' shivering jar
  And pealing wide—or ringing near
  Its echoes on the throbbing ear
The deathshot hissing from afar—
The shock—the shout—the groan of war—

---

brand: sword.

[16]Seeing the Giaour in Albanian dress and leading a band of Albanian mercenaries or bandits, Hassan assumes that the Giaour has abandoned the Christian faith.

Reverberate along that vale,
More suited to the shepherd's tale:
Though few the numbers—theirs the strife,
That neither spares nor speaks for life!
Ah! fondly youthful hearts can press,
To seize and share the dear caress;
But Love itself could never pant
For all that Beauty sighs to grant,
With half the fervour Hate bestows
Upon the last embrace of foes,
When grappling in the fight they fold
Those arms that ne'er shall lose their hold;
Friends meet to part—Love laughs at faith;—
True foes, once met, are joined till death!

* * * * *

With sabre shiver'd to the hilt,
Yet dripping with the blood he spilt;
Yet strain'd within the sever'd hand
Which quivers round that faithless brand;
His turban far behind him roll'd,
And cleft in twain its firmest fold;
His flowing robe by falchion torn,
And crimson as those clouds of morn
That streak'd with dusky red, portend
The day shall have a stormy end;
A stain on every bush that bore
A fragment of his palampore,[D]
His breast with wounds unnumber'd riven,
His back to earth, his face to heaven,
Fall'n Hassan lies—his unclos'd eye
Yet lowering on his enemy,
As if the hour that seal'd his fate,
Surviving left his quenchless hate;
And o'er him bends that foe with brow
As dark as his that bled below.—

* * * * *

"Yes, Leila sleeps beneath the wave,
But his shall be a redder grave;

---

falchion: broad, short sword.

Her spirit pointed well the steel
Which taught that felon heart to feel.
He call'd the Prophet, but his power
Was vain against the vengeful Giaour:
He call'd on Alla—but the word
Arose unheeded or unheard.
Thou Paynim[17] fool!—could Leila's prayer
Be pass'd, and thine accorded there?
I watch'd my time, I leagu'd with these,
The traitor in his turn to seize;
My wrath is wreak'd, the deed is done,
And now I go—but go alone."

* * * * *

* * * * *

The browzing camels' bells are tinkling—
His Mother looked from her lattice high,
She saw the dews of eve besprinkling
The pasture green beneath her eye,
She saw the planets faintly twinkling,
" 'Tis twilight—sure his train is nigh."—
She could not rest in the garden-bower,
But gazed through the grate of his steepest tower—
"Why comes he not? his steeds are fleet,
Nor shrink they from the summer heat;
Why sends not the Bridegroom his promised gift,
Is his heart more cold, or his barb less swift?
Oh, false reproach! yon Tartar now
Has gained our nearest mountain's brow,
And warily the steep descends,
And now within the valley bends;
And he bears the gift at his saddle bow—
How could I deem his courser slow?
Right well my largess shall repay
His welcome speed, and weary way."—
The Tartar lighted at the gate,
But scarce upheld his fainting weight;
His swarthy visage spake distress,

Paynim: pagan or heathen; insulting term to describe a Muslim, the inverse of *giaour.*

[17] In lines 675–88, the Giaour speaks for the first time in the poem.

But this might be from weariness;
His garb with sanguine spots was dyed,
But these might be from his courser's side;—
He drew the token from his vest—
Angel of Death! 'tis Hassan's cloven crest!
His calpac[E] rent—his caftan red—
"Lady, a fearful bride thy Son hath wed—
Me, not from mercy, did they spare,
But this empurpled pledge to bear.
Peace to the brave! whose blood is spilt—
Woe to the Giaour! for his the guilt."

* * * * *

A turban[F] carv'd in coarsest stone,
A pillar with rank weeds o'ergrown,
Whereon can now be scarcely read
The Koran verse that mourns the dead;
Point out the spot where Hassan fell
A victim in that lonely dell.
There sleeps as true an Osmanlie
As e'er at Mecca bent the knee;
As ever scorn'd forbidden wine,
Or pray'd with face towards the shrine,
In orisons resumed anew
At solemn sound of "Alla Hu!"[G]
Yet died he by a stranger's hand,
And stranger in his native land—
Yet died he as in arms he stood,
And unaveng'd, at least in blood.
But him the maids of Paradise
  Impatient to their halls invite,
And the dark Heaven of Houri's eyes
  On him shall glance for ever bright;
They come—their kerchiefs green they wave,[H]
And welcome with a kiss the brave!

---

caftan: full-length, long-sleeved garment worn under a coat or tunic and tied at the waist.
Osmanlie: Turk; descendant of Osman (see 188 n. 8). Lines 723–86 are narrated from a Turkish Muslim perspective.
Mecca: the most holy city of Islam, to which Muslims attempt to make at least one pilgrimage during their lives.

Who falls in battle 'gainst a Giaour,
Is worthiest an immortal bower.

* * * * *

But thou, false Infidel! shalt writhe
Beneath avenging Monkir's[I] scythe;
And from its torment 'scape alone
To wander round lost Eblis'[J] throne;
And fire unquench'd, unquenchable—
Around—within—thy heart shall dwell,[18]
Nor ear can hear, nor tongue can tell
The tortures of that inward hell!—
But first, on earth as Vampire[K] sent,
Thy corse shall from its tomb be rent;
Then ghastly haunt thy native place,
And suck the blood of all thy race,
There from thy daughter, sister, wife,
At midnight drain the stream of life;
Yet loathe the banquet which perforce
Must feed thy livid living corse;
Thy victims ere they yet expire
Shall know the daemon for their sire,
As cursing thee, thou cursing them,
Thy flowers are wither'd on the stem.
But one that for thy crime must fall—
The youngest—most belov'd of all,
Shall bless thee with a *father's* name—
That word shall wrap thy heart in flame!
Yet must thou end thy task, and mark
Her cheek's last tinge, her eye's last spark,
And the last glassy glance must view
Which freezes o'er its lifeless blue;
Then with unhallowed hand shalt tear
The tresses of her yellow hair,
Of which in life a lock when shorn,
Affection's fondest pledge was worn;
But now is borne away by thee,
Memorial of thine agony!
Wet with thine own best blood shall drip,[L]

---

[18] Byron is alluding here to *Vathek* and drawing on Beckford's depiction of the Muslim underworld (see 154).

Thy gnashing tooth and haggard lip;
Then stalking to thy sullen grave—
Go—and with Gouls and Afrits rave;[19]
Till these in horror shrink away
From spectre more accursed than they!

* * * * *

"How name ye yon lone Caloyer?[20]
  His features I have scann'd before
In mine own land—'tis many a year,
  Since, dashing by the lonely shore,
I saw him urge as fleet a steed
As ever serv'd a horseman's need.
But once I saw that face—yet then
It was so mark'd with inward pain
I could not pass it by again;
It breathes the same dark spirit now,
As death were stamped upon his brow."

" 'Tis twice three years at summer tide
  Since first among our freres he came;
And here it soothes him to abide
  For some dark deed he will not name.
But never at our vesper prayer,
Nor e'er before confession chair
Kneels he, nor recks he when arise
Incense or anthem to the skies,
But broods within his cell alone,
His faith and race alike unknown.
The sea from Paynim land he crost,
And here ascended from the coast,
Yet seems he not of Othman race,
But only Christian in his face:
I'd judge him some stray renegade,
Repentant of the change he made,
Save that he shuns our holy shrine,

Caloyer: member of an order of Greek (Orthodox Christian) monks.
freres: brothers or friars in the Caloyer monastery. One of these friars speaks lines 798–831 and 883–915.

[19]*Ghuls* and *afrits* are demons in Islamic tradition (see *Vathek* 113 and 126 n. 34.
[20]The speaker of lines 787–97 is apparently the Muslim narrator of lines 180–287.

Nor tastes the sacred bread and wine.
Great largess to these walls he brought,
And thus our abbot's favour bought;
But were I Prior, not a day
Should brook such stranger's further stay,
Or pent within our penance cell
Should doom him there for aye to dwell.
Much in his visions mutters he
Of maiden 'whelmed beneath the sea;
Of sabres clashing—foemen flying,
Wrongs aveng'd—and Moslem dying.
On cliff he hath been known to stand,
And rave as to some bloody hand
Fresh sever'd from its parent limb,
Invisible to all but him,
Which beckons onward to his grave,
And lures to leap into the wave."

* * * * *

* * * * *

Dark and unearthly is the scowl
That glares beneath his dusky cowl—
The flash of that dilating eye
Reveals too much of times gone by—
Though varying—indistinct its hue,
Oft will his glance the gazer rue—
For in it lurks that nameless spell
Which speaks—itself unspeakable—
A spirit yet unquelled and high
That claims and keeps ascendancy,
And like the bird whose pinions quake—
But cannot fly the gazing snake—
Will others quail beneath his look,
Nor 'scape the glance they scarce can brook.
From him the half-affrighted Friar
When met alone would fain retire—
As if that eye and bitter smile
Transferred to others fear and guile—
Not oft to smile descendeth he,

---

pinions: wings.

And when he doth 'tis sad to see
That he but mocks at Misery.
How that pale lip will curl and quiver!
Then fix once more as if for ever—
As if his sorrow or disdain
Forbade him e'er to smile again.—
Well were it so—such ghastly mirth
From joyaunce ne'er deriv'd its birth.—
But sadder still it were to trace
What once were feelings in that face—
Time hath not yet the features fixed,
But brighter traits with evil mixed—
And there are hues not always faded,
Which speak a mind not all degraded
Even by the crimes through which it waded—
The common crowd but see the gloom
Of wayward deeds—and fitting doom—
The close observer can espy
A noble soul, and lineage high.—
Alas! though both bestowed in vain,
Which Grief could change—and Guilt could stain—
It was no vulgar tenement
To which such lofty gifts were lent,
And still with little less than dread
On such the sight is riveted.—
The roofless cot decayed and rent,
  Will scarce delay the passer by—
The tower by war or tempest bent,
While yet may frown one battlement,
  Demands and daunts the stranger's eye—
Each ivied arch—and pillar lone,
Pleads haughtily for glories gone!

"His floating robe around him folding,
  Slow sweeps he through the columned aisle—
With dread beheld—with gloom beholding
  The rites that sanctify the pile.
But when the anthem shakes the choir,
And kneel the monks—his steps retire—

---

cot: cottage.

By yonder lone and wavering torch
His aspect glares within the porch;
There will he pause till all is done—
And hear the prayer—but utter none.
See—by the half-illumin'd wall
His hood fly back—his dark hair fall—
That pale brow wildly wreathing round,
As if the Gorgon there had bound
The sablest of the serpent-braid
That o'er her fearful forehead strayed.
For he declines the convent oath,
And leaves those locks unhallowed growth—
But wears our garb in all beside;
And—not from piety but pride
Gives wealth to walls that never heard
Of his one holy vow nor word.—
Lo!—mark ye—as the harmony
Peals louder praises to the sky—
That livid cheek—that stoney air
Of mixed defiance and despair!
Saint Francis! keep him from the shrine!
Else may we dread the wrath divine
Made manifest by awful sign.—
If ever evil angel bore
The form of mortal, such he wore—
By all my hope of sins forgiven
Such looks are not of earth nor heaven!"

To love the softest hearts are prone,
But such can ne'er be all his own;
Too timid in his woes to share,
Too meek to meet, or brave despair;
And sterner hearts alone may feel
The wound that time can never heal.
The rugged metal of the mine
Must burn before its surface shine,
But plung'd within the furnace-flame,
It bends and melts—though still the same;
Then tempered to thy want, or will,
'Twill serve thee to defend or kill;
A breast-plate for thine hour of need,
Or blade to bid thy foeman bleed;

But if a dagger's form it bear,
Let those who shape its edge, beware!
Thus passion's fire, and woman's art,
Can turn and tame the sterner heart;
From these its form and tone are ta'en,
And what they make it, must remain,
But break—before it bend again.

* * * * *

* * * * *

If solitude succeed to grief,
Release from pain is slight relief;
The vacant bosom's wilderness
Might thank the pang that made it less.
We loathe what none are left to share—
Even bliss—'twere woe alone to bear;
The heart once left thus desolate,
Must fly at last for ease—to hate.
It is as if the dead could feel
The icy worm around them steal,
And shudder, as the reptiles creep
To revel o'er their rotting sleep
Without the power to scare away
The cold consumers of their clay!
It is as if the desart-bird,[M]
  Whose beak unlocks her bosom's stream;
  To still her famish'd nestlings' scream,
Nor mourns a life to them transferr'd;
Should rend her rash devoted breast,
And find them flown her empty nest.
The keenest pangs the wretched find
  Are rapture to the dreary void—
The leafless desart of the mind—
  The waste of feelings unemploy'd—
Who would be doom'd to gaze upon
A sky without a cloud or sun?
Less hideous far the tempest's roar,
Than ne'er to brave the billows more—
Thrown, when the war of winds is o'er,
A lonely wreck on fortune's shore,
'Mid sullen calm, and silent bay,
Unseen to drop by dull decay;—

Better to sink beneath the shock
Than moulder piecemeal on the rock!

* * * * *

"Father![21] thy days have pass'd in peace,
 Mid counted beads, and countless prayer;
To bid the sins of others cease,
 Thyself without a crime or care,
Save transient ills that all must bear,
Has been thy lot, from youth to age,
And thou wilt bless thee from the rage
Of passions fierce and uncontroul'd,
Such as thy penitents unfold,
Whose secret sins and sorrows rest
Within thy pure and pitying breast.
My days, though few, have pass'd below
In much of joy, but more of woe;
Yet still in hours of love or strife,
I've scap'd the weariness of life;
Now leagu'd with friends, now girt by foes,
I loath'd the languor of repose;
Now nothing left to love or hate,
No more with hope or pride elate;
I'd rather be the thing that crawls
Most noxious o'er a dungeon's walls,
Than pass my dull, unvarying days,
Condemn'd to meditate and gaze—
Yet, lurks a wish within my breast
For rest—but not to feel 'tis rest—
Soon shall my fate that wish fulfil;
 And I shall sleep without the dream
Of what I was, and would be still,
 Dark as to thee my deeds may seem—
My memory now is but the tomb
Of joys long dead—my hope—their doom—
Though better to have died with those
Than bear a life of lingering woes—
My spirit shrunk not to sustain
The searching throes of ceaseless pain;

[21] Lines 971–1328 are spoken by the Giaour, presumably to the Abbot ("Father") of the Caloyer monastery.

Nor sought the self-accorded grave
Of ancient fool, and modern knave:
Yet death I have not fear'd to meet,
And in the field it had been sweet
Had danger wooed me on to move
The slave of glory, not of love.
I've brav'd it—not for honour's boast;
I smile at laurels won or lost.—
To such let others carve their way,
For high renown, or hireling pay;
But place again before my eyes
Aught that I deem a worthy prize;—
The maid I love—the man I hate—
And I will hunt the steps of fate,
(To save or slay—as these require)
Through rending steel, and rolling fire;
Nor need'st thou doubt this speech from one
Who would but do—what he *hath* done.
Death is but what the haughty brave—
The weak must bear—the wretch must crave—
Then let Life go to him who gave:
I have not quailed to danger's brow—
When high and happy—need I *now*?

* * * * *

"I lov'd her, friar! nay, adored—
    But these are words that all can use—
I prov'd it more in deed than word—
There's blood upon that dinted sword—
    A stain its steel can never lose:
'Twas shed for her, who died for me,
    It warmed the heart of one abhorred:
Nay, start not—no—nor bend thy knee,
    Nor midst my sins such act record,
Thou wilt absolve me from the deed,
For he was hostile to thy creed!
The very name of Nazarene
Was wormwood to his Paynim spleen,
Ungrateful fool! since but for brands,
Well wielded in some hardy hands;
And wounds by Galileans given,

The surest pass to Turkish heav'n;[22]
For him his Houris still might wait
Impatient at the prophet's gate.
I lov'd her—love will find its way
Through paths where wolves would fear to prey,
And if it dares enough, 'twere hard
If passion met not some reward—
No matter how—or where—or why,
I did not vainly seek—nor sigh:
Yet sometimes with remorse in vain
I wish she had not lov'd again.
She died—I dare not tell thee how,
But look—'tis written on my brow!
There read of Cain the curse and crime,[23]
In characters unworn by time:
Still, ere thou dost condemn me—pause—
Not mine the act, though I the cause;
Yet did he but what I had done
Had she been false to more than one;
Faithless to him—he gave the blow,
But true to me—I laid him low;
Howe'er deserv'd her doom might be,
Her treachery was truth to me;
To me she gave her heart, that all
Which tyranny can ne'er enthrall;
And I, alas! too late to save,
Yet all I then could give—I gave—
'Twas some relief—our foe a grave.
His death sits lightly; but her fate
Has made me—what thou well may'st hate.
His doom was seal'd—he knew it well,
Warn'd by the voice of stern Taheer,
Deep in whose darkly boding ear[N]
The deathshot peal'd of murder near—
As filed the troop to where they fell!
He died too in the battle broil—
A time that heeds nor pain nor toil—

---

[22] *Nazarene* and *Galileans* are here both terms for Christians; the Giaour claims that being killed in battle by Christians guarantees passage to Paradise according to Muslim belief.

[23] Cain, the first murderer in the Bible, was marked (traditionally on his brow) by God so that, though expelled from Eden, he would not be killed (see Genesis 4.1–16).

One cry to Mahomet for aid,
One prayer to Alla—all he made:
He knew and cross'd me in the fray—
I gazed upon him where he lay,
And watched his spirit ebb away;
Though pierced like Pard by hunters' steel,
He felt not half that now I feel.
I search'd, but vainly search'd to find,
The workings of a wounded mind;
Each feature of that sullen corse
Betrayed his rage, but no remorse.
Oh, what had Vengeance given to trace
Despair upon his dying face!
The late repentance of that hour,
When Penitence hath lost her power
To tear one terror from the grave—
And will not soothe, and can not save!

* * * * *

"The cold in clime are cold in blood,
Their love can scarce deserve the name;
But mine was like the lava flood
That boils in Aetna's breast of flame,
I cannot prate in puling strain
Of ladye-love, and beauty's chain;
If changing cheek, and scorching vein—
Lips taught to writhe, but not complain—
If bursting heart, and mad'ning brain—
And daring deed, and vengeful steel—
And all that I have felt—and feel—
Betoken love—that love was mine,
And shewn by many a bitter sign.
'Tis true, I could not whine nor sigh,
I knew but to obtain or die.
I die—but first I have possest,
And come what may, I *have been* blest;
Shall I the doom I sought upbraid?
No—reft of all—yet undismay'd

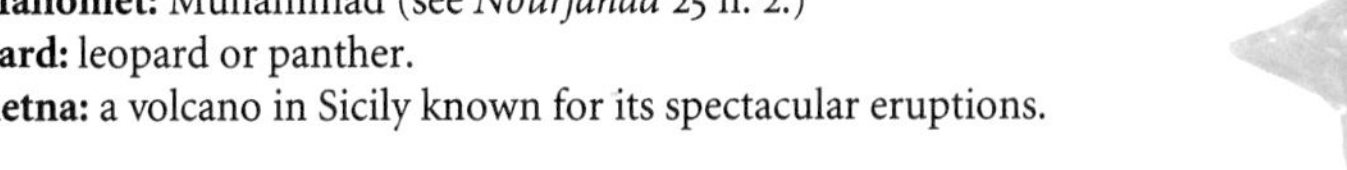

Mahomet: Muhammad (see *Nourjahad* 25 n. 2.)
Pard: leopard or panther.
Aetna: a volcano in Sicily known for its spectacular eruptions.

But for the thought of Leila slain,
Give me the pleasure with the pain,
So would I live and love again.
I grieve, but not, my holy guide!
For him who dies, but her who died;
She sleeps beneath the wandering wave,
Ah! had she but an earthly grave,
This breaking heart and throbbing head
Should seek and share her narrow bed.
She was a form of life and light—
That seen—became a part of sight,
And rose—where'er I turned mine eye—
The Morning-star of Memory!

"Yes, Love indeed is light from heaven—
  A spark of that immortal fire
With angels shar'd—by Alla given,
  To lift from earth our low desire.
Devotion wafts the mind above,
But Heaven itself descends in love—
A feeling from the Godhead caught,
To wean from self each sordid thought—
A Ray of him who form'd the whole—
A Glory circling round the soul!
I grant *my* love imperfect—all
That mortals by the name miscall—
Then deem it evil—what thou wilt—
But say, oh say, *hers* was not guilt!
She was my life's unerring light—
That quench'd—what beam shall break my night?
Oh! would it shone to lead me still,
Although to death or deadliest ill!—
Why marvel ye? if they who lose
  This present joy, this future hope,
  No more with sorrow meekly cope—
In phrenzy then their fate accuse—
In madness do those fearful deeds
  That seem to add but guilt to woe,
Alas! the breast that inly bleeds
  Hath nought to dread from outward blow—
Who falls from all he knows of bliss,
Cares little into what abyss.—

Fierce as the gloomy vulture's now
To thee, old man, my deeds appear—
I read abhorrence on thy brow,
And this too was I born to bear!
'Tis true, that, like that bird of prey,
With havock have I mark'd my way—
But this was taught me by the dove—
To die—and know no second love.
This lesson yet hath man to learn,
Taught by the thing he dares to spurn—
The bird that sings within the brake,
The swan that swims upon the lake,
One mate, and one alone, will take.
And let the fool still prone to range,
And sneer on all who cannot change—
Partake his jest with boasting boys,
I envy not his varied joys—
But deem such feeble, heartless man,
Less than yon solitary swan—
Far—far beneath the shallow maid
He left believing and betray'd.
Such shame at least was never mine—
Leila—each thought was only thine!—
My good, my guilt, my weal, my woe,
My hope on high—my all below.
Earth holds no other like to thee,
Or if it doth, in vain for me—
For worlds I dare not view the dame
Resembling thee, yet not the same.
The very crimes that mar my youth
This bed of death—attest my truth—
Tis all too late—thou wert—thou art
The cherished madness of my heart!

"And she was lost—and yet I breathed,
But not the breath of human life—
A serpent round my heart was wreathed,
And stung my every thought to strife.—
Alike all time—abhorred all place,
Shuddering I shrunk from Nature's face,
Where every hue that charmed before
The blackness of my bosom wore:—

The rest—thou dost already know,
And all my sins and half my woe—
But talk no more of penitence,
Thou see'st I soon shall part from hence—
And if thy holy tale were true—
The deed that's done can'st *thou* undo?[24]
Think me not thankless—but this grief
Looks not to priesthood for relief.°
My soul's estate in secret guess—
But would'st thou pity more—say less—
When thou can'st bid my Leila live,
Then will I sue thee to forgive;
Then plead my cause in that high place
Where purchased masses proffer grace—
Go—when the hunter's hand hath wrung
From forest-cave her shrieking young,
And calm the lonely lioness—
But soothe not—mock not *my* distress!

"In earlier days, and calmer hours,
  When heart with heart delights to blend,
Where bloom my native valley's bowers
  I had—Ah! have I now?—a friend!—
To him this pledge I charge thee send—
Memorial of a youthful vow;
I would remind him of my end,—
  Though souls absorbed like mine allow
Brief thought to distant friendship's claim,
Yet dear to him my blighted name.
'Tis strange—he prophesied my doom,
  And I have smil'd—(I then could smile—)
When Prudence would his voice assume,
  And warn—I reck'd not what—the while—
But now remembrance whispers o'er
Those accents scarcely mark'd before.
Say—that his bodings came to pass,
  And he will start to hear their truth,
  And wish his words had not been sooth,
Tell him—unheeding as I was—

[24]Like Vathek, the Giaour claims to have sinned beyond redemption: compare *Vathek* 148.

Through many a busy bitter scene
Of all our golden youth had been—
In pain, my faultering tongue had tried
To bless his memory ere I died;
But heaven in wrath would turn away,
If Guilt should for the guiltless pray.
I do not ask him not to blame—
Too gentle he to wound my name;
And what have I to do with fame?
I do not ask him not to mourn,
Such cold request might sound like scorn;
And what than friendship's manly tear
May better grace a brother's bier?
But bear this ring—his own of old—
And tell him—what thou dost behold!
The wither'd frame, the ruined mind,
The wrack by passion left behind—
A shrivelled scroll, a scatter'd leaf,
Sear'd by the autumn blast of grief!

* * * * *

"Tell me no more of fancy's gleam,
No, father, no, 'twas not a dream;
Alas! the dreamer first must sleep,
I only watch'd, and wish'd to weep;
But could not, for my burning brow
Throbb'd to the very brain as now.
I wish'd but for a single tear,
As something welcome, new, and dear;
I wish'd it then—I wish it still,
Despair is stronger than my will.
Waste not thine orison—despair
Is mightier than thy pious prayer:
I would not, if I might, be blest,
I want no paradise—but rest.
'Twas then, I tell thee, father! then
I saw her—yes—she liv'd again;
And shining in her white symar,[P]
As through yon pale grey cloud—the star
Which now I gaze on, as on her
Who look'd and looks far lovelier;
Dimly I view its trembling spark—

To-morrow's night shall be more dark—
And I—before its rays appear,
That lifeless thing the living fear.
I wander, father! for my soul
Is fleeting towards the final goal;
I saw her, friar! and I rose,
Forgetful of our former woes;
And rushing from my couch, I dart,
And clasp her to my desperate heart;
I clasp—what is it that I clasp?
No breathing form within my grasp,
No heart that beats reply to mine,
Yet, Leila! yet the form is thine!
And art thou, dearest, chang'd so much,
As meet my eye, yet mock my touch?
Ah! were thy beauties e'er so cold,
I care not—so my arms enfold
The all they ever wish'd to hold.
Alas! around a shadow prest,
They shrink upon my lonely breast;
Yet still—'tis there—in silence stands,
And beckons with beseeching hands!
With braided hair, and bright-black eye—
I knew 'twas false—she could not die!
But he is dead—within the dell
I saw him buried where he fell;
He comes not—for he cannot break
From earth—why then art thou awake?
They told me, wild waves roll'd above
The face I view, the form I love;
They told me—'twas a hideous tale!
I'd tell it—but my tongue would fail—
If true—and from thine ocean-cave
Thou com'st to claim a calmer grave;
Oh! pass thy dewy fingers o'er
This brow that then will burn no more;
Or place them on my hopeless heart—
But, shape or shade!—whate'er thou art,
In mercy, ne'er again depart—
Or farther with thee bear my soul,
Than winds can waft—or waters roll!—

* * * * *

"Such is my name, and such my tale,
Confessor—to thy secret ear,
I breathe the sorrows I bewail,
And thank thee for the generous tear
This glazing eye could never shed.
Then lay me with the humblest dead,
And save the cross above my head,
Be neither name nor emblem spread—
By prying stranger to be read,
Or stay the passing pilgrim's tread."
He pass'd—nor of his name and race
Hath left a token or a trace,
Save what the father must not say
Who shrived him on his dying day;
This broken tale was all we knew
Of her he lov'd, or him he slew.[Q]

[*Byron's notes to* The Giaour *are reproduced here as published during Byron's lifetime, with minimal further annotation. The notes often overlap with those that Samuel Henley produced for* Vathek *(159–79), which Byron would have read in the first English edition of 1786.* Ed.]

NOTE a, line 3.

That tomb, which, gleaming o'er the cliff. A tomb above the rocks on the promontory, by some supposed the sepulchre of Themistocles.

NOTE b, line 22.

Sultana of the Nightingale. The attachment of the nightingale to the rose is a well-known Persian fable—if I mistake not, the "Bulbul of a thousand tales" is one of his appellations.

NOTE c, line 40.

Till the gay mariner's guitar. The guitar is the constant amusement of the Greek sailor by night, with a steady fair wind, and during a calm, it is accompanied always by the voice, and often by dancing.

NOTE d, line 81.

Where cold Obstruction's apathy.

Ay, but to die and go we know not where,
To lie in cold obstruction.
—*Measure for Measure,* Act III. 130. Sc. 2.

[From Claudio's lines on death in William Shakespeare's *Measure for Measure* 3.1.117–18. Ed.]

NOTE e, line 89.

The first—last look—by death reveal'd. I trust that few of my readers have ever had an opportunity of witnessing what is here attempted in description, but those who have will probably retain a painful remembrance of that singular beauty which pervades, with few exceptions, the features of the dead, a few hours, and but for a few hours after "the spirit is not there." It is to be remarked in cases of violent death by gun-shot wounds, the expression is always that of languor, whatever the natural energy of the sufferer's character; but in death from a stab the countenance preserves its traits of feeling or ferocity, and the mind its bias, to the last.

NOTE f, line 151.

Slaves—nay the bondsmen of a slave. Athens is the property of the Kislar Aga, (the slave of the seraglio and guardian of the women), who appoints the Waywode.—A pandar and eunuch—these are not polite yet true appellations—now *governs* the *governor* of Athens!

NOTE g, line 190.

'Tis calmer than thy heart, young Giaour. Infidel.

NOTE h, line 225.

In echoes of the far tophaike. "Tophaike," musquet.—The Bairam is announced by the cannon at sunset; the illumination of the Mosques, and the firing of all kinds of small arms, loaded with *ball,* proclaim it during the night.

NOTE i, line 251.

Swift as the hurled on high jerreed. Jerreed, or Djerrid, a blunted Turkish javelin, which is darted from horseback with great force and precision. It is a favourite exercise of the Mussulmans; but I know not if it can be called a *manly* one, since the most expert in the art are the Black Eunuchs of Constantinople.—I think, next to these, a Mamlouk at Smyrna was the most skilful that came within my own observation.

NOTE j, line 282.

He came, he went, like the Simoom. The blast of the desart, fatal to every thing living, and often alluded to in eastern poetry.

NOTE k, line 343.

To bless the sacred "bread and salt." To partake of food—to break bread and salt with your host—insures the safety of the guest, even though an enemy; his person from that moment is sacred.

NOTE l, line 351.

Since his turban was cleft by the infidel's sabre. I need hardly observe, that Charity and Hospitality are the first duties enjoined by Mahomet; and to say truth, very generally practised by his disciples. The first praise that can be bestowed on a chief, is a panegyric on his bounty; the next, on his valour.

NOTE m, line 355.

And silver-sheathed ataghan. The ataghan, a long dagger worn with pistols in the belt, in a metal scabbard, generally of silver; and, among the wealthier, gilt, or of gold.

NOTE n, line 357.

An Emir by his garb of green. Green is the privileged colour of the prophet's numerous pretended descendants; with them, as here, faith (the family inheritance) is supposed to supersede the necessity of good works; they are the worst of a very indifferent brood.

NOTE o, line 358.

Ho! who art thou?—this low salam. Salam aleikoum! aleikoum salam! peace be with you; be with you peace—the salutation reserved for the faithful;—to a Christian, "Urlarula," a good journey; or saban hiresem, saban serula; good morn, good even; and sometimes, "may your end be happy"; are the usual salutes.

Note p, line 389.

The insect-queen of eastern spring. The blue-winged butterfly of Kashmeer, the most rare and beautiful of the species.

Note q, line 434.

Or like the Scorpion girt by fire. Alluding to the dubious suicide of the scorpion, so placed for experiment by gentle philosophers. Some maintain that the position of the sting, when turned towards the head, is merely a convulsive movement; but others have actually brought in the verdict "Felo de se" [suicide]. The scorpions are surely interested in a speedy decision of the question; as, if once fairly established as insect Catos, they will probably be allowed to live as long as they think proper, without being martyred for the sake of a hypothesis. [Marcus Porcius Cato (95–46 B.C.), Roman statesman who famously committed suicide during the course of the Civil Wars. Ed.]

Note r, line 449.

When Rhamazan's last sun was set. The cannon at sunset close the Rhamazan; see note h.

Note s, line 468.

By pale Phingari's trembling light. Phingari, the moon.

Note t, line 479.

Bright as the jewel of Giamschid. The celebrated fabulous ruby of Sultan Giamschid, the embellisher of Istakhar; from its splendour, named Schebgerag, "the torch of night;" also, the "cup of the sun," &c.—In the first editions "Giamschid" was written as a word of three syllables, so D'Herbelot has it; but I am told Richardson reduces it to a dissyllable, and writes "Jamshid." [D'Herbelot and Richardson are identified in the notes to *Vathek.* Ed.] I have left in the text the orthography of the one with the pronunciation of the other.

Note u, line 483.

Though on Al-Sirat's arch I stood. Al-Sirat, the bridge of breadth less than the thread of a famished spider, over which the Mussulmans must *skate* into Paradise, to which it is the only entrance; but this is not the worst, the river beneath being hell itself, into which, as may be expected, the unskilful and tender of foot contrive to tumble with a "facilis descensus Averni," ["Easy is the descent to Avernus," well-known line from Virgil's epic poem *The Aeneid* (6.126) describing the descent of Aeneas into the underworld. Ed.] not very pleasing in prospect to the next passenger. There is a shorter cut downwards for the Jews and Christians.

Note v, line 488.

And keep that portion of his creed. A vulgar error; the Koran allots at least a third of Paradise to well-behaved women; but by far the greater number of Mussulmans interpret the text their own way, and exclude their moieties from heaven. Being enemies to Platonics, they cannot discern "any fitness of things" in the souls of the other sex, conceiving them to be superseded by the Houris.

Note w, line 494.

The young pomegranate's blossoms strew. An oriental simile, which may, perhaps, though fairly stolen, be deemed "plus Arabe qu'en Arabie." ["More Arabian than in Arabia." Ed.]

Note x, line 496.

Her hair in hyacinthine flow. Hyacinthine, in Arabic, "Sunbul," as common a thought in the eastern poets as it was among the Greeks.

Note y, line 506.

The loveliest bird of Franguestan. "Franguestan," Circassia.

Note z, line 568.

Bismillah! now the peril's past. Bismillah—"In the name of God;" the commencement of all the chapters of the Koran but one, and of prayer and thanksgiving.

Note A, line 593.

Then curl'd his very beard with ire. A phenomenon not uncommon with an angry Mussulman. In 1809, the Capitan Pacha's whiskers at a diplomatic audience were no less lively with indignation than a tiger cat's, to the horror of all the dragomans; the portentous mustachios twisted, they stood erect of their own accord, and were expected every moment to change their colour, but at last condescended to subside, which, probably, saved more heads than they contained hairs.

Note B, line 603.

Nor raised the craven cry, Amaun! "Amaun," quarter, pardon.

Note C, line 612.

I know him by the evil eye. The "evil eye," a common superstition in the Levant, and of which the imaginary effects are yet very singular on those who conceive themselves affected.

Note D, line 666.

A fragment of his palampore. The flowered shawls generally worn by persons of rank.

Note E, line 717.

His calpac rent—his caftan red. The "Calpac" is the solid cap or centre part of the head-dress; the shawl is wound round it, and forms a turban.

Note F, line 723.

A turban carv'd in coarsest stone. The turban—pillar—and inscriptive verse, decorate the tombs of the Osmanlies, whether in the cemetery or the wilderness. In the mountains you frequently pass similar mementos; and on enquiry you are informed that they record some victim of rebellion, plunder, or revenge.

Note G, line 734.

At solemn sound of "Alla Hu!" "Alla Hu!" the concluding words of the Muezzin's call to prayer from the highest gallery on the exterior of the Minaret. On a still evening, when the Muezzin has a fine voice (which they frequently have) the effect is solemn and beautiful beyond all the bells in Christendom.

Note H, line 743.

They come—their kerchiefs green they wave. The following is part of a battlesong of the Turks:—"I see—I see a dark-eyed girl of Paradise, and she waves a handkerchief, a kerchief of green; and cries aloud, Come, kiss me, for I love thee," &c.

Note I, line 748.

Beneath avenging Monkir's scythe. Monkir and Nekir are the inquisitors of the dead, before whom the corpse undergoes a slight noviciate and preparatory training for damnation. If the answers are none of the clearest, he is hauled up with a scythe and thumped down with a red hot mace till properly seasoned, with a variety of subsidiary probations. The office of these angels is no sinecure; there are but two; and the number of orthodox deceased being in a small proportion to the remainder, their hands are always full.

Note J, line 750.

To wander round lost Eblis' throne. Eblis the Oriental Prince of Darkness.

Note K, line 755.

But first, on earth as Vampire sent. The Vampire superstition is still general in the Levant. Honest Tournefort tells a long story, which Mr. Southey, in the notes on Thalaba, quotes about these "Vroucolochas," as he calls them. [Robert Southey had included a long note on the vampire superstition, then little known in Britain, to book 8, line 146 of his Orientalist epic poem *Thalaba the Destroyer* (1801). Ed.] The Romaic term is "Vardoulacha." I recollect a whole family being terrified by the scream of a child, which they imagined must proceed from such a visitation. The Greeks never mention the word without horror. I find that "Broucolokas" is an old legitimate Hellenic appellation—at least is so applied to Arsenius, who, according to the Greeks, was after his death animated by the Devil.—The moderns, however, use the word I mention.

Note L, line 781.

Wet with thine own best blood shall drip. The freshness of the face, and the wetness of the lip with blood, are the never-failing signs of a Vampire. The stories told in Hungary and Greece of these foul feeders are singular, and some of them most *incredibly* attested.

Note M, line 951.

It is as if the desart-bird. The pelican is, I believe, the bird so libelled, by the imputation of feeding her chickens with her blood.

NOTE N, line 1077.

Deep in whose darkly boding ear. This superstition of a second-hearing (for I never met with downright second-sight in the East) fell once under my own observation.—On my third journey to Cape Colonna early in 1811, as we passed through the defile that leads from the hamlet between Keratia and Colonna, I observed Dervish Tahiri riding rather out of the path, and leaning his head upon his hand, as if in pain.—I rode up and enquired. "We are in peril," he answered. "What peril? we are not now in Albania, nor in the passes to Ephesus, Messalunghi, or Lepanto; there are plenty of us, well armed, and the Choriates have not courage to be thieves?"—"True, Affendi, but nevertheless the shot is ringing in my ears."—"The shot!—not a tophaike has been fired this morning."—"I hear it notwithstanding—Bom—Bom—as plainly as I hear your voice."—"Psha."—"As you please, Affendi; if it is written, so will it be."—I left this quickeared predestinarian, and rode up to Basili, his Christian compatriot; whose ears, though not at all prophetic, by no means relished the intelligence.—We all arrived at Colonna, remained some hours, and returned leisurely, saying a variety of brilliant things, in more languages than spoiled the building of Babel, upon the mistaken seer. Romaic, Arnaout, Turkish, Italian, and English were all exercised, in various conceits, upon the unfortunate Mussulman. While we were contemplating the beautiful prospect, Dervish was occupied about the columns.—I thought he was deranged into an antiquarian, and asked him if he had become a *"Palao-castro"* man [a connoisseur of old fortresses]: "No," said he, "but these pillars will be useful in making a stand"; and added other remarks, which at least evinced his own belief in his troublesome faculty of *fore-hearing.*—On our return to Athens, we heard from Leoné (a prisoner set ashore some days after) of the intended attack of the Mainotes, mentioned, with the cause of its not taking place, in the notes to Childe Harolde, Canto 2d.—[Byron refers to a note on Cape Colonna appended to a note to canto 2, stanza 12, of his poem *Childe Harold's Pilgrimage* (1812). ED.] I was at some pains to question the man, and he described the dresses, arms, and marks of the horses of our party so accurately, that with other circumstances, we could not doubt of *his* having been in "villanous company," and ourselves in a bad neighbourhood.—Dervish became a soothsayer for life, and I dare say is now hearing more musquetry than ever will be fired, to the great refreshment of the Arnaouts of Berat, and his native mountains.—I shall mention one trait more of this singular race.—In March 1811, a remarkably stout and active Arnaout came (I believe the 50th on the same errand,) to offer himself as an attendant, which was declined: "Well, Affendi," quoth he, "may you live!—you would have found me useful. I shall leave the town for the hills tomorrow, in the winter I return, perhaps you will then receive me."—Dervish, who was present, remarked as a thing of course, and of no consequence, "in the mean time he will join the Klephtes," (robbers), which was true to the letter.—If not cut off, they come down in the winter, and pass it unmolested in some town, where they are often as well known as their exploits.

NOTE O, line 1207.

Looks not to priesthood for relief. The monk's sermon is omitted. It seems to have had so little effect upon the patient, that it could have no hopes from the reader. It may be sufficient to say, that it was of a customary length, (as may be perceived from the interruptions and uneasiness of the penitent), and was delivered in the nasal tone of all orthodox preachers.

NOTE P, line 1273.

And shining in her white symar. "Symar"—Shroud.

NOTE Q, line 1334.

The circumstance to which the above story relates was not very uncommon in Turkey. A few years ago the wife of Muchtar Pacha complained to his father of his son's supposed infidelity; he asked with whom, and she had the barbarity to give in a list of the twelve handsomest women in Yanina. They were seized, fastened up in sacks, and drowned in the lake the same night! One of the guards who was present informed me, that not one of the victims uttered a cry, or shewed a symptom of terror at so sudden a "wrench from all we know, from all we love." [Misquoted from Edward Young's poem, *Night Thoughts on Life, Death, and Immortality* (1742–45), 2.655: "A wrench from all we love, from all we are." ED.] The fate of Phrosine, the fairest of this sacrifice, is the subject of many a Romaic and Arnaut ditty. The story in the text is one told of a young Venetian many years ago, and now nearly forgotten.—I heard it by accident recited by one of the coffee-house story-tellers who abound in the Levant, and sing or recite their narratives.—The additions and interpolations by the translator will be easily distinguished from the rest by the want of Eastern imagery; and I regret that my memory has retained so few fragments of the original.

For the contents of some of the notes I am indebted partly to D'Herbelot, and partly to that most eastern, and, as Mr. Weber [Henry Weber, compiler of *Tales of the East* (1812). ED.] justly entitles it, "sublime tale," the "Caliph Vathek." I do not know from what source the author of that singular volume may have drawn his materials; some of his incidents are to be found in the "Bibliotheque Orientale"; but for correctness of costume, beauty of description, and power of imagination, it far surpasses all European imitations; and bears such marks of originality, that those who have visited the East will find some difficulty in believing it to be more than a translation. As an Eastern tale, even Rasselas must bow before it; his "Happy Valley" will not bear a comparison with the "Hall of Eblis." [Byron ranks Beckford's *Vathek* above Samuel Johnson's *Rasselas* (1759) as the finest British Oriental tale, helping to establish its importance for later writers. ED.]

Part Two

CONTEXTS:
THE RISE OF LITERARY ORIENTALISM

Arabian Nights Entertainments:

CONSISTING OF

One Thousand and One

STORIES,

TOLD BY

The Sultaness of the *Indies*, to divert the Sultan from the Execution of a Bloody Vow he had made to Marry a Lady every Day, and have her cut off next Morning, to avenge himself for the Disloyalty of his first Sultaness, &c.

Containing

A better Account of the Customs, Manners, and Religion of the Eastern Nations, *viz. Tartars, Persians*, and *Indians*, than is to be met with in any Author hitherto publish'd.

Translated into *French* from the *Arabian* MSS. by M. *Galland*, of the Royal Academy; and now done into English.

ARABIAN NIGHTS ENTERTAINMENTS

The *Arabian Nights Entertainments,* also called *The Thousand and One Nights,* is a major collection of stories originally assembled in Arabic and inspired by various Arabic, Persian, and Indian popular tales over a number of centuries. The tales became famous in Europe thanks to the polished French translation by Antoine Galland, issued in installments from 1704 to 1717. Galland's *Les Mille et une nuits* was in turn done into English by an anonymous "Grub Street" (hack) translator, from about 1706 on, with new and expanded editions appearing nearly every year. The tales are nested within a frame story, in which the witty Scheherazade uses her narrative gifts to delay her death at the hands of her husband, the Sultan Schahriar. Deceived by his first wife, Schahriar takes a succession of new wives who are promptly killed the morning after the consummation of each marriage. By engaging Schahriar in her skilfully told tales, with their endings inevitably held back for the next evening, Scheherazade manages to defer her execution until Schahriar's insane jealousy and homicidal possessiveness are finally cured by the wisdom of the very tales she uses to entrance him. The "Fourteenth Night" includes a tale (told within a longer tale of Sindbad) that reflects back on the themes of jealousy, distrust, female ingenuity, and the obsessive control of female sexuality that animate the framing narrative of Schahriar, Scheherazade, and her sister, Dinarzade. The text below follows the 1713 edition of the Grub Street translation. [Ed.]

Preface

There's no occasion to prepossess the Reader with an Opinion of the Merit and Beauty of the following Work. There needs no more but to read it to satisfy any Man, that hitherto nothing so Fine of this Nature, has appeared in any Language.

From *Arabian Nights Entertainments.* 4th ed. London: Bell, 1713.

What can be more Ingenious, than to Compose such a prodigious Quantity of pleasant Stories, whose Variety is surprizing, and whose Connexion is so wonderful. We know not the Name of the Author of so great a Work; but probably it is not all done by one Hand; for how can we suppose that one Man alone, could have Invention enough to make so many fine Things.

If Stories of this sort be pleasant and diverting, because of the Wonders they usually contain; these have certainly the Advantage above all that have yet been publish'd, because they are full of surprising Events, which engage our Attention, and shew how much the *Arabians* surpass other Nations in Composures of this sort.

They must also be pleasing, because of the Account they give us of the Customs and Manners of the Eastern Nations, and of the Ceremonies of their Religion, as well Pagan as Mahometan, which are better describ'd here, than in any Author that has wrote of 'em, or in the Relations of Travellers. All the Eastern Nations, Persians, Tartars, and Indians, are here distinguish'd, and appear such as they are, from the Sovereign to the meanest Subject; so that without the Fatigue of going to see those People in their respective Countries, the Reader has here the pleasure to see them act, and hear them speak. Care has been taken to preserve their Characters, and to keep their Sense; nor have we varied from the Text, but when Modesty obliged us to it. The Translator flatters himself, that those who understand *Arabick,* and will be at the pains to compare the Original with the Translation, must agree, that he has shew'd the *Arabians* to the *French,* with all the Circumspection that the Niceness of the *French* Tongue, and of the Time requires; and if those who read these Stories have but any Inclination to profit by the Examples of Vertue and Vice, which they will here find exhibited, they may reap an advantage by it, that is not to be reap'd in other Stories, which are more proper to corrupt than to reform our Manners.

The Fourteenth Night

An Hour before Day, *Dinarzade* awak'd her Sister, and says to her, you will certainly be as good as your word, Madam, and tell us out the Story of the Fisher-man; to assist your Memory, I will tell you where you left off. It was where the Grecian King maintain'd the Innocence of his Physician *Dorban,* against his Visier. I remember it, says *Scheherazade,* and am ready to give you Satisfaction.

Sir, continues she, addressing her self to *Schahriar,* That which the Grecian King said about King Sindbad, rais'd the Visier's curiosity, who says to

---

Mahometan: Muslim.
Visier: vizier, from the Arabic *wazir,* the lieutenant or first minister of a king or sultan.

him, Sir, I pray your Majesty to pardon me, if I have the boldness to demand of you, what the Visier of King Sindbad said to his Master, to divert him from cutting off the Prince his Son. The Grecian King had the Complaisance to satisfy him; That Visier, says he, after having represented to King Sindbad, that he ought to beware, lest on the Accusation of a Mother-in-law, he should commit an Action, which he might afterwards repent of, told him this Story.

THE STORY OF THE HUSBAND AND PARROT

A Certain Man had a fair Wife, whom he lov'd so dearly, that he could scarce allow her to be out of his sight. One day being oblig'd to go abroad about urgent Affairs, he came to a place where all sorts of Birds were sold, and there bought a Parrot, which not only spoke very well, but could also give an account of everything that was done before it. He brought it in a Cage to his House, pray'd his Wife to put it in her Chamber, and to take care of it, during a Journey he was oblig'd to undertake, and then went out.

At his return, he took care to ask the Parrot, concerning what had pass'd in his absence, and the Bird told him things, that gave him occasion to upbraid his Wife. She thought some of her Slaves had betray'd her, but all of 'em swore they had been faithful to her, and they all agreed that it must have been the Parrot, that had told Tales.

Upon this the Wife bethought herself of a way, how she might remove her Husband's Jealousy, and at the same time revenge herself of the Parrot, which she effected thus. Her Husband being gone another Journey, she commanded a Slave in the Night-time, to turn a Hand-mill under the Parrot's Cage, she ordered another to throw Water in form of Rain over the Cage, and a third to take a Glass, and turn it to the Right and to the Left before the Parrot, so as the reflections of the Candle might shine on its Face. The Slaves spent great part of the Night, in doing what their Mistress commanded them, and acquitted themselves very dexterously.

Next day the Husband return'd, and examin'd the Parrot again, about what had pass'd during his absence. The Bird answer'd, Good Master, the Lightning, Thunder and Rain, did so much disturb me all Night, that I cannot tell how much I suffered by it. The Husband, who knew that there had been neither Thunder, Lightning, nor Rain, that Night, fansied that the Parrot, not having told him the Truth in this, might also have lyed to him in the other; upon which he took it out of the Cage, and threw it with so much force to the ground, that he kill'd it. Yet afterwards he understood by his Neighbours, that the poor Parrot had not lyed to him, when it gave him

---

Glass: mirror.

an account of his Wife's base Conduct, which made him repent he had kill'd it. *Scheherazade* stopp'd here, because she saw it was Day.

All that you tell us, Sister, says *Dinarzade*, is so curious, that nothing can be more agreeable. I shall be willing to divert you, answers *Scheherazade*, if the Sultan my Master, will allow me time to do it. *Schahriar*, who took as much pleasure to hear the Sultaness, as *Dinarzade*, arose, and went about his affairs, without ordering the Visier to cut her off.

THE SPECTATOR NO. 578

Jointly edited and largely written by Sir Richard Steele (1672–1729) and Joseph Addison (1672–1719), the *Spectator* ran from March 1711 to December 1712 and again (under Addison alone) from June to December 1714. Ostensibly the work of a small club of gentlemen, the *Spectator* (which appeared daily) quickly became extremely popular with the new bourgeois readership that helped transform eighteenth-century literature and culture in Britain. It treated moral subjects in a witty, entertaining manner while providing a range of literary and social criticism that partly reflected and partly helped to shape the taste of its era. A number of issues either touch on or are wholly given over to Oriental subjects, including a series of Eastern tales. Addison's "Vision of Mirzah," published in Number 159 (1 September 1711), helped to establish the eighteenth-century vogue for Oriental moral allegories, which found its way into children's literature, such as Ellenor Fenn's *Fairy Spectator* (1789), as well as periodical and popular fiction for adults. Number 578 (9 August 1714) playfully juxtaposes John Locke's disembodied theory of personal identity, developed in his *Essay Concerning Human Understanding* (1690), with a Persian tale featuring the magical transmigration of souls from one body to another. The tale (which may have been contributed by Addison's cousin, Eustace Budgell) was condensed from Ambrose Philips's *Thousand and One Days: Persian Tales* (1714), a translation of François Pétis de la Croix's *Les Mille et un jour: Contes Persans* (1710–12). The same tale, or a close variant, was later adapted by the Italian dramatist Carlo Gozzi in his comedy *Il Re Cervo* (1762). Recast by Andrei Serban at the American Repertory Theater as *The King Stag* (1984), with theatrical motifs borrowed from Japanese and Indone-

---

From *The Spectator: A New Edition*. Ed. Henry Morley. London: Routledge, 1883. Vol. 3.

sian traditions and Asian-inspired sets, puppets, and costumes designed by Julie Taymor, Gozzi's revived fairytale play suggests that the mingling of "European" and "Oriental" conventions, forms, and motifs has yet to play itself out as a hallmark of "Western" culture. [ED.]

Monday, August 9, 1714

Eque feris humana in corpora transit,
Inque feras Noster
—Ovid.[1]

There has been very great Reason, on several Accounts, for the learned World to endeavour at settling what it was that might be said to compose *personal Identity.*

Mr. Lock[e], after having premised that the Word *Person* properly signifies a thinking intelligent Being that has Reason and Reflection, and can consider it self as it self; concludes That it is Consciousness alone, and not an Identity of Substance, which makes this personal Identity or Sameness. Had I the same Consciousness (says that Author) that I saw the Ark and *Noah's* Flood, as that I saw an Overflowing of the *Thames* last Winter; or as that I now write; I could no more doubt that I who write this now, that saw the *Thames* overflow last Winter, and that viewed the Flood at the general Deluge, was the same *Self,* place that *Self* in what Substance you please, than that I who write this am the same *My self* now whilst I write, (whether I consist of all the same Substance material or immaterial or no) that I was Yesterday; For as to this Point of being the same *Self,* it matters not whether this present *Self* be made up of the same or other Substances.[2]

I was mightily pleased with a Story in some Measure applicable to this Piece of Philosophy, which I read the other Day in the *Persian Tales,* as they are lately very well translated by Mr. *Philips;*[3] and with an Abridgement whereof I shall here present my Readers.

I shall only premise that these Stories are writ after the Eastern Manner, but somewhat more correct.

---

[1] "And [the spirit] passes from our human bodies into beasts," Ovid, *Metamorphoses* 15.167–68. [ED.]

[2] John Locke, *An Essay Concerning Human Understanding* (1690), 2.27.16. [ED.]

[3] Francois Pétis de la Croix, *The Thousand and One Days: Persian Tales,* trans. Ambrose Philips (1714), vol. 1 (days 57–60). [ED.]

"*Fadlallah*, a Prince of great Virtues, succeeded his Father *Bin-Ortoc*, in the Kingdom of *Mousel.* He reigned over his faithful Subjects for some time, and lived in great Happiness with his beauteous Consort Queen *Zemroude;* when there appeared at his Court a young *Dervis* of so lively and entertaining a Turn of Wit, as won upon the Affections of every one he conversed with. His Reputation grew so fast every Day, that it at last raised a Curiosity in the Prince himself to see and talk with him. He did so, and far from finding that common Fame had flatter'd him, he was soon convinced that every thing he had heard of him fell short of the Truth.

"*Fadlallah* immediately lost all Manner of Relish for the Conversation of other Men; and as he was every Day more and more satisfied of the Abilities of this Stranger, offered him the first Posts in his Kingdom. The young *Dervis,* after having thanked him with a very singular Modesty, desired to be excused, as having made a Vow never to accept of any Employment, and preferring a free and independent State of Life to all other Conditions.

"The King was infinitely charmed with so great an Example of Moderation; and tho' he could not get him to engage in a Life of Business, made him however his chief Companion and first Favourite.

"As they were one Day hunting together, and happened to be separated from the rest of the Company, the *Dervis* entertained *Fadlallah* with an Account of his Travels and Adventures. After having related to him several Curiosities which he had seen in the *Indies, It was in this Place,* says he, *that I contracted an Acquaintance with an old* Brachman, *who was skilled in the most hidden Powers of Nature: He died within my Arms, and with his parting Breath communicated to me one of the most valuable of his Secrets, on Condition I should never reveal it to any Man.* The King immediately reflecting on his young Favourite's having refused the late Offers of Greatness he had made him, told him he presumed it was the Power of making Gold. *No Sir,* says the *Dervis, it is somewhat more wonderful than that; it is the Power of re-animating a dead Body, by flinging my own Soul into it.*

"While he was yet speaking a Doe came bounding by them; and the King, who had his Bow ready, shot her through the Heart; telling the *Dervis,* that a fair Opportunity now offered for him to show his Art. The young Man immediately left his own Body breathless on the Ground, while at the same Instant that of the Doe was re-animated, she came to the King, fawned upon him, and after having play'd several wanton Tricks, fell again upon the Grass; at the same Instant the Body of the *Dervis* recovered its Life. The

---

Mousel: Mosul, a region and city north of Baghdad in present-day Iraq.
Dervis: dervish, a Muslim holy man or religious ascetic, often ascribed magical powers in Orientalist writing.
Brachman: Brahman, member of the highest, priestly caste among Hindu societies.

King was infinitely pleased at so uncommon an Operation, and conjured his Friend by every thing that was sacred to communicate it to him. The *Dervis* at first made some Scruple of violating his Promise to the dying *Brachman;* but told him at last that he found he could conceal nothing from so excellent a Prince; after having obliged him therefore by an Oath to Secrecy, he taught him to repeat two Cabalistick Words, in pronouncing of which the whole Secret consisted. The King, impatient to try the Experiment, immediately repeated them as he had been taught, and in an Instant found himself in the Body of the Doe. He had but little Time to contemplate himself in this new Being; for the treacherous *Dervis* shooting his own Soul into the Royal Corps, and bending the Prince's own Bow against him, had laid him dead on the Spot, had not the King, who perceiv'd his Intent, fled swiftly to the Woods.

"The *Dervis,* now triumphant in his Villany, returned to *Mousel,* and filled the Throne and Bed of the unhappy *Fadlallah.*

"The first thing he took Care of, in order to secure himself in the Possession of his new-acquired Kingdom, was to issue out a Proclamation, ordering his Subjects to destroy all the Deer in the Realm. The King had perished among the rest, had he not avoided his Pursuers by re-animating the Body of a Nightingale which he saw lie dead at the Foot of a Tree. In this new Shape he winged his Way in Safety to the Palace, where perching on a Tree which stood near his Queen's Apartment, he filled the whole Place with so many melodious and melancholy Notes as drew her to the Window. He had the Mortification to see that instead of being pitied, he only moved the Mirth of his Princess, and of a young Female Slave who was with her. He continued however to serenade her every Morning, till at last the Queen, charmed with his Harmony, sent for the Bird-catchers, and ordered them to employ their utmost Skill to put that little Creature into her Possession. The King, pleased with an Opportunity of being once more near his beloved Consort, easily suffered himself to be taken; and when he was presented to her, tho' he shewed a Fearfulness to be touched by any of the other Ladies, flew of his own Accord, and hid himself in the Queen's Bosom. *Zemroude* was highly pleased at the unexpected Fondness of her new Favourite, and ordered him to be kept in an open Cage in her own Apartment. He had there an Opportunity of making his Court to her every Morning, by a thousand little Actions which his Shape allowed him. The Queen passed away whole Hours every Day in hearing and playing with him. *Fadlallah* could even have thought himself happy in this State of Life,

---

Cabalistick: cabalistic (secret or magical); see *Vathek* 153.
Corps: corpse, body.

had he not frequently endured the inexpressible Torment of seeing the *Dervis* enter the Apartment and caress his Queen even in his Presence.

"The Usurper, amidst his toying with the Princess, would often endeavour to ingratiate himself with her Nightingale; and while the enraged *Fadlallah* peck'd at him with his Bill, beat his Wings, and shewed all the Marks of an impotent Rage, it only afforded his Rival and the Queen new Matter for their Diversion.

"*Zemroude* was likewise fond of a little Lap-Dog which she kept in her Apartment, and which one Night happened to die.

"The King immediately found himself inclined to quit the shape of the Nightingale, and enliven this new Body. He did so, and the next Morning *Zemroude* saw her favourite Bird lie dead in the Cage. It is impossible to express her Grief on this Occasion, and when she called to mind all its little Actions, which even appeared to have somewhat in them like Reason, she was inconsolable for her Loss.

"Her Women immediately sent for the *Dervis,* to come and comfort her, who after having in vain represented to her the Weakness of being grieved at such an Accident, touched at last by her repeated Complaints; *Well Madam,* says he, *I will exert the utmost of my Art to please you. Your Nightingale shall again revive every Morning and serenade you as before.* The Queen beheld him with a Look which easily shewed she did not believe him; when laying himself down on a Sofa, he shot his Soul into the Nightingale, and *Zemroude* was amazed to see her Bird revive.

"The King, who was a Spectator of all that passed, lying under the Shape of a Lap Dog, in one Corner of the Room, immediately recovered his own Body, and running to the Cage with the utmost Indignation, twisted off the neck of the false Nightingale.

"*Zemroude* was more than ever amazed and concerned at this second Accident, till the King entreating her to hear him, related to her his whole Adventure.

"The Body of the *Dervis,* which was found Dead in the Wood, and his Edict for killing all the Deer, left her no Room to doubt of the Truth of it: But the Story adds, That out of an extream Delicacy (peculiar to the Oriental Ladies) she was so highly afflicted at the innocent Adultery in which she had for some time lived with the *Dervis,* that no Arguments even from *Fadlallah* himself could compose her Mind. She shortly after died with Grief, begging his Pardon with her last Breath for what the most rigid Justice could not have interpreted as a Crime.

"The King was so afflicted with her Death, that he left his Kingdom to one of his nearest Relations, and passed the rest of his Days in Solitude and Retirement."

THE RAMBLER NO. 120

Samuel Johnson

One of the most celebrated British writers of his era, Samuel Johnson (1709–84) made important contributions as a poet, biographer, lexicographer, essayist, and writer of prose fiction. Thanks to the efforts of James Boswell, his follower and companion, who brought out the massive *Life of Samuel Johnson* in 1791, Johnson also became famous as a great talker and a monumental character. Johnson's own major works include *London* (1738) and *The Vanity of Human Wishes* (1749), which together established his reputation as a leading Neoclassical poet; the *Dictionary of the English Language* (1755), the first English work of its kind; and the *Lives of the English Poets* (1779–81). *Rasselas, Prince of Abyssinia,* published in 1759, vies with Beckford's *Vathek* as the leading work of eighteenth-century British Orientalist fiction. In stark contrast to Beckford, however, Johnson's purpose is primarily—some might say remorselessly—moralistic, though given its wit, its philosophical musings, and its famous digressions on poetry, the imagination, and the inexhaustible nature of desire, *Rasselas* can hardly be dismissed as mere didacticism. Johnson was well-practiced both in didactic fiction and "Oriental" writing by the time he composed *Rasselas* (allegedly in a single week), having written a number of Oriental tales for his biweekly journal, the *Rambler* (1750–52). Aimed, like the *Spectator* before it, at a bourgeois readership, but more somber in tone and less topical in subject matter, the *Rambler* included essays, character studies, Eastern allegories and fables, and literary criticism, nearly all of it produced by Johnson himself. *Rambler* 120, issued on Saturday, May 11, 1751, is set in Samarcand (Samarquand), a major trading center in Central Asia during the reign of Genghis (Jenghiz) Khan (c. 1167–1227), founder of the Mongol Empire. Johnson gives an Eastern coloring to some of his most persistent themes—the instability of life, the limitations of prosperity, the emptiness of earthly desires—while touching on stock Orientalist notions of luxury, tyranny, and the childlike pursuit of pleasure. [Ed.]

From *The Works of Samuel Johnson.* Oxford: Talboys, 1825. Vol. 3.

Saturday, May 11, 1751

Redditum Cyri solio Phraaten,
Dissidens plebi, numero beatorum
Eximit virtus, populumque falsis
Dedocet uti Vocibus.
—Horace *Odes* 2.2.17–21

True virtue can the crowd unteach
Their false mistaken forms of speech;
Virtue, to crowds a foe profest,
Disdains to number with the blest
Phraates, by his slaves ador'd,
And to the Parthian crown restor'd.
—Francis[1]

In the reign of Jenghiz Can, conqueror of the east, in the city of Samarcand, lived Nouradin the merchant, renowned throughout all the regions of India, for the extent of his commerce, and the integrity of his dealings. His warehouses were filled with all the commodities of the remotest nations; every rarity of nature, every curiosity of art, whatever was valuable, whatever was useful, hasted to his hand. The streets were crowded with his carriages; the sea was covered with his ships; the streams of Oxus[2] were wearied with conveyance, and every breeze of the sky wafted wealth to Nouradin.

At length Nouradin felt himself seized with a slow malady, which he first endeavoured to divert by application, and afterwards to relieve by luxury and indulgence; but finding his strength every day less, he was at last terrified, and called for help upon the sages of physick; they filled his apartments with alexipharmicks, restoratives, and essential virtues; the pearls of the ocean were dissolved, the spices of Arabia were distilled, and all the powers of nature were employed to give new spirits to his nerves, and new

---

alexipharmicks: antidotes.

[1] Philip Francis's translation of Horace's *Odes* appeared in 1742–43. The lines are a loose translation of the stanza from Horace; Phraates killed his father on the way to becoming King of Parthia. [Ed.]

[2] The Oxus (Amu-Darya) River runs through central Asia, south of Samarcand in present-day Uzbekistan. [Ed.]

balsam to his blood. Nouradin was for some time amused with promises, invigorated with cordials, or soothed with anodynes; but the disease preyed upon his vitals, and he soon discovered with indignation, that health was not to be bought. He was confined to his chamber, deserted by his physicians, and rarely visited by his friends; but his unwillingness to die flattered him long with hopes of life.

At length, having passed the night in tedious languor, he called to him Almamoulin, his only son, and dismissing his attendants, "My son," says he, "behold here the weakness and fragility of man; look backward a few days, thy father was great and happy, fresh as the vernal rose, and strong as the cedar of the mountain; the nations of Asia drank his dews, and art and commerce delighted in his shade. Malevolence beheld me, and sighed: 'His root,' she cried, 'is fixed in the depths; it is watered by the fountains of Oxus; it sends out branches afar, and bids defiance to the blast; Prudence reclines against his trunk, and Prosperity dances on his top.' Now, Almamoulin, look upon me withering and prostrate; look upon me and attend. I have trafficked, I have prospered, I have rioted in gain; my house is splendid, my servants are numerous; yet I displayed only a small part of my riches; the rest, which I was hindered from enjoying by the fear of raising envy, or tempting rapacity, I have piled in towers, I have buried in caverns, I have hidden in secret repositories, which this scroll will discover. My purpose was, after ten months more spent in commerce, to have withdrawn my wealth to a safer country; to have given seven years to delight and festivity, and the remaining part of my days to solitude and repentance; but the hand of death is upon me; a frigorifick torpor encroaches upon my veins; I am now leaving the produce of my toil, which it must be thy business to enjoy with wisdom." The thought of leaving his wealth filled Nouradin with such grief, that he fell into convulsions, became dilirious, and expired.

Almamoulin, who loved his father, was touched awhile with honest sorrow, and sat two hours in profound meditation, without perusing the paper which he held in his hand. He then retired to his own chamber, as overborne with affliction, and there read the inventory of his new possessions, which swelled his heart with such transports, that he no longer lamented his father's death. He was now sufficiently composed to order a funeral of modest magnificence, suitable at once to the rank of Nouradin's profession, and the reputation of his wealth. The two next nights he spent in visiting the towers and the caverns, and found the treasures greater to his eye than to his imagination.

---

frigorifick torpor: freezing insensibility.

Almamoulin had been bred to the practice of exact frugality, and had often looked with envy on the finery and expenses of other young men: he therefore believed, that happiness was now in his power, since he could obtain all of which he had hitherto been accustomed to regret the want. He resolved to give a loose to his desires, to revel in enjoyment, and feel pain and uneasiness no more.

He immediately procured a splendid equipage, dressed his servants in rich embroidery, and covered his horses with golden caparisons. He showered down silver on the populace, and suffered their acclamations to swell him with insolence. The nobles saw him with anger, the wise men of the state combined against him, the leaders of armies threatened his destruction. Almamoulin was informed of his danger: he put on the robe of mourning in the presence of his enemies, and appeased them with gold, and gems, and supplication.

He then sought to strengthen himself by an alliance with the princes of Tartary, and offered the price of kingdoms for a wife of noble birth. His suit was generally rejected, and his presents refused; but the princess of Astracan once condescended to admit him to her presence. She received him, sitting on a throne, attired in the robe of royalty, and shining with the jewels of Golconda; command sparkled in her eyes, and dignity towered on her forehead. Almamoulin approached and trembled. She saw his confusion and disdained him: "How," says she, "dares the wretch hope my obedience, who thus shrinks at my glance? Retire, and enjoy thy riches in sordid ostentation; thou wast born to be wealthy, but never canst be great."

He then contracted his desires to more private and domestick pleasures. He built palaces, he laid out gardens, he changed the face of the land, he transplanted forests, he levelled mountains, opened prospects into distant regions, poured fountains from the tops of turrets, and rolled rivers through new channels.

These amusements pleased him for a time; but languor and weariness soon invaded him. His bowers lost their fragrance, and the waters murmured without notice. He purchased large tracts of land in distant provinces, adorned them with houses of pleasure, and diversified them with accommodations for different seasons. Change of place at first relieved his satiety, but all the novelties of situation were soon exhausted; he found his heart vacant, and his desires, for want of external objects, ravaging himself.

He therefore returned to Samarcand, and set open his doors to those whom idleness sends out in search of pleasure. His tables were always covered with delicacies; wines of every vintage sparkled in his bowls, and his

---

Astracan: Astrakhan, a khanate (principality ruled by a khan) in central Asia.
Golconda: city in India famous for its diamond mines.

lamps scattered perfumes. The sound of the lute, and the voice of the singer, chased away sadness; every hour was crowded with pleasure; and the day ended and began with feasts and dances, and revelry and merriment. Almamoulin cried out, "I have, at last, found the use of riches; I am surrounded by companions, who view my greatness without envy; and I enjoy at once the raptures of popularity, and the safety of an obscure station. What trouble can he feel, whom all are studious to please, that they may be repaid with pleasure? What danger can he dread, to whom every man is a friend?"

Such were the thoughts of Almamoulin, as he looked down from a gallery upon the gay assembly regaling at his expense; but, in the midst of this soliloquy, and officer of justice entered the house, and, in the form of legal citation, summoned Almamoulin to appear before the emperor. The guests stood awhile aghast, then stole imperceptibly away, and he was led off without a single voice to witness his integrity. He now found one of his most frequent visitants accusing him of treason, in hopes of sharing his confiscation; yet, unpatronized and unsupported, he cleared himself by the openness of innocence, and the consistence of truth; he was dismissed with honour, and his accuser perished in prison.

Almamoulin now perceived with how little reason he had hoped for justice or fidelity from those who live only to gratify their senses; and, being now weary with vain experiments upon life and fruitless researches after felicity, he had recourse to a sage, who, after spending his youth in travel and observation, had retired from all human cares, to a small habitation on the banks of Oxus, where he conversed only with such as solicited his counsel. "Brother," said the philosopher, "thou hast suffered thy reason to be deluded by idle hopes, and fallacious appearances. Having long looked with desire upon riches, thou hast taught thyself to think them more valuable than nature designed them, and to expect from them, what experience has now taught thee, that they cannot give. That they do not confer wisdom, thou mayest be convinced, by considering at how dear a price they tempted thee, upon thy first entrance into the world, to purchase the empty sound of vulgar acclamation. That they cannot bestow fortitude or magnanimity, that man may be certain, who stood trembling at Astracan, before a being not naturally superiour to himself. That they will not supply unexhausted pleasure, the recollection of forsaken palaces, and neglected gardens, will easily inform thee. That they rarely purchase friends, thou didst soon discover, when thou wert left to stand thy trial uncountenanced and alone. Yet think not riches useless; there are purposes to which a wise man may be delighted to apply them; they may, by a rational distribution to those who want them, ease the pains of helpless disease, still the throbs of restless anxiety, relieve innocence from oppression, and raise imbecility to cheerfulness and vigour. This they will enable thee to perform, and this will afford the only happiness ordained for our present state, the confidence of divine favour, and the hope of future rewards."

LETTER 33

Oliver Goldsmith

A friend and protégé of Samuel Johnson, Oliver Goldsmith (c. 1730–74) similarly produced widely acclaimed works in a range of genres, including poetry, fiction, the "polite" essay, and stage comedy. Like Frances Sheridan and Maria Edgeworth, Goldsmith was Anglo-Irish; after settling in England in 1756, Goldsmith was treated as something of an outsider, even by his friends in the Johnson circle. Although his works included *The Deserted Village* (1770), a much admired poem in the mode of Johnson and Alexander Pope, the popular novel of sentiment *The Vicar of Wakefield* (1766), and the hit comedy *She Stoops to Conquer* (1773), Goldsmith often had to resort to hackwork, ephemeral journalism, and anonymous writing for children to earn his living. The last placed him within the orbit of John Newbery, an innovative publisher of juvenile fiction including *The History of Little Goody Two-Shoes* (1765), the prototypical didactic children's tale which may have been written by Goldsmith. From January 1760 through August 1761, Newbery included Goldsmith's "Chinese Letters" in regular installments of his new journal, the *Public Ledger*, and Goldsmith republished them in book form as *The Citizen of the World* in 1762. The letters are purportedly written by Lien Chi Altangi, a Chinese philosopher visiting England, and by the Chinese and European correspondents who write back to him. Following the precedent of Montesquieu's brilliant *Lettres persanes* (*Persian Letters*) of 1721, Goldsmith deploys an imagined Chinese perspective to cast a distancing, ironic light on English customs, institutions, prejudices, and pretensions. As Letter 33 demonstrates in telling detail, European notions of the Orient are themselves ironized in this undervalued work of British Orientalist literature. It was initially published in the *Public Ledger* (numbered there as 31) on 25 April 1760. [Ed.]

From *The Citizen of the World. Miscellaneous Works.* Paris: Baudry's, 1837. Vol. 3.

From Lien Chi Altangi, to Fum Hoam, first president of the Ceremonial Academy at Pekin, in China

I am disgusted, O Fum Hoam, even to sickness disgusted. Is it possible to bear the presumption of those islanders, when they pretend to instruct me in the ceremonies of China! They lay it down as a maxim, that every person who comes from thence must express himself in metaphor; swear by Alla, rail against wine, and behave, and talk, and write like a Turk or Persian. They make no distinction between our elegant manners, and the voluptuous barbarities of our eastern neighbours. Wherever I come, I raise either diffidence or astonishment: some fancy me no Chinese, because I am formed more like a man than a monster; and others wonder to find one born five thousand miles from England, endued with common sense. Strange, say they, that a man who has received his education at such a distance from London, should have common sense; to be born out of England, and yet have common sense! Impossible! He must be some Englishman in disguise; his very visage has nothing of the true exotic barbarity.

I yesterday received an invitation from a lady of distinction, who it seems had collected all her knowledge of eastern manners from fictions every day propagated here, under the titles of eastern tales, and oriental histories: she received me very politely, but seemed to wonder that I neglected bringing opium and a tobacco-box; when chairs were drawn for the rest of the company, I was assigned my place on a cushion on the floor. It was in vain that I protested the Chinese used chairs as in Europe; she understood decorums too well to entertain me with the ordinary civilities.

I had scarce been seated according to her directions, when the footman was ordered to pin a napkin under my chin: this I protested against, as being no way Chinese; however, the whole company, who it seems were a club of connoisseurs, gave it unanimously against me, and the napkin was pinned accordingly.

It was impossible to be angry with people, who seemed to err only from an excess of politeness, and I sat contented, expecting their importunities were now at an end; but as soon as ever dinner was served, the lady demanded whether I was for a plate of *Bears' claws,* or a slice of *Birds' nests*? As these were dishes with which I was utterly unacquainted, I was desirous of eating only what I knew, and therefore begged to be helped from a piece of beef that lay on the side-table: my request at once disconcerted the whole company. A Chinese eat beef! that could never be! there was no local propriety in Chinese beef, whatever there might be in Chinese pheasant. Sir, said my entertainer, I think I have some reasons to fancy myself a judge of these matters: in short, the Chinese never eat beef; so that I must be permitted to recommend the Pilaw, there was never better dressed at Pekin; the saffron and rice are well boiled, and the spices in perfection.

I had no sooner begun to eat what was laid before me, than I found the whole company as much astonished as before; it seems I made no use of my chop-sticks. A grave gentleman, whom I take to be an author, harangued very learnedly (as the company seemed to think) upon the use which was made of them in China: he entered into a long argument with himself about their first introduction, without once appealing to me, who might be supposed best capable of silencing the enquiry. As the gentleman therefore took my silence for a mark of his own superiour sagacity, he was resolved to pursue the triumph: he talked of our cities, mountains, and animals, as familiarly as if he had been born in Quamsi, but as erroneously as if a native of the moon. He attempted to prove that I had nothing of the true Chinese cut in my visage; shewed that my cheek-bones should have been higher, and my forehead broader; in short, he almost reasoned me out of my country, and effectually persuaded the rest of the company to be of his opinion.

I was going to expose his mistakes, when it was insisted, that I had nothing of the true eastern manner in my delivery. This gentleman's conversation (says one of the ladies, who was a great reader) is like our own, mere chit-chat and common sense: there is nothing like sense in the true eastern style, where nothing more is required but sublimity. Oh! for a history of Aboulfaouris, the grand voyager, of genii, magicians, rocks, bags of bullets, giants, and enchanters, where all is great, obscure, magnificent, and unintelligible! I have written many a sheet of eastern tale myself, interrupts the author, and I defy the severest critic to say but that I have stuck close to the true manner. I have compared a lady's chin to the snow upon the mountains of Bomek; a soldier's sword, to the clouds that obscure the face of heaven. If riches are mentioned, I compared them to the flocks that graze the verdant Tefflis; if poverty, to the mists that veil the brow of mount Baku. I have used *thee* and *thou* upon all occasions; I have described fallen stars and splitting mountains, not forgetting the little Houries, who make a very pretty figure in every description. But you shall hear how I generally begin: "Eben-ben-bolo, who was the son of Ban, was born on the foggy summits of Benderabassi. His beard was whiter than the feathers which veil the breast of the Penguin; his eyes were like the eyes of doves when washed

---

Pilaw: pilaf, a Middle Eastern, not a Chinese dish.
Pekin: Beijing, present-day capital of China.
Quamsi: Kwangsi (Guangxi), southern province of China.
bullets: small round balls—here perhaps magical pellets or gold.
Houries: houris, perpetual virgins who serve the Muslim faithful in Paradise (see *Nourjahad* 46).

by the dews of the morning; his hair, which hung like the willow weeping over the glassy stream, was so beautiful that it seemed to reflect its own brightness; and his feet were as the feet of a wild deer which fleeth to the tops of the mountains." There, there, is the true eastern taste for you; every advance made towards sense is only a deviation from sound. Eastern tales should always be sonorous, lofty, musical, and unmeaning.

I could not avoid smiling to hear a native of England attempt to instruct me in the true eastern idiom; and after he looked round some time for applause, I presumed to ask him, whether he had ever travelled into the east; to which he replied in the negative. I demanded whether he understood Chinese or Arabic; to which also he answered as before. Then how, sir, said I, can you pretend to determine upon the eastern style, who are entirely unacquainted with the eastern writings? Take, sir, the word of one who is *professedly* a Chinese, and who is *actually* acquainted with the Arabian writers, that what is palmed upon you daily for an imitation of eastern writing, no way resembles their manner, either in sentiment or diction. In the east, similes are seldom used, and metaphors almost wholly unknown; but in China particularly, the very reverse of what you allude to takes place; a cool phlegmatic method of writing prevails there. The writers of that country, ever more assiduous to instruct than to please, address rather the judgment than the fancy. Unlike many authors of Europe, who have no consideration of the reader's time, they generally leave more to be understood than they express.

Besides, Sir, you must not expect from an inhabitant of China the same ignorance, the same unlettered simplicity, that you find in a *Turk, Persian,* or native of *Peru.* The Chinese are versed in the sciences as well as you, and are masters of several arts unknown to the people of Europe. Many of them are instructed not only in their own national learning, but are perfectly well acquainted with the languages and learning of the west. If my word in such a case is not to be taken, consult your own travellers on this head, who affirm, that the scholars of Pekin and Siam sustain theological theses in Latin. *The college of Masprend, which is but a league from Siam* (says one of your travellers),[1] *came in a body to salute our ambassador. Nothing gave me more sincere pleasure than to behold a number of priests, venerable both from age and modesty, followed by a number of youths of all nations, Chinese, Japanese, Tonquinese, of Cochin China, Pegu, and Siam, all willing to pay their*

Siam: now called Thailand.
Tonquinese: from Tonkin (northern region of present-day Vietnam).
Cochin China: southern region of Vietnam.
Pegu: southern region of Burma (Myanmar).

[1] "*Journal ou Suite du Voyage de Siam, en forme de Lettres familières, fait en 1685,* par M.L.D.C., p. 174. Edit. Amstelod. 1686." [Goldsmith's note.]

respects in the most polite manner imaginable. A Cochin Chinese made an excellent Latin oration upon this occasion; he was succeeded, and even outdone, by a student of Tonquin, who was as well skilled in the western learning as any scholar of Paris. Now, sir, if youths, who never stirred from home, are so perfectly skilled in your laws and learning, surely more must be expected from one like me, who have travelled so many thousand miles; who have conversed familiarly for several years with the English factors established at Canton,[2] and the missionaries sent us from every part of Europe. The unaffected of every country nearly resemble each other, and a page of our Confucius and of your Tillotson have scarcely any material difference.[3] Paltry affectation, strained allusions, and disgusting finery, are easily attained by those who choose to wear them; and they are but too frequently the badges of ignorance, or of stupidity, whenever it would endeavour to please.

I was proceeding in my discourse, when, looking round, I perceived the company no way attentive to what I attempted, with so much earnestness, to enforce. One lady was whispering her that sat next, another was studying the merits of a fan, a third began to yawn, and the author himself fell fast asleep. I thought it, therefore, high time to make a retreat; nor did the company seem to show any regret at my preparations for departure; even the lady who had invited me, with the most mortifying insensibility, saw me seize my hat and rise from my cushion; nor was I invited to repeat my visit, because it was found that I aimed at appearing rather a reasonable creature, than an outlandish ideot. Adieu.

MURAD THE UNLUCKY

Maria Edgeworth

A novelist ranked in her own time with Jane Austen, Maria Edgeworth (1768–1849) also made major contributions to educational theory and to children's literature, which she helped to create in its modern form. Her father, the Anglo-Irish landowner Richard Lovell Edgeworth, brought liberal reformist principles to the management

---

From *Tales and Novels.* London: Routledge, 1893. Vol. 2.

factors: business agents, merchants.

[2] Like nearby Hong Kong and Macao, Canton was an early center for Chinese-European trade. [Ed.]

[3] Confucius is the Europeanized name for K'ung fu-tzu (559–479 B.C.), major Chinese philosopher. John Tillotson (1630–94), archbishop of Canterbury, was highly regarded for his sermons and religious thought. [Ed.]

of his estate and his family alike. As the eldest daughter, Maria took on a primary role in educating her brothers and sisters in the innovative, "rational," experience-based methods favored by her father and inspired by the educational theories of John Locke and Jean-Jacques Rousseau. *Practical Education* (1798), written jointly by Edgeworth and her father, brought the pedagogical methods and specific lessons they had pioneered into systematic form and became the most influential educational treatise of its time. The same methods are further illustrated in the many works for children written by the Edgeworths or by Maria alone, from *The Parent's Assistant* (1796) through *Harry and Lucy Concluded* (1825). Her novels for adults, including *Castle Rackrent* (1800), *Belinda* (1801), *Patronage* (1814), and *Helen* (1834), embody a subtler version of her progressive didacticism in a lively and complex fashion. *Popular Tales* (1804), in which "Murad the Unlucky" was first published, represents an early attempt to produce entertaining yet "improving" fiction for the growing lower-class and lower-middle-class British reading public. In juxtaposing the fortunes of the hapless Murad and his eminently prudent brother, Saladin, the tale implicitly argues for the superiority of European over "Oriental" values while endorsing a bourgeois ethic of work, discipline, and delayed gratification. [Ed.]

CHAPTER I

It is well known that the grand seignior amuses himself by going at night, in disguise, through the streets of Constantinople; as the caliph, Haroun Alraschid,[1] used formerly to do in Bagdad.

One moonlight night, accompanied by his grand vizier, he traversed several of the principal streets of the city, without seeing any thing remarkable. At length, as they were passing a rope-maker's, the sultan recollected the Arabian story of Cogia-Hassan Alhabal, the rope-maker, and his two friends, Saad and Saadi, who differed so much in their opinion concerning the influence of fortune over human affairs.

---

grand vizier: the first minister of a King or Sultan.
story of Cogia-Hassan Alhabal: a story in the *Arabian Nights Entertainments.*

[1] For Harun al-Rashid, see *Vathek* 80 n. 1. The "grand seignior" is the Sultan of Turkey and ruler of the Ottoman Empire, with its capital at Constantinople (now called Istanbul). [Ed.]

"What is your opinion on this subject?" said the grand seignior to his vizier.

"I am inclined, please your majesty," replied the vizier, "to think that success in the world depends more upon prudence than upon what is called luck, or fortune."

"And I," said the sultan, "am persuaded that fortune does more for men than prudence. Do you not every day hear of persons who are said to be fortunate or unfortunate? How comes it that this opinion should prevail amongst men, if it be not justified by experience?"

"It is not for me to dispute with your majesty," replied the prudent vizier.

"Speak your mind freely; I desire and command it," said the sultan.

"Then I am of opinion," answered the vizier, "that people are often led to believe others fortunate, or unfortunate, merely because they only know the general outline of their histories; and are ignorant of the incidents and events in which they have shown prudence or imprudence. I have heard, for instance, that there are at present, in this city, two men, who are remarkable for their good and bad fortune: one is called *Murad the Unlucky,* and the other *Saladin the Lucky.* Now I am inclined to think, if we could hear their stories, we should find that one is a prudent and the other an imprudent character."

"Where do these men live?" interrupted the sultan. "I will hear their histories from their own lips, before I sleep."

"Murad the Unlucky lives in the next square," said the vizier.

The sultan desired to go thither immediately. Scarcely had they entered the square, when they heard the cry of loud lamentations. They followed the sound till they came to a house of which the door was open, and where there was a man tearing his turban, and weeping bitterly. They asked the cause of his distress, and he pointed to the fragments of a china vase, which lay on the pavement at his door.

"This seems undoubtedly to be beautiful china," said the sultan, taking up one of the broken pieces; "but can the loss of a china vase be the cause of such violent grief and despair?"

"Ah, gentlemen," said the owner of the vase, suspending his lamentations, and looking at the dress of the pretended merchants, "I see that you are strangers: you do not know how much cause I have for grief and despair! You do not know that you are speaking to Murad the Unlucky! Were you to hear all the unfortunate accidents that have happened to me, from the time I was born till this instant, you would perhaps pity me, and acknowledge I have just cause for despair."

Curiosity was strongly expressed by the sultan; and the hope of obtaining sympathy inclined Murad to gratify it, by the recital of his adventures.

"Gentlemen," said he, "I scarcely dare invite you into the house of such an unlucky being as I am; but, if you will venture to take a night's lodging under my roof, you shall hear at your leisure the story of my misfortunes."

The sultan and the vizier excused themselves from spending the night with Murad; saying that they were obliged to proceed to their khan, where they should be expected by their companions: but they begged permission to repose themselves for half an hour in his house, and besought him to relate the history of his life, if it would not renew his grief too much to recollect his misfortunes.

Few men are so miserable as not to like to talk of their misfortunes, where they have, or where they think they have, any chance of obtaining compassion. As soon as the pretended merchants were seated, Murad began his story in the following manner:

"My father was a merchant of this city. The night before I was born, he dreamed that I came into the world with the head of a dog, and the tail of a dragon; and that, in haste to conceal my deformity, he rolled me up in a piece of linen, which unluckily proved to be the grand seignior's turban; who, enraged at his insolence in touching his turban, commanded that his head should be struck off.

"My father awaked before he lost his head, but not before he had lost half his wits from the terror of his dream. He considered it as a warning sent from above, and consequently determined to avoid the sight of me. He would not stay to see whether I should really be born with the head of a dog, and the tail of a dragon; but he set out, the next morning, on a voyage to Aleppo.

"He was absent for upwards of seven years; and during that time, my education was totally neglected. One day I inquired from my mother why I had been named Murad the Unlucky? She told me that this name was given to me in consequence of my father's dream; but she added that, perhaps, it might be forgotten, if I proved fortunate in my future life. My nurse, a very old woman, who was present, shook her head, with a look which I shall never forget, and whispered to my mother loud enough for me to hear, 'Unlucky he was, and is, and ever will be. Those that are born to ill luck cannot help themselves; nor can any, but the great prophet, Mahomet himself, do anything for them. It is a folly for an unlucky person to strive with their fate: it is better to yield to it at once.'

"This speech made a terrible impression upon me, young as I then was; and every accident that happened to me afterwards confirmed my belief in

---

khan: inn.
Aleppo: major trade-route city located in present-day Syria.
Mahomet: Muhammad (see *Nourjahad* 25 n. 2).

my nurse's prognostic. I was in my eighth year when my father returned from abroad. The year after he came home my brother Saladin[2] was born, who was named Saladin the Lucky, because the day he was born, a vessel freighted with rich merchandise for my father arrived safely in port.

"I will not weary you with a relation of all the little instances of good fortune by which my brother Saladin was distinguished, even during his childhood. As he grew up, his success in everything he undertook was as remarkable as my ill luck in all that I attempted. From the time the rich vessel arrived, we lived in splendour; and the supposed prosperous state of my father's affairs was of course attributed to the influence of my brother Saladin's happy destiny.

"When Saladin was about twenty, my father was taken dangerously ill; and as he felt that he should not recover, he sent for my brother to the side of his bed, and, to his great surprise, informed him that the magnificence in which we had lived had exhausted all his wealth; that his affairs were in the greatest disorder; for, having trusted to the hope of continual success, he had embarked in projects beyond his powers.

"The sequel was he had nothing remaining to leave to his children but two large china vases, remarkable for their beauty, but still more valuable on account of certain verses inscribed upon them in an unknown character, which were supposed to operate as a talisman or charm in favour of their possessors.

"Both these vases my father bequeathed to my brother Saladin; declaring he could not venture to leave either of them to me, because I was so unlucky that I should inevitably break it. After his death, however, my brother Saladin, who was blessed with a generous temper, gave me my choice of the two vases; and endeavoured to raise my spirits, by repeating frequently that he had no faith either in good fortune or ill fortune.

"I could not be of his opinion, though I felt and acknowledged his kindness in trying to persuade me out of my settled melancholy. I knew it was in vain for me to exert myself, because I was sure that, do what I would, I should still be Murad the Unlucky. My brother, on the contrary, was nowise cast down, even by the poverty in which my father left us: he said he was sure he should find some means of maintaining himself, and so he did.

"On examining our china vases, he found in them a powder of a bright scarlet colour; and it occurred to him that it would make a fine dye. He tried it, and after some trouble, it succeeded to admiration.

---

[2] Saladin is the Europeanized form of Salah-ed Din (c. 1138–93), a celebrated Muslim caliph who warred successfully with the Crusaders and is known in European literature for chivalry and generosity. [Ed.]

"During my father's lifetime, my mother had been supplied with rich dresses, by one of the merchants who was employed by the ladies of the grand seignior's seraglio. My brother had done this merchant some trifling favours; and, upon application to him, he readily engaged to recommend the new scarlet dye. Indeed it was so beautiful, that, the moment it was seen, it was preferred to every other colour. Saladin's shop was soon crowded with customers; and his winning manners and pleasant conversation were almost as advantageous to him as his scarlet dye. On the contrary, I observed that the first glance at my melancholy countenance was sufficient to disgust every one who saw me. I perceived this plainly; and it only confirmed me the more in my belief in my own evil destiny.

"It happened one day that a lady, richly appareled and attended by two female slaves, came to my brother's house to make some purchases. He was out, and I alone was left to attend to the shop. After she had looked over some goods, she chanced to see my china vase, which was in the room. She took a prodigious fancy to it, and offered me any price if I would part with it; but this I declined doing, because I believed that I should draw down upon my head some dreadful calamity, if I voluntarily relinquished the talisman. Irritated by my refusal, the lady, according to the custom of her sex, became more resolute in her purpose; but neither entreaties nor money could change my determination. Provoked beyond measure at my obstinacy, as she called it, she left the house.

"On my brother's return, I related to him what had happened, and expected that he would have praised me for my prudence; but, on the contrary, he blamed me for the superstitious value I set upon the verses on my vase; and observed that it would be the height of folly to lose a certain means of advancing my fortune, for the uncertain hope of magical protection. I could not bring myself to be of his opinion; I had not the courage to follow the advice he gave. The next day the lady returned, and my brother sold his vase to her for ten thousand pieces of gold. This money he laid out in the most advantageous manner, by purchasing a new stock of merchandise. I repented, when it was too late; but I believe it is part of the fatality attending certain persons, that they cannot decide rightly at the proper moment. When the opportunity has been lost, I have always regretted that I did not do exactly the contrary to what I had previously determined upon. Often, whilst I was hesitating, the favourable moment passed.[3] Now this is what I call being unlucky. But to proceed with my story.

---

seraglio: harem (see *Nourjahad* 24 n. 1.).

[3] "Whom the gods wish to destroy, they first deprive of understanding." [Edgeworth's translation of a proverb going back to classical Greek times. Ed.]

"The lady, who bought my brother Saladin's vase, was the favourite of the sultan, and all-powerful in the seraglio. Her dislike to me, in consequence of my opposition to her wishes, was so violent, that she refused to return to my brother's house, while I remained there. He was unwilling to part with me; but I could not bear to be the ruin of so good a brother. Without telling him my design, I left his house, careless of what should become of me. Hunger, however, soon compelled me to think of some immediate mode of obtaining relief. I sat down upon a stone, before the door of a baker's shop: the smell of hot bread tempted me in, and with a feeble voice I demanded charity.

"The master baker gave me as much bread as I could eat, upon condition that I should change dresses with him, and carry the rolls for him through the city this day. To this I readily consented; but I had soon reason to repent of my compliance. Indeed, if my ill luck had not, as usual, deprived me at this critical moment of memory and judgment, I should never have complied with the baker's treacherous proposal. For some time before, the people of Constantinople had been much dissatisfied with the weight and quality of the bread furnished by the bakers. This species of discontent has often been the sure forerunner of an insurrection; and, in these disturbances, the master bakers frequently lose their lives. All these circumstances I knew; but they did not occur to my memory, when they might have been useful.

"I changed dresses with the baker; but scarcely had I proceeded through the adjoining streets with my rolls, before the mob began to gather round me, with reproaches and execrations. The crowd pursued me even to the gates of the grand seignior's palace; and the grand vizier, alarmed at their violence, sent out an order to have my head struck off; the usual remedy, in such cases, being to strike off the baker's head.

"I now fell upon my knees, and protested I was not the baker for whom they took me; that I had no connexion with him; and that I had never furnished the people of Constantinople with bread that was not weight. I declared I had merely changed clothes with a master baker, for this day; and that I should not have done so, but for the evil destiny which governs all my actions. Some of the mob exclaimed that I deserved to lose my head for my folly; but others took pity on me, and whilst the officer, who was sent to execute the vizier's order, turned to speak to some of the noisy rioters, those who were touched by my misfortune opened a passage for me through the crowd, and thus favoured, I effected my escape.

"I quitted Constantinople: my vase I had left in the care of my brother. At some miles distance from the city, I overtook a party of soldiers. I joined them; and learning that they were going to embark with the rest of the grand seignior's army for Egypt, I resolved to accompany them. If it be, thought I, the will of Mahomet that I should perish, the sooner I meet my fate the better. The despondency into which I was sunk was attended by so great a degree of indolence, that I scarcely would take the necessary means to preserve my existence. During our passage to Egypt, I sat all day long upon the deck of the vessel, smoking my pipe; and I am convinced that if a storm had risen, as I expected, I should not have taken my pipe from my mouth, nor should I have handled a rope, to save myself from destruction. Such is the effect of that species of resignation or torpor, whichever you please to call it, to which my strong belief in *fatality* had reduced my mind.

"We landed, however, safely, contrary to my melancholy forebodings. By a trifling accident, not worth relating, I was detained longer than any of my companions in the vessel when we disembarked; and I did not arrive at the camp till late at night. It was moonlight, and I could see the whole scene distinctly. There was a vast number of small tents scattered over a desert of white sand; a few date trees were visible at a distance; all was gloomy, and all still; no sound was to be heard but that of the camels, feeding near the tents; and, as I walked on, I met with no human creature.

"My pipe was now out, and I quickened my pace a little towards a fire, which I saw near one of the tents. As I proceeded, my eye was caught by something sparkling in the sand: it was a ring. I picked it up, and put it on my finger, resolving to give it to the public crier the next morning, who might find out its rightful owner: but by ill luck, I put it on my little finger, for which it was much too large; and as I hastened towards the fire to light my pipe, I dropped the ring. I stooped to search for it amongst the provender on which a mule was feeding; and the cursed animal gave me so violent a kick on the head, that I could not help roaring aloud.

"My cries awakened those who slept in the tent, near which the mule was feeding. Provoked at being disturbed, the soldiers were ready enough to think ill of me; and they took it for granted that I was a thief, who had stolen the ring I pretended to have just found. The ring was taken from me by force; and the next day I was bastinadoed for having found it: the officer persisting in the belief that stripes would make me confess where I had concealed certain other articles of value, which had lately been missed in the camp. All this was the consequence of my being in a hurry to light my pipe, and of my having put the ring on a finger that was too little for it; which no one but Murad the Unlucky would have done.

"When I was able to walk again after my wounds were healed, I went into one of the tents distinguished by a red flag, having been told that these were coffee-houses. Whilst I was drinking coffee, I heard a stranger near

bastinadoed: beaten with a stick, staff, or cudgel (especially on the soles of the feet).

me complaining that he had not been able to recover a valuable ring he had lost; although he had caused his loss to be published for three days by the public crier, offering a reward of two hundred sequins to whoever should restore it. I guessed that this was the very ring which I had unfortunately found. I addressed myself to the stranger, and promised to point out to him the person who had forced it from me. The stranger recovered his ring; and, being convinced that I had acted honestly, he made me a present of two hundred sequins, as some amends for the punishment which I had unjustly suffered on his account.

"Now you would imagine that this purse of gold was advantageous to me: far the contrary; it was the cause of new misfortunes.

"One night, when I thought that the soldiers who were in the same tent with me were all fast asleep, I indulged myself in the pleasure of counting my treasure. The next day, I was invited by my companions to drink sherbet with them. What they mixed with the sherbet which I drank, I know not; but I could not resist the drowsiness it brought on. I fell into a profound slumber; and, when I awoke, I found myself lying under a date tree, at some distance from the camp.

"The first thing I thought of, when I came to my recollection, was my purse of sequins. The purse I found still safe in my girdle; but, on opening it, I perceived that it was filled with pebbles, and not a single sequin was left. I had no doubt that I had been robbed by the soldiers with whom I had drunk sherbet; and I am certain that some of them must have been awake the night I counted my money; otherwise, as I had never trusted the secret of my riches to any one, they could not have suspected me of possessing any property; for, ever since I kept company with them, I had appeared to be in great indigence.

"I applied in vain to the superior officers for redress: the soldiers protested they were innocent; no positive proof appeared against them, and I gained nothing by my complaint but ridicule and ill-will. I called myself, in the first transport of my grief, by that name which, since my arrival in Egypt, I had avoided to pronounce: I called myself Murad the Unlucky! The name and the story ran through the camp; and I was accosted afterwards, very frequently, by this appellation. Some indeed varied their wit, by calling me Murad with the purse of pebbles.

"All that I had yet suffered is nothing compared to my succeding misfortunes.

"It was the custom at this time, in the Turkish camp, for the soldiers to amuse themselves with firing at a mark. The superior officers remonstrated

---

sequins: gold coins.
sherbet: drink made with fruit juices and sugared water, often cooled with snow.

against this dangerous practice,[4] but ineffectually. Sometimes a party of soldiers would stop firing for a few minutes, after a message was brought them from their commanders; and then they would begin again, in defiance of all orders. Such was the want of discipline in our army, that this disobedience went unpunished. In the meantime, the frequency of the danger made most men totally regardless of it. I have seen tents pierced with bullets, in which parties were quietly seated smoking their pipes, whilst those without were preparing to take fresh aim at the red flag on the top.

"This apathy proceeded, in some, from unconquerable indolence of body; in others, from the intoxication produced by the fumes of tobacco and of opium; but in most of my brother Turks it arose from the confidence which the belief in predestination inspired. When a bullet killed one of their companions, they only observed, scarcely taking the pipes from their mouths, 'Our hour is not yet come: it is not the will of Mahomet that we should fall.'

"I own that this rash security appeared to me, at first, surprising; but it soon ceased to strike me with wonder; and it even tended to confirm my favourite opinion, that some were born to good and some to evil fortune. I became almost as careless as my companions, from following the same course of reasoning. It is not, thought I, in the power of human prudence to avert the stroke of destiny. I shall perhaps die to-morrow; let me therefore enjoy to-day.

"I now made it my study, every day, to procure as much amusement as possible. My poverty, as you will imagine, restricted me from indulgence and excess; but I soon found means to spend what did not actually belong to me. There were certain Jews who were followers of the camp, and who, calculating on the probability of victory for our troops, advanced money to the soldiers; for which they engaged to pay these usurers exorbitant interest. The Jew to whom I applied traded with me also upon the belief that my brother Saladin, with whose character and circumstances he was acquainted, would pay my debts, if I should fall. With the money I raised from the Jew I continually bought coffee and opium, of which I grew immoderately fond. In the delirium it created, I forgot all my misfortunes, all fear of the future.

"One day, when I had raised my spirits by an unusual quantity of opium, I was strolling through the camp, sometimes singing, sometimes dancing, like a madman, and repeating that I was not now Murad the Unlucky. Whilst these words were on my lips, a friendly spectator, who was in possession of his sober senses, caught me by the arm, and attempted to

[4] "Antis's Observations on the Manners and Customs of the Egyptians." [Edgeworth's note. The reference is to John Antes, *Observations* . . . (London: Stockdale, 1800). Ed.]

drag me from the place where I was exposing myself. 'Do you not see,' said he, 'those soldiers, who are firing at a mark? I saw one of them, just now, deliberately taking aim at your turban; and, observe, he is now reloading his piece.' My ill luck prevailed even at this instant, the only instant in my life when I defied its power. I struggled with my adviser, repeating, 'I am not the wretch you take me for; I am not Murad the Unlucky.' He fled from the danger himself: I remained, and in a few seconds afterwards a ball reached me, and I fell senseless on the sand.

"The ball was cut out of my body by an awkward surgeon, who gave me ten times more pain than was necessary. He was particularly hurried, at this time, because the army had just received orders to march in a few hours, and all was confusion in the camp. My wound was excessively painful, and the fear of being left behind with those who were deemed incurable added to my torments. Perhaps, if I had kept myself quiet, I might have escaped some of the evils I afterwards endured; but, as I have repeatedly told you, gentlemen, it was my ill fortune never to be able to judge what was best to be done, till the time for prudence was past.

"During that day, when my fever was at the height, and when my orders were to keep my bed, contrary to my natural habits of indolence, I rose a hundred times, and went out of my tent in the very heat of the day, to satisfy my curiosity as to the number of the tents which had not been struck, and of the soldiers who had not yet marched. The orders to march were tardily obeyed, and many hours elapsed before our encampment was raised. Had I submitted to my surgeon's orders, I might have been in a state to accompany the most dilatory of the stragglers; I could have borne, perhaps, the slow motion of a litter, on which some of the sick were transported; but in the evening, when the surgeon came to dress my wounds, he found me in such a situation that it was scarcely possible to remove me.

"He desired a party of soldiers, who were left to bring up the rear, to call for me the next morning. They did so; but they wanted to put me upon the mule which I recollected, by a white streak on its back, to be the cursed animal that had kicked me, whilst I was looking for the ring. I could not be prevailed upon to go upon this unlucky animal. I tried to persuade the soldiers to carry me, and they took me a little way; but, soon growing weary of their burden, they laid me down on the sand, pretending that they were going to fill a skin with water at a spring they had discovered, and bade me lie still, and wait for their return.

"I waited and waited, longing for the water to moisten my parched lips; but, no water came—no soldiers returned; and there I lay, for several hours, expecting every moment to breathe my last. I made no effort to move, for I was now convinced my hour was come; and that it was the will of Mahomet that I should perish in this miserable manner, and lie unburied like a dog; a death, thought I, worthy of Murad the Unlucky.

"My forebodings were not this time just; a detachment of English soldiers passed near the place where I lay: my groans were heard by them, and they humanely came to my assistance. They carried me with them, dressed my wound, and treated me with the utmost tenderness. Christians though they were, I must acknowledge that I had reason to love them better than any of the followers of Mahomet, my good brother only excepted.

"Under their care I recovered; but scarcely had I regained my strength before I fell into new disasters. It was hot weather, and my thirst was excessive. I went out with a party, in hopes of finding a spring of water. The English soldiers began to dig for a well, in a place pointed out to them by one of their men of science. I was not inclined to such hard labour, but preferred sauntering on in search of a spring. I saw at a distance something that looked like a pool of water; and I pointed it out to my companions. Their man of science warned me by his interpreter, not to trust to this deceitful appearance; for that such were common in this country, and that, when I came close to the spot, I should find no water there. He added, that it was at a greater distance than I imagined; and that I should, in all probability, be lost in the desert, if I attempted to follow this phantom.

"I was so unfortunate as not to attend to his advice: I set out in pursuit of this accursed delusion, which assuredly was the work of evil spirits, who clouded my reason, and allured me into their dominion. I went on, hour after hour, in expectation continually of reaching the object of my wishes; but it fled faster than I pursued, and I discovered at last that the Englishman, who had doubtless gained his information from the people of the country, was right; and that the shining appearance, which I had taken for water, was a mere deception.

"I was now exhausted with fatigue: I looked back in vain after the companions I had left; I could see neither men, animals, nor any trace of vegetation in the sandy desert. I had no resource but, weary as I was, to measure back my footsteps, which were imprinted in the sand.

"I slowly and sorrowfully traced them as my guides in this unknown land. Instead of yielding to my indolent inclinations, I ought, however, to have made the best of my way back, before the evening breeze sprung up. I felt the breeze rising, and unconscious of my danger, I rejoiced, and opened my bosom to meet it; but what was my dismay when I saw that the wind swept before it all trace of my footsteps in the sand. I knew not which way to proceed; I was struck with despair, tore my garments, threw off my

---

phantom: mirage.

turban, and cried aloud; but neither human voice nor echo answered me. The silence was dreadful. I had tasted no food for many hours, and I now became sick and faint. I recollected that I had put a supply of opium into the folds of my turban; but, alas! when I took my turban up, I found that the opium had fallen out. I searched for it in vain on the sand, where I had thrown the turban.

"I stretched myself out upon the ground, and yielded without further struggle to my evil destiny. What I suffered from thirst, hunger, and heat, cannot be described! At last I fell into a sort of trance, during which images of various kinds seemed to flit before my eyes. How long I remained in this state I know not; but I remember that I was brought to my senses by a loud shout, which came from persons belonging to a caravan returning from Mecca. This was a shout of joy for their safe arrival at a certain spring, well known to them in this part of the desert.

"The spring was not a hundred yards from the spot where I lay; yet, such had been the fate of Murad the Unlucky, that he missed the reality, whilst he had been hours in pursuit of the phantom. Feeble and spiritless as I was, I sent forth as loud a cry as I could, in hopes of obtaining assistance; and I endeavoured to crawl to the place from which the voices appeared to come. The caravan rested for a considerable time whilst the slaves filled the skins with water, and whilst the camels took in their supply. I worked myself on towards them; yet, notwithstanding my efforts, I was persuaded that, according to my usual ill fortune, I should never be able to make them hear my voice. I saw them mount their camels! I took off my turban, unrolled it, and waved it in the air. My signal was seen! The caravan came towards me!

"I had scarcely strength to speak: a slave gave me some water; and, after I had drunk, I explained to them who I was, and how I came into this situation.

"Whilst I was speaking, one of the travellers observed the purse which hung to my girdle: it was the same the merchant, for whom I recovered the ring, had given to me; I had carefully preserved it, because the initials of my benefactor's name, and a passage from the Koran, were worked upon it. When he gave it to me, he said that, perhaps, we should meet again in some other part of the world, and he should recognize me by this token. The person who now took notice of the purse was his brother; and when I related to him how I had obtained it, he had the goodness to take me under his protection. He was a merchant, who was now going with the caravan to

---

Mecca: the most holy city of Islam, to which Muslims attempt to make at least one pilgrimage during their lives.

Grand Cairo: he offered to take me with him, and I willingly accepted the proposal, promising to serve him as faithfully as any of his slaves. The caravan proceeded, and I was carried with it.

CHAPTER II

"The merchant, who was become my master, treated me with great kindness; but, on hearing me relate the whole series of my unfortunate adventures, he exacted a promise from me, that I would do nothing without first consulting him. 'Since you are so unlucky, Murad,' said he, 'that you always choose for the worst when you choose for yourself, you should trust entirely to the judgment of a wiser or a more fortunate friend.'

"I fared well in the service of this merchant, who was a man of a mild disposition, and who was so rich that he could afford to be generous to all his dependants. It was my business to see his camels loaded and unloaded at proper places, to count his bales of merchandise, and to take care that they were not mixed with those of his companions. This I carefully did, till the day we arrived at Alexandria; when, unluckily, I neglected to count the bales, taking it for granted that they were all right, as I had found them so the preceding day. However, when we were to go on board the vessel that was to take us to Cairo, I perceived that three bales of cotton were missing.

"I ran to inform my master, who, though a good deal provoked at my negligence, did not reproach me as I deserved. The public crier was immediately sent round the city, to offer a reward for the recovery of the merchandise; and it was restored by one of the merchants' slaves, with whom we had travelled. The vessel was now under sail; my master and I and the bales of cotton were obliged to follow in a boat; and when we were taken on board, the captain declared he was so loaded that he could not tell where to stow the bales of cotton. After much difficulty, he consented to let them remain upon deck; and I promised my master to watch them night and day.

"We had a prosperous voyage, and were actually in sight of shore, which the captain said we could not fail to reach early the next morning. I stayed, as usual, this night upon deck; and solaced myself by smoking my pipe. Ever since I had indulged in this practice at the camp at El Arish, I could not exist without opium and tobacco. I suppose that my reason was this night a little clouded with the dose I took; but, towards midnight, I was sobered by terror. I started up from the deck on which I had stretched myself; my turban was in flames; the bale of cotton on which I had rested was all on fire. I awakened two sailors, who were fast asleep on deck. The consternation became general, and the confusion increased the danger. The captain and my master were the most active, and suffered the most in extinguishing the flames: my master was terribly scorched.

"For my part, I was not suffered to do any thing; the captain ordered that I should be bound to the mast; and, when at last the flames were extinguished, the passengers, with one accord, besought him to keep me bound hand and foot, lest I should be the cause of some new disaster. All that had happened was, indeed, occasioned by my ill luck. I had laid my pipe down, when I was falling asleep, upon the bale of cotton that was beside me. The fire from my pipe fell out, and set the cotton in flames. Such was the mixture of rage and terror with which I had inspired the whole crew, that I am sure they would have set me ashore on a desert island, rather than have had me on board for a week longer. Even my humane master, I could perceive, was secretly impatient to get rid of Murad the Unlucky, and his evil fortune.

"You may believe that I was heartily glad when we landed, and when I was unbound. My master put a purse containing fifty sequins into my hand, and bade me farewell. 'Use this money prudently, Murad, if you can,' said he, 'and perhaps your fortune may change.' Of this I had little hopes, but determined to lay out my money as prudently as possible.

"As I was walking through the streets of Grand Cairo, considering how I should lay out my fifty sequins to the greatest advantage, I was stopped by one who called me by my name, and asked me if I could pretend to have forgotten his face. I looked steadily at him, and recollected to my sorrow that he was the Jew Rachub, from whom I had borrowed certain sums of money at the camp at El Arish. What brought him to Grand Cairo, except it was my evil destiny, I cannot tell. He would not quit me; he would take no excuses; he said he knew that I had deserted twice, once from the Turkish and once from the English army; that I was not entitled to any pay; and that he could not imagine it possible that my brother Saladin would own me, or pay my debts.

"I replied, for I was vexed by the insolence of this Jewish dog, that I was not, as he imagined, a beggar; that I had the means of paying him my just debt, but that I hoped he would not extort from me all that exorbitant interest which none but a Jew could exact. He smiled, and answered that, if a Turk loved opium better than money, this was no fault of his; that he had supplied me with what I loved best in the world; and that I ought not to complain, when he expected I should return the favour.

"I will not weary you, gentlemen, with all the arguments that passed between me and Rachub. At last we compromised matters; he would take nothing less than the whole debt: but he let me have at a very cheap rate a chest of second-hand clothes, by which he assured me I might make my fortune. He brought them to Grand Cairo, he said, for the purpose of selling them to slave merchants, who, at this time of the year, were in want of them to supply their slaves; but he was in haste to get home to his wife and family, at Constantinople, and therefore he was willing to make over to a friend the profits of this speculation. I should have distrusted Rachub's professions of friendship, and especially of disinterestedness; but he took me with him to the khan, where his goods were, and unlocked the chest of clothes to show them to me. They were of the richest and finest materials, and had been but little worn. I could not doubt the evidence of my senses; the bargain was concluded, and the Jew sent porters to my inn with the chest.

"The next day I repaired to the public market-place; and, when my business was known, I had choice of customers before night: my chest was empty—and my purse was full. The profit I made, upon the sale of these clothes, was so considerable, that I could not help feeling astonishment at Rachub's having brought himself so readily to relinquish them.

"A few days after I had disposed of the contents of my chest, a Damascene merchant, who had bought two suits of apparel from me, told me, with a very melancholy face, that both the female slaves who had put on these clothes were sick. I could not conceive that the clothes were the cause of their sickness; but soon afterwards, as I was crossing the market, I was attacked by at least a dozen merchants, who made similar complaints. They insisted upon knowing how I came by the garments, and demanded whether I had worn any of them myself. This day I had for the first time indulged myself with wearing a pair of yellow slippers, the only finery I had reserved for myself out of all the tempting goods. Convinced by my wearing these slippers that I could have had no insidious designs, since I shared the danger, whatever it might be, the merchants were a little pacified; but what was my terror and remorse the next day, when one of them came to inform me that plague-boils had broken out under the arms of all the slaves who had worn this pestilential apparel! On looking carefully into the chest, we found the word Smyrna written, and half effaced, upon the lid. Now, the plague had for some time raged at Smyrna; and, as the merchants suspected, these clothes had certainly belonged to persons who had died of that distemper. This was the reason why the Jew was willing to sell them to me so cheap; and it was for this reason that he would not stay at Grand Cairo himself to reap the profits of his speculation. Indeed, if I had paid attention to it at the proper time, a slight circumstance might have revealed the truth to me. Whilst I was bargaining with the Jew, before he opened the chest, he swallowed a large dram of brandy, and stuffed his nostrils with sponge dipped in vinegar: this he told me he did to prevent his perceiving the smell of musk, which always threw him into convulsions.

Damascene: from Damascus; Syrian.

"The horror I felt, when I discovered that I had spread the infection of the plague, and that I had probably caught it myself, overpowered my senses; a cold dew spread over all my limbs, and I fell upon the lid of the fatal chest in a swoon. It is said that fear disposes people to take the infection; however this may be, I sickened that evening, and soon was in a raging fever. It was worse for me whenever the delirium left me, and I could reflect upon the miseries my ill fortune had occasioned. In my first lucid interval, I looked round and saw that I had been removed from the khan to a wretched hut. An old woman, who was smoking her pipe in the farthest corner of my room, informed me that I had been sent out of the town of Grand Cairo by order of the cadi, to whom the merchants had made their complaint. The fatal chest was burnt, and the house in which I had lodged razed to the ground. 'And if it had not been for me,' continued the old woman, 'you would have been dead, probably, at this instant; but I have made a vow to our great prophet, that I would never neglect an opportunity of doing a good action: therefore, when you were deserted by all the world, I took care of you. Here, too, is your purse, which I saved from the rabble; and, what is more difficult, from the officers of justice: I will account to you for every para that I have expended; and will moreover tell you the reason of my making such an extraordinary vow.'

"As I believed that this benevolent old woman took great pleasure in talking, I made an inclination of my head to thank her for her promised history, and she proceeded; but I must confess I did not listen with all the attention her narrative doubtless deserved. Even curiosity, the strongest passion of us Turks, was dead within me. I have no recollection of the old woman's story. It is as much as I can do to finish my own.

"The weather became excessively hot: it was affirmed by some of the physicians, that this heat would prove fatal to their patients;[5] but, contrary to the prognostics of the physicians, it stopped the progress of the plague. I recovered, and found my purse much lightened by my illness. I divided the remainder of my money with my humane nurse, and sent her out into the city, to inquire how matters were going on.

"She brought me word that the fury of the plague had much abated; but that she had met several funerals, and that she had heard many of the merchants cursing the folly of Murad the Unlucky, who, as they said, had brought all this calamity upon the inhabitants of Cairo. Even fools, they

---

cadi: an officer of justice.
para: a coin of small value.

[5] "Antis's Observations on the Manners and Customs of the Egyptians." [Edgeworth's note.]

say, learn by experience. I took care to burn the bed on which I had lain, and the clothes I had worn: I concealed my real name, which I knew would inspire detestation, and gained admittance, with a crowd of other poor wretches, into a lazaretto, where I performed quarantine, and offered up prayers daily for the sick.

"When I thought it was impossible I could spread the infection, I took my passage home. I was eager to get away from Grand Cairo, where I knew I was an object of execration. I had a strange fancy haunting my mind; I imagined that all my misfortunes, since I left Constantinople, had arisen from my neglect of the talisman upon the beautiful china vase. I dreamed three times, when I was recovering from the plague, that a genius appeared to me, and said, in a reproachful tone, 'Murad, where is the vase that was intrusted to thy care?'

"This dream operated strongly upon my imagination. As soon as we arrived at Constantinople, which we did, to my great surprise, without meeting with any untoward accidents, I went in search of my brother Saladin, to inquire for my vase. He no longer lived in the house in which I left him, and I began to be apprehensive that he was dead; but a porter, hearing my inquiries, exclaimed, 'Who is there in Constantinople that is ignorant of the dwelling of Saladin the Lucky? Come with me, and I will show it to you.'

"The mansion to which he conducted me looked so magnificent, that I was almost afraid to enter lest there should be some mistake. But, whilst I was hesitating, the doors opened, and I heard my brother Saladin's voice. He saw me almost at the same instant that I fixed my eyes upon him, and immediately sprang forward to embrace me. He was the same good brother as ever, and I rejoiced in his prosperity with all my heart. 'Brother Saladin,' said I, 'can you now doubt that some men are born to be fortunate, and others to be unfortunate? How often you used to dispute this point with me!'

"'Let us not dispute it now in the public street,' said he, smiling; 'but come in and refresh yourself, and we will consider the question afterwards at leisure.'

"'No, my dear brother,' said I, drawing back, 'you are too good: Murad the Unlucky shall not enter your house, lest he should draw down misfortunes upon you and yours. I come only to ask for my vase.'

"'It is safe,' cried he; 'come in, and you shall see it: but I will not give it up till I have you in my house. I have none of these superstitious fears: pardon me the expression, but I have none of these superstitious fears.'

"I yielded, entered his house, and was astonished at all I saw! My brother did not triumph in his prosperity; but, on the contrary, seemed intent only

---

lazaretto: hospital; isolated building (or ship) for quarantined patients.

upon making me forget my misfortunes: he listened to the account of them with kindness, and obliged me by the recital of his history; which was, I must acknowledge, far less wonderful than my own. He seemed, by his own account, to have grown rich in the common course of things, or rather, by his own prudence. I allowed for his prejudices, and, unwilling to dispute farther with him, said, 'You must remain of your opinion, brother; and I of mine: you are Saladin the Lucky, and I Murad the Unlucky; and so we shall remain to the end of our lives.'

"I had not been in his house four days when an accident happened, which showed how much I was in the right. The favourite of the sultan, to whom he had formerly sold his china vase, though her charms were now somewhat faded by time, still retained her power, and her taste for magnificence. She commissioned my brother to bespeak for her, at Venice, the most splendid looking-glass that money could purchase. The mirror, after many delays and disappointments, at length arrived at my brother's house. He unpacked it, and sent to let the lady know it was in perfect safety. It was late in the evening, and she ordered it should remain where it was that night; and that it should be brought to the seraglio the next morning. It stood in a sort of ante-chamber to the room in which I slept; and with it were left some packages, containing glass chandeliers for an unfinished saloon in my brother's house. Saladin charged all his domestics to be vigilant this night, because he had money to a great amount by him, and there had been frequent robberies in our neighbourhood. Hearing these orders, I resolved to be in readiness at a moment's warning. I laid my scimitar beside me upon a cushion; and left my door half open, that I might hear the slightest noise in the ante-chamber, or the great staircase. About midnight, I was suddenly awakened by a noise in the ante-chamber. I started up, seized my scimitar, and the instant I got to the door, saw, by the light of the lamp which was burning in the room, a man standing opposite to me, with a drawn sword in his hand. I rushed forward, demanding what he wanted, and received no answer; but, seeing him aim at me with his scimitar, I gave him, as I thought, a deadly blow. At this instant, I heard a great crash; and the fragments of the looking-glass, which I had shivered, fell at my feet. At the same moment, something black brushed by my shoulder: I pursued it, stumbled over the packages of glass, and rolled over them down the stairs.

"My brother came out of his room, to inquire the cause of all this disturbance; and when he saw the fine mirror broken, and me lying amongst the glass chandeliers at the bottom of the stairs, he could not forbear exclaiming, 'Well, brother! you are indeed Murad the Unlucky.'

"When the first emotion was over, he could not, however, forbear laughing at my situation. With a degree of goodness, which made me a thousand times more sorry for the accident, he came down stairs to help me up, gave me his hand, and said, 'Forgive me, if I was angry with you at first. I am sure you did not mean to do me any injury; but tell me how all this has happened?'

"Whilst Saladin was speaking, I heard the same kind of noise which had alarmed me in the ante-chamber; but, on looking back, I saw only a black pigeon, which flew swiftly by me, unconscious of the mischief he had occasioned. This pigeon I had unluckily brought into the house the preceding day; and had been feeding and trying to tame it for my young nephews. I little thought it would be the cause of such disasters. My brother, though he endeavoured to conceal his anxiety from me, was much disturbed at the idea of meeting the favourite's displeasure, who would certainly be grievously disappointed by the loss of her splendid looking-glass. I saw that I should inevitably be his ruin, if I continued in his house; and no persuasions could prevail upon me to prolong my stay. My generous brother, seeing me determined to go, said to me, 'A factor, whom I have employed for some years to sell merchandise for me, died a few days ago. Will you take his place? I am rich enough to bear any little mistakes you may fall into, from ignorance of business; and you will have a partner who is able and willing to assist you.'

"I was touched to the heart by this kindness, especially at such a time as this. He sent one of his slaves with me to the shop in which you now see me, gentlemen. The slave, by my brother's directions, brought with us my china vase, and delivered it safely to me, with this message: 'The scarlet dye that was found in this vase, and in its fellow, was the first cause of Saladin's making the fortune he now enjoys: he therefore does no more than justice, in sharing that fortune with his brother Murad.'

"I was now placed in as advantageous a situation as possible; but my mind was ill at ease, when I reflected that the broken mirror might be my brother's ruin. The lady by whom it had been bespoken was, I well knew, of a violent temper; and this disappointment was sufficient to provoke her to vengeance. My brother sent me word this morning, however, that though her displeasure was excessive, it was in my power to prevent any ill consequences that might ensue. 'In my power!' I exclaimed; 'then, indeed, I am happy! Tell my brother there is nothing I will not do to show him my gratitude, and to save him from the consequences of my folly.'

"The slave who was sent by my brother seemed unwilling to name what was required of me, saying that his master was afraid I should not like to grant the request. I urged him to speak freely, and he then told me the favourite declared nothing would make her amends for the loss of the

---

factor: business agent or merchant.

mirror but the fellow vase to that which she had bought from Saladin. It was impossible for me to hesitate; gratitude for my brother's generous kindness overcame my superstitious obstinacy; and I sent him word I would carry the vase to him myself.

"I took it down this evening from the shelf on which it stood; it was covered with dust, and I washed it, but unluckily, in endeavouring to clean the inside from the remains of the scarlet powder, I poured hot water into it, and immediately I heard a simmering noise, and my vase, in a few instants, burst asunder with a loud explosion. These fragments, alas! are all that remain. The measure of my misfortunes is now completed! Can you wonder, gentlemen, that I bewail my evil destiny? Am I not justly called Murad the Unlucky? Here end all my hopes in this world! Better would it have been if I had died long ago! Better that I had never been born! Nothing I ever have done or attempted has prospered. Murad the Unlucky is my name, and ill-fate has marked me for her own."

CHAPTER III

The lamentations of Murad were interrupted by the entrance of Saladin. Having waited in vain for some hours, he now came to see if any disaster had happened to his brother Murad. He was surprised at the sight of the two pretended merchants, and could not refrain from exclamations on beholding the broken vase. However, with his usual equanimity and good-nature, he began to console Murad; and, taking up the fragments, examined them carefully, one by one joined them together again, found that none of the edges of the china were damaged, and declared he could have it mended so as to look as well as ever.

Murad recovered his spirits upon this. "Brother," said he, "I comfort myself for being Murad the Unlucky, when I reflect that you are Saladin the Lucky. See, gentlemen," continued he, turning to the pretended merchants, "scarcely has this most fortunate of men been five minutes in company before he gives a happy turn to affairs. His presence inspires joy: I observe your countenances, which had been saddened by my dismal history, have brightened up since he has made his appearance. Brother, I wish you would make these gentlemen some amends for the time they have wasted in listening to my catalogue of misfortunes, by relating your history, which, I am sure, they will find rather more exhilarating."

Saladin consented, on condition that the strangers would accompany him home, and partake of a social banquet. They at first repeated the former excuse of their being obliged to return to their inn; but at length the sultan's curiosity prevailed, and he and his vizier went home with Saladin the Lucky, who, after supper, related his history in the following manner:—

"My being called Saladin the Lucky first inspired me with confidence in myself; though I own that I cannot remember any extraordinary instances of good luck in my childhood. An old nurse of my mother's, indeed, repeated to me twenty times a day, that nothing I undertook could fail to succeed, because I was Saladin the Lucky. I became presumptuous and rash; and my nurse's prognostics might have effectually prevented their accomplishment, had I not, when I was about fifteen, been roused to reflection during a long confinement, which was the consequence of my youthful conceit and imprudence.

"At this time there was at the Porte a Frenchman, an ingenious engineer, who was employed and favoured by the sultan, to the great astonishment of many of my prejudiced countrymen. On the grand seignior's birth-day he exhibited some extraordinarily fine fireworks; and I, with numbers of the inhabitants of Constantinople, crowded to see them. I happened to stand near the place where the Frenchman was stationed; the crowd pressed upon him, and I amongst the rest; he begged we would, for our own sakes, keep at a greater distance, and warned us that we might be much hurt by the combustibles which he was using. I, relying upon my good fortune, disregarded all these cautions; and the consequence was, that as I touched some of the materials prepared for the fireworks, they exploded, dashed me upon the ground with great violence, and I was terribly burnt.

"This accident, gentlemen, I consider as one of the most fortunate circumstances of my life; for it checked and corrected the presumption of my temper. During the time I was confined to my bed, the French gentleman came frequently to see me. He was a very sensible man; and the conversations he had with me enlarged my mind, and cured me of many foolish prejudices, especially of that which I had been taught to entertain, concerning the predominance of what is called luck, or fortune, in human affairs. 'Though you are called Saladin the Lucky,' said he, 'you find that your neglect of prudence has nearly brought you to the grave even in the bloom of youth. Take my advice, and henceforward trust more to prudence than to fortune. Let the multitude, if they will, call you Saladin the Lucky; but call yourself, and make yourself, Saladin the Prudent.'

"These words left an indelible impression on my mind, and gave a new turn to my thoughts and character. My brother, Murad, has doubtless told you that our difference of opinion, on the subject of predestination, produced between us frequent arguments; but we could never convince one another, and we each have acted, through life, in consequence of our different beliefs. To this I attribute my success and his misfortunes.

---

the Porte: the Ottoman court at Constantinople, by extension the Turkish government.

"The first rise of my fortune, as you have probably heard from Murad, was owing to the scarlet dye, which I brought to perfection with infinite difficulty. The powder, it is true, was accidentally found by me in our china vases; but there it might have remained to this instant, useless, if I had not taken the pains to make it useful. I grant that we can only partially foresee and command events; yet on the use we make of our own powers, I think, depends our destiny. But, gentlemen, you would rather hear my adventures, perhaps, than my reflections; and I am truly concerned, for your sakes, that I have no wonderful events to relate. I am sorry I cannot tell you of my having been lost in a sandy desert. I have never had the plague, nor even been shipwrecked: I have been all my life an inhabitant of Constantinople, and have passed my time in a very quiet and uniform manner.

"The money I received from the sultan's favourite for my china vase, as my brother may have told you, enabled me to trade on a more extensive scale. I went on steadily with my business; and made it my whole study to please my employers, by all fair and honourable means. This industry and civility succeeded beyond my expectations: in a few years, I was rich for a man in my way of business.

"I will not proceed to trouble you with the journal of a petty merchant's life; I pass on to the incident which made a considerable change in my affairs.

"A terrible fire broke out near the walls of the grand seignior's seraglio:[6] as you are strangers, gentlemen, you may not have heard of this event, though it produced so great a sensation in Constantinople. The vizier's superb palace was utterly consumed; and the melted lead poured down from the roof of the mosque of St. Sophia. Various were the opinions formed by my neighbours, respecting the cause of the conflagration. Some supposed it to be a punishment for the sultan's having neglected, one Friday, to appear at the mosque of St. Sophia; others considered it as a warning sent by Mahomet, to dissuade the Porte from persisting in a war in which we were just engaged. The generality, however, of the coffee-house politicians contented themselves with observing that it was the will of Mahomet that the palace should be consumed. Satisfied by this supposition, they took no precaution to prevent similar accidents in their own houses. Never were fires so common in the city as at this period; scarcely a night passed without our being wakened by the cry of fire.

"These frequent fires were rendered still more dreadful by villains, who were continually on the watch to increase the confusion by which they

[6]"*Vide* Baron de Tott's Memoirs." [Edgeworth's note. The reference is to Baron François de Tott's *Memoirs,* translated into English in 1785. Ed.].

profited, and to pillage the houses of the sufferers. It was discovered that these incendiaries frequently skulked, towards evening, in the neighbourhood of the bezestein, where the richest merchants store their goods; some of these wretches were detected in throwing *coundaks,*[7] or matches, into the windows; and if these combustibles remained a sufficient time, they could not fail to set the house on fire.

"Notwithstanding all these circumstances, many even of those who had property to preserve continued to repeat, 'It is the will of Mahomet,' and consequently to neglect all means of preservation. I, on the contrary, recollecting the lesson I had learned from the sensible foreigner, neither suffered my spirits to sink with superstitious fears of ill luck, nor did I trust presumptuously to my good fortune. I took every possible means to secure myself. I never went to bed without having seen that all the lights and fires in the house were extinguished, and that I had a supply of water in the cistern. I had likewise learned from my Frenchman that wet mortar was the most effectual thing for stopping the progress of flames: I therefore had a quantity of mortar made up in one of my outhouses, which I could use at a moment's warning. These precautions were all useful to me: my own house, indeed, was never actually on fire, but the houses of my next door neighbours were no less than five times in flames, in the course of one winter. By my exertions, or rather by my precautions, they suffered but little damage; and all my neighbours looked upon me as their deliverer and friend: they loaded me with presents, and offered more indeed than I would accept. All repeated that I was Saladin the Lucky. This compliment I disclaimed, feeling more ambitious of being called Saladin the Prudent. It is thus that what we call modesty is often only a more refined species of pride. But to proceed with my story.

"One night I had been later than usual at supper, at a friend's house: none but the watch were in the streets, and even they, I believe, were asleep.

---

bezestein: bezesteen, a bazaar or marketplace.

[7]"'A *coundak* is a sort of combustible that consists only of a piece of tinder wrapped in brimstone matches, in the midst of a small bundle of pine shavings. This is the method usually employed by incendiaries—they lay this match by stealth behind a door, which they find open, or on a window; and after setting it on fire, they make their escape. This is sufficient often to produce the most terrible ravages in a town where the houses, built with wood and painted with oil of spike, afford the easiest opportunity to the miscreant who is disposed to reduce them to ashes. The method employed by the incendiaries, and which often escapes the vigilance of the masters of the houses, added to the common causes of fires, gave for some time very frequent causes of alarm.'—*Translation of Memoirs of Baron de Tott,* vol. i." [Edgeworth's note.]

"As I passed one of the conduits, which convey water to the city, I heard a trickling noise; and, upon examination, I found that the cock of the water-spout was half turned, so that the water was running out. I turned it back to its proper place, thought it had been left unturned by accident, and walked on; but I had not proceeded far before I came to another spout and another, which were in the same condition. I was convinced that this could not be the effect merely of accident, and suspected that some ill-intentioned persons designed to let out and waste the water of the city, that there might be none to extinguish any fire that should break out in the course of the night.

"I stood still for a few moments, to consider how it would be most prudent to act. It would be impossible for me to run to all parts of the city, that I might stop the pipes that were running to waste. I first thought of wakening the watch and the firemen, who were most of them slumbering at their stations; but I reflected that they were perhaps not to be trusted, and that they were in a confederacy with the incendiaries; otherwise, they would certainly, before this hour, have observed and stopped the running of the sewers in their neighbourhood. I determined to waken a rich merchant, called Damat Zade, who lived near me, and who had a number of slaves, whom he could send to different parts of the city, to prevent mischief, and give notice to the inhabitants of their danger.

"He was a very sensible, active man, and one that could easily be wakened: he was not, like some Turks, an hour in recovering their lethargic senses. He was quick in decision and action; and his slaves resembled their master. He despatched a messenger immediately to the grand vizier, that the sultan's safety might be secured; and sent others to the magistrates, in each quarter of Constantinople. The large drums in the janissary aga's tower beat to rouse the inhabitants; and scarcely had this been heard to beat half an hour before the fire broke out in the lower apartments of Damat Zade's house, owing to a *coundak,* which had been left behind one of the doors.

"The wretches who had prepared the mischief, came to enjoy it, and to pillage; but they were disappointed. Astonished to find themselves taken into custody, they could not comprehend how their designs had been frustrated. By timely exertions, the fire in my friend's house was extinguished; and though fires broke out, during the night, in many parts of the city, but little damage was sustained, because there was time for precautions; and by the stopping of the spouts, sufficient water was preserved. People were awakened, and warned of the danger, and they consequently escaped unhurt.

---

janissary aga: principal officer of the janissaries, or sultan's guard.

"The next day, as soon as I made my appearance at the bezestein, the merchants crowded round, called me their benefactor, and the preserver of their lives and fortunes. Damat Zade, the merchant whom I had awakened the preceding night, presented to me a heavy purse of gold, and put upon my finger a diamond ring of considerable value; each of the merchants followed his example, in making me rich presents: the magistrates also sent me tokens of their approbation; and the grand vizier sent me a diamond of the first water, with a line written by his own hand: 'To the man who has saved Constantinople.' Excuse me, gentlemen, for the vanity I seem to show in mentioning these circumstances. You desired to hear my history, and I cannot therefore omit the principal circumstance of my life. In the course of four-and-twenty hours, I found myself raised, by the munificent gratitude of the inhabitants of this city, to a state of affluence far beyond what I had ever dreamed of attaining.

"I now took a house suited to my circumstances, and bought a few slaves. As I was carrying my slaves home, I was met by a Jew, who stopped me, saying, in his language, 'My lord, I see, has been purchasing slaves: I could clothe them cheaply.' There was something mysterious in the manner of this Jew, and I did not like his countenance; but I considered that I ought not to be governed by caprice in my dealings, and that, if this man could really clothe my slaves more cheaply than another, I ought not to neglect his offer merely because I took a dislike to the cut of his beard, the turn of his eye, or the tone of his voice. I therefore bade the Jew follow me home, saying that I would consider of his proposal.

"When we came to talk over the matter, I was surprised to find him so reasonable in his demands. On one point, indeed, he appeared unwilling to comply. I required not only to see the clothes I was offered, but also to know how they came into his possession. On this subject he equivocated; I therefore suspected there must be something wrong. I reflected what it could be, and judged that the goods had been stolen, or that they had been the apparel of persons who had died of some contagious distemper. The Jew showed me a chest, from which he said I might choose whatever suited me best. I observed, that as he was going to unlock the chest, he stuffed his nose with some aromatic herbs. He told me that he did so to prevent his smelling the musk with which the chest was perfumed: musk, he said, had an extraordinary effect upon his nerves. I begged to have some of the herbs which he used himself; declaring that musk was likewise offensive to me.

"The Jew, either struck by his own conscience, or observing my suspicions, turned as pale as death. He pretended he had not the right key, and could not unlock the chest; said he must go in search of it, and that he would call on me again.

"After he had left me, I examined some writing upon the lid of the chest that had been nearly effaced. I made out the word Smyrna, and this was sufficient to confirm all my suspicions. The Jew returned no more: he sent some porters to carry away the chest, and I heard nothing of him for some time, till one day when I was at the house of Damat Zade, I saw a glimpse of the Jew passing hastily through one of the courts, as if he wished to avoid me. 'My friend,' said I to Damat Zade, 'do not attribute my question to impertinent curiosity, or to a desire to intermeddle with your affairs, if I venture to ask the nature of your business with the Jew, who has just now crossed your court?'

"'He has engaged to supply me with clothing for my slaves,' replied my friend, 'cheaper than I can purchase it elsewhere. I have a design to surprise my daughter, Fatima, on her birthday, with an entertainment in the pavilion in the garden; and all her female slaves shall appear in new dresses on the occasion.'

"I interrupted my friend, to tell him what I suspected relative to this Jew and his chest of clothes. It is certain that the infection of the plague can be communicated by clothes, not only after months but after years have elapsed. The merchant resolved to have nothing more to do with this wretch, who could thus hazard the lives of thousands of his fellow-creatures for a few pieces of gold: we sent notice of the circumstance to the cadi, but the cadi was slow in his operations; and, before he could take the Jew into custody, the cunning fellow had effected his escape. When his house was searched, he and his chest had disappeared: we discovered that he sailed for Egypt, and rejoiced that we had driven him from Constantinople.

"My friend, Damat Zade, expressed the warmest gratitude to me. 'You formerly saved my fortune: you have now saved my life; and a life yet dearer than my own, that of my daughter Fatima.'

"At the sound of that name I could not, I believe, avoid showing some emotion. I had accidentally seen this lady; and I had been captivated by her beauty, and by the sweetness of her countenance; but as I knew she was destined to be the wife of another, I suppressed my feeling, and determined to banish the recollection of the fair Fatima for ever from my imagination. Her father, however, at this instant, threw into my way a temptation, which it required all my fortitude to resist. 'Saladin,' continued he, 'it is but just that you, who have saved our lives, should share our festivity. Come here on the birthday of my Fatima: I will place you in a balcony, which overlooks the garden, and you shall see the whole spectacle. We shall have a *feast of tulips*, in imitation of that which, as you know, is held in the grand seignior's gardens. I assure you, the sight will be worth seeing; and besides, you will have a chance of beholding my Fatima, for a moment, without her veil.'

"'That,' interrupted I, 'is the thing I most wish to avoid. I dare not indulge myself in a pleasure which might cost me the happiness of my life. I will conceal nothing from you, who treat me with so much confidence. I have already beheld the charming countenance of your Fatima, but I know that she is destined to be the wife of a happier man.'

"Damat Zade seemed much pleased by the frankness with which I explained myself; but he would not give up the idea of my sitting with him, in the balcony, on the day of the feast of tulips; and I, on my part, could not consent to expose myself to another view of the charming Fatima. My friend used every argument, or rather every sort of persuasion, he could imagine to prevail upon me: he then tried to laugh me out of my resolution; and, when all failed, he said, in a voice of anger, 'Go, then, Saladin; I am sure you are deceiving me: you have a passion for some other woman, and you would conceal it from me, and persuade me you refuse the favour I offer you from prudence, when, in fact, it is from indifference and contempt. Why could you not speak the truth of your heart to me with that frankness with which one friend should treat another?'

"Astonished at this unexpected charge, and at the anger which flashed from the eyes of Damat Zade, who till this moment had always appeared to me a man of a mild and reasonable temper, I was for an instant tempted to fly into a passion and leave him: but friends, once lost, are not easily regained. This consideration had power sufficient to make me command my temper. 'My friend,' replied I, 'we will talk over this affair tomorrow: you are now angry, and cannot do me justice; but tomorrow you will be cool: you will then be convinced that I have not deceived you; and that I have no design but to secure my own happiness, by the most prudent means in my power, by avoiding the sight of the dangerous Fatima. I have no passion for any other woman.'

"'Then,' said my friend, embracing me, and quitting the tone of anger which he had assumed only to try my resolution to the utmost, 'then, Saladin, Fatima is yours.'

"I scarcely dared to believe my senses! I could not express my joy! 'Yes, my friend,' continued the merchant, 'I have tried your prudence to the utmost; it has been victorious, and I resign my Fatima to you, certain that you will make her happy. It is true, I had a greater alliance in view for her: the pacha of Maksoud has demanded her from me; but I have found, upon private inquiry, he is addicted to the intemperate use of opium: and my daughter shall never be the wife of one who is a violent madman one half the day, and a melancholy idiot during the remainder. I have nothing to apprehend from the pacha's resentment, because I have powerful friends with the grand vizier who will oblige him to listen to reason, and to submit quietly to a disappointment he so justly merits. And now, Saladin, have you any objection to seeing the feast of tulips?'

"I replied only by falling at the merchant's feet, and embracing his knees. The feast of tulips came, and on that day I was married to the charming Fatima! The charming Fatima I continue still to think her, though she has now been my wife some years. She is the joy and pride of my heart; and, from our mutual affection, I have experienced more felicity than from all the other circumstances of my life, which are called so fortunate. Her father gave me the house in which I now live, and joined his possessions to ours; so that I have more wealth even than I desire. My riches, however, give me continually the means of relieving the wants of others; and therefore I cannot affect to despise them. I must persuade my brother Murad to share them with me, and to forget his misfortunes: I shall then think myself completely happy. As to the sultana's looking-glass, and your broken vase, my dear brother," continued Saladin, "we must think of some means——"

"Think no more of the sultana's looking-glass, or of the broken vase," exclaimed the sultan, throwing aside his merchant's habit, and showing beneath it his own imperial vest. "Saladin, I rejoice to have heard, from your own lips, the history of your life. I acknowledge, vizier, I have been in the wrong, in our argument," continued the sultan, turning to his vizier. "I acknowledge that the histories of Saladin the Lucky, and Murad the Unlucky, favour your opinion, that prudence has more influence than chance in human affairs. The success and happiness of Saladin seem to me to have arisen from his prudence: by that prudence, Constantinople has been saved from flames, and from the plague. Had Murad possessed his brother's discretion, he would not have been on the point of losing his head, for selling rolls which he did not bake: he would not have been kicked by a mule, or bastinadoed for finding a ring: he would not have been robbed by one party of soldiers, or shot by another: he would not have been lost in a desert, or cheated by a Jew: he would not have set a ship on fire; nor would he have caught the plague, and spread it through Grand Cairo: he would not have run my sultana's looking-glass through the body, instead of a robber: he would not have believed that the fate of his life depended on certain verses on a china vase: nor would he, at last, have broke this precious talisman, by washing it with hot water. Henceforward, let Murad the Unlucky be named Murad the Imprudent: let Saladin preserve the surname he merits, and be henceforth called Saladin the Prudent."

So spake the sultan, who, unlike the generality of monarchs, could bear to find himself in the wrong; and could discover his vizier to be in the right, without cutting off his head. History farther informs us that the sultan offered to make Saladin a pacha, and to commit to him the government of a province; but Saladin the Prudent declined this honour, saying he had no ambition, was perfectly happy in his present situation, and that, when this was the case, it would be folly to change, because no one can be more than happy. What farther adventures befel Murad the Imprudent are not recorded; it is known only that he became a daily visitor to the *Teriaky*; and that he died a martyr to the immoderate use of opium.[8]

[REVIEW OF *THE GIAOUR*]

Francis Jeffrey

As a frequent and highly regarded reviewer, as well as the co-founder and longtime editor of the *Edinburgh Review,* Francis Jeffrey (1773–1805) was one of the most influential critics of Romantic-era Britain. His reviewing style could be unsparing—his critique of Wordsworth's *Excursion* famously begins, "This will never do"—but his acute literary judgment was widely acknowledged and his reviews of the British Romantic poets include some of the most telling critical assessments ever made in print. Byron's relation to the *Edinburgh Review* was for a time quite a hostile one. Following Henry Brougham's blistering, unsigned attack on his early volume *Hours of Idleness* in the January 1808 number of the *Edinburgh Review,* Byron responded with *English Bards and Scotch Reviewers* (1809), a verse satire that attacked Jeffrey personally. When Jeffrey published a generous, perceptive review of the first two cantos of *Childe Harold's Pilgrimage* in 1812, however, the feud abruptly ended. Jeffrey's account of *The Giaour,* with its clear summary of the narrative's basic trajectory,

---

Edinburgh Review July 1813: 299–309.

[8] "Those among the Turks who give themselves up to an immoderate use of opium are easily to be distinguished by a sort of rickety complaint, which this poison produces in course of time. Destined to live agreeably only when in a sort of drunkenness, these men present a curious spectacle, when they are assembled in a part of Constantinople called Teriaky or Tcharkissy, the market of opium-eaters. It is there that, towards the evening, you may see the lovers of opium arrive by the different streets which terminate at the Solymania (the greatest mosque in Constantinople): their pale and melancholy countenances would inspire only compassion, did not their stretched necks, their heads twisted to the right or left, their back-bones crooked, one shoulder up to their ears, and a number of other whimsical attitudes, which are the consequences of the disorder, present the most ludicrous and the most laughable picture.—*Vide* De Tott's Memoirs." [Edgeworth's note.]

remains a valuable introduction to Byron's challenging poem. The review speaks to the contemporary appeal of "Turkish" fragments and "Oriental *costume*" in poetry at a time when the prose Oriental tale had lost much of its force and popularity. [ED.]

This, we think, is very beautiful—or, at all events, full of spirit, character, and originality;—nor can we think that we have any reason to envy the Turkish auditors of the entire tale, while we have its fragments thus served up by a *restaurateur* of such taste as Lord Byron. Since the increasing levity of the present age, indeed, has rendered it impatient of the long stories that used to delight our ancestors, the taste for fragments, we suspect, has become very general; and the greater part of polite readers would now no more think of sitting down to a whole Epic, than to a whole ox:—And truly, when we consider how few long poems there are, out of which we should not wish very long passages to have been omitted, we will confess, that it is a taste which we are rather inclined to patronize—notwithstanding the obscurity it may occasionally produce, and the havoc it must necessarily make, among the proportions, developments, and *callidae juncturae* of the critics. The truth is, we suspect, that after we once know what it contains, no long poem is ever read, but in fragments;—and that the connecting passages, which are always skipped after the first reading, are often so tedious as to deter us from thinking of a second;—and in very many cases so awkwardly and imperfectly brought out, that it is infinitely less laborious to *guess at* the author's principle of combination, than to follow out his full explanation of it.

In the present instance, however, we do not think that we are driven upon such an alternative; for though we have heard that some persons of slender sagacity, or small poetical experience, have been at a loss to make out the thread of the story, it certainly appears to us to be as free from obscurity as any *poetical* narrative with which we are acquainted—and is plain and elementary in the highest degree, when compared with the *lyric* compositions either of the Greeks, or of the Orientals. For the sake of such humble readers, however, as are liable to be perplexed by an *ellipsis,* we subjoin the following brief outline,—by the help of which they will easily be able to connect the detached fragments from which it is faithfully deduced.

---

callidae juncturae: deft linkages, skillful rhetorical design.

Giaour is the Turkish word for Infidel, and signifies, upon this occasion, a daring and amorous youth, who, in one of his rambles into Turkey, had been smitten with the charms of the favourite of a rich Emir; and had succeeded not only in winning her affections, but in finding opportunities for the indulgence of their mutual passion. By and by, however, Hassan discovers their secret intercourse; and in a frenzy of jealous rage, sews the beauteous Leila up in a sheet—rows her out, in a calm evening, to a still and deep part of the channel—and plunges her into the dark and shuddering flood. The Giaour speedily comes to the knowledge of this inhuman vengeance; and, mad with grief and resentment, joins himself to a band of plundering Arnauts, and watches the steps of the cruel Hassan, who, after giving out that Leila had eloped from his Serai, proceeds, in a few days, with a gorgeous and armed train, to woo a richer and more noble beauty. The Giaour sets upon him as he is issuing from a rocky defile, and after a sanguinary contest, immolates him to the shade of the murdered Leila. Then, perturbed in spirit, and perpetually haunted by the vision of that lovely victim, he returns to his own country, and takes refuge in a convent of Anchorets;—not, however, to pray or repent, but merely for the solitude and congenial gloom of that lonely retreat. Worn out with the agony of his recollections, and the constant visitation of his stormy passions, he there dies at the end of a few miserable years; and discloses to the pious priest whom pity and duty had brought to the side of his couch, as much of his character and history as the noble author has thought fit to make known to his readers.

Such is the simple outline of this tale,—which Turk or Christian might have conceived as we have given it, without any great waste of invention—but to which we do not think any other but Lord Byron himself could have imparted the force and the character which are conspicuous in the fragments that are now before us. What the noble author has most strongly conceived and most happily expressed, is the character of the Giaour;—of which, though some of the elements are sufficiently familiar in poetry, the sketch which is here given appears to us in the highest degree striking and original. The fiery soul of the Marmion and Bertram of Scott, with their love of lofty daring, their scorn of soft contemplation or petty comforts, and their proud defiance of law, religion, and conscience itself,—are combined with something of the constitutional gloom and the mingled disdain and regret for human nature, which were invented for Childe Harold;

Marmion and Bertram: characters in Sir Walter Scott's narrative poems *Marmion* (1808) and *The Lady of the Lake* (1810).
Childe Harold: the hero of Byron's semiautobiographical and highly successful poem, *Childe Harold's Pilgrimage* (1812–18).

while the stern features of that lofty portraiture are softened down by the prevalence of an ardent passion for the gentlest of human beings, and shaded over by the overwhelming grief which the loss of her had occasioned. The poetical effect of the picture, too, is not lowered, in the present instance, by the addition of any of those debasing features, by which Mr. Scott probably intended to give a greater air of nature and reality to his representations. The Giaour has no sympathy with Marmion in his love of broad meadows and fertile fields—nor with Bertram, in his taste for plunder and low debauchery; and while he agrees with them in placing in the first rank of honour, the savage virtues of dauntless courage and terrible pride, knows far better how much more delightfully the mind is stirred by a deep and energetic attachment. The whole poem, indeed, may be considered as an exposition of the doctrine, that the enjoyment of high minds is only to be found in the unbounded vehemence and strong tumult of the feelings; and that all gentler emotions are tame and feeble, and unworthy to move the soul that can bear the agency of the greater passions. It is the force and feeling with which this sentiment is expressed and illustrated, which gives the piece before us its chief excellence and effect; and has enabled Lord Byron to turn the elements of an ordinary tale of murder into a strain of noble and impassioned poetry.

The images are sometimes strained and unnatural—and the language sometimes harsh and neglected, or abrupt and disorderly; but the effect of the whole is powerful and pathetic; and, when we compare the general character of the poem to that of the more energetic parts of Campbell's O'Connor's Child, though without the softness, the wildness, or the occasional weakness, of that enchanting composition, and to the better parts of Crabbe's lyrical tales,[1] without their coarseness or details,—we have said more to recommend this little volume to all true lovers of poetry, than if we had employed a much larger space than it occupies with a critique and analysis of its contents. It is but fair, however, that the reader should be enabled to judge, from a few specimens, of the justness or accuracy of this comparative estimate. He may take, first, the following little sketch of an Oriental beauty.

> Her eye's dark charm 'twere vain to tell—
> But gaze on that of the Gazelle,
> It will assist thy fancy well [. . .][2]

---

[1] Thomas Campbell, "O'Connor's Child, or The Flower of Love-Lies-Bleeding," *Gertrude of Wyoming and Other Poems*, 2nd ed. (1810); George Crabbe, *Tales in Verse* (1812). [Ed.]

[2] Jeffrey here quotes lines 473–79 and 494–503. [Ed.]

The drowning of this lovely, loving, and unresisting creature, is described with great force and feeling. Hassan comes, in profound silence with a silent band, bearing gently among them a silent and heaving burden in a white sheet. They row out in a still and golden evening from the rocky shore, and silently slip their burden into the water. [. . .][3]

These, in our opinion, are the most beautiful passages of the poem—and some of them of a beauty which it would not be easy to eclipse by many citations in the language. Different readers, however, may think differently; and some will probably be better pleased with the following parallel of hunting butterflies and courting beauties. The idea is not quite original—and the parallel is pushed too far into detail; but it is written not only with great elegance and ingenuity, but with a degree of feeling, that does not always appear in those plays of the imagination. [. . .][4]

There is infinite beauty and effect, though of a painful and almost oppressive character, in the following extraordinary passage; in which the author has illustrated the beautiful, but still and melancholy aspect, of the once busy and glorious shores of Greece, by an image more true, more mournful, and more exquisitely finished, than any that we can now recollect in the whole compass of poetry. [. . .][5]

The Oriental *costume* is preserved, as might be expected, with admirable fidelity through the whole of this poem, and the Turkish original of the tale is attested, to all but the bolder sceptics of literature, by the great variety of untranslated words which perplex the unlearned reader in the course of these fragments. *Kiosks, Caiques* and *Muezzins,* indeed, are articles with which all readers of modern travels are forced to be pretty familiar; but *Chiaus, palampore,* and *ataghan,* are rather more puzzling: they are well sounding words, however; and as they probably express things for which we have no appropriate words of our own, we shall not now object to their introduction. But we cannot extend the same indulgence to *Phingari,* which signifies merely the moon; which, though an humble monosyllable,

---

[3] After quoting lines 374–87, Jeffrey singles out several more passages for favorable comment: "the death of Hassan" (lines 655–74); the "original and energetic" vampire passage (lines 755–84); and the Giaour's "own dying and passionate confessions," especially lines 971–99, 1029–38, 1056–79, and 1099–1126. [Ed.]

[4] Jeffrey quotes lines 388–421, then singles out two more passages as "exceptionable": lines 916–36, "striking and original" in sentiment but neither "poetical" nor "elegant" and developed with too much "minuteness"; and lines 422–38, forceful in "conception and expression" but flawed by "harshness" in diction and "an air of studied ingenuity in the thought, which is very remote from the general style either of the piece or its author." [Ed.]

[5] Jeffrey quotes lines 68–102. [Ed.]

we maintain to be a very good word either for verse or prose, and can, on no account, allow to be supplanted, at this time of day, by any such new and unchristian appellation.

The faults of diction which may be charged against the noble author are sufficiently apparent in several of the passages we have quoted, and need not be farther specified. They are faults, some of them of carelessness, and some, we think, of bad taste—but as they are not very flagrant in either way, it would probably do the author no good to point them out particularly to his notice. The former, we suspect, he would not take the trouble to correct,—and of the existence of the latter we are not sure that we should easily convince him.

We hope, however, that he will go on, and give us more fragments from his Oriental collections; and, powerful as he is in the expression of the darker passions and more gloomy emotions from which the energy and the terrors of poetry are chiefly derived, we own we should like now and then to meet in his pages with something more cheerful, more amiable, and more tender. The most delightful, and, after all, the most poetical of all illusions are those by which human happiness and human virtue and affection are magnified beyond their natural dimensions, and represented in purer and brighter colours than nature can furnish, even to partial observation. Such enchanting pictures not only gladden life by the glories which they pour on the imagination—but exalt and improve it, by raising the standard both of excellence and enjoyment beyond the vulgar level of sober precept and actual example; and produce on the ages and countries which they adorn, something of the same effect, with the occasional occurrence of great and heroic characters in real life—those moral *avatars*, by whose successive advents the dignity of our nature is maintained against a long series of degradations, and its divine original and high destination made palpable to the feelings of all to whom it belongs. The sterner and more terrible poetry which is conversant with the guilty and vindictive passions, is not indeed without its use both in purging and in exalting the soul: But the delight which it yields is of a less pure, and more overpowering nature; and the impressions which it leaves behind are of a more dangerous and ambiguous tendency. Energy of character and intensity of emotion are sublime in themselves, and attractive in the highest degree as objects of admiration; but the admiration which they excite, when presented in combination with worthlessness and guilt, is one of the most powerful corrupters and perverters of our moral nature; and is the more to

---

avatars: incarnations of a deity in Hindu mythology.

be lamented, as it is most apt to exert its influence on the noblest characters. The poetry of Lord Byron is full of this perversion; and it is because we conceive it capable of producing other and still more delightful sensations than those of admiration, that we wish to see it employed upon subjects less gloomy and revolting than those to which it has hitherto been almost exclusively devoted.

Part Three

RECENT CRITICISM

Frances Sheridan: Morality and Annihilated Time

Margaret Anne Doody

[. . .] The investigation of past and present was Sheridan's contribution to the novel as a genre. She took much from Richardson, who is good on families, but even Richardson never presented this tight patterning of generational interrelation. For Sheridan, past and present lapse into one another, conflate. Memory takes precedence of experience. It is as if consciousness lapses into intervals of dreamlike, if vivid, activity, only to awaken and return to some inevitable and more solid (if terrible) recurrence of the past, which is reality. It is no wonder that a critic of part 1 of *Miss Sidney Bidulph* worried lest "the too popular doctrine of predestination seems here to be encouraged."[1] There is some kind of predestination at work, though it seems less Providential than psychological, and less psychological than visionary. Actions are related to powerful "spots of time" which are conditioning but not redemptive.

The elements that I have extrapolated from *Miss Sidney Bidulph* appear in full force in Mrs. Sheridan's Oriental tale, *The History of Nourjahad.* Published anonymously in 1767, this tale was written at the same time as the continuation of *Miss Sidney Bidulph.* According to Sheridan's granddaughter, the idea of the tale came to its author after a sleepless night spent "reflecting upon the inequality in the conditions of men" and the dependence of happiness or misery upon "the due regulation of the passions, rather than on the outward dispensations of Providence." The idea for her story then occurred to her.

> Mrs. Sheridan represented it as entering her mind like a kind of vision or dream, between sleep and waking; and though this account is very

---

From *Fetter'd or Free? British Women Novelists, 1670–1815*. Ed. Mary Anne Schofield and Cecilia Macheski. Athens: Ohio UP, 1986.

[1] *London Magazine* (March 1761): 168. [Doody's essay begins with a discussion (omitted here) of Sheridan's epistolary novel, *The Memoirs of Miss Sidney Bidulph* (1761). ED.]

> extraordinary, persons of a fertile and poetical imagination themselves, will see nothing impossible in it. She communicated the sketch of the story the next morning to her eldest daughter. . . .[2]

At the outset of the story, Nourjahad, the friend and contemporary of the young Sultan of Persia, Schemzeddin, seems destined for great office in the state, but the sultan, to test him, asks him what he would like if any of his wishes could be granted. Nourjahad honestly answers, with his boundless wishes: "I should desire to be possessed of inexhaustible riches, and to enable me to enjoy them to the utmost, to have my life prolonged to eternity" (25).[3] Seeing the sultan's displeasure with his fantasy, Nourjahad hastily makes a more prudent statement, but to himself, when again alone, he admits that his first wishes were his real desires. In the dead of night an apparition comes like a dream to his bedchamber; a gloriously handsome angelic youth tells Nourjahad he is his guardian genius, and that his wishes can be granted. He confers upon him a boundless treasure, and offers him also a vial whose contents confer eternal existence. But the genius warns Nourjahad that if he behaves iniquitously and abuses his gifts, he will be punished by "the temporary death of sleep" (27)—a sleep that may last for months, years, or centuries. Nourjahad rejoices next morning to find his dream is true, transfers his treasure of gold and gems to a secret cave, and begins a course of extravagance.

The young man is somewhat disconcerted to find that the sultan, in displeasure with him and his suspicious access to wealth, soon has him put under house arrest, but with so many pleasures at his disposal within his own palatial mansion and grounds, Nourjahad endures the privation of liberty, flattering himself that he will soon—given his immortality—outlive the sultan. He acquires a seraglio of exotic beauties, and falls in love with one of his women, the lovely Mandana. He neglects the poets and sages he had first hired, and gives himself entirely to physical pleasure. At the end of one banquet, in defiance of Mohammedan law, he drinks wine and gets drunk. He awakens to find he has slept for four years and twenty days; his beloved Mandana is dead, having died well over three years ago in giving birth to his little son.

Regret makes Nourjahad keener than ever to give a loose to appetite. With the sultan's permission he acquires a summer palace, and enhances his seraglio with new purchases. Flown with delight and pride, he appoints a festival day in which his establishment will be called Paradise. His seraglio,

---

[2] Alicia LeFanu, *Memoirs of the Life and Writings of Mrs. Frances Sheridan* (London: Whittaker, 1824), 4–5.

[3] All parenthetical references are to this New Riverside Edition. [Ed.]

led by his new favorite, Cadiga, will personate the houris, while he enacts the part of Mohammed. Taking a short nap before the festivities begin, he wakens to find that he has slept for forty years and eleven months. The withered hags who greet his awakening with joy are the ladies of his seraglio. Cadiga, who was entrusted with Nourjahad's secret by his faithful slave Hasem and has thus kept the palace in order until his restoration, tries to expostulate with him on his immoral life. But self-indulgence, loneliness, and disorientation have made Nourjahad cruel: "Go tell thy prophet so!" he cries and stabs Cadiga (56).

Next morning he awakens to find that he has slept twenty years. Cadiga's brother, Cozro, to whom she entrusted the secret before she expired of the dagger thrust, had faithfully looked after Nourjahad's interests. Cozro kept his promise to Cadiga, refraining, as she made him swear, from revenge. Impressed by the moral strength of Cozro, and by the knowledge of his own wickedness, Nourjahad reforms. He will spend his money on aiding the poor. His reward for this charity is to be arrested by the officers of the new sultan, Schemzeddin's late-born Schemerzad. In his charitable pursuits Nourjahad has broken the laws of mourning for the old sultan, the late Schemzeddin, and is suspected of a treasonable attempt to gain popularity and raise a revolt among the people. Believing that Cozro, his agent in giving alms and now more friend than slave, has been executed, Nourjahad in prison prays to Mohammed that the fatal gifts be taken back; his guardian genius appears and assures him that this is done.

Now mortal once again, Nourjahad confronts the enraged young sultan and expresses his willingness to die. But the old sultan's son turns out to be none other than Schemzeddin himself; old Hasem appears as the vizier, and Mandana, still living—and young and beautiful—is recognizable as the guardian genius also, though she now appears to be in her true role as a member of Schemzeddin's harem. The sultan had arranged all in order to reform his friend. Nourjahad has lived in illusion, and the actions which he had supposed took place over a period of more than sixty years have all happened within fourteen months. He did not kill Cadiga. The young beauties of his seraglio and the withered hags were different persons. Mandana's son (who later went to the bad) was imaginary. Most of the treasure was fake.

The story of Nourjahad teaches "the folly of unreasonable wishes" (the subtitle of the tale in a children's version),[4] as well as the unreason of letting

[4]*Nourjahad; or, The Folly of Unreasonable Wishes,* an Eastern Tale with Three Coloured Engravings (London: Printed for Tabart and Co. at the Juvenile and School Library, 1805). This is a greatly abridged and simplified version of the tale, priced at sixpence; the erotic touches, such as the rose-bud birthmark on Cadiga's breast, are omitted in the version for the very young. The pictures are attractive, if crude.

appetite triumph over humanity. Like so much Augustan literature, this tale preaches the need of acknowledging limitations and mortality in order to be fully human. Nourjahad's fantasies resemble Gulliver's ecstatic imaginings when he first hears of the immortal Struldbruggs in book 3 of *Gulliver's Travels*—that work by another Irish writer, a friend of Frances Sheridan's father-in-law. Nourjahad also bears a marked relationship to *Rasselas,* without resembling Johnson's story—there are, for instance, erotic elements completely absent in Johnson's work.

If *Nourjahad* is an Augustan piece, it is also a Romantic one; its influence can be felt in the exoticism of *Vathek* (1786), and in the fantastic elements in stories by William Godwin and Mary Shelley, authors who are also interested in the movement of time and in the psychological effects of peculiar immortalities.

What is really significantly new about Frances Sheridan's tale is its playing with time. Nourjahad experiences two time spans at once—but he is aware only of the longer one. His illusory protracted experience seems in duration and complexity more like real human life than does his saner existence, the shorter "real time" operated in by Schemzeddin. Nourjahad is for instance, made to experience, comically, the vicissitudes of fashion; when he tries to create yet another seraglio, after his forty-year sleep, he can find no girls to his taste—where, oh where, are the beauties of yesteryear? Cadiga the old informs him that

> the taste for beauty is quite altered since that time: You may assure yourself that none will be offered to your acceptance that will exceed these. Were I and my companions, whom you once so much admired, to be restored to our youth again, we should not now be looked upon: such is the fantastic turn of the age. (53)

Perhaps only a woman could have thought of this, but it should be pointed out that *Nourjahad* is consistent in maintaining a masculine point of view, just as it is consistent—and respectful—in its use of Mohammedanism. The main characters are male (women have only a subordinate walk-on part to play in the narrative) and masculine views, ambitions, and sexuality are sympathetically treated. This marks a change from *Miss Sidney Bidulph,* in which female experience and views are paramount, though in both novels the male characters are led to discover the power and importance of heterosexual love which mingles friendship and affection with erotic desire—the eighteenth-century ideal. Both novels, however, show a sympathy with men of strong sex drives who are tempted into excess. Nourjahad, given the license of the Persian seraglio, can discover his true love, Mandana, without suffering as Faulkland does for other adventures.[5] And of course, Mandana, given the license of her position as member of a seraglio, does not worry about seduction nor in the conclusion stick at any scruples or "punctilio" regarding Nourjahad's connections with Cadiga & Co. It is noticeable that the excessively indulgent hero of the moral tale wins his true love, for all his debauchery, while the more virtuous hero of the romantic novel remains eternally denied consummation with his beloved, who is likewise his Nemesis as well as guardian genius.

What goes wrong in *Miss Sidney Bidulph* would seem at first glance to go even more wrong in *Nourjahad,* but in the latter work the road of excess leads not only to the palace of wisdom, but also to happiness and fulfillment. Nourjahad's unreasonable wishes only *appear* to wreak havoc for a time; morally, they are easily identifiable and corrigible. *Miss Sidney Bidulph* too is a story of unreasonable wishes, but the most unreasonable wishes are precisely the moral ideals. Lady Bidulph's—and Sidney's—wishes to do right, to behave with heroic justice to other women and, like the sultan, to mete out just returns to lascivious men, are destined for unsuccess. Only life's experience over time can prove to the would-be doer of right the disparity between external reality and private judgment. The true difficulty of doing right can be known only over a lifetime, just as the true difficulty of achieving pleasure can be proved to Nourjahad only after what seems a span of two generations' worth of time. Nourjahad can have a second chance; Sidney cannot.

Yet, until the end and the surprise turning of the closure with the sudden revelation of the sultan's trick, Nourjahad's experience is very like Sidney's after all. Both characters learn melancholy, and find everything they have hoped and worked for with apparent prudence slipping through their fingers. Experience changes them; indeed, perhaps Nourjahad's processes of psychological change are deeper and more interesting than Sidney's. Yet they cannot escape the consequences of the past, in external situation and in internal condition. A reviewer in the *Monthly Review* had doubts about *Miss Sidney Bidulph,* wondering whether such pictures of unhappiness could have a moral end: "It is much to be questioned if such pictures of human life, however justly they may be copied from nature, are well adapted to serve the cause of virtue."[6] *Nourjahad* met more unreserved critical admiration because its overt morality is simpler, more acceptable and cheerful than that of the long novel. Yet we can doubt whether morality—or rather, the "moral"—interested Sheridan primarily. In both the somber-shaded novel and the optimistic tale similar themes can be traced.

---

[5] Faulkland is the name of the errant hero of *Sidney Bidulph.* [Ed.]

[6] *Monthly Review* (Sept. 1768): 238.

As I have indicated, Sheridan's new contribution in both narratives is found in her handling of *time.* In the apparently realistic *Miss Sidney Bidulph* as in the dreamlike and dream-originated *Nourjahad,* time proceeds in a spiral, or rather a helix, doubling back on itself. In both, the inner meaning of a series of actions or happenings can be understood only by circling back to an original point or time, a point of departure. Sidney's (and her daughters') periods of activity and pseudodecision (moral and social activity) are as vivid, lengthy and ironic as Nourjahad's pleasure seeking. The major decisive actions of characters in *Miss Sidney Bidulph* (for example, Sidney's first rejection of Faulkland, her marriage to Arnold, Dolly's interruption of her sister's wedding) take place in dreamlike states. These "realities" seem like illusions; they scatter and reform, as in a lapse of consciousness, and they return like recurring dreams. However far the Bidulph women may seem to advance in time (and they do proceed from cradle to grave in moral time) the characters all return, as if subject to reiterated and inevitable sleep of reason, to the condition in which individual desires or decisions are blotted out. Progressive time is annihilated.

The whole narrative of *Miss Sidney Bidulph* can be seen metaphorically in the light of what *Nourjahad* is literally—the story of a continuing consciousness (in this case a kind of group consciousness which endures through three generations of women) doomed to "the temporary death of sleep" (27) as well as to the sleep of death. Which is more real—the activity or the dreamlike return to reenactment? Consciousness itself cannot triumph over the reiterated fate—the past—which makes almost every character succumb in a deathly reversion to Lady Bidulph's story. Characters awaken after this lapse and find everything altered, and yet after they have tried to cope with the disorienting and puzzling new conditions, they are still eventually doomed to fall again into that lacuna in time. They are constantly immobilized and rendered oblivious at that a-temporal point to which all their actions, however ambitious or frenetic, tend. Time is conflated in *Miss Sidney Bidulph,* as it is more happily in *Nourjahad.* The past is simultaneous with the present. But in *Nourjahad,* the past time, the time the sultan knows, the "real" time, is redemptive, whereas in *Miss Sidney Bidulph* the past can never be redeemed, and cannot heal or be healed.

Sheridan's view of time and the effect of the past is a somber one, however cheerfully she tried to render it at the end of *Nourjahad.* And in the Oriental tale, too, the most vivid effects concern the hero's fatiguing immortality of error, stuck at age twenty-three over a period of sixty years, and his bewilderment after each fit of oblivion. That Sheridan's views are somber does not mean that they are unattractive. Her handling of time is quite exciting, and it brings something new to fiction. I believe that her works were an influence on the Brontës' novels. One of her later, indirect, inheritors is Virginia Woolf (one thinks of *The Years*). Sheridan's novels were translated into French, and may have had an effect on the French novel; perhaps ultimately, indirectly and among many other influences, her novel was to affect *A La Recherche du Temps Perdu.*

Yet I believe too that that grave sense of time, and the sense of helplessness in relation to time and the past, are feminine insights, or at least in the eighteenth century could have been expressed only by a female writer. Such insights, that is, could have been expressed only by a sensibility with a deep knowledge of the meaning of powerlessness, and of lack of control over fate, as well as a comprehension of the hardship involved in encountering the outside world with moral ideals, or with warm desires. It is in her larger aesthetic view of the nature of time, rather than in particular opinions about female education or sexual morality, that Sheridan is truly a "feminist," and her treatment of time is her contribution—not only to feminism but to the Novel at large—that is, to humanism and humane experience.

The Empire of Love

Felicity A. Nussbaum

[. . .] Frances Sheridan's enormously popular *History of Nourjahad* (1767), following her well-liked *Memoirs of Miss Sidney Bidulph* (1761), reverses the terms of women's entrapment in the harem so that the male sovereign, Nourjahad, is confined to his quarters by a moralistic sultan, Schemzeddin. Intended to become the first in a series of moral tales to be dedicated to the Prince of Wales, *The History of Nourjahad* was translated into French, Russian, and Polish, as well as staged as a melodrama in 1802 and as a musical play, *Illusion,* in 1813.[1] In the novel one is tempted to compare Nourjahad's confinement to the domestic containment of Englishwomen at mid-century, for whom release was experienced through the romance of improbable trances, angels bearing enormous gifts, and wealth imagined

---

From *Torrid Zones: Maternity, Sexuality, and Empire in Eighteenth-Century English Narratives.* Baltimore: Johns Hopkins UP, 1995.

[1]See B. G. McCarthy, *The Later Women Novelists,* (Cork, Ire.: Cork University Press, 1946), 21. Other oriental tales include Ellis Cornelia Knight's *Dinarbas* (1790) and Maria Edgeworth's *Murad the Unlucky* (1804). Sheridan's novel was published posthumously; she died in 1766. See the entry on Sheridan in *A Dictionary of British and American Women Writers, 1660–1800,* ed. Janet Todd (Totawa, N.J.: Rowman and Allanheld, 1985).

to be buried deep in the earth: for Nourjahad, "this paradise was to be his prison" (45).[2] Like women, he finds release from his confinement through untrammeled imagination. His confinement unmans him: "He grew lazy and effeminate" (33). Nourjahad escapes from physical entrapment through luxury, exotic drama, and the imagination, characteristics that align him with women: "I will not waste my hours, said he, in fruitless languishment for what I cannot at present attain, but make the most of the good which now offers itself to my acceptance" (144–45). While Rasselas and Nekayah[3] stoically attempt to reconcile themselves to the limitations of a life in which much is to be endured and little enjoyed, Nourjahad's desires send him dipping deeper into the subterranean treasure cave of unlimited wealth granted him by a celestial visitor. As the central character, Nourjahad is made morally ambiguous. He virtuously and unflaggingly tells the truth to the doubting sultan Schemzeddin, yet lavishly indulges himself to assuage his discontent at being physically confined. Schemzeddin, like Imlac,[4] is a judicious and moral counselor.

Forbidden to travel, Nourjahad experiences the world through his seraglio, which is "adorned with a number of the most beautiful female slaves, of almost every nation, whom he purchased at a vast expense" (33). Nourjahad is less than licentious, however, because he unvaryingly remains faithful to one woman of the harem, Mandana: "By Mandana he found himself equally beloved; a felicity very rare amongst Eastern husbands; and longing to unbosom himself to one, on whose tenderness and fidelity he could rely, to her he disclosed the marvellous story of his destiny" (33). Nourjahad's apparently disreputable character is complicated by his nearly monogamous fidelity to Mandana, the favored mistress who escapes domestic tyranny through becoming a specter. As a *man* confined to the domestic, he finds his release in the imagination.

According to Sheridan's bizarre little tale, Nourjahad supposedly falls asleep for two years, then four, then twenty, then forty, each time awakening to discover that his world has been transformed. His slumbers in each case occur because of some particularly egregious demonstration of greed or intemperance, though in fact he has been secretly drugged, duped, and presented with masquerades by the sultan. Among his extravagant projects to entertain himself is the creation of a theater of virgins who impersonate the Houriis (beautiful virgins given as a reward to true believers). Nourja-

---

[2] Frances Sheridan, *The History of Nourjahad.* All parenthetical references are to this New Riverside Edition. [Ed.]

[3] The title character and his sister in Samuel Johnson's *Rasselas* (1759). [Ed.]

[4] Imlac is the advisor to Rasselas and Nekayah in *Rasselas.* [Ed.]

had represents Mahomet, and Cadiga, who is his favorite mistress after Mandana's supposed death, acts as Mahomet's wife. Nourjahad falls asleep and awakens, fearing that his women will indulge "themselves in liberties without that restraint to which they were accustomed in his presence" (47). In the interim while he has slept, however, the seraglio has become "a train of wrinkled and deformed old hags" (48). Consequently, the self-indulgent Nourjahad reflects on human mortality and determines to fill up the seraglio anew with fresh young beauties or "I shall be at a loss how to divert the tedious hours which may yet remain of my confinement" (52). He recounts his disappointments in shopping for women in the marketplace: "One had features too large, and another's were too small; the complexion of this was not brilliant, and the air of that wanted softness; this damsel was too tall, and the next was ill proportioned" (53). Nourjahad contradictorily represents the least desirable qualities of stereotypical Eastern tyrants while he remains susceptible to traditional domestic values.

After Mandana apparently dies during one of Nourjahad's long sleeps, Cadiga's lone voice of morality counters his despotism in arguing for the laws of society and for kindness to one's fellow creatures. Nourjahad shockingly silences her by murdering her. Because the text focuses on Nourjahad's subjectivity rather than Mandana's or Cadiga's, the resulting insurrection in the seraglio is startling in its intensity. Clearly, the women's power is greater than might have been at first assumed. "Thou hadst rendered thyself so odious to thy women, that not one of them retained the smallest degree of love or fidelity towards thee," Cadiga intones. "In spite of my vigilance they made thy hated seraglio the scene of their unlawful pleasures; and at length having bribed the eunuchs who guarded them, they all in one night fled from their detested walls, taking with them the slaves who had assisted them in their purpose" (58). The offensive act that leads to the women's insurrection is the murder of Cadiga, a woman who dies attempting to make Nourjahad recognize his own failure of virtue. Women escape tyranny in this novel through collective action.

The beloved Mandana, it is revealed much later in the best romance tradition, has only feigned her death. Disguised and cross-dressed as a youth, she becomes the agent of Nourjahad's reformation away from romance to "reality" and virtue, and then reveals herself:

> The angelic youth, snatching from his head a circlet of flowers intermixed with precious stones, which encompassed his brows, and shaded a great part of his forehead; and at the same time throwing off a head of artificial hair which flowed in golden ringlets down his shoulders; a fine fall of brown hair which was concealed under it succeeded, dropping in light curls on his neck and blushing cheeks; and Nourjahad, in

> the person of his seraphic guide, discovered his beloved and beautiful Mandana! (73)[5]

All the fantastical events turn out to be a hoax, reality is restored, and Nourjahad reenters the human community invoking the moral that passion and greed should be tempered. Sheridan's romance, though apparently contributing to a virtuous woman's murder, is stripped of its deleterious effects and activates moral reform. When the veil of romance lifts in *Nourjahad,* virtue is revealed. The reader retroactively reconstitutes the way that the sultan and Mandana rather than Nourjahad actually had possessed the power to shape the story, and they reveal that the apparent romance elements are simply mundane tricks. Further, the belief that romance corrupts women's morals is thoroughly controverted, since a romance fiction effectively *cures* Nourjahad of his libidinous and licentious excesses. In *The History of Nourjahad,* dead and murdered characters resurrect themselves according to romance conventions. As in *The Female Quixote* a cross-dressed figure is the agent of crisis, but in *Nourjahad* that agent speaks and cajoles rather than simply discomfits others by her presence.[6]

In *The Female Quixote* the cross-dressed prostitute seems to urge Arabella to confront romance with prostitution and to combine the virtuous but deluded woman with the insurrectional powers of the sexually ambiguous and transgressive. When the veil of romance is lifted in *The Female Quixote,* Arabella's alignment with the maid and the prostitute is exposed. Instead of building feminist community from that alignment, Lennox turns the encounter with the prostitute into a negative example, and Arabella relinquishes romance to yield to the preachings of the exemplary countess and doctor. The revolutionary potential of romance is thwarted. But in *Nourjahad* the cross-dressed favorite of the seraglio devolves into a virtuous, monogamous woman who is the agent of her master's deliverance. Both her sexual and cultural Otherness are erased in the body of virtue. Romance is abandoned, but only after its transformative power is realized. In Sheridan's tale the confrontation occurs between the cross-dressed Mandana and the entrapped Nourjahad rather than between women. Nourjahad marries Mandana, and the seraglio, as well as polygamy, completely slips from mind.

---

[5] Margaret Anne Doody, "Frances Sheridan: Morality and Annihilated Time," in *Fetter'd or Free: British Women Novelists, 1670–1815,* ed. Mary Anne Schofield and Cecilia Macheski (Athens, Ohio: Ohio University Press, 1986), 353, believes, on the contrary, that "*Nourjahad* is consistent in maintaining a masculine point of view" and that "women have only a subordinate walk-on part to play in the narrative."

[6] Charlotte Lennox's *The Female Quixote* (1752), is discussed by Nussbaum in the earlier part of this chapter, omitted here. [Ed.]

Like Lennox's Arabella and even Austen's Emma, Nourjahad is infuriatingly misguided. Like Arabella, who encourages suitors to pursue their adventures even until death, Nourjahad actually stabs the bearer of truth, his seraglio slave, Cadiga, when she cries, "Thou art not fit to live" (56). Just as Arabella is known as mad, yet intelligent and worthy, Nourjahad is condemned as evil and greedy but deserving of redemption because of his capacity for reform. While *The Female Quixote* is comic and satiric, *The History of Nourjahad* is fantastic and sentimental. The doctor cures Arabella of romance, Pekuah recognizes the vanity of human wishes, and the sultan and Mandana remedy Nourjahad's indulgence of luxury and cruelty. Nourjahad's dilemma is the human condition—how to be happy in an imperfect world—and his unsatisfactory solution is to luxuriate in riches. But the irony for Nourjahad is that he is held prisoner in his home by the sultan, who affects to doubt his story of celestial visitations and who controls his redemptive experience. The romance he envisions is the sultan's intentionally deceptive construction. The romance elements in *Nourjahad* prove to be the effect of the sultan's well-meant deception and Mandana's willing collusion. Nourjahad is feminized, and Mandana regains dominion over him through the empire of love. Romance is a narrative ruse which, through its ability to manipulate consciousness, does the cultural work of producing moral good.

Like Arabella, who flirts with losing her reputation by unwittingly impersonating a prostitute, Nourjahad risks his moral stature as well—but his sexual virtue is not under contest and his maintaining a seraglio is never questioned. Sheridan uses the sultan to invent a reality and hence a romance for Nourjahad but uses a woman, Mandana, to bring him to a recognition of moral duty. The potential for the real harm that romance can do—as in the supposed murder of Cadiga—is dispelled through the deus ex machina of the sultan's revelations of his intrigues. In both *The Female Quixote* and *The History of Nourjahad* male authority finally wins out. Benevolence and charity, sympathy and tenderness, bridge the gap between the isolation of delusion and human community; as the doctor puts it, "It is impossible to read these Tales without lessening part of that Humility, which by preserving in us a Sense of our Alliance with all human nature, keeps us awake to Tenderness and Sympathy, or without impairing that Compassion which is implanted in us as an Incentive to Acts of Kindness."[7] *Nourjahad* is a woman's vision of male power and authority employed for good ends through a woman's agency.

---

[7]Charlotte Lennox, *The Female Quixote, or The Adventures of Arabella,* ed. Margaret Dalziel (Oxford: Oxford UP, 1991), 381. [Ed.]

Romance becomes a way to disguise and absorb the historical and geographical empire into the figural empire of love. What must be veiled or blushed over is woman's "manliness" (associated with the prostitute and exotic women), her transgressive sexuality, and her potential to escape and extend the private empire of love. In Lennox and Sheridan, women's power to produce alternative narratives about love's empire is limited to the domestic realm as a condition for the articulation of a narrative of the empire of adventure that enables the oppression of other women. The empire of love is a powerful enabling fiction, but a metaphor nevertheless, while men's imperial dominion involves actual territory and the legitimating power to colonize the world. Their imperial domain intrudes upon the domestic in spite of seeming to be distant and irrelevant. The empire of love is implicated in other kinds of empire, and the domestic is dangerously, evocatively intertwined with the exotic.

Beckford's Heaven of Boys

Adam Potkay

Lord Byron's amour with Caroline Lamb has afforded biographers any number of spicy anecdotes, though none perhaps as rich as this:

> One day [in the wake of their affair] she entered his apartment at the Albany, and finding him out, picked up Beckford's *Vathek* from the table and wrote on the first page: "Remember me!" When Byron saw what she had done, in the irritation of the moment he wrote under those words:
>
> Remember thee! remember thee!
> Till Lethe quench life's burning stream
> Remorse and shame shall cling to thee,
> And haunt thee like a feverish dream!

Leslie Marchand's *Byron: A Portrait* offers this story without remark, a silence that suggests reticence. Louis Crompton, however, observes what's obvious to anyone familiar with William Beckford: the novel in which Caroline Lamb left her *memento amori* was written by a gentleman who, thirty years earlier, had fled England to avoid being prosecuted for pederasty. Since Caroline knew of Byron's own youthful exploits with younger boys, her choice of *Vathek* is certainly intended to point a moral and probably meant to suggest the threat of exposure. But the choice of *Vathek* establishes more

Raritan Summer 1993. (All parenthetical references are to this New Riverside Edition.)

than just an ominous parallel between its author's life and Byron's own. With exquisite irony (and not without a deeper pathos), Caroline writes "Remember me!" on the first page of a novel that ends by furiously damning the memory of women and presenting as its ideal a paradise without them, happier far.

However, the irony is apparently lost on Byron. While irony demands distance, Byron's retort suggests that *Vathek* is a tale he is quite uncritically living. The stanza he writes under Caroline's line simply reproduces Vathek's own sentiment at the novel's end. Trapped in the hellish "palace of Eblis," Vathek damns his mother, a woman named Carathis, for his fate: she is, he says, "the sole cause of my perdition," an "execrable woman!" (355). (Vathek merely realizes here what the narrator has known all along, for Carathis is earlier introduced to the reader as being "as wicked as woman could be; which is not saying a little," 99.) As the "remorse" of Byron's stanza "clings" ambiguously to his bitter memory of Caroline and to Caroline's own conscience, so Vathek makes the offending woman share in the pain he feels, summoning his mother to join him in the hell she has putatively made for him.

Vathek relies, in part, on the all-too-familiar logic that when someone must take the blame, *cherchez la femme.* The novel condemns women for inciting men to aspire: Vathek is initially goaded by Carathis to abandon his childlike indolence and go in quest of the treasures of the preadamite sultans in the halls of Eblis; he is later egged on by Nouronihar, a princess he acquires along the way, for whom the promised carbuncle of Giamschid is a sufficient lure away from her sportive playmate, the adolescent boy Gulchenrouz. Carathis and Nouronihar are largely held accountable for "that restless ambition," to quote the novel's penultimate paragraph, "which, aiming at discoveries reserved for beings of a supernatural order, perceives not, through its infatuated pride, that the condition of man upon earth is to be—humble and ignorant" (158). Where ignorance is devoutly to be wished, *all* knowledge becomes forbidden knowledge. The novel concludes, "Thus the Caliph Vathek, for the sake of empty pomp and forbidden power, had sullied himself with a thousand crimes, became a prey to grief without end, and remorse without mitigation: whilst the humble, the despised Gulchenrouz passed whole ages in undisturbed tranquillity, and in the pure happiness of childhood" (158).

As this last sentence makes clear, the moral of *Vathek* is finally neither Faustian lesson nor simple misogynist topos. It involves the more surprising notion that growing up at all—acquiring any kind of knowledge—is inherently damning. Happiness is childhood, or, more specifically, early adolescence, for while Gulchenrouz "has passed his thirteenth year," one suspects he's just barely done so. Gulchenrouz's blessing is never to pass another year, but rather to remain perpetually adolescent, "in nests still higher than the clouds," along with the fifty "handsomest boys" of Persia. Vathek's intention was to have sacrificed these boys to the Giaour, a messenger of Eblis—just as it was Carathis's plan to offer up the "palpitating heart" of Gulchenrouz—but all alike are saved by a deus ex machina, "a good old genius, whose fondness for the company of children, had made it his sole occupation to protect them." Gulchenrouz's entry into the paradise of boys is the novel's one picture of salvation:

> He admitted without fear the congratulations of his little friends, who were all assembled in the nest of the venerable genius, and vied with each other in kissing his serene forehead and beautiful eye-lids.—Remote from the inquietudes of the world; the impertinence of harems, the brutality of eunuchs, and the inconstancy of women; there he found a place truly congenial to the delights of his soul. In this peaceable society his days, months, and years glided on; nor was he less happy than the rest of his companions: for the genius, instead of burthening his pupils with perishable riches, and vain sciences, conferred upon them the boon of perpetual childhood. (143–44)

Male reciprocity, unlimited mutuality, the communion of kind: these are the attributes of a paradise in which boys placidly reflect one another for all eternity.

And this is the book that Byron kept on his table, referred to in print as a "sublime tale," and reportedly called in conversation "his gospel." His admiration for *Vathek* was early conceived, and long sustained. Beyond any personal sympathy he may have felt for Beckford—whom he dubbed, with dubious tone, "the great Apostle of Paederasty" and "the Martyr of Prejudice"—Byron was first and foremost fascinated with Beckford's novel, which he most fully addressed in a manuscript stanza from *Childe Harold:*

> Unhappy Vathek! in an evil hour
> Gainst Nature's voice seduced to deed accurst,
> Once Fortune's minion, now thou feel'st her Power!
> Wrath's vials on thy lofty head have burst.
> In wit, in genius, as in wealth the first,
> How wondrous bright thy blooming morn arose!
> But thou wert smitted with unhallowed thirst
> Of nameless crime, and thy sad day must close
> To scorn, and solitude unsought—the worst of woes.

As the scandal of Beckford's life has always been better known than the plot of his novel, it seems natural, upon first glancing at Byron's lines, to read "Vathek" as an alias for "Beckford," and the "nameless crime" as a taste for boys. But "Vathek" can be read as more than a mere alias. Indeed, Byron's stanza provides a perfectly lucid commentary on the Caliph's "unhallowed thirst" for untold power and knowledge—a crime always incited, apparently, by mothers and brides. Taken as a reading of the novel, Byron's lines express a marked sympathy with its will to recoil from curious knowledge, from experience itself, and, implicitly, from women. We can well imagine that Byron felt the allure of Beckford's paradise of boys; certainly, this is what Caroline Lamb seems to have imagined. Her "Remember me," whether as plea or threat, warns Byron against denying their liaison, which she might consider a rite of passage, and investing in a puerile fable bound to sour into mere impossibility. Oblivious to admonition, Byron merely conjures his favorite image of the Lethean waters that will wash away all memory of experience, and to allow him to become pristine and inviolable, a boy again.

Of course, as publication history amply attests, Byron's call for Lethe struck a responsive chord in a sizable readership. For all his Childe's talk of alienation, Byron knew that he himself was no island, and he is, perhaps, never less alone than in his puerile longings. The fantasy of being a boy among boys is neither a peculiarity of Byron's biography and Beckford's *Vathek,* nor is it solely an episode in the history of what will come to be called homosexuality. It's a far more pervasive fantasy, and the fact that it is now a thoroughly familiar one—which we are apt to call the "Peter Pan syndrome," and which we have most recently seen glamorized in *Brideshead Revisited*'s Sebastian Flyte and his teddy bear—should not obscure the fact of its being, at least in literature, an eighteenth-century *invention.*

The desire to be a boy among boys is an utterly novel aspect of the Age of Enlightenment, and one that must be properly distinguished from the pedigreed desire to be a man enjoying boys. Byron's famous stanzas on Don Juan's education show a full awareness of what "Greek Love" entailed, and in a Latin text probably familiar to Byron (if not Juan), Suetonius details Tiberius's entertainments at Capri, which included "training little boys, whom he called his 'minnows,' to chase him while he went swimming and get between his legs to lick and nibble him." Yet for Tiberius, surrounding oneself with boys is altogether opposed to identifying with them. Similarly, paradise contains beautiful boys in the Koran, and pederasty figures more generally in both the Islamic literature and the oriental tales available to Beckford and Byron. In all these cases, however, boys exist for the pleasure of men.

Literature before the eighteenth century doubtless affords examples of boys or young men loath to grow up; that the fair young man of Shakespeare's sonnets should so insistently be told to marry and reproduce indeed implies a certain unwillingness to do so. But the poet of the sonnets doesn't wish that the young man could remain young forever or gravely lament the fact that he cannot. The first poet to do so unequivocally would appear to be Thomas Gray, in "An Ode on a Distant Prospect of Eton College." With Polixenes of *The Winter's Tale*—but without a Hermione to rebuff him maturely—the poet of the Eton Ode longs "to be a boy eternal" alongside other "pretty lordlings," far from the "temptations [that] have since been born to 's."

Gray's poem charts the distance between "a sprightly Race" of schoolboys, blessedly free from self-consciousness or any type of care, and the speaker's own unhappy consciousness of "Misfortune," "the fury Passions," and everything else that distinguishes "Men." Following Gray, poets very often cast longing backward glances at a lost paradise of humble and ignorant boyhood; Byron's *Hours of Idleness* is hardly remarkable for containing a poem entitled "On a Distant View of the Village and School of Harrow on the Hill." What is remarkable is how captivating this genre of recollection became, despite how little it resembles anyone's schooldays. The glamorizing of schoolboys owes something, of course, to the prosaic fact that attending public schools had become a national habit of the well born in England by the mid-eighteenth century. But this fact alone can hardly explain the adult fantasy of wishing oneself a boy again, especially when, as Gray well knew, public school was not really such a congenial place for budding poets. As Gibbon soberly remarked of Gray's lines, "The poet may gaily describe the short hours of recreation; but he forgets the daily tedious labours of the school, which is approached each morning with anxious and reluctant steps." Moreover, the educational ideal of public school can't account—except ironically—for Gray's influential image of an Eden where "Ignorance is Bliss" and "'Tis Folly to be wise."

Neither can the simple matter of public school segregation adequately explain his image of an Eden without Eve. An almost mythic animus lurks behind a poem in which, if women figure at all, they do so only as the implicit causes of fallen passions such as "pineing Love" and "Jealousy with rankling Tooth." This animus is more clearly displayed in a letter Gray himself would later write to his young student Bonstetten, warning him against the "allurements of painted Women"; it is still more vivid in Johann Müller's engraving of Richard Bentley's "Design" for the Eton Ode (1753). Horace Walpole explained the design: "Boys at their sports, near the chapel of Eton, the god of the Thames sitting by: the passions, misfortunes, and diseases, coming down upon them. On either side, terms representing Jealousy and Madness." Madness is the figure that frames the central scene on the right, a Medusa figure with torch in hand, while Jealousy is the despondent, androgynous figure on the left; the "passions" that descend upon the boys are similarly all feminine forms. In no uncertain terms, women are cast as the enclosing threat to the focal idyll of "boys," who are in turn depicted as duly Hellenized young men. Moreover, Bentley and Müller evoke the homoeroticism merely implicit in Gray's prospect by placing a distinct compositional emphasis on the jutting posteriors of two of the young men, one bathing in, and one stooping beside, the Thames. However, the decidedly homoerotic cast of the Eton poem and design (along with much of Beckford and some of Byron) should not lead us to assume that the paradise of boys was primarily a ghettoized vision in the eighteenth century. Some forty years after Gray composed his Ode, Johnson could disapprove of it on the grounds that it "suggests nothing . . . which every beholder does not equally think and feel."

But by the time that every man shared Gray's tragic vision of boyhood's fragility, Beckford had introduced a strangely compelling comedy in which boyhood need never end. The Eton Ode is an elegy; the fate of Gulchenrouz in *Vathek* is an idyll. Beckford indeed expresses in European letters the same idyll of "never-ending youth" that Johann Winckelmann located at the heart of Greek statuary, in his ground-breaking *History of Ancient Art.* As a neo-Hellenic fantasy of incorruptible adolescence, Gulchenrouz supplies *Vathek* with a counterpoint to the Caliph Vathek, who is irredeemably damned through growing up. The novel is in effect the first antibildungsroman, ironically poised at the threshold of the nineteenth-century novel of education.

The outset of Beckford's tale provides an allegory of infancy, in which Vathek is comfortably ensconced in his "palaces of the five senses" (80)—an image of oriental sensuality, certainly, but also an illustration of the pancorporal sexuality that precedes the putatively genital-centered sexuality of the adult. In the first third of the novel, Vathek generally acts out the Calvinist conception of the infant as a tyrant of desire. His appetite for food is predominant, and when, in a scene of not untypical grotesqueness, his demands fall upon the (literally) deaf ears of his fifty "mute negresses," he, "having totally forgotten their deafness began to cuff, pinch, and bite them" (100). Kicking is his other common response to frustrated desire, as when a number of his guards are unfortunately found "lying lifeless around him": "In the paroxism of his passion he fell furiously upon the poor carcases, and kicked them till evening without intermission" (85). While servants, quick or dead, are fair game for such abuse, Vathek— here, at one with Beckford—especially relishes kicking, tricking, and treading on venerable elders, eunuchs, and holy men, who are invariably presented as doddering old fools. No briars are about to bind his joys and desires.

Vathek thus starts out as an infantile character, little more than an id, at once ludicrous and, in an iconoclastic way, oddly heroic. Women serve as the agents of his subsequent education. His absurdly wicked mother Carathis, who is first seen putting her son to bed and protecting him from a populace reasonably offended by his various high jinks, ultimately diverts his appetite for food into a more wordly ambition for power and glory. He sets off on his quest for the subterranean palace of Eblis largely at her prompting. But Vathek truly crosses out of infancy only through the heterosexual passion he conceives along the way for the princess Nouronihar. Mistakenly thinking at one point that Nouronihar has died, Vathek significantly loses his appetite, believing it "will not soon be the case" that he will "feel hungry" (134). (The reader has grown so accustomed to Vathek's hunger that the sentence is startling.) It is when Carathis becomes incensed at the dilatoriness of her son's love affair that he first defies, however partially, a maternal authority until then absolute:

> Dread lady! you shall be obeyed; but I will not drown Nouronihar. She is sweeter to me than a Myrabolan comfit; and is enamoured of carbuncles; especially that of Giamschid; which hath also been promised to be conferred upon her: she, therefore, shall go along with us; for I intend to repose with her upon the sofas of Soliman: I can sleep no more without her. (141)

Vathek remains blissfully ignorant of Nouronihar's real motive in sleeping with him: as the narrator repeatedly tells us, she has more "ardour" for the carbuncle than for "the amorous monarch," whom she manipulates to suit her own ends (135). Clearly, whether in the hands of Carathis or Nouronihar, Vathek never ceases to be a puppet of women's power and thirst for power. Growing up in *Vathek* means more or less blindly coming under the sway of female ambitions. Vathek's eyes are opened only after his quest has irretrievably damned him; only in the dungeons of Eblis is his own experience explained to him by the preadamite king Soliman Ben Daoud, who similarly "suffered [himself] to be seduced by the love of women, and a curiosity that could not be restrained by sublunary things" (154). The sequence of this sentence is ostensibly causal.

According to the logic of the novel, Carathis, who follows upon Vathek's heels to Eblis, assuredly deserves to be damned, whereas the reader feels a certain illogical regret at Nouronihar's fate, if only because it might have been avoided had she remained Gulchenrouz's playmate. Her own fall proceeds from abandoning the perfect narcissism of their relationship, glowingly described by the narrator: "Nouronihar loved her cousin, more than her own beautiful eyes. Both had the same tastes and amusements; the same long, languishing looks; the same tresses; the same fair complexions; and, when Gulchenrouz appeared in the dress of his cousin, he seemed to be more feminine than even herself" (123). This description of Gulchenrouz's epicene beauty harkens back to Winckelmann's admiration for ancient statues of Hercules, in which "the distinction of sex [is left] almost doubtful, as the beauty of a young man should be." By the same token, Gulchenrouz's casual transvestism may allude to representations of Hercules's sojourn with Omphale. His physical appeal is not at all virile, a point made still clearer in the narrative detail that while he could "draw the bow," he could not "dart the lance" (123). As bowman, he recalls a youthful, puckish Eros, yet Gulchenrouz never has to grow up and "dart the lance"; he is, rather, an Eros eternally without a Psyche. Nouronihar's original ability to mirror her little cousin might have been her salvation, but she comes instead to yearn for Vathek and carbuncles—she becomes, in the novel's terms, a woman. And heterosexuality, in *Vathek,* always leads to hell. Gulchenrouz, by contrast, is transported to a paradise in which he may forever enjoy the pleasure of being a boy passively reflecting other boys. Gibbon deplored Gray's portrayal of "a state of happiness arising only from the want of foresight and reflection," but, in any irony that adheres to the word, the joy of "reflection" is precisely the key to Gray's, and Beckford's, paradise of boys.

Why should this fantasy have become so powerful and pervasive in the later eighteenth century? While any answer must remain broadly speculative, I'll try to taper the breadth of my successive theses. Most generally, the paradise of boys motif contests the ascendent myths of modernity: progressive technological, social, and moral change; a break with the unexamined pieties of the past; "man's emergence," in Kant's phrase, "from his self-imposed non-age." The loneliness of becoming—which, not for Kant alone, means becoming ever more autonomous and responsible—calls forth nostalgia for the comforts of simply being, in the way that adults sometimes think that children simply are. Boys in particular (girls, it seems, are never discussed) are thought to exist without consciousness, without will, undifferentiated from animals, from other boys, from the natural settings in which our fancies invariably place them. While this primitivist vision of boyhood wouldn't have been unrecognizable to Shakespeare, he would have been at least surprised by the urgency with which eighteenth-century authors invoke it. Polixenes recalls his "unfledged days" with merely pleasant grief; he would hardly have sympathized with Gray's grim reluctance to leave boyhood behind, or Beckford's anarchic denial of the need to grow up.

Moreover, even Polixenes—who, as Hermione amusedly notes, implies in passing that wives are "devils"—could scarcely comprehend the bitterness with which later authors blame women for forcing them to grow up. Perhaps the novel emotional demands of what Lawrence Stone calls the ideology of the companionate marriage made (and makes) growing up seem more dreadful than it might otherwise be. Similarly, the attraction of a segregated paradise attests to, even as it rejects, the increasing sexual integration of polite society. Not only did the family circle become a more prominent institution, and the Parisian salon flourish, but the entire eighteenth-century "republic of letters" allowed for a greater accommodation of women, both as audience (Hume, for one, was all but prepared to "resign into their Fair Hands the sovereign Authority over [this] Republic"), and as authority (in the proliferation of popular women novelists, essayists, and letter writers). Traditionally, sexual segregation, attended by varying shades of misogynist sentiment, had been more or less the norm; only in the later eighteenth century does it begin to become a conscious revolt. Beckford and Byron variously rebel against both the rising estimation of women in society, and the concomitant rise of a polite discourse of stylistic and passional restraint, authorized by an ideal of women's natural modesty.

Between Beckford's rebellion and Byron's there lies that portion of Wordsworth which, as Trilling observed, "defends the violence and fearfulness of literature from the 'progressive' ideas of his day." Trilling refers here to book 5 of *The Prelude,* in which lone poetic madness and eschatological vision are preferred over the domestic life of men for whom it is enough "to take charge / Their wives, their children, and their virgin loves." The same book draws the well-known contrast between the Infant Prodigy, whose self-consciousness has been cultivated according to Maria and Richard Edgeworth's enlightened educational theory, and the Winander Boy, whose heart and mind reflect the dizzying sublimities of nature as passively as nature reflects itself, like "that uncertain heaven, received / Into the bosom of the steady lake." The Infant Prodigy has foresight and reflection, in Gibbon's sense; the Winander Boy simply reflects that which surrounds him. In the elegy that follows upon the recollection of the Winander Boy's early death, Wordsworth unites him with "his mates," "a race of real children" who now all seem to be interred, and all of whom are commemorated for having been in life happily free from volition, "mad at their sports like withered leaves in winds." The Winander Boy is Wordsworth's Gulchenrouz, preserved from the corruptions of thought and experience by abruptly and magically disappearing while still young, and reappearing, if only in the poet's imaginative vision, amidst a veritable paradise of boys.

It is, however, in the broad outlines of Byron's literary career that we may find the Romantics' most thorough engagement with the themes of *Vathek.* Byron early conceived an inclination to glorify his boyhood: his "Distant View of Harrow" begins,

> Ye scenes of my childhood, whose loved recollection
> Embitters the present, compared with the past;
> Where science first dawn'd on the powers of reflection,
> And friendships were form'd, too romantic to last;
> Where fancy yet joys to retrace the resemblance

Of comrades, in friendship and mischief allied;
How welcome to me your ne'er fading remembrance,
Which rests in the bosom, though hope is denied!

In the first stanza the speaker's attitude towards the dawn of science is not unambiguous, and neither is the meaning of *reflection,* which may refer either to cogitation or, in light of the following stanza, the boys' ability romantically to reflect or "resemble" one another. Boyhood attachments are the only memories that Byron is glad are "ne'er fading," and indeed he did much in his life to preserve them, such as always carrying with him a lock of John Edelston's hair. "I certainly love him more than any human being," Byron wrote shortly before leaving Cambridge, "and neither time nor distance have had the least effect on my (in general) changeable disposition."

Yet since most of us, unlike John Edelston, don't die young, the Byronic hero confronts the problem that "The Tree of Knowledge is not that of Life." *Manfred* depicts the damning knowledge—of good and evil, of things seen and unseen, and especially of one's own intolerable isolation—that follows upon a shattered idyll. In the aftermath of his fatal affair with his sister Astarte, Manfred remembers, "She was like me in lineaments; her eyes / Her hair, her features, all, to the very tone / Even of her voice, they said were like mine." We unavoidably see Byron and his sister Augusta reflected in this passage, but we might just as readily see the unfallen love of Gulchenrouz and Nouronihar. Sexual experience—penetrating the reflective surface—is the unnameable crime that defaces Manfred's paradise with Astarte, and issues (by now expectably) in their deaths.

Yet according to the high Byronic vision, sexual knowledge is as daring as it is damning. Taking a certain pride in feeling himself a damned creature, Byron was apt to satirize a writer such as Keats, who hadn't yet crossed out of adolescence; Byron's letters refer contemptuously to "Johnny Keats's piss a bed poetry," his "Onanism of Poetry." Keats's great odes, however, seem relatively grown up; his fascination with the frozen adolescent figures on a Grecian urn is merely regretful, conventionally Gray-like. *Don Juan* is a far less responsible fantasy of sexual adventures that, magically, do not entail experience. Byron chose for his last and greatest poem a character who, for all his varied episodic adventures, never has to grow up or learn anything. Juan brings to Haidee's island—and even to Gulbeyaz's harem, and Catherine's court—the same undeflowered innocence he should properly have lost with Julia. Though lent a certain irony, in part, by the poem's more seasoned narrator, the character of Juan still remains perpetually Edenic. He remembers nothing. Byron, not so blessed as this, would die in Greece, in love with an adolescent boy in whom he could no longer see his own reflection.

The Orientalism of Byron's *Giaour*

Marilyn Butler

Orientalism is a major theme of English Romanticism. Much, even perhaps most, of the best poetry of Byron and Shelley is set between Greece and the Hindu Kush, a region which in their day signified the crumbling Ottoman empire and the insecure overland route to British India. This was the Debateable Land between a Europe locked in a war involving at one time or another every major state, and the supposedly wealthy empire and trading monopoly which Britain had secured in the East. The geographical significations should be taken at face value, since these are materialist poets, for whom the place of a poem's setting means what it says, and the time is always in some sense the present. Hazlitt came to view Byron's contemporaneity as a reproach: "his Lordship's Muse spurns the olden time, and affects all the supercilious airs of a modern fine lady and an upstart."[1] John Hamilton Reynolds thought his friend Keats scored over Byron by getting away from specifics of time and place. Keats "does not make a home for his mind in one land—its productions are an universal story, not an eastern tale."[2] Whether these two are right about the value of what Byron did, they are surely not wrong as to the fact. Whatever the East came afterwards to represent as an abstraction—a paradisal religious region of the mind for German academics, a place of sexual release and fantasy for French artists—in English culture in the Napoleonic war period it is also the site of a pragmatic contest among the nations for world power.

When Byron left England for the Mediterranean on 2 July 1809 he surely expected the focus of his trip to be more European than *Childe Harold* I and II, considered as a single poem, actually is. He visited exotic lands now fallen into slavery, but showing symptoms of heroic resistance: first Portugal and Spain, afterwards Albania and Greece. Colourful freedom-fighters, present-day equivalents of Scott's highly saleable Border rievers and Highland chieftains, must have been the bait that took Byron initially to the Iberian peninsula. After the French invaded Spain and Portugal in 1807, some of the Spanish peasantry rose against them in the spring of 1808, and were supported that August by the landing of a British army. Byron a year

From *Byron and the Limits of Fiction.* Liverpool: Liverpool UP, 1988.

[1] William Hazlitt, "Lord Byron," *The Spirit of the Age* (1825); reprinted in *Byron: The Critical Heritage,* ed. Andrew Rutherford (London, 1970), p. 269.

[2] J. H. Reynolds, review of *Endymion* in *The Alfred,* 6 October 1818; reprinted in *Keats: The Critical Heritage,* ed. G. M. Matthews (London, 1971), p. 119.

later arrives not quite as a tourist, more as a literary type of war correspondent, an early Hemingway. The whole of *Childe Harold* I and II in its original form, most of it written in Greece between 31 October 1809 and 28 March 1810, has the stamp of investigative journalism, in which the poetic reporter looks for signs of rebellion and (since he is highly partisan) satirizes the natives when, as in Portugal and Greece, he finds them supine.

For Byron the exercise is decidedly not designed to help the British war effort. Conservative intellectuals had rushed to make capital for Britain out of these uprisings by peasants against the theoretically democratic French. Wordsworth in *The Convention of Cintra* and Coleridge in *The Friend* both extolled the Spanish people for confirming Burke's view of human nature as *naturally* religious, traditional, socially bonded to a little platoon rather than to the abstract concepts of liberty and fraternity. Liberals like Byron and Francis Jeffrey were correspondingly embarrassed by Spanish resistance to the French, which had to be acknowledged as popular, but was also rightist, Catholic, and ideologically uncongenial to them. Byron contrives to dilute the topic in his first two Cantos of *Childe Harold* by placing it in a wider context and even trumping it with the yet more glorious possibility of an uprising in Greece, the spiritual home of liberty.

Significantly, Byron was not alone in linking the Spanish struggle with matters further east. Three of the most serious older poets then writing, Landor, Scott and Southey, all chipped in with works on the Peninsula, managing to choose the very same episode, which had a hero, Don Roderick, who could claim to be the father of all Spanish freedom fighters through his resistance to the Moorish invasion in the early eighth century. The subject was made obvious by its analogies with recent events at the Spanish court. The Moors were invited into Spain by a traitor, Count Julian, as an act of revenge after his daughter, la Cava, had been raped by Don Roderick. King Charles IV of Spain, or his Prime Minister Manuel de Godoy, the Queen's paramour, made the Treaty of Fountainebleau which in 1807 brought the French into the Peninsula. Still, and perhaps by chance, by the time Landor published his tragedy *Count Julian* (1812), and Scott and Southey their long narrative poems on Roderick, in 1812 and 1814, the fact that they were describing the Islamic occupation of a Christian country looked up-to-the-minute for a quite new reason. It became increasingly likely that there would be a war of liberation in the eastern Mediterranean, and there, in Greece, the religions of conqueror and conquered were as they had been in eighth-century Spain.

Southey, the most hawkish as a war poet of these three, was also the last to publish, so that his *Roderick, the Last of the Goths* had less topical impact than most of his work. Already by 1809 Southey liked to represent war with Napoleon not simply as a fight against an alien despotism, but, more popularly, as a Christian crusade of later days. In July 1811, when Byron got back to Britain, he found plenty of signs of a more resolute war policy than when he had left, and signs too of a vigorous Evangelical campaign in favour of proselytism in the East. It was in relation to India that the Evangelical pressure-group known as the Clapham Sect first mounted the campaign that for Wilberforce even outdid the abolition of slavery as a national moral crusade. Hitherto it had been the policy of the British East India Company, strongly supported by Parliament, to leave the Indian social structure undisturbed, or if parts were defunct, as was the case with Hindu law, to revive them. It was a cornerstone of Company policy to respect the spheres of influence of Hindu and Moslem religious leaders. But as long ago as 1792 the Evangelical Charles Grant, a servant of the Company first in India, now at its London headquarters in Leadenhall Street, wrote a tract which challenged the old policy of religious coexistence not merely on religious but on moral and social grounds. Writing for the minister under Pitt responsible for Indian affairs, Henry Dundas, Grant argued that Hinduism was not, as Warren Hastings and William Jones had argued in the 1770s and 1780s, a social creed rooted in immemorial village customs which also found expression in an indigenous code of law. In fact the laws of Manu, a code on which Jones as chief justice in Calcutta expended immense labour, were, Grant asserted, chaotic and in their origins despotic, an imposition on the populace from above. The "cruel genius" which pervaded them was the ethos of Hinduism, and it encouraged fraud, lying and the abuse of people of inferior caste.[3]

Grant's long paper, though not published until admitted as evidence in the parliamentary debates of 1813, was circulated in India House and Evangelical circles in 1797, and frequently seems to have been echoed in the first decade of the new century, as Grant's Evangelical faction struggled for control of the London end of the company's affairs. From 1802 Southey took up the campaign to allow Christian missionaries in among the Indian population, initially in reviews for the Dissenter-owned *Annual Review*, then in 1805 in his epic *Madoc*. The epic first took shape in 1794 as a romantic tale of a twelfth-century quest to the New World in search of social and religious freedom—a historical analogue to the pantisocracy plan—but Southey revamped it extensively between 1803 and 1805. The final version makes a strong case for the mass conversion of native peoples where, as in pre-Conquest Mexico, their own religion was cruel and oppressive.

---

[3]Charles Grant, "Observations on the State of Society among the Asiatic Subjects of Great Britain, particularly with respect to Morals, and on the means of Improving It. Written chiefly in the Year 1792," *Parliamentary Papers*, 1812–13, X, Paper 282, p. 66.

Southey's Mexico worships a serpent cult served by priests who practise human sacrifice and keep a cruel despotism in power. It is a paradigm of a socially unacceptable religion which has close resemblances to Grant's portrayal of Hinduism in 1792, for both these analyses of religions concentrate on their impact on the welfare of the common people, what Grant called the tendency of Hinduism to forge "a life of abject slavery and unparalleled depravity." Indeed, in an article written a year before his Hindu epic, *The Curse of Kehama* (1810), Southey draws attention to the similarity between the two religions: "Except the system of Mexican priestcraft, no fabric of human fraud has ever been discovered so deadly as the Braminical."[4]

The Curse of Kehama is an extravagant Gothic epic about a wicked Hindu rajah, or would-be emperor of the world, an eastern alter ego of Napoleon Bonaparte. We meet him at the funeral of his son, who was killed by the father of a girl he was attempting to rape; a resisting child-widow and several slaves are flung onto the pyre. After the ceremony, the Rajah uses supernatural powers (which Hinduism allows bad men to acquire) to punish the man who killed his son, a peasant called Ladurlad. He must endure an eternal life in endless pain, consumed with an inward fire which no natural element, not air or water or earth, will have the power to cool:

> I charm thy life
> From the weapons of strife,
> From stone and from wood,
> From fire and from flood,
> From the serpent's tooth,
> And the beasts of blood:
> From Sickness I charm thee,
> And Time shall not harm thee,
> But Earth which is mine,
> Its fruits shall deny thee;
> And Water shall hear me,
> And know thee and fly thee;
> And the Winds shall not touch thee
> When they pass by thee,
> And the Dews shall not wet thee,
> When they fall nigh thee:
> And thou shalt seek Death
> To release thee, in vain;
> Thou shalt live in thy pain,

---

[4] [Robert Southey], "Periodical Accounts, relative to the Baptist Missionary Society, &c," *Quarterly Review*, 1 (1809), 194. Cf. Grant, p. 44.

While Kehama shall reign,
With a fire in thy heart,
And a fire in thy brain;
And sleep shall obey me,
And visit thee never,
And the curse shall be on thee
For ever and ever.
(*Curse of Kehama,* 1810, I, 19–21)

Kehama's memorable curse, given in the languages of folk poetry and folk magic, symbolizes Hinduism as Grant describes it, a religion cruel in its ideas and relentlessly despotic in social practice.

Kehama is eventually defeated by the peasant Ladurlad and his daughter Kailyal, whose quest takes them allegorically through the experience of religious conversion. Though their final apotheosis translates them to a heaven too doctrinally unspecific to be certainly Christian, they end believing in one supreme Deity who cares for his human creatures, and can intervene on their behalf. Unlike the Hinduism sketched by Grant, and summarized indeed by Southey in a long, violent article in the first number of the *Quarterly Review,* the religion that Ladurlad finds upholds the socially-conserving concept of justice as well as the personally-consoling concept of mercy.

In July 1811 Byron thus found that a topic overlapping that of his new poem—the small Eastern nation absorbed into a foreign empire—had been recently used by a rival poet to advocate a nationalistic religious policy for the British in *their* empire. At first sight it could benefit the Greeks if they engaged the sympathy of a powerful and wealthy stratum of British public opinion. But Byron plainly saw mostly disadvantages in representing Greek liberation as a Christian struggle. One arose from what he knew of Greek politics: in return for religious freedom the leaders of the Greek Orthodox church operated, according to a modern historian, "as guarantors of the loyalty of the Orthodox populations to the Ottoman empire."[5] The second was longer-term and more telling. The imminent fall of the Ottoman empire was certain to lead to a scramble for pickings by the Christian European powers, who now in the later war years found the swelling religious revival handing them new moral justifications for annexing Eastern populations. If only to protect Greece's chances of real independence, it was most important for Byron to play down the religious implications of the brewing storm there. Within a month of his return, in August 1811, he sent a new note for *Childe Harold* II, stanzas 3–9, to his friend R. C.

[5] Richard Clogg, *The Movement for Greek Independence, 1770–1821* (London, 1976), p. xiii.

Dallas, who was helping him with arrangements for publication. Dallas advised him not to publish it, and Byron agreed; it appears in McGann's new Oxford edition in the version Dallas published in his *Recollections:*

> In this age of bigotry, when the puritan and priest have changed places, and the wretched catholic is visited with the "sins of his fathers", even unto generations far beyond the pale of the commandment, the cast of opinion in these stanzas will doubtless meet with many a contemptuous anathema. But let it be remembered, that the spirit they breathe is desponding, not sneering, scepticism; that he who has seen the Greek and Moslem superstitions contending for mastery over the former shrines of Polytheism,—who has left in his own country "Pharisees, thanking God that they are not like Publicans and Sinners", and Spaniards in theirs, abhorring the Heretics, who have holpen them in their need,—will be not a little bewildered, and begin to think, that as only one of them can be right, they may most of them be wrong. With regard to morals, and the effect of religion on mankind, it appears, from all historical testimony, to have had less effect in making them love their neighbours, than inducing that cordial christian abhorrence between sectaries and schismatics. The Turks and Quakers are the most tolerant; if an Infidel pays heratch to the former, he may pray how, when, and where he pleases; and the mild tenets, and devout demeanour of the latter, make their lives the truest commentary on the Sermon of the Mount.[6]

In 1814, two years after publication, Byron added ten new stanzas to *Childe Harold* Canto II, which focus upon the danger that foreign intervention will lead to fresh enslavement, that the Greeks must free themselves, and that religion is not the issue.[7]

The first of Byron's oriental poems written under the influence of the new, more polarized attitudes to the East was *The Giaour,* composed late 1812–March 1813, published in its first state in May 1813, and added to throughout that year. These dates coincide with the height of the Evangelical campaign to mobilize public opinion behind missions to India, a policy still opposed by the majority of directors of the East India Company as well as by the majority of members of Parliament. It was William Wilberforce, an M.P. of great eloquence and great moral authority, who saw that the Administration and the Commons could not be carried without an extra-parliamentary campaign. Wilberforce organized support not merely among Anglicans and old, respectable Dissent, but among enthusiastic

---

[6] Byron, note to *Childe Harold,* II.3–9, published in R. C. Dallas, *Recollections of the Life of Lord Byron* (1824), pp. 171–72; reprinted in *Lord Byron: The Complete Poetical Works,* ed. J. J. McGann (Oxford, 1980–93), II, 283.

[7] Cf. especially Canto II, stanzas 27, 77–83, 89–90.

popular sectarians more genuinely given to proselytizing, such as the Baptists, who in the teeth of official disapproval had been sending missions to India for a decade and a half.[8] The campaign worked; the volume and the fervour of public support induced Parliament to include in the Charter Act of 1813 a "pious clause" which permitted missions to be sent to India and allowed for the establishment of an Anglican bishopric there. Though the practical effects were much slower than enthusiasts expected, the symbolic consequences were great. The secular Enlightenment intellectuals who had advocated governing India by old, Indian ways were now to be steadily driven back by a coalition of middle-class ideologues, Evangelicals and utilitarians, who believed in changing India for something better.

Byron's concept of other nations' independence was that of an Enlightenment intellectual, who respected the autonomy of other cultures, but was inclined to admire them precisely for their otherness, their unreformed feudal "romantic" features. The decisive shift in the British public's perception of an Eastern population which was signalled in 1813 irked him partly because, like the Spanish uprising, it exposed the fault line in late Enlightenment liberalism, its equivocal attitude to mass movements. By marshalling popular opinion at home, Christians had won permission to go out and teach a populace abroad. Southey, one of the leading advocates of this Christianized and popular form of imperialism, remained Byron's chief literary antagonist throughout his life, and it is of course a great mistake to accept unexamined Byron's portrayals of Southey in *Don Juan* and *The Vision of Judgement* as merely a paid government hack. Southey was the only one of the trio of "Lake Poets" to remain a genuine populist, the more troubling because by 1810 he was a Tory populist, and Tory populism almost certainly commanded more general British support than "jacobinism" ever did. His influence, and that of the campaign of 1813, is felt profoundly in *The Giaour*. It is telling for example that Islam in that poem is the religion of leaders as well as followers, and can be illustrated from elegant courtly literature, while Christianity has no spokesmen in the poem but ignorant zealots.

As learned annotated verse, set in part of the Ottoman empire, Byron's *Childe Harold* II and *The Giaour* have often been spoken of as formally indebted to the first of Southey's romance epics, *Thalaba* (1801). Byron does indeed share with this poem by Southey a format, a concern with Islam, and a battery of sources in eighteenth-century learned Western orientalism. J. J.

---

[8] For the controversy over renewing the Company's charter, and especially over the insertion of the "pious clause," see Eric Stokes, *English Utilitarians and India* (Oxford, 1959), pp. 28ff., and Ainslie Embree, *Charles Grant and British Rule in India* (London, 1962), especially pp. 141ff.

McGann lists other debts, some of them structurally or textually significant, such as the fragment form, which Byron found in Samuel Rogers's *The Vision of Columbus* (1812).[9] But images, phrasing and formalistic details do not necessarily get to the centre of a poem, nor distinguish it from others, nor explain why it had to be written. *The Giaour* opposes two men who love the same woman, one a Moslem, the other a (nominal) Christian, and it is concerned with their creeds' attitudes to sexual love, to death and to an individual afterlife. In his treatment of the social implications of different religions, Byron often seems to be matching the materialism and pragmatism of his newly evangelized opponent Southey, though Byron's tone remains jeeringly, perhaps by implication snobbishly sceptical, and his political drift is quite different. The argument of this paper is that for its central subject, and indeed for much of its power and urgency, *The Giaour* is indebted to a current controversy, in part outside "literature" as narrowly conceived, but already reflected in literature. Texts by Grant and Southey, some in verse, represent the ideological attitudes and social interests to which Byron was opposed at a level far more fundamental than his taste for the orientalizing of, say, Beckford.

Unlike *Childe Harold* II, which precedes it, and the Oriental romances to come, *The Giaour,* a love story, appears to have nothing directly to do with Greek independence. The "Giaour" of the title (the word means foreigner or infidel) tries to save his mistress Leila, a slave in Hassan's harem, from being tied in a sack and thrown into the sea as a ritual, socially-approved punishment for her adultery. When he fails, he joins a band of Albanian brigands in order to ambush Hassan and kill him. In spite of incidental resemblances to (for example) Scott's *Marmion, The Giaour* begins very emphatically in the present day and in a mood to reject the romance of history. The first narrator, an educated Westerner, contemplates modern Greeks under Turkish rule, and finds them so enfeebled that he cannot bring himself to tell a story of heroic Greeks in olden times (ll.143–58). At this point indeed his narration fails completely, and we switch to the "Turkish Fragment" announced in the poem's subtitle, supposedly a popular ballad narrated by a Moslem in a coffee-house. The complex narrational method balances the Western and Eastern points of view and impedes the Western reader from reading Hassan with Western sympathies, since to the Moslem fisherman who witnesses the violent main action it is the Giaour, not Hassan, who is the alien—"I know thee not, I loathe thy race" (l. 191). Byron's Oriental tale out-Southeys Southey by being "naturalistically" anti-Western. This does not prevent him from framing the fisherman in a more educated

---

[9] McGann, *Complete Poetical Works,* III, 415.

and cosmopolitan context, or from overlaying his voice with the sardonic commentary provided in Byron's dense, witty and idiosyncratic notes.

Byron's notes, here more personal as well as more generally informative than in any other of the tales, put greater emphasis on the Moslem governors than on the Christian governed, for, in this story of Athens, the native Greeks are virtually invisible. Similarly, though the turbulent, tormented Christian Giaour is the poem's hero, it takes some while for him to become the focus of attention. For at least half the story we are exploring the religion and psyche of Hassan, his Turkish antagonist, and noticing that he is socialized in his world, while the Giaour seems friendless there, except for Leila. The notes convey undisguised admiration for the warlike qualities taught by Mohammedanism—the courage instilled in warriors, for example, by their belief that if they fall in battle they will be welcomed to Paradise by a beautiful woman, or houri. Byron also derives satisfaction from revealing to his readers the dislike with which Christians are regarded in the East. But his respect for Turks does not extend to their regime in Athens, which he roundly abuses—"A pandar and a eunuch . . . now *govern* the *governor* of Athens" (l. 151n).

Byron often retains an urbane Voltairean detachment when he writes of the Moslem's conception of the afterlife:

> Monkir and Nekir are the inquisitors of the dead, before whom the corpse undergoes a slight noviciate and preparatory training for damnation. If the answers are none of the clearest, he is hauled up with a scythe and thumped down with a red hot mace till properly seasoned, with a variety of subsidiary probations. The office of these angels is no sinecure; there are but two; and the number of orthodox deceased being in a small proportion to the remainder, their hands are always full.[10]

But this at least is colourful, and thus, like the other Moslem superstitions Byron treats, relatively attractive. The notes are more consistently derisory where they touch on Christianity. "The monk's sermon is omitted. It seems to have had so little effect upon the patient, that it could have no hopes from the reader" (l. 1207n). It is noticeable, too, that Hassan dies consoled by the knowledge that he can expect rewards in heaven because he is killed by an infidel. The sympathetic Moslem fisherman takes pious pleasure from this fact (though Byron ironically defamiliarizes such piety by his sly emphasis on the non-Hebraic, non-ascetic notion of the houris). Mohammedanism performs at least two useful social functions, it seems: to console people and to draw them together. But from the monk who later in

---

[10] Byron's note to *Giaour*, l. 748.

the poem attends the deathbed of the Giaour there is no such fellow-feeling. The monk views the Giaour as a damned soul:

> If ever evil angel bore
> The form of mortal, such he wore.
> (ll. 912–13)

Any possibility of Christian solidarity vanishes when the Giaour rejects the monk's half-hearted consolation and takes over the burden of the narration, with a "confession" as theologically perverse as that of Pope's Eloisa: he will not hear of a Heaven which omits the sexual happiness he has known and lost on earth:

> Who falls from all he knows of bliss
> Cares little into what abyss.
> (ll. 1157–58)

In his philosophy it is not the monk's transcendental Deity, but Leila, who is

> My good, my guilt, my weal, my woe,
> My hope on high—my all below.
> (ll. 1182–83)

In a dying vision which echoes the Mohammedan belief in the houri, he sees the ghost of the drowned Leila. Unlike Hassan, the ungodly Giaour is loath to believe in apparitions, yet he begs her to stay and let him share her fate, even bodily, rather than leave him to enter some future existence without her:

> But, shape or shade!—whate'er thou art,
> In mercy, ne'er again depart—
> Or farther with thee bear my soul,
> Than winds can waft—or waters roll!
> (ll. 1315–18)

As a love story, one of those classic late-Enlightenment triangles of the *Werther* type that oppose the free and intuitive behaviour of illicit lovers to the religious propriety of the legal husband, *The Giaour* achieves a greater simplicity and intensity than the tales which succeed it, *The Bride of Abydos* and *The Corsair*. However accidentally it was put together, the effect is elegantly compact. To withhold the Giaour's own voice, to deny us entry to his consciousness, until he comes to utter his fiercely heterodox dying "confession", is to give him the special status of one speaking from the grave, the domain long since of the only people he has cared about, his mistress and his enemy. As a humane and personal morality, the Giaour's creed is plainly Byron's: he sincerely hates a religion that instructs a man to tie his wife in a sack and throw her into the sea for infidelity. Hassan's pious docility puts him in the same category as two of the Old Testament's Just Men Byron later depicted, Abel, who loves God better than his brother Cain, and Noah, who lets drown the girl his son loves, because she is not on the list of those God wants saved from the Flood. Byron's morality prefers the personal and human to the abstract and divine, a point he characteristically makes by redeeming a character technically criminal through the trait of total sexual loyalty to a single individual. (Women may have this reckless sexual loyalty too, especially in his later work—Myrrha in *Sardanapalus,* Aholibamah in *Heaven and Earth.*) But nowhere perhaps is there a study of the Byronic humanist so concentrated, intense, and personally felt, so skilfully central and unimpeded, as in the last five hundred lines of *The Giaour,* where the intellectually superior hero confronts the dense priestly bigot trying to prepare him for a Christian afterlife.

For all the elaboration of its fragmented format, the poem achieves simplicity through its ferocious concentration on one moral issue—whether love between human beings is not superior to and perhaps incompatible with belief in either of the two great monotheistic religions. The two halves of the poem can be seen in the end as equally preoccupied with this issue. Byron enforces the point by symmetrically ending the first "Moslem" part with a meditation on the afterlife, first as the pious Hassan will encounter it, then, anticipating the end, as the Giaour eventually should. The Moslem section ends with the fisherman's curse, a pronouncement which rises to the strange fanatical intensity so characteristic of this poem, and, in Byron's perception, of the discourse of religion itself:

> And fire unquench'd, unquenchable—
> Around—within—thy heart shall dwell,
> Nor ear can hear, nor tongue can tell
> The tortures of that inward hell!—
> But first, on earth as Vampire sent,
> Thy corse shall from its tomb be rent;
> Then ghastly haunt thy native place,
> And suck the blood of all thy race,
> There from thy daughter, sister, wife,
> At midnight drain the stream of life;
> Yet loathe the banquet which perforce
> Must feed thy livid living corse;
> Thy victims ere they yet expire
> Shall know the daemon for their sire,
> As cursing thee, thou cursing them,
> Thy flowers are wither'd on the stem.
> But one that for thy crime must fall—

The youngest—most belov'd of all,
Shall bless thee with a *father's* name—
That word shall wrap thy heart in flame!
Yet must thou end thy task, and mark
Her cheek's last tinge, her eye's last spark . . .
Wet with thine own best blood shall drip,
Thy gnashing tooth and haggard lip;
Then stalking to thy sullen grave—
Go—and with Gouls and Afrits rave.
(ll. 751–72, 781–84)

In gloating over the Giaour's hell to come, in the arms of human loved ones, the fisherman ironically anticipates his voluntary dying preference of eternity under any conditions with Leila. But the curse is also a religious statement, though it represents the dark underside of religion, its primitive superstition and its cruelty. Rhetorically it makes the centerpiece of the poem, though only Byron's note fully reveals how ideologically appropriate this is. His source for the folk belief in vampirism, common to the Balkans and the Levant, is a note to Book VIII of Southey's *Thalaba,* a work which overall maintains the kindliness and orderliness of monotheistic religions. But the notion of the curse and some if its details, for example the perpetual fire about the victim's heart, also recall the most celebrated moment in the more recent *Curse of Kehama,* where the very same author accused polytheistic religions of a peculiar tendency to superstition and cruelty. (It is strange, all things considered, that the motif of the vampire was released into nineteenth-century Western literature by two competing progressivist critics of regressive religions.)

Poems inevitably take on the ambivalences of the human consciousness in which they are moulded. But, viewed as polemic, *The Giaour* is hardly muddled or likely to be practically ineffectual. The story "proves" Turkish rule ethically unacceptable to civilized Westerners, without ever showing the Christian church in a more favourable light. The plain fact is that the poem has good Moslems but no good Christians. The poem's villains are the two great monotheistic codes, Christianity and Islam, *comparable* instruments of personal control over the lives of men and women, and potentially of political control by great powers over the destiny of small nations.

Byron's next oriental romances, *The Bride of Abydos* (1813), *The Corsair* (1814) and *Lara* (1814), deal more directly than *The Giaour* with the theme of Greek liberation, but lack its psychological intensity and rhetorical power. Their political contribution is to familiarize a British (and, rapidly, a European) readership with the idea that the fight within Greece would not be led by "respectable" leaders of society, churchmen, landowners or wealthy merchants, but by irregulars of little or no social standing, the bandits or "klefts" in hill country, and pirates on the sea. Rigas Velestinlis (1757–1798) was a real-life revolutionary who was also the associate of bandits, Lambros Katzonis a real-life pirate. Byron alludes to both in his note to Canto II, l. 380 of *The Bride of Abydos,* and, however lightly stressed here, it is of course no accident that all his eastern Mediterranean heroes fight the Turks as either bandits or pirates:

> Lambro Canzani, a Greek, famous for his efforts in 1789–90 for the independence of his country; abandoned by the Russians he became a pirate, and the Archipelago was the scene of his enterprizes. He is said to be still alive at Petersburg. He and Riga are the two most celebrated of the Greek revolutionists.[11]

It must be because of clues of this kind that Francis Jeffrey, reviewing *The Corsair* and *The Bride of Abydos* in the *Edinburgh Review,* suddenly refers in a rather coded, unspecific fashion to the historical probability that modern poetry (like Byron's) will be political:

> This is the stage of society in which fanaticism has its second birth, and political enthusiasm its first true development—when plans of visionary reform, and schemes of boundless ambition are conceived, and almost realized by the energy with which they are pursued—the era of revolutions and projects—of vast performances, and infinite expectations.[12]

But the trouble with these sequels is that in them Byron develops what was probably the most titillating theme in *The Giaour* for its not very politicized drawing-room audience, the hero's terrible sense of sexual guilt and loss. An action presumably intended to simulate a heroic national struggle reads like a trumpery and undermotivated yarn in a colourful setting, a vehicle for a hero who could have been encountered in a Western drawing-room. Byron lacked what both Southey and Shelley had, a positive belief in political change. His difficulty is graphically demonstrated by his love of leaders who have nowhere to take their followers to. His Conrads and Laras are as much strangers, as socially isolated, as the Giaour, and Sardanapalus could have been an admirable ruler, but only if he had not been born millennia before his time. Byron's best sustained nationalist writing is probably in the *Hebrew Melodies,* that collection made direct, ac-

---

[11] McGann, III, 441: Byron's note to *Bride of Abydos,* II.380.

[12] Francis Jeffrey, "The Corsair: a Tale and the Bride of Abydos: a Turkish Tale," *Edinburgh Review,* 23 (1814); reprinted in *Byron: The Critical Heritage,* p. 55.

cessible, popularly Zionist through being set to the genuine folk and religious music collected in the synagogues by Isaac Nathan.[13]

It was only by chance and in a travestied form that any of the Oriental tales made their way into English popular political mythmaking. Peter Manning has surveyed thefts made of Byron's copyright by the radical publisher William Hone, who began in 1816 by pirating especially the more political, pro-Napoleonic poems of that year. It was not until 1817 that Hone brought out a sentimentalized prose paraphrase of *The Corsair* (for fourpence, in contrast to Murray's edition of the poem at five shillings and sixpence), prompted, Manning suggests, by its sudden notoriety in October 1817. In June 1817 a group of Nottinghamshire working men from Pentridge mounted a protest which, partly through the efforts of government *agents provocateurs,* turned into an uprising. It was quickly put down, and the leaders were brought to trial at Derby in October, charged with high treason. Manning recounts how Byron became implicated in the defence:

> Jeremiah Brandreth, the "Nottingham Captain," who had in the course of the rising killed a man, was found guilty on the eighteenth [of October], as was William Turner on the twenty-first. Faced with these convictions, the defence sought to exonerate the third man charged, Isaac Ludlam, by arguing that he had only "Yielded to the overpowering force of their extraordinary leader." No doubt remembering Byron's maiden speech in parliament in 1812 against the death penalty for this very same class of rioting Nottingham weavers, Denman, a Whig, attempted to establish the irresistible magnetism of Brandreth by comparing him to Byron's Corsair: ". . . I have . . . found him so wonderfully depicted by a noble poet of our own time, and one of the greatest geniuses of any age, that I shall take the liberty of now reading that prophetic description. It will perfectly bring before you his character, and even his appearance, the commanding qualities of his powerful but uncultivated mind, and the nature of his influence over those that he seduced to outrage."[14]

Denman proceeded to quote to the court some thirty lines of *The Corsair,* including the description (l. 179–82) of the "spell" Conrad cast over his followers, but the tactic failed, and Ludlam was condemned along with

[13]For the *Hebrew Melodies,* and especially Byron's concern for the authenticity of Isaac Nathan's music, see Frederick Burwick, "Identity and Tradition in the *Hebrew Melodies*" and Paul Douglass, "Isaac Nathan's Settings for *Hebrew Melodies,*" in *English Romanticism: The Paderborn Symposium*, ed. R. Breuer, W. Huber and R. Schowerling, *Studien zur Englischen Romantik*, I (Essen, 1985).

[14]Peter J. Manning, "The Hone-ing of Byron's *Corsair,*" in *Textual Criticism and Literary Interpretation*, ed. J. J. McGann (Chicago, 1985), pp. 112–13.

the other two. In November, a week after the execution of Brandreth and the others, the papers were full of accounts of the prosecution of the radical bookseller Richard Carlile for publishing radical parodies by Hone; in December, Hone himself was on trial for that offence. It seems to have been at this point that Byron's Corsair entered the popular consciousness, shorn of his foreign nationalist specificity, and thus of the characteristics that meant most to Byron and to liberals of his type. Hone's prose love-story preserves little but the invitation to the reader to identify with an idealistic criminal, a modern Robin Hood, an ill-defined, non-socialized focus for political discontent not unlike the modern urban terrorist.

In the long run, Byron was to be successfully attacked more as an anticlerical writer sapping the faith and morals of individuals than as a misleader of the riotous masses. After he left England for good in 1816, a sustained campaign began, not ended even with his death, on the Gothic self-projection perhaps most tellingly pioneered in the vampirish Giaour. Coleridge connects Byron with the subversive Gothic taste in *The Courier* in August 1816. This is that curious, deeply revealing and pregnant passage, afterwards absorbed into the *Biographia Literaria* as chapter XXIII, in which Coleridge, by contrasting Byron's self-absorbed and self-absolved demon-heroes with the properly-punished sinners of Christian literature (such as Don Juan), seems incidentally to have incited Byron to reply with his greatest poem. Lesser critics (Coleridge's nephew J. T. Coleridge, Southey, Reginald Heber) from 1818 mounted an intensifying campaign on his Satanism that led equally logically to the most spectacularly heterodox of all his works, *Cain.*[15]

If *The Giaour* represents the aspect of Byron his religious antagonists most wanted to attack, this is not only because of its protagonist, but because of its wholesale critique of Christianity as a social creed, an instrument of government at home as well as abroad. Byron did not often deal with such topics on a level of generality, but he did eventually return to this one in the mythological tragedy which is also a pre-Shavian comedy, *Sardanapalus* (1821). Here the monarch concerned is a debauchee and a divorcee who cavorts with his mistress in a newly-built pavilion. He also has the misfortune, as a secularist and pacifist, to be king of a nation seized with belief in a divine mission to conquer India. Sardanapalus is thus both the newly-crowned George IV, unhappily cast as leader of a serious, professional, efficient middle-class nation, and the equally déraciné Byron, whose role in the public limelight requires him to take up uncongenially

[15] For this campaign and its implications for Byron's dramas of 1821, see my "Romantic Manicheism," in *The Sun Is God*, ed. J. B. Bullen (Oxford: Clarendon Press; New York: Oxford University Press, 1989).

responsible positions. A study of a post-religious consciousness, *Sardanapalus* is the most complex and searching of Byron's self-projections. But it is also the most social and political. In returning to the type of national dilemma he first properly confronted in *The Giaour,* how to determine the goals of government among the sometimes contending and sometimes collusive forces of religion, nationalism and progressivism, Byron if nothing else added a dimension to his studies of private disaffection and existential despair.

WORKS CITED

Alexander, Boyd. *England's Wealthiest Son: A Study of William Beckford.* London: Centaur, 1962.

Ali, Muhsin Jassim. *Scheherazade in England: A Study of Nineteenth-Century English Criticism of the* Arabian Nights. Washington: Three Continents, 1981.

Aravamudan, Srinivas. *Tropicopolitans: Colonialism and Agency, 1688–1804.* Durham: Duke UP, 1999.

Barrell, John. *The Infection of Thomas De Quincey: A Psychopathology of Imperialism.* New Haven: Yale UP, 1991.

Beckford, William. *Vathek.* Ed. Roger Lonsdale. London: Oxford UP, 1970.

Byron, George Gordon. *Byron's Letters and Journals.* Ed. Leslie A. Marchand. 12 vols. London: Murray, 1973–82.

———. *Complete Poetical Works.* Ed. Jerome J. McGann. 7 vols. Oxford: Clarendon, 1980–93.

Chapman, Guy. *Beckford.* New York: Scribner's, 1937.

Conant, Martha Pike. *The Oriental Tale in England in the Eighteenth Century.* 1908. Rpt. New York: Octagon, 1966.

Crompton, Louis. *Byron and Greek Love: Homophobia in Nineteenth-Century England.* Berkeley: U of California P, 1985.

Edgeworth, Maria. *Tales and Novels.* 10 vols. London: Routledge, 1893.

Goldsmith, Oliver. *The Miscellaneous Works of Oliver Goldsmith, with an Account of His Life and Writings.* Ed. Washington Irving. 4 vols. Paris: Baudry's, 1837.

Johnson, Samuel. *The Works of Samuel Johnson, L.L. D.* 9 vols. Oxford: Talboys, 1825.

Kiely, Robert. *The Romantic Novel in England.* Cambridge: Harvard UP, 1972.

Leask, Nigel. *British Romantic Writers and the East: Anxieties of Empire.* Cambridge: Cambridge UP, 1992.

———. "'Wandering through Eblis': Absorption and Containment in Romantic Exoticism." *Romanticism and Colonialism: Writing and Empire, 1780–1830.* Ed. Tim Fulford and Peter J. Kitson. Cambridge: Cambridge UP, 1998. 165–188.

Lefanu, Alicia. *Memoirs of the Life and Writings of Mrs. Frances Sheridan, Mother of the Late Right Hon. Richard Brinsley Sheridan, and Author of "Sidney Bidulph," "Nourjahad," and "The Discovery."* London: Whittaker, 1824.

Lew, Joseph. "The Necessary Orientalist? *The Giaour* and Nineteenth-Century Imperialist Misogyny." *Romanticism, Race, and Imperial Culture, 1780–1834.* Ed. Alan Richardson and Sonia Hofkosh. Bloomington: Indiana UP, 1996. 265–82.

Lowe, Lisa. *Critical Terrains: French and British Orientalisms.* Ithaca: Cornell UP, 1991.

MacKenzie, John M. *Orientalism: History, Theory, and the Arts.* Manchester: Manchester UP, 1995.

Mahmoud, Fatma Moussa. "Beckford, *Vathek,* and the Oriental Tale." *William Beckford of Fonthill, 1760–1844: Bicentenary Essays,* ed. Mahmoud. Cairo: Cairo Studies in English, 1960. 63–121.

Makdisi, Saree. *Romantic Imperialism: Universal Empire and the Culture of Modernity.* Cambridge: Cambridge UP, 1998.

Mallarmé, Stéphane. "Préface à *Vathek.*" *Oeuvres Complètes.* Ed. Henri Mondor and G[eorges] Jean-Aubry. Paris: Gallimard, 1945. 549–65.

Mannsåker, Frances. "Elegancy and Wildness: Reflections of the East in the Eighteenth-Century Imagination." *Exoticism in the Enlightenment.* Ed. G. S. Rousseau and Roy Porter. Manchester: Manchester UP, 1990. 175–95.

Nussbaum, Felicity A. *Torrid Zones: Maternity, Sexuality, and Empire in Eighteenth-Century English Narratives.* Baltimore: Johns Hopkins UP, 1995.

Porter, Dennis. "*Orientalism* and Its Problems." 1983. Rpt. in *Colonial Discourse and Post-Colonial Theory: A Reader.* Ed. Patrick Williams and Laura Chrisman. New York: Columbia UP, 1994. 150–61.

Said, Edward. *Orientalism.* New York: Vintage, 1979.

Sardar, Ziauddin. *Orientalism.* Buckingham: Open UP, 1999.

Schwab, Raymond. *The Oriental Renaissance: Europe's Rediscovery of India and the East, 1680–1880.* Trans. Gene Patterson-Black and Victor Reinking. New York: Columbia UP, 1984.

Sharafuddin, Mohammed. *Islam and Romantic Orientalism: Literary Encounters with the Orient.* London: Tauris, 1994.

Suleri, Sara. *The Rhetoric of English India.* Chicago: U of Chicago P, 1992.

FOR FURTHER READING

Ahmad, Aijaz. *In Theory: Classes, Nations, Literatures.* London: Verso, 1992.

Aravamudan, Srinivas. "In the Wake of the Novel: The Oriental Tale as National Allegory." *Novel* 33 (1999): 5–31.

Bayly, C. A. *Imperial Meridian: The British Empire and the World, 1780–1830.* London: Longman, 1989.

Bhabha, Homi K. *The Location of Culture.* New York: Routledge, 1994.

Brice, William C., ed. *An Historical Atlas of Islam.* Leiden: Brill, 1981.

Brown, Laura. *Ends of Empire: Women and Ideology in Early Eighteenth-Century English Literature.* Ithaca: Cornell UP, 1993.

Caracciolo, Peter L., ed. *The* Arabian Nights *in English Literature: Studies in the Reception of* The Thousand and One Nights *into British Culture.* New York: St. Martin's, 1988.

Glassé, Cyril. *The Concise Encyclopedia of Islam.* San Francisco: Harper, 1989.

Harlow, Barbara, and Mia Carter, eds. *Imperialism and Orientalism: A Documentary Sourcebook.* Oxford: Blackwell, 1999.

Irwin, Robert. *The* Arabian Nights: *A Companion.* London: Lane, 1994.

Kidwai, Abdur Raheem. *Orientalism in Lord Byron's "Turkish Tales":* The Giaour *(1813),* The Bride of Abydos *(1813),* The Corsair *(1814), and* The Siege of Corinth *(1813).* Lewiston: Mellen UP, 1995.

Le Yaouanc, Colette. *L'Orient dans la Poesie anglaise de l'epoque romantique, 1798–1824.* Paris: Champion, 1975.

Liu, Alan. "Toward a Theory of Common Sense: Beckford's *Vathek* and Johnson's *Rasselas.*" *Texas Studies in Language and Literature* 26 (1984): 183–217.

Macfie, A. L., ed. *Orientalism: A Reader.* Edinburgh: Edinburgh UP, 2000.

Mack, Robert L., ed. *Arabian Nights' Entertainments.* Oxford: Oxford UP, 1995.

Majeed, Javed. *Ungoverned Imaginings: James Mill's* The History of British India *and Orientalism.* Oxford: Clarendon, 1992.

Marchand, Leslie A. *Byron: A Biography.* New York: Knopf, 1957.

Marshall, P. J., and Glyndwr Williams. *The Great Map of Mankind: British Perceptions of the World in the Age of Enlightenment.* London: Dent, 1982.

Melman, Billie. *Women's Orients: English Women and the Middle East, 1718–1918.* Ann Arbor: U of Michigan P, 1992.

Oueijan, Naji B. *A Compendium of Eastern Elements in Byron's Oriental Tales.* New York: Lang, 1999.

Pratt, Mary Louise. *Imperial Eyes: Travel Writing and Transculturation.* London: Routledge, 1992.

Said, Edward. *Culture and Imperialism.* New York: Knopf, 1993.

Smith, Hamilton Jewett. *Oliver Goldsmith's* The Citizen of the World: *A Study.* New Haven: Yale UP, 1926.

Spivak, Gayatri Chakravorty. *A Critique of Postcolonial Reason: Toward a History of the Vanishing Present.* Cambridge: Harvard UP, 1999.

Williams, Glyndwr. *The Expansion of Europe in the Eighteenth Century: Overseas Rivalry, Discovery, and Exploitation.* New York: Walker, 1966.

CREDITS

Margaret Doody, from "Frances Sheridan: Morality and Annihilated Time," in *Fetter'd or Free?* ed. Mary Anne Schofield and Cecilia Macheski (Athens: Ohio University Press, 1986), pp. 350–56. Reprinted with permission from Ohio University Press, Athens, Ohio.

Nussbaum, Felicity A. *Torrid Zones: Maternity, Sexuality, and Empire in Eighteenth-Century English Narratives,* pp. 129–134. © 1995 Felicity A. Nussbaum. Reprinted by permission of The Johns Hopkins University Press.

Adam Potkay. "Beckford's Heaven of Boys" is reprinted by permission from *Raritan: A Quarterly Review.* Vol. XIII, No. 1 (Summer 1993).

Marilyn Butler, "The Orientalism of Byron's *Giaour,*" in *Byron and the Limits of Fiction,* ed. Bernard Beatty and Vincent Newey, pp. 78–96. Copyright 1988 by Liverpool University Press. Reprinted by permission.